For – Mrs Bates –
from her very sincere
friend Mary B.
1861.

CHRISTIAN

BELIEVING AND LIVING.

SERMONS

BY

F. D. HUNTINGTON, D. D.,

PREACHER TO THE UNIVERSITY, AND PLUMMER PROFESSOR OF
CHRISTIAN MORALS IN HARVARD COLLEGE.

BOSTON:
CROSBY, NICHOLS, AND COMPANY,
117 Washington Street.
1860.

University Press, Cambridge:
Electrotyped and Printed by Welch, Bigelow, & Co.

CONTENTS.

SERMON I.

SERMON II.

SERMON III.

SERMON IV.

SERMON V.

SERMON VI.

SERMON VII.

SERMON VIII.

SERMON IX.

SERMON X.

SERMON XI.

SERMON XII.

SERMON XIII.

SERMON XIV.

SERMON XV.

SERMON XVI.

SERMON XVII.

SERMON XVIII.

SERMON XIX.

SERMON XX.

SERMON XXI.

SERMON XXII.

SERMON XXIII.

SERMON XXIV.

SERMON XXV.

SERMON I.

THE CHRISTIAN CALLING.

YE SEE YOUR CALLING.—1 Cor. i. 26.

THE word "calling" applied to a human life in the Christian sense, and by a Christian authority like Paul, is a condensed confession of faith. It means the great primary truth of religion, viz. that our erring life is governed by a will above it, and is capable of receiving influences of attraction from the Spirit of God. Take up that single truth, trace it out to its legitimate results, admit all its practical obligations, let in upon your own mind both the solemn sense of duty and the clear illumination for sorrow that it brings with it, accept its necessary incidents of penitence, renewal, redemption, and you find that, including its connections and consequences, it is a majestic compendium of religious doctrine.

There is another and at present a more secular application of the same term. A man's common employment—the means of his livelihood—is spoken of as his "calling," or his vocation. But this usage discovers the same origin; for it must have sprung up in days of a livelier faith, when it was verily believed that each man's business in the world was a sacred appointment, and that he himself, while about his ordinary work, was on a divine errand. A living faith not only justifies that view, but requires it. For it supposes that in the soul which has confessed its calling, where Christ is "formed within," there is a power of holy consecration supreme over all the choices and pursuits of the mind. We are thus carried up to a conception of Christian discipleship that has been too far lost out of the modern habits of living, and even out of the belief and worship of the Church. We have glimpses of a holy manhood and womanhood beyond the mark of our secularized, diluted, or perhaps formalized and ossified Christianity. We catch a breath of the fragrant piety which once hallowed the earth and sweetened the air. We feel that miraculous touch which has always brought healing and vigor to the languid pulse and feeble muscles. We behold, with sight too dim, but in a splendor that cannot be wholly veiled, "the prize of the high calling of God in Christ Jesus."

The expression stirs some feeling of mystery. More is suggested than the understanding clearly grasps. It is so, in a degree, with every elevated, prophetic utterance of spiritual truth. For that always borders upon the unknown, shades off into the infinite, and leaves us to discern spiritually what we cannot reduce to the terms of knowledge. Religion itself, as the invisible bond that holds us consciously, confidingly, to the Eternal One, is mysterious. Yet a life *without* this sense of a Hand guiding it, a Spirit moving it, a God in Christ calling to it, is really far more perplexing and unaccountable than with that key to its changes. For then, severed from a Father, it is not only a mystery, but a contradiction; not only a riddle to the reason, but, sooner or later, with all its failures and miseries, a painful puzzle to the heart, or even an agonizing mockery to our sense of right, — an enigma that neither genius, nor stoicism, nor sensuality, nor suicide can solve. Persons of sensitive natures have to shut their eyes and refuse to think of it. Hardier observers speculatively turn it over, like some anomalous specimen in science, in the fingers of their philosophy, with no clew to its secret.

But there is something here, too, that is plain enough to common sense, and, to earnest moods at least, very welcome. How many weeks will any of us be able to live without coming to some spot where it will be felt as a rational comfort to believe that all our way, step by step, trial by trial, surprise, success, failure, loss, removal, was ordered for us by Him who sees the end from the beginning? If there is a "calling," there is One who calls, and who when calling has a right to be heard. It follows that there is one object in existence so pre-eminent, that to accomplish that is to fulfil the great purpose of our being, and to fail of that is to miss the chief end. These are very intelligible ideas, easily seized by every mind, and indeed seeming to be naturally suited to serious and reverential habits of thought, looking but a little way below the surface. It is only triflers, too frivolous to think, who conceive of their life as without a plan, and have never heard the call of the Master, "Go, work to-day in my vineyard."

So true is this, that it has been observed of the most efficient and commanding men in the history of the world, that they were apt to represent themselves as led on by some Power beyond themselves, — instigated, possessed, or inspired by a strange force above their control, — a Demon, a Genius, a Destiny, or a

Deity. And certainly the successful establishing of this impression respecting any leader, legislator, or reformer, has always proved a powerful element of popular fascination. To be held the princely child of an unseen guardianship, an elect avenger of the gods, or an inspired instrument of Fate, has always clothed a hero in extraordinary superiority. And whether you take it as the honest conviction of the claimant to such a mission, or as the superstition of his followers, this seems to be an indirect natural testimony that the strongest achievements of man bear in their very bosom an involuntary witness that there is more than man behind them.

But the Apostle refers to something higher and holier than any dreamy sentiment like this. Standing on the verities of the Gospel, speaking, observe, to those that have heard it and nominally assented to it, he summons them to a more solemn and searching sense of what it requires of them: "Ye see your calling, brethren." The truth is clear; you see it. It is not of men, but of God, who calls. Christ has lived, and he asks living followers. He has died, a sacrifice, and he asks the spirit of self-sacrifice, the death of evil, in you. He has risen, living evermore; and whatsoever gift of his love ye shall ask, believing, ye shall receive. These are your guaranties, your commission, your grounds of action. This is your calling. It is not, then, our life in general, every kind of life, the life of mere accidental impulse or of moral insensibility, the life of self-interest, the life of fashion-following or fame-seeking, — it is not an irreligious life at all, in any of its unsightly and empty forms, that is "your calling." It is the life of a disciple of Christ, penetrated in every part by his spirit, warmed by his zeal, baptized into his pure blood, sanctified by his indwelling presence, purged of dead works and a servile obedience by his quickening grace, "hid" with him, and so "made manifest" and "glorified" with him.

It is remarkable how perseveringly the New Testament clings to this particular conception of the Christian relation, setting it forward in all possible connections of phrase, and putting it in contact with each element of the Christian system, as if there were a vitality in it that must not by any means be missed. Disciples are said to be "the called of Jesus," "called out of darkness into marvellous light," "called unto liberty," "called to peace," "called to eternal life," "called" first, to be afterwards "justified and glorified," "called to inherit a blessing," "called in one body" and "one hope," "called by God's grace" to "holiness," to "his kingdom and glory," with "a holy calling," "a heavenly calling." The Apostles are "called" from one place, work, suffering, joy, to another, in the journeying and progress of their apostleship. To "walk worthy of the vocation," is made the business of a careful conscience. To make our "calling and election sure," is the grand victory of our warfare. The promise that subdues all anxiety as to the result is in the words, "Faithful is he which calleth you."

Let us notice, in order, the prominent teachings of this language.

I. In the first place, it is conveyed in it, as it is in the whole drift of the primitive teaching of the Apostles, that the business of a Christian life is something special and distinctive, — a "calling" by itself. That is, in its nature and spirit, it is something to be distinguished from all other occupations, all schemes of thought, systems of philosophy, enterprises of the will, or plans of education. It is such that no one of these things can be mistaken for it, nor substituted in place of it. A Christian character springs from its own root, grows by its own laws, and bears its own peculiar fruit. It finds a distinct provision in every human soul for developing it, — a religious capacity, an organ of faith, a spiritual want, reaching dimly after God, and never meant to be satisfied but in the gift of his Holy Spirit. It is therefore to be gone about as an attainment, grand but simple, practicable for all men, the noblest of all objects. It has its own conditions, of effort, preparation, faithful use of appointed means. Seek, and ye shall find; ask, and ye shall receive. The inward eye must be turned toward the Revelation of God. There must be definite action, a fixing of attention, a concentration of the mind, a full purpose of the will. This must have a beginning, which the New Testament everywhere speaks of as being born into a new life. There must be a stirring and moving of the soul awakened from death toward its Deliverer, with complete faith in him, which Christ constantly calls coming to him. Then there must be a growing into greater strength and goodness, without end. Here, therefore, is a new principle of conduct. It is a divine calling. Paul speaks as if no pursuit were to be thought of in comparison with it. It is the errand on which we are all sent into the world, — to gain the character, to live the life, that will be nearest to God here, and will be immortal by its secret fellowship with Him who is its Resurrection, — Life of life.

II. Secondly, this idea of a "calling" individualizes not only the Christian obligation, but the Christian person. Paul had no conception of a social Christianity apart from the personal righteousness of the men that make up society. That is one of the plausible fictions of people who find speculative abstractions more to their taste than the self-denying drudgeries of daily duty, and a Christianity on paper a cheap substitute for Christianity *in the heart.* Ye see the calling, Paul says,— and it is *your* calling. This is personal language. It is addressed to individual men and women. It is the uniform and thorough dealing of the Christian doctrine. That truth knows nothing of public virtue except as it is found in the breasts and the conduct of private persons, who take their virtue with them, and keep it with them, when they enter into public relations. It reaches society and institutions only through the souls that are open to its persuasion and loyal to its control. It is quite vain for us to congratulate each other on a state of general integrity and order, if we tolerate depravity in ourselves, or excuse it in the usages of the class to which we happen to belong. If we have a community here of a thousand people, in which we want to see the Christian graces flourishing, our only way is to go to work and turn one and another of the thousand into a Christian person, each beginning with himself. Everybody feels the advantage of a general good name; the least deserving take a pride in it when it is secured;— one of those indirect and involuntary tributes to the power and truth of religion which are more unanswerable than volumes of formal arguments. But are we willing to pay the price,—the contribution of our own personal uprightness and vigilance? Or are we mean enough to wish to take a share of the credit, while practising the very sins that this fair repute is wanted to conceal? The worst enemies our faith has to suffer from are those that always take complacency in its benefits as a civil economy, but always make it bend to their own inclination in the indulgences of passion and the obliquities of self-interest. Its open deniers — those who call themselves infidels — have a small and incredulous audience. There is not one of the creeds — the most rigid — but has more hearty and contented adherents than the no-creed of blank negation. And commonly, the more explicit impiety or irreverence becomes, the less its chance of popularity. The mortal wound is given by those who take up Christianity as a social policy, a name to conjure with, a commercial convenience, trying to make that pass for the holy reality of Christ. The only people that can take any benefit from this insincerity are those that are too undiscriminating to mark the difference between words and things. And even for these, the difference is constantly forcing itself to light; the mask is constantly liable to drop, through the unguarded inconsistencies and the providential uncoverings of hollow proprieties. How weary and indignant God must be at hearing these Pharisaic praises of a Christian religion, a Christian legislation, a Christian literature, a Christian country, from speakers and writers who allow Christianity to conquer no one of their propensities to pleasure or to pride! Have you never known a community tacitly, not avowedly, — there is too much instinctive shame left for that, — but actually, and by a common understanding, established on the rule to recognize the practical control of Christianity up to a certain point, — and beyond that point, a mutual, silent conspiracy to let questionable matters alone? How would that bear the preaching of Paul, or of Paul's Master? The truth is, the fashions and assemblages of society, instead of being an exposure and a judgment to irreligious hearts, are often made their protection. We speak of bad men hiding in solitude. Far more of them hide in company. Personal obligation, with its strict and solemn answers of each penitent and awakened soul to the call of its Lord, is sunk, or frittered away, in the cowardly compliances of a vulgar prosperity. The original Gospel breaks in upon this giddiness. It says, Unto you I call, soul by soul. The vocation is an individual matter. Ye see it, each for himself. Hast thou faith, have it to thyself. There is no impersonal character, no pardon by proxy, no collective salvation. The work is for each. "Repent," is for each. "Thou shalt love the Lord thy God," is for each. "Take up the cross and come after me," is for each. "Ye see your calling."

Thus we have found that this Apostolic view of practical Christianity as a "calling" individualizes, first, the Christian principle, as having a place distinct from all other principles, and, secondly, individualizes the Christian life, as having all its awful obligations, its joys and sanctions, centred upon each personal conscience and heart.

III. Be reminded, further, that, notwithstanding all this, Christ's truth is a matter, not of partial, but of universal application. The Christian spirit, the Christian revelation, the Christian privilege and promises, are not meant for a class of men culled out arbitrarily here and there; not for a few persons of special constitutional proclivities that way, nor for a few others whose circumstances and situation in the world happen to predispose them for a spiritual plane of being, making it easy for them to reach it. The Bible makes no such limitations, no reservations, no exceptions. "Whosoever will,"—"All men everywhere,"—"In every nation,"—"From the least even unto the greatest";—these are the broad terms of the Gospel charter, the strict terms of the Gospel requisition. Nor is the Christian calling a whit the less universal and impartial for the reason that, as we were just now showing, it is special, requiring a personal consecration. On the contrary, its speciality is the very ground of its universality. God himself, as the Infinite Spirit, is far more readily recognized as having to do with the whole human race, for the distinctness of his personality. The more personal, the nearer to all. The forces of nature lose nothing of their diffusive or penetrative action by the distinctness of the laws that govern them. The more definite, the more important, and the more searching you make the Christian command to be, the more will the principles of its righteousness send their pressure into every department of life, and the spirit of its charity diffuse its fragrance into every nook and corner of the household of humanity. Nothing in the administration of Christianity is better proved by trial than this.

If there were any variations excusing men from this calling, they might be suspected to exist either (1.) in the unlike constitutions of men's minds, or (2.) in their unlike external conditions, or (3.) in the unlike ages when they appear;—in other words, either in their nature, their place, or their time. Yet how far these things are from really constituting, in the Christian view, an apology for disregarding the duty of a disciple!

Take the inequalities of intellectual equipment.

There is not much likelihood of men's seeking a release from taking up the Christian work and cross on a plea of mental infirmity. One of the last confessions extorted from vanity is that of inferiority there. More probably the pretence of exemption will arise in the opposite quarter, and be a pretence of gifts or a culture superior to the need of faith, independent of the humiliating doctrines of the Crucified. Yet in this very passage we have a sublime strain of prophetic utterance from Paul, coming with such irresistible power of inspiration, and with such self-attesting credentials of the Spirit of Truth in its majestic affirmations, as to supersede argument, and leave the poor conceits of irreligious knowledge and genius to contempt. "Where is the wise? Where is the disputer of this world? Hath not God made foolish the wisdom of the world? The world by wisdom knew not God. The foolishness of God is wiser than men. For the preaching of the cross is to them that perish, foolishness, but unto them which are called, Christ, the power of God and the wisdom of God."

Or take the excuse of unfavorable outward fortunes. What are those fortunes? Poverty and hardship? Unto the poor the Gospel was first preached, and in every age the facts show that it is with them that its simple and consoling truths have found their most cordial and fruitful reception. Wealth and station, then? But unto whom much is given, of them shall much be required. The ten talents must answer for ten talents more returned unto the Lord who reckoneth. Or is it the busy and contented state of pecuniary mediocrity or a competency? Yet that is the very state which, of all others, a wise man is represented as praying for, and which common sense would pronounce most favorable to a useful and healthy piety. Indeed, nothing is plainer than that the whole honest spirit of our religion disallows the evasive notion that any position can liberate the spiritual child of God from loving his Maker, serving his Saviour, and living in godly charity with his fellow-men.

And, thirdly, the changing aspects of the times are just as powerless to acquit any single conscience of its accountability for a Christian walk and conversation. Principles do not change with periods. The Christ of whom it is written that he is the same yesterday, to-day, and for ever, is not subject to fluctuation, either in the measure of his affection or in his demands for allegiance. If the tendencies of an age are materialistic, so much the more need of men and women whom the world cannot purchase, nor the flesh seduce, nor the Devil deceive. If the times are hard and unbelieving, it is out of such epochs, by men whose faith is a light shining in a dark place, — lamps in the cave, — that the noblest revolutions have sprung, the abominable idols of the den have been discovered, and new days of hope have dawned. If the times are prosperous, then it is a call for money and commerce and learning to spread the Christian kingdom, setting up the cross wherever the heathen imagine a vain thing. Or if they are corrupt and vile, then it is for brave witnesses to live this loftier life, to stand unstained by all pollutions, and, though vice should combine with the voluptuousness of Corinth an American energy, mix the appetites of the ancient Paganism with the insolence of the new, and revive the sorceries of the familiar spirits of old among the destructive theories begotten in the prurient imaginations of yesterday, yet to keep themselves unspotted from the world.

The true lesson when some fresh outbreak of iniquity in the very seats of law puts back the hopes of civilization, or some almost incredible story of crime alarms the security and sickens the senses of the land, is not a general distrust of man or of woman; it is not a weighing off, by human judgment, of guilt against guilt, as if we held the balances of Omniscience; it is not to lend a frightened ear to those sweeping suspicions which are the tempter's capital, and the poison of all peace; it is not even a diminished confidence in the principle and the honor which in Christ's new-born souls still live, — thank God! and live because He lives, — as dear and sacred and mighty warders of the purity of home as ever; but it is this rather, — that there is no safeguard on earth for any one single virtue but the calling wherewith the Christian is called; no sufficing restraint on the wild and riotous depravity of man, but a reverent faith in God; no incorruptible keeper of a household or a heart, but a principle of right such as that Redeemer planted, who was holy, and harmless, and undefiled, and separate from sinners.

My friends, a near and natural illustration of this uniformity of the Christian calling and responsibility occurs in the very composition of an assembly of Christian worshippers.

Ye see your calling, families. On every domestic sanctuary, its sympathies, its cares, its wear and waste of sensibility, its wealth and joy of love, tenderness, pity, and tears, Christ lays the law of a consecrated and holy economy. Set thy house in order; for these earthly tabernacles are to be dissolved. And while they last, they take in no calm, no abiding light, save through invisible windows that open upward into the unshadowed and undivided Heaven.

Ye see your calling, parents. To exercise your trust, I will not say religiously, but even honorably, you will have to feel that the Christian character of every child committed to your charge, and living in sight of your life, is immeasurably the most urgent interest of your parental office. The religious welfare of these souls, you will confess, does not rest on the same basis as their social, literary, worldly advancement, but, high as that is, on a higher and stronger. Whatever hinders or endangers that, in speech or example or neglect, inflicts a wrong too terrible to trace. The lines of its bad influence run out, beyond where any eye or thought can follow them. There is a cause of Christian earnestness to be carried forward; a work of Christian training to be done; a privilege of Christian comfort and sympathy and mutual help to be diffused, by self-denial, watchfulness, counsel, and prayer, — a calling wherewith all who are intrusted with the solemn embassy of paternity or maternity are alike called.

And ye see your calling, men of action. "I have written unto you, young men, because ye are strong, and the word of God abideth in you." Is there not something more, in this vocation, than some of you have fairly apprehended? Something on which conscience, waking to a livelier activity, will take, if you will let it, a stronger and firmer hold? You have a field not surpassed, you will say, for Christian opportunity in the world; powers that never will be freer, nor less compromised with the usages of evil; standards of public opinion that are in your own hands, to be nobly moulded by you, if the good will stand together, or for you to be ignobly moulded by, if you are servile; temptations to be overcome, prizes to be won. You have a Church of Christ inviting you and offering you its gracious aids and benedictions. However sin may have spoilt the past, do not despair. If you sit weeping with Mary by the sepulchre of some buried joy, a voice may yet break in on your grief, "The Master is come and calleth for thee." If you lie blind and weak by the wayside with Bartimeus, the animating news may yet lift you to your feet, "Rise! he calleth thee."

To-day, then, fellow-worshippers, we are to put it to ourselves, whether this cause of our Redeemer does not signify either more or less than our treatment makes it: whether, if its claim is genuine, and its doctrine valid, it does not require of us a more explicit, profound, all-controlling acknowledgment; whether consistency does not enjoin it upon us to enthrone this faith over all the practice of our life, — making every abode of kindred bodies a home of Christian hearts; making all the social pleasures and the literary competitions of youth to be just, generous, blameless; — all honors to be gained and knowledge laid up, heartily, for a usefulness whose record is beyond this world; and all our public affairs so ordered as to lay the foundations of intellectual eminence and civil glory on this only sure and stable Rock, the Gospel of Christ.

If we both see and follow this calling of our Lord, — when he calls again, and calls "his own by name," it will be to glory and honor and immortality.

SERMON II.

THE ANSWER OF FAITH.

AND ERE THE LAMP OF GOD WENT OUT IN THE TEMPLE OF THE LORD, WHERE THE ARK OF GOD WAS, AND WHEN SAMUEL WAS LAID DOWN TO SLEEP, THE LORD CALLED SAMUEL, AND HE ANSWERED, "HERE AM I; SPEAK, FOR THY SERVANT HEARETH." — 1 Sam. iii. 3, 4, 10.

IF pride should object that the text is only the language of a child, it will be enough to answer, that he was a child of faith, which is wiser than the wisest brain, and to recall and put with it the unquestionable words of Christ: "Except ye become as little children, ye cannot enter into the kingdom of heaven."

Setting aside the unbelief that rejects it, and the unconcern that neglects it, there are undoubtedly two views taken of the nature of the thing we call Christianity. One represents the world as a field of *man's* work, and so calls on men to put forth their self-impelled activity in it; the other represents it as a scene of the work of God in Christ, and calls on men to witness his presence, to welcome his spirit, and to make themselves willing and obedient instruments in his hand. A perfect reconciliation of these would be Christianity realized; but in their divorcement is the denial of the incarnation, the very matter of heresy, the loss of the supernatural

Gospel gift, and the bereavement of the immortal hope. Self-will would be the spring of life in the one case, faith in the other. One would ask of its *own* mind, "What shall I do?" The other of the *Divine*, "What wilt thou have me do?" The one stimulates itself by the friction of human effort on its own level; the other opens itself in prayer to be stimulated by an inspiration from above. One says, every morning, at every beginning of a task, or every turn in the way, "Lord, here am I; send me; lead me"; the other, "Fellow-men, here I am; make room for my wit and my enterprise." One is Samuel in the temple; the other is Saul fronting the Philistines. Both say, "I will arise," but one adds, "and will go to my Father, and will arise for that purpose." Both resolve, "I will work out my salvation," but one first confesses, "It is God that worketh in me both to will and to do." So it was from the very beginning. In the twilight of history stand two figures, — brothers, — patriarchs. Both tended their flocks, and wrought in "sad sincerity" all the day; but before one of them, when the night fell, and he slept in the pasture, with a stone for his pillow, the angels of God ascended and descended, and earth no less than heaven became a Bethel, house of God. One would give us Saul of Tarsus, rushing on in his headstrong and unhallowed zeal to Damascus to persecute the best benefactor he ever knew; the other is *Paul* the Apostle, penetrated by the voice of Jesus, humbled by the light above him, "not disobedient to the heavenly vision," saying, "I can do all things, through Christ strengthening me."

We need not undervalue either the toiling hand or the trusting heart. Work is too noble and too much needed to be even indirectly disparaged. The world everywhere waits for more of it,—fruitful, righteous, cheerful work. The earth is to be subdued; and it can be subdued in no other way. Loads of oppression are to be lifted off. Ignorance is to be instructed. Strong poor men are to be guided to their task, and paid their wages. Weak poor men are to be helped, till they grow strong. Superstition is to be flooded with pure light. Error is to be discrowned. Partition-walls of prejudice and pride are to be broken through. Nature is to be made the servant of man, and her forces tools in the grasp of thought. No; the question is not whether men shall work, but how they shall work to a purpose, i. e. work rightly. Here the voice of Christ speaks, and speaks unmistakably. It says, To work rightly, to work effectually, you must work *from God*,—consciously, faithfully, piously, *from God*. His Christ must be your leader; his Spirit your law; his will your motive. Not as out of yourself alone, but out of him, must your power come. And faith is the feeling that confesses it; prayer is the hand that draws it down. He who knew all that is in man testifies this again and again. It was to convince us of it, that he came into the world. If we are Christians, we shall hold that no work is done well that is not done religiously. Philosophy is not here our authority; we have an altar, of which they have no right to eat who serve that tabernacle. Yet the highest philosophy would say the same thing. To be efficient, labor must be hearty; and when we say the heart goes into it, we mean simply that faith goes into it. In moral enterprises, a thing must be believed in before it can be done. We are born into a spiritual estate, and we cannot live worthily of it, nor be educated into a fit adjustment to it, till we behold the facts, the verities, the obligations, the destiny, that pertain to us by virtue of our spiritual inheritance. No life is truly lived that is not lived in the spirit of him who arose in the temple and answered the heavenly summons with his reverent, "Speak, Lord, for thy servant heareth." For he seems like only a prophecy of that other child born later for a yet diviner ministry, who also spoke in the temple and said, "Wist ye not that I must be about my Father's business?"

The first word of the Bible Luther ever read, out of the Bible itself, at Erfurth, his biography tells us, was the story of Hannah and "her child lent to the Lord for ever"; and the beautiful narrative, so full of fresh, prophetic meaning to his ritual-laden spirit, drew him on to the study of the whole Holy Word, till, through the text, "The just shall live by faith," as through the gates of the morning, the full, clear light of the new day broke in upon his soul. The story of Eli, so striking that it has passed into the arts as well as religion, places us at a most significant crisis in the ecclesiastical fortunes of the chosen nation. It is the grand moment of transition from the priest to the prophet. Wafted incense, the fat of beasts, gorgeous sacerdotal vestments, the sacrificial pomp of the priesthood, — hitherto these have been the only medium of intercourse between earth and heaven. But now a new order of worship, more spiritual, more simple, more real, is to be installed. The day of the prophet has come, — bold rebuker of kings and chieftains, — sharp discerner between light and darkness, between truth and lies, — the unsparing censor of the corruptions of government, of the abuses of law, of the idolatries and worldliness of the people. Superannuated Eli, representative of the priestly formalism, slumbers in the temple-court. Young Samuel, first of the prophets, type at once and herald of the new ministry of righteousness, wakes by night, hears the whisper of God's spirit, and answers with the promptitude of a vigilant faith. "The priestly system," it has been well said, "boasts of being immutable and unimprovable; all its veneration is for the past, not sympathetic nor prospective; it turns its back upon the living, and bows the head and bends the knee to departed ages. It involves a distant Deity, a mean humanity, a servile worship, a physical sanctity, and a retrospective reverence." But now comes the prophet "commissioned from the Divine nature to sanctify the human. His business is to bring the finite will and the infinite into immediate and thrilling contact. An earnest speech, a brave and holy life, truth of sympathy, severity of conscience, because freshness and loftiness of faith, — these natural sanctities are his implements of power. The prophetic character involves the ideas of a spiritual Deity, a noble humanity, a loving worship, individual holiness, and a prospective veneration."

At this precise point of history the priest gives way, the prophet appears. Old Eli sleeps by his altar; Samuel, with eager faculties, hears that voice which no sacerdotal ear could hear, and answers, "Speak, Lord; thy servant heareth."

It is a transition symbolical of what may go on in the individual heart, yours or mine. When we pass from a mere outward compliance with religious forms to a hearty adoption of their life; when we turn from sleepy ceremonies that satisfy, to the searching devotions that humiliate and so arouse us; when we cease building on a proud moral complacency, and come straight to our

Father, in our Redeemer, and beseech him to speak, and long to hear, instead of veiling his presence behind natural laws or second causes; — then we have made the whole passage from Jewish externalism, which dies, to Christian spirituality, which is immortal. We have gone from works that have no living root, barren and fruitless, to the faith that ever works by love, and so yields fruit for ever, an hundred-fold. The theory of the priest is, that Heaven is to be propitiated by a round of meritorious acts or forms. The truth of Christian prophecy is, that we reach salvation, and find heaven, just so far as we practically believe in our Saviour, and walk and speak, and buy and sell, and marry and die, in his spirit.

Now, different periods, places, communities, have their peculiar perils. The business of Christianity is to meet with its positive and inexhaustible power just the impending, pressing danger. Its reconciling spirit is one, universal, unchangeable; but its forms of application are not stereotyped, nor its protests everywhere the same. With the recluses of Port Royal, and the monks of St. Edmondsbury, work needed more to be preached than faith; and the resolute preacher who roused the dreamers to action was the true prophet of the Lord. But contemplation is not much our habit. Quietism is not the modern excess. Dreaming is not our American weakness. Everything tends of itself to external demonstration. All the wheels of prosperous enterprise are running. Action is spontaneous. Indolence may debilitate individuals; but the strong, swift march of the multitude tramples them down, or crowds them aside. So work needs less, just here, to be preached than faith. Let us think not of the wants of other centuries, but of our own wants. We want to charge all this human enginery, this useful doing, with the spring or motive power of true good in God, and so convert it to Christ. This is Christianity. This is what churches are built for, Sabbaths are appointed, worship is kept up. You might have many true things, noble virtues, — manliness, honesty, temperance, kindness, courage, — discoursed upon, without these. These are for religion, to keep alive the conviction and love of Christ in men, to make them feel just what Samuel felt in *his* temple, that a personal God speaks, to be obeyed, and a Christ has come, to be formed within.

Get on in the world; get wealth; get position; enjoy yourself; and in doing this follow your own best ideas as you find them in a general culture of your powers and in the laws of the world, by consulting your moral sense, and the judgments of society; do about right, as the standards of respectability require: — is this, or not, a prevailing doctrine of man's highest relations? Is this what has come about in the name of "religion," and what passes for the piety of the churches? The result will inevitably be, first, a lifeless form of devotion, a pretending to pray where there is no prayer; next, a perception of this hollowness by sharp-sighted minds; next, a terrible recoil of scepticism, and a standing aloof from sacred institutions, on the part of men who, however far from faith, are yet too clean to touch a lie; to be followed, I suppose, if the laws of human nature hold good, by some honest, penitent return to a living intercourse with the living Eternal Spirit that has waited patiently all the while. This for the general action of Christendom, — the history of the Church at large. But, meantime, where is the individual? Where are we?

Are we taking up and wearing the name of religion, while our souls are not calling earnestly upon God, and not beseeching, through evil report and through good report, through convivial temptations and fashionable excitements, and profitable dishonesties, and household irritations, to do his will bravely, and abide in his peace contentedly? Can we say in the midst of every company, every plan for the future, every hope of promotion, every bargain, every study, every covert of darkness, "Lord, I wait thy command; speak, thy servant heareth, and will obey"? If not, then that thing we call religion is something else. That happens, only in a different direction, which happened on a large scale under the Papal hierarchy in the Middle Ages, when religion came to mean a set of monastic vows, — when a "religious" person was not a righteous man, or a godly woman, or a devout child anywhere, but a member of a separate community shut out from the world, — and when a "religious" house was not the dwelling of a Christian family, adoring and serving God, but of some Dominican or Franciscan order. The idea of a real relation to God will have gone out, and a notion of mortal power and luxury have come in in its place. Honesty requires that the name shall be changed with the thing.

An intelligent traveller in South Africa states that among the more degraded tribes he found one, where no word was known in the language for a "Supreme Being." There was a word remembered but dimly by only here and there an old man, — one or two in a thousand, — but entirely lost to the mass of the people, signifying, "Him that is above." By gradual steps the very name of the Supreme had faded out, after the vanishing faith in him, from the savage soul. What will it be to the real advantage of our civilization when God himself has been put out of all our thoughts, and men live on daily in utter disregard of his presence and his law, if only by virtue of our superior mastery over the arts of expression we preserve the articulate sound that names him, — the sound by which believing ancestors once heartily called upon him, and each holy tongue said, "Speak, Lord; for thy servant heareth," — but nothing beside. "Not every one that saith unto me, Lord, Lord, shall enter into the kingdom of heaven."

If we look into the average life of Christendom to-day, we find there much bad keeping between the religious language and the habit of religious thought, — or rather the habit of those anxious thoughts which occupy the place that belongs to religion. In other words, Are even the better thought and purpose of men really religious, or ethical only? Does life fix itself habitually in God, take its departure from him, appeal to him, ever return to him, and seek eternal rest and harmony in him? or does it strike out in a bold and eager search after something of its own, feeling along by its own hand over an unbounded sea, without any lamp in the sky, or any unvarying finger to determine a fixed point, "dim sounding on its perilous way," not having God in all its thoughts? If the latter, then, while the old language remains to fill up solemn occasions, to sustain the appearances of worship, to build meeting-houses, and write Sunday-school books, and repeat public prayers, to appease the traditional demand for pious observance, the heart of the whole matter is still wanting; then there is an actual contradiction between the phraseology of the subject and the sense of it, — between the convictions in which such men live, and the speech and ceremony they are afraid to drop.

Now, this is nothing else than cant, the base resort of timidity; superstition, if it springs from a nameless fear of evil, — hypocrisy, if it springs from a love of superstitious people's approval, or a desire to keep on terms of commerce with old respectability; but in either case a ghastly piece of pretension, — a falsehood. Then the world is right in charging upon ecclesiastical functionaries, and even upon Sabbath assemblies, unreality, or worse. Nothing in the world can bring sincerity back but a reopening of the interior gates and avenues between each human soul and Christ, — nothing but a free and faithful turning of the dependent heart to the personal Lord of its life; nothing but the filial and reverential feeling of the Prophet-child, looking ever up with obedient faith, "Lord, here am I; speak, for thy servant heareth!"

It seems to me the testimony of an unprejudiced layman of our times — one of the most penetrating readers of the laws of impression, and one of the most original thinkers — has value, when he says, incidentally, "I believe the reason that preaching is so ineffectual is, that it oftener calls on men to work for God, than to behold God working for them. If," he adds, "for every rebuke that we utter of men's vices, we put forth a claim upon their hearts; if for every assertion of God's demands from them we could substitute a display of his kindness to them, I think there would be fewer deaf children sitting in the market-place."

Leave criticism aside. Our business is with ourselves. We are a company of persons, suppose, seeking in common how to live righteously, to be helped by each other's experience, and encouraged by each other's discoveries. Trying other things, have we tried fairly the power of intercourse by faith with the Spirit? Trying our own strength, have we tried God's? Troubled with our own cares, business perplexities, household sorrows and fears, or with the frightful tendencies of the times, have we taken all these, in salutary and believing confidence, to our Father, as little children take their troubles to father or to mother?

That our religion, in its explicit and holiest sense, is the veritable guide of our life, the support under it, the inspiration quickening it, the comfort healing it, the promise irradiating it; that a man has learnt how to live only when his daily cry is precisely that old cry, "Thy servant heareth; here am I at thy bidding, for thy service, send me"; — this is shown in the fact that such a doctrine stands in exact agreement with the only true theory of the origin of life itself. We talk of our dependence on Providence. Who is Providence? That language means nothing, unless it means that of everything which exists God is, every instant, the ever-new, ever-conscious, ever-active Creator. Strictly speaking, there is but one life. Our personality, individual diversities, moral freedom, are all carefully secured, yet secured every moment by the Spirit himself afresh. "Man lives only from God." Every moment this creative life flows in. Creation is perpetual. We are told of whole forests springing from a single root. The universe itself is such a manifold growth, in affiliated parts. Every form in nature is a branch. The Northman's fable of the universal tree, whose divine sap is the energy by which all things are and consist, was not so far from the true cosmogony, or doctrine of creation, as many a baptized creed which locates its Deity at a distance from his creatures in space, and far back before the flood in time. These throbbing hearts that warm the world are only pulses from one central and everlasting heart of love. Those unfading stars that light the sky, and shine serenely on one another, are only so many tongues of a kindred flame, burning up from one conscious and eternal fire. Our breath, which the ancients called *spiritus*, is the breathing spirit of the Infinite One. "Thou takest away their breath," said the believing Psalmist, "they die, and return to their dust." The whole Bible is written to teach us what we are so slow to learn, that we live in God, and shall be held and judged for ever in the righteous laws of his own justice and truth. "In the beginning God created," is the sublime key-note of the *Old* Testament. "I can do all things through Christ which strengtheneth me," is the blessed consolation of the New. What absurdity and crime, what enormity of ingratitude, as well as defiance of retribution, must it be, to cast off the parental hand, — to hide from the only source of good, — to rebel at the only beauty that never fades, and the only love that never cools! It was, in the beginning, as it ever will be, guilt, and craft, and fear, that hid from God's face, when he was heard coming in the garden. It was, as it ever will be, innocence, and candor, and simple trust, that answered promptly as a welcome in the place of prayer, "Lord, here am I; speak, for thy servant heareth!"

But life is not only given and regiven; it has to be consecrated, redeemed from sin, and spiritually sanctified. So this doctrine throws equal light on the ministry of Christ in the world. In fact, your whole view of that ministry will take its shape from the way this subject lies in your belief. Christ did not come to show us how a human existence can be moulded, and the world's evils be vanquished, by a resolute self-will. It is amazing with what a barren notion of "Christ, the example," some Christian readers have been satisfied; as if the Son of God had stood apart from the vital seats of motive-power, the springs of love and faith in men, and only exhibited to the eye of admiration an external model of excellence, which his followers were to set themselves, with cool faculties, to copy. The highest spiritual works are not accomplished in that way. Exemplary virtue is never the loftiest virtue. Imitation of any model, however high, is not the noblest action of the soul. Influence, as the very etymology of the word might teach, is another thing from that. All our best helps are spiritual gifts or forces from soul to soul. Christ came to be a divine personal influence in the world; i. e. that in and through his Person the Divine life might veritably and literally *flow into* the breasts of mankind. He came not to tell us the manner of living, but to communicate, to pour in, upon all willing and receiving hearts, the power of living, — the energy that acts itself spontaneously into holy thoughts and deeds. To that end the Divine and the human elements are perfectly blended in him. He is the Divine Humanity *in* Jesus of Nazareth; the Word from the beginning; the "Man of Sorrows," and "before Abraham was," Son of Mary, and Son of God. This constitutes a mediator. In order that God might gain that love and that trust, — in order that man might lay hold of him in a *personal* "way, and truth, and life," in a Saviour made in all points like himself, and even tempted as he is, the Father was manifested in the Son. The world's poor, aching heart longed to see and to feel that heavenly compassion, that Divine goodness, and it came. Bethlehem and Calvary were the answer to that want. And so, Christendom over, wherever Christ has been most personally reverenced, and loved, and clung to, and sung, and celebrated, and followed, there his religion has had its most positive planting, and exercised its most effectual control. So, it is said, his true disciples are "partakers" of his life; whoso "receiveth" him — not heareth him merely, or looketh on him, but "receiveth" him — "hath life eternal." We are to eat his flesh, and drink his blood, the strong, true figure says. He is to be formed within us. He gives himself. This comports with the purest and simplest philosophy of the spiritual nature. Surely, if Christ merely set himself up as a pattern of human virtue to be imitated, he did not understand himself, nor his work. Then he could not have said, "As I live by the Father, so ye shall live by me"; "I in them, and thou, Father, in me, that all may be made perfect in one."

Objections can be imagined. It may be said, that when we make it man's first duty to wait on God, as a worshipper and servant of his Spirit, we encourage a tame, abject feeling, by making everything hang in subjection on one being. But what kind of a being? Suppose he is Perfect Goodness, and can no more destroy his child's guarded liberty than he can be untrue to himself. Suppose he is Boundless Light, and holds his children subject only that he may pour the more steadily upon them his spotless brightness, in which they may walk the more safely. Suppose he is Infinite Affection, so that the more entirely we are his, the more we are exalted, enlarged, and raised in the dignity of man's estate. So we learn the difference between the servility that bows to any finite masterdom, and the joyous inspiration of waiting obediently on Him "whose service is perfect freedom."

In fact, I think some natural analogies must have explained to us, that the most inspiring of all things is to feel the direct action of a greater and more generous spirit than our own. Hence it is that we enter into the great instances of self-denial, and grow disinterested by them; that martyrs' sufferings awaken aspiration and stir zeal; that glorious charities kindle enthusiasm and brotherly love in the dullest soul. It is not that the cold understanding sees something there for the cold will to adopt, as a fine virtue for a yet colder selfishness or pride to practise. It is that the uncalculating overflow of noble sympathies in a person whose contact we feel, bears on many responsive natures with it, and that personal goodness exerts an attraction and an authority of which we can only mark the tendency and feel the blessing, without explaining the method, or estimating the extent. And when we ascend from mortal measures of this power to the unsearchable, we take with us an humble illustration how the one spiritual force which most liberates and exalts manhood is faith reverently waiting to hear the order, and run on the errands of our Lord, how obedience to him becomes the perfect emancipation of the soul.

Or it might be said, that to depend on another, though he be infinitely high and holy, puts the grand work of man's salvation out of his own hands, and encourages personal negligence and sloth. And so we might conclude, but for the plain and familiar spiritual principle, that no motive on earth is so efficient to prompt action, to rouse energy, to stimulate invention, to sustain endurance and sacrifice, as personal love. Unless this principle holds, more than half of the world's literature is a lie, and its charm is in its doing violence to the dictates of our nature, instead of echoing them. Take the nearest illustration. For the first dozen years of his life, and often more, each of us, as a rule, is subject to his parents. It is a subjection of trust and affection on the one side, of love and tenderness on the other, and so the best possible image of the parentage in heaven. Does it indispose the heart for service? Does it prevent the child's activity? Or does it, in healthy and normal cases, beget the sacred passion for grateful obedience, and the life-long eagerness to render work for work, and love for love?

The facts of experience come in, and turn the imaginary objection into a positive proof. For where have the most practical of human charities, and the grand ameliorations of philanthropy, had their birth and growth? Has it not been in the strong-holds of religion, — in the climate of Christian faith, — in the breasts of believers? History makes her undeniable answer. The love of God has created and warmed the love of man. Faith has fed charity. Prayer has inspired beneficence. In the martyrdoms of the Church, in the hospitals of pestilence and war, on both continents, where rude soldiers and dying lepers have invoked blessings on the sisters of mercy, and kissed the passing shadows of those angels of human compassion, as fast as one section falls before the contagion, or faints with famine, another presses up to fill the empty places; the thinned companies close their ranks with celestial, cheerful courage, and the august ministry of Nazareth goes on. Not seldom the most contemplative of the mystics have been the most abundant in alms-deeds. Many of the Quietists, accused of an inactive and selfish piety, were really the practical philanthropists of their time. One of the chief masters of the sect of German devotees called "The Friends of God," of the fourteenth century, set down by their enemies as visionaries and dreamers, is found writing these words, worthy of any humanity-preacher of the nineteenth: "For my part, I would rather there were less of excitement and transport, less of mere sweet emotion, so that a man were diligent and right manful in working, for in such exercise do we best know ourselves. These raptures are not the highest order of devotion. And this I say, that if it happened to me, that I had to forsake that lofty, inward work, to go and prepare comfort for some sick person, I should go cheerfully, believing not only that God would be with me, but that he would vouchsafe me, it may be, even greater grace and blessing in that external work, undertaken out of true love in the service of my neighbor, than I should receive in my season of loftiest contemplation." All fair history confirms what right reason would expect, that there is no fountain of good labors so rich and unfailing as a heart that ever waits and calls on God.

So the doctrine proves itself complete; not narrow and one-sided, but broad and all-embracing. Out of this holy waiting upon God comes the resolute action for men; out of this childlike looking upward into the spiritual world, the manliest pressing forward into enterprises for the world around you; out of the believing prayer, each duty of the day. It was when Hannah's son laid down to sleep, ere the lamp of God went out in the temple, — the ark of sacred promise resting at his side, — that the voice called. Faith hallows the evening and the morning, and makes them a day of the Lord. The consecrated disciple rises to each new encounter with his lot, in a reverent vigilance for every beckoning of God's hand. He falls asleep, each night, with a sacred curiosity to hear that further revelation of the great secret and mystery of being which the daybreak is sure to tell from the Spirit. He finds a path through the intricacies of earthly duty, by a simple reference to the benignity of the Lord, — like the Psalmist, who fled from the onset of his enemies, and the strife of tongues, to the "pavilion of the Most High." He quiets the importunities of his own unbelieving mind by confessing, "Thou wilt show me the path of life"; like Sir Thomas Browne, who says he conquered his "sturdy doubts and boisterous objections in no martial posture, but on his knees."

The revelations of God are not ended, if only there are earnest eyes to see them, though the lamp has gone out in the Hebrew temple. His voice has not ceased speaking, if childlike trust listens, though the ark of the elder covenant has floated away into darkness. His glory is not quenched on the open face of creation, though it shines no longer in the Shekinah over the wings of the cherubim. Each obedient and thoughtful heart may take up the supplication, as the poetry of faith has paraphrased it, — sermon passing into song, and exhortation into prayer: —

"Still, as of old, thy precious word
Is by the nations dimly heard;
The hearts its holiness hath stirred
Are weak and few.
Wise men the secret dare not tell;
Still in thy temple slumbers well
Good Eli: O, like Samuel,
Lord, here am I!

"Few years, no wisdom, no renown,
Only my life can I lay down;
Only my heart, Lord, to thy throne
I bring; and pray
A child of thine I may go forth,
And spread glad tidings through the earth,
And teach sad hearts to know thy worth!
Lord, here am I!

"Young lips may teach the wise, Christ said;
Weak feet sad wanderers home have led;
Small hands have cheered the sick one's bed
With freshest flowers:
O, teach me, Father! heed their sighs,
While many a soul in darkness lies
And waits thy message; make me wise!
Lord, here am I!

"And make me strong; that, staff and stay,
And guide and guardian of the way,
To thee-ward I may bear, each day,
Some fainting soul.
Speak, for I hear; make pure in heart,
Thy face to see; thy truth impart,
In hut and hall, in church and mart!
Lord, here am I!

"I ask no heaven till earth be thine,
Nor glory-crown, while work of mine
Remaineth here; when earth shall shine
Among the stars,
Her sins wiped out, her captives free,
Her voice a music unto thee,
For crown, new work give thou to me!
Lord, here am I!"

When the heavy weights of discouragement hang upon our will, — when the riddle of the world's success and failure vexes the understanding, — when all our strivings look like baffled blows upon the air, — when the name of virtue, put near any deed of ours, seems like a mockery and a satire on all we are and do, — when changed faces create a solitude in the midst of society, or unanswered affections turn festivities into mournful struggles with despair, or empty seats in our houses and our hearts make us cry out, in the long night of life, "Would God it were morning,"—then what better thing to do, there in the dark, than to wait, in the spirit of the consecrated child,—ere the lamp of God goes quite out,—to listen, and the moment the voice of God speaks, in whatever tone, to arise and answer faithfully, "Lord, I am here, thy servant; speak, for thy servant heareth!"

Then God himself, he that created thee, will answer: "Fear not; I have called thee by thy name, and thou art mine; I have redeemed thee: when thou passest through the waters, I will be with thee; and through the rivers, they shall not overflow thee. When thou walkest through the fire, thou shalt not be burned, neither shall the flame kindle upon thee. I am thy God, thy Saviour. Ye shall be my sons and my daughters, saith the Lord Almighty."

There is order in the spiritual world, as it lies within and above us. Life without Christ is anarchy. A sincere piety is the master sentiment of the soul, governing all things. Charity to man,—the bright hopes of a better future for the race,—all rest at last on that. One of Raphael's frescos in the Vatican represents the three Christian Graces. Charity stands in the midst of poverty and weakness, little children resting in her arms, and clinging to her robes. Hope lifts her hands, and turns her face upward in prophetic expectation. But Faith, on which both seem to lean, only "clasps, patiently and tenderly and inseparably, the cross on which her Master died."

SERMON III.

THE FAITH-FACULTY.

THE THINGS OF THE SPIRIT OF GOD . . . . . ARE SPIRITUALLY DISCERNED. — 1 Cor. ii. 14.

THIS is addressed to persons supposed to have some concern about gaining a Christian character, and to be seeking the way. It presumes us to be risen above the stolidity of a mere sensual satisfaction into a posture of spiritual inquiry. It especially meets two mistakes, not uncommon, nor without plausibility; — that of supposing that the whole measure of Christian obligation is filled out by a development of moral sensibility and moral performance; and that of supposing that all Christian truth can be received and tested by the intellect.

If that is the best definition of education which makes it consist in giving a man the right use of his powers, the education will be best which assigns to each of his powers its own use, and does not require of one to do the work of another. Respecting those faculties of man that are more purely intellectual, this is generally allowed. But it is just as true of what is called his religious or spiritual nature; and in the practical acknowledgment of that truth will come a great wave of spiritual light, a great gain of religious power, — if indeed such a discovery shall not be found indispensable finally to any commanding action of the Christian faith in the world.

Why should I, or why should you, not having done so before, set about the business of being a Christian, — in secret principle, in open confession, in consistent conduct? This, in short, is the question. Christianity stands on earth, the Gospel is published, Christ himself was born at Bethlehem, and died at Calvary, and inspires his disciples, to give the answer. But that it may be received as an answer, that in us which the voices speak to must hear; that door through which only the heavenly guests can enter, must be open.

Every good that is possible to man finds something in him to lay hold of it; material nourishment, a body; the air, lungs; light, eyes; enterprises, a will; property, the passion of ownership; beauty, taste; science, an understanding; friends, affection. On the other hand, every faculty in him has its external object, and an appropriate exercise in reaching towards it. This is the adaptation of the creature to his place; the mutual fitness between man and his home, — every part of man and some part of his surroundings. Without this complete adjustment, nature would be a riddle, the mind a mockery, history a failure, and our Maker certainly not God.

So far as the outward condition is concerned, this is easily found out. Even in the more external movements of *the intellect*, having to do with our immediate wants, and necessary to provide for our comfort, it is acknowledged. If we fail to own it when we come to our deeper life, passing from man as a mind to man as a soul, — or from man as he thinks and understands, to man as he feels, aspires, and believes, — it will not be because the analogy fails, but only because we enter a region we have kept less familiar, and whose objects lie farther from the senses; — the senses meantime crowding in and engrossing attention.

Every competent authority, however, affirms that man is provided with a spiritual power, for discerning, receiving, and doing spiritual things. The Word, experience, the system of nature in other departments, and the human constitution itself, agree in that. There are spiritual realities. How do we know it, or what is it to us when we do know it, if there is not an implanted faculty in us, capable of becoming conversant with those realities? There is, to vary the expression, a spiritual world, — including beings and facts and laws of its own. How strange if there were not some part of ourselves made to touch it, — opening out on that side, — and, if treated purely, if dealt with according to its own conditions, forming a bond of kindred and sympathy between our whole nature and that world unseen! Or, if you prefer, there is a body of religious truth, imposing corresponding duties on us, which we can apprehend, and commune with, and draw from, only by a distinct energy, whose germ God planted, meant for that end, and for no other.

How God himself exists, an Infinite Person; how his spirit acts on human spirits; the divinity of the man Christ Jesus; the possibility and power of redemption; how sin can be forgiven; the certainty of a future life; the great laws of religious improvement and decay, including the facts of salvation and retribution, or

Heaven and Hell; the being of persons not living in visible bodies;—these are among the things obviously belonging to that world, that body of truth, that scene of spiritual realities, and are really known to us only through a spiritual discernment, or faculty of faith,—as outward nature is known by the senses, and its scientific relations by the understanding.

After this enumeration, nothing need be said of the relative rank of this spiritual part of man among the human powers. The interests it embraces, the infinitude it touches,—the fact that by it we are related to God, and to Eternity, so that our boundless weal or woe depends upon it,—all this lifts it at once into unquestionable supremacy. If it exists at all, it is the royal thing in us, and rules by divine right.

Now, if we begin to say that we will know religion only through some of the faculties given us for knowing something else, that we will not set about being Christians except by means of the understanding, or the memory, or sensible proof; if, when we are called on to believe, we reply, we will not believe because we cannot demonstrate,—whereas if we could demonstrate there would be no occasion at all to believe; if we say, we will not trust in God, nor pray, nor credit the Christian Incarnation, nor accept the New Testament, because these are things not rationally made out, because we have stationed logic as gate-keeper to let nothing pass that cannot be framed into a syllogism;—then do we not call off a part of our powers to do a work not their own, and for which they are not fit? Do we not miss a good, possibly an infinite one, by that mismanagement? Do we not abuse ourselves, just as if we should insist on judging poetry by rules of reasoning, or learning algebra by our affections, or trying to remember a language we never studied? You say, you cannot reason out the whole Gospel teaching. Very well; the Gospel never said you could, nor asked you to try. The Gospel approaches that part of your nature which the Creator made to receive it. The things of the Spirit are spiritually discerned.

On the other hand, if we leave out of practice and out of culture one of the faculties, or groups of faculties, planted in us for growth; if we fail to direct it to its proper objects, and to nourish it on its natural food, then, like other unused powers, it will wither and die. So much will be not only taken from the efficiency and the symmetry of our being, but we forfeit all the wisdom meant to come by that avenue. Other forces, which this ought to have counterbalanced and checked, will grow rank and pernicious. Nor shall we ever quite know how much we have lost, — what glories and joys may have been shut out, — what bright and heavy-laden processions from the gates of heaven may have passed by, such as might have filled our houses with honor, while we were busy making terms with those sharp extortioners and publicans of the brain.

One chief difficulty probably consists in the fact that this spiritual faculty, while distinct, is yet so intimately and so variously connected with others. It is so connected, because man is a complex being; just as *each* of our powers is modified by its companions. As the imagination affects the judgment, as the affections modify the will, as the memory restrains the fancy and helps the understanding, or as the logical faculty cools the passions, so the spiritual faculty may, more or less, mix with all these, and, in turn, be strengthened or weakened by their suggestions. It was intended to be so. Yet, out of that necessity doubtless comes a danger that faith will not get her due ; and for the cause just now assigned, — that her objects are more remote, while the appetites are not only exorbitant but somehow disordered, and fallen from their estate of purity.

All our powers exercise reciprocal influences. To a degree, they are not only related, but interdependent, for they are parts of one living, organic creature. In their perfect balance would be the perfection of character. Depravity, of all sorts, unsettles that balance. It pulls the sovereign from its throne, sets up a usurper in selfishness, raises an insurrection of passions, and leaves the whole commonwealth in discord. Worst of all, and first of all, it clogs the channels whereby illumination and energy flow in from above, and so at once multiplies our enemies, and robs us of our weapons of defence.

Another obstacle to the right appreciation of this faculty grows out of the indefiniteness of the place assigned it in any metaphysical classification. It is easy to see what recognized powers are adjacent to it ; — the affections, because the character of God and the first Christian duty is love ; conscience, because the discrimination between right and wrong draws the line where religion comes in contact with and re-enforces morality, or practical righteousness ; reverence, because without that there would be no worship ; the desire of excellence, and a sense of the Infinite, if these are to be reckoned distinct natural powers, because both of them would bring important elements to what is the common understanding of religion. Possibly, if philosophy had completed its analysis, all that we mean by the distinct spiritual faculty would be found embraced under some of its names. It is enough that we know the faculty by its effects; that we can have a growing consciousness of it, if we will; and that the whole resultant action of all its elements is *faith*, — the New Testament faith, — not mere belief, not mere trust, still less mere opinion, or vague feeling, but faith. We may call it, then, without error, the *faith-faculty*.

Very largely, it is subject to the same conditions, as to its cultivation, with the other faculties.

For instance, it is increased by a separate and special discipline of its own, as the rest are; with its own apparatus, tuition, and practice. As the understanding has its school, the affections their home, the artistic faculty its manipulations and galleries, the natural sciences their lectures and cabinets, so the spiritual power has its own modes of impression and multiplication, — in the Bible and its filial literature, — in meditation, rising into devotion, — in the Church and its ordinances.

Or, secondly, the faith-faculty may be assisted indirectly by the healthy exercise of all the other powers. No exclusive possession is claimed for it. It rather penetrates than excludes; rather leavens than destroys; rather sanctifies than slays. All that is, in the good sense, natural, it tries to purify and preserve; only when it meets those natural *sins* which are really the perversions and degradations of nature as God made it, does it lay the axe to the root of the tree, and overturn, and make the old die that the new may be born. Otherwise it welcomes all the other powers to its service, in their co-ordinate, harmonious operation. Christianity has a body of facts, to which it refers for testimony, — facts of history, facts of human nature, — and therefore it wants the understanding to grasp and hold them. So long as the understanding keeps to its own province, and does not presume beyond its limits, there is agreement. So have these Christian facts a system of laws, relations, and doctrines under and among them ; and, therefore, the faith-faculty asks for science to arrange them. So long as science does not trespass over her own domain, to pass upon what is not hers, there is only concord still. So has religion, for its impressions and effects, symbols and forms of beauty, and calls in the aids of poetry and art, architecture and music. So long as taste does not undertake to dictate to piety, and substitute her æsthetics for religious principle, all is harmonious. Once more, the sequences of moral and religious truth involve processes of reasoning; hence theology is thankful for sound logic, and only when it grows meddlesome and arrogant, does the higher authority have to rebuke it as foolishness, a babbler, — "science falsely so called." And, in general, since sophistry and error are apt to encumber the simplicity of the Gospel with artificial matter, the close-thinking intellect is serviceable in clearing the human additions away, and undoing a false reasoning with a true.

But, apart from all mixtures and modifications, the spiritual sight has a sphere of its own. Things are shown to it not shown to the strongest brain. A knowledge breaks upon the earnest heart, waiting at the Master's feet, which makes the wisdom of the world but folly. Rendering unto the understanding the things of the understanding, we must render unto faith the things that are faith's. We are not to say that till we can compass the heavenly world with our intellectual measuring line, and clear up every difficulty, we will not believe ; any more than we are to say, that till we can have logic set to music, we will not learn logic; or that, till the propositions of geometry are put to us in brilliant rhetoric we will not study geometry. A burst of feeling, or an impassioned appeal, may find a graceful place, and have a persuasive effect, now and then, in a legal argument; but, whatever else we may think of it, we cannot say it is a part of the argument. And a purely intellectual process may render invaluable aid to religious truth, but it will not make it a whit more true, nor necessarily bear it in on those seats of feeling and faith, where it must get a lodgment, if it is to renew the fountains of life.

It is to the faith-faculty that revelation is offered. Indeed, revelation would be impossible without it; and it is only for want of opening it, and looking through it, that some men doubt whether a revelation has been made. As the word signifies, revelation is an uncovering, or showing, of what was before unseen,—utterly profitless, of course, except there is a vision to behold what is shown. Patmos, the Mount of Transfiguration, the banks of the Jordan, Gethsemane, would be all spots of common earth and without illumination but for that. When the voice from above, in reply to the Saviour's prayer, "Father, glorify thy name," answered, "I have both glorified it, and will glorify it again," some of them that stood by, rationalists, said that it thundered; others, spiritually-minded, said that an angel spoke to him. To a really spiritual mind it will seem no strange thing that, when an epoch like the advent of Christ arrives, and the whole course of the world is to be changed, the habits of the material scene should yield to the stress of the spirit, and the time of the Messiah be signalized by that spiritual world breaking through a little, and giving tokens of its reality,—what we call miracle. To appreciate the revelation will require a vision in sympathy with the Christ revealed. Yet, doubtless, the showing of the things stimulates and quickens the vision. Perhaps it is significant of this, that the word "vision" is used for both, — the faculty seeing, and the thing seen, — both being related and mutually dependent.

Revelation, not being a book of psychology, does not describe the exact place that spiritual discernment has in a metaphysical system, nor even, as we have seen, give to it a metaphysical name. It simply refers to it by its action, its function, which is faith. Of that all the Bible is full, letting us see the faculty by its fruit, — the practical not the speculative way. After the name of the Author of our religion, faith is the chief term of the Bible; and it is the correlate to that name. The Word is forever calling on men to believe. Have faith. To many people, whose spiritual life has never been awakened and exercised, this word sounds vague, abstract, technical: sounds as of the pulpit, and not of the living world. Yet, in the light of this truth, as we have seen it, how simple and how natural! Have faith! That is, exercise this faith-faculty. Use it; and by using it, strengthen it. Open the soul. Let the light in. Let the prayer be, "Lord, I believe; help thou mine unbelief."

It is very remarkable, if we read the Evangelists with this view, how constantly Christ addresses himself to this inward vision. He evidently expects to accomplish nothing without it. His parables, his warnings, his tender entreaties, were all adapted to open and quicken it. Till that was done, his message could not get entrance. So he stands waiting, with unspeakable compassion and love, before every heedless, unbelieving, unrepenting heart: "Behold I stand at the door, and knock." He waits for the inward eye to open. He does everything, says everything, that is possible to help it to open. Without that, nothing avails. Even miracles would be useless. The healer of sightless men came to cure a worse blindness than any that shuts out the light of the sun. His errand on earth was not to restore a few sick, or palsied, or buried bodies. He did that only to reach in, to startle, to raise up, the deaf, dumb, paralytic, slumbering soul within. It was the Lazarus of a lost humanity he was seeking, when he cried, "Come forth," "Loose him, and let him go." Accordingly, before he put forth these special wonders, how often he looked in on the hearts about him, to see if there was that indispensable readiness that would justify the miracle, or make it really beneficent. Sometimes it was simply a common question, as if to fix the mind: to Bartimeus, "What wilt thou that I should do unto thee?" Sometimes it was a searching requirement, uncovering instantly all the hidden reservation, and exposing the weak illusion: to the young man: "Sell all thou hast, and give to the poor." Sometimes, as to Matthew: "Believest thou this?" When the leper cried, at once, "Lord, if thou wilt, thou canst make me clean," he did not delay, but put forth his hand and healed him. When the centurion had such humility as to decline the visit of the Lord of life to his unworthy roof, he exclaimed, "I have not found so great faith, no, not in Israel." And when the Syrophenician woman came pleading for her lunatic daughter, he let her cry long after him, till he had proved her: "It is not meet to take the children's bread, and to cast it to dogs." Yet, when she had the lowliness and the trust to say, "Yea, Lord, yet the dogs under the table eat of the crumbs which fall from their master's table," and showed herself content even with the cast-off blessings of a more favored people, he spake again that great benediction, "Great is thy faith, be it unto thee even as thou wilt." And so, forever and forever, we shall be spiritually enriched just as much as we are willing and ready to be. They that love much are forgiven much; and "the things of the Spirit are spiritually discerned."

We can apply the same principle to seeking for what are called the "Evidences for Christianity." As often conducted, that study is chiefly a dry exercise of the understanding. It is all very well. The understanding's own difficulties are met; intellectual objections are removed; the sceptic's allegations are logically answered, perhaps, and the Gospel history is reconciled with reason. A very noble enterprise, on the outworks. Only it does not make a believer, in Christ's sense. It does not bring the interior life into sympathy with the Saviour. It does not give spiritual discernment. It does not bring us to live joyfully and affectionately with our Lord.

Faith comes another way,—by its own faculty. It has been said, by a bold statement, that we are to believe Jesus Christ was the Son of God because he said he was. It sounds credulous, at first. And it is not the whole of the truth. But there is a profound meaning in it, and it was a profound thinker that said it. We *are* to believe Christ is the Son of God because *he* says he is; that is, because such a person as he, with his character and nature, with all that we at once see and feel him to be, if we give ourselves up to a simple impression of his Divine Goodness,—because *he*, with his own spirit, his love, and look, and tone, says he is. There is an evidence of Christianity; not an argument, but an apprehension; not a balancing of affirmatives and negatives, but a direct sight. Standing before him on the mount, sitting at his feet, looking up at him on the cross, we believe. Without reasoning upon it, without deduction, or premise, or analysis, we consent. We use *those* steps at our leisure, to confirm, or to settle subsidiary matters. But by faith, we say it is so; it is borne in upon us as a conviction, like the goodness of the friend we love; and no dialectics will make it more true. It is as true as it can be; and you are just as likely, more likely, to *act* upon such a conviction, in any common case, than on the result of an argumentative process.

Or, take up any of the Saviour's great sayings, where principles are announced so broad as to encompass the whole zone of duty,—truths so vast as to link heaven and earth together; what are they still but verbal sounds, save as there is a spiritual discernment? "I am the Resurrection and the Life,"—that unparalleled sentence, of more moment to each of us than all the wealth and all the knowledge and all the news circulating through all the civilization and societies of the world; over how many listless ears and indifferent minds it will pass to-day, as fruitless as the mourning mother's repetition of the familiar name to the daughter that was dead! "Thou shalt love the Lord thy God with all thy heart":—what is it to us, if our earnest hearts within us are not asking *what* we shall do, and whom we shall love. "I pray, O Father, that they may be one, as we are":—is there any logic in the books, or any science in the schools, that will make that prayer clearer to your soul, or that will abate, one particle, its eternal beauty and grandeur when the love of your own soul has really prayed it once? Take the Beatitudes, one by one. And as their immortal promises fall on the outward sense,—mercy for the merciful, comfort for them that mourn, the kingdom of heaven for the poor in spirit, filial places for the peacemakers, celestial fellowship with the Prophets for those persecuted for righteousness' sake, and for the pure in heart the beatific vision of God,—what does all this boundless *Beatus*, "Blessed," signify, except there be some spiritual discernment to catch an image of the joy? To the sensual, to the profane, to the soul that is shut upward and open only toward the earth, cold in devotion and eager only with its appetites, or cased in that intellectual selfishness that shrinks as it freezes, what great desire, or aspiration, can that "Blessed" bring?

It is not to be forgotten that in the practical direction of the Christian life, in the various applications of Christian truth to duties, there is need of the best intellectual force. Religion is constantly calling mental activity to her service. For instance, in the First Epistle to the Corinthians, you find a large discussion of questions of judgment,—questions, rather, of conscience, primarily, but such that only judgment, reflection, intellectual powers, can rightly settle them. They are properly matters of Christian casuistry. Christianity was a new religion. It had to be put into many old practices, social relations, civil and ecclesiastical institutions. These involved more or less important questions. They were not the great things of Revelation. Revelation is occupied with grand original truths, comprehensive facts, immense disclosures of a world of unseen life. So it can plant *them* in the convictions of men, it is less concerned about the rest. It knows the rest will come, in due time, by the working of the accepted Spirit.

Yet naturally the minds of the first Christians would be greatly exercised on the practical side of their new religion, getting it at work in their life, into contact with their habits and employments, adjusted to their former notions and outward ordinances. Faith, in itself, is an unchangeable principle; but when it acts by human agents, in human affairs, its operations will be variable. Paul would help these first Christians in that matter. He was able. He had their confidence. He had a strong dialectic power, and a ripe culture, as well as spiritual illumination. So he taught them, about circumcision, about tongues, about going to law, about marriage, and feasts, and church discipline, — all with reference to a fair working out of the Christian ideas. But then he knew, all the while, these were not the great things of faith. Those, which were really the subjects of his inspiration, were stated in few words. It was in them, after all, that his specialty, as an apostle, lay; and he often and gladly returned to them. Whenever he comes to them it is with veneration, with holy feet. Then he says, "Spiritual things are spiritually discerned."

It is a great hour for a man, when he wakes up to this conviction that there is a world of truth which he is to receive, grow familiar with, and live in, otherwise than through his mind, or his bodily senses. It is a new being. It is his regeneration. The term is not too strong. Christ uses it, deliberately, repeatedly. For that change is not merely the addition of a new sense, on a level with his other senses. It is a wakening to a world not only new, but one which, if seen to exist at all, is seen to be of supreme beauty, dignity, brilliancy. It pours another atmosphere over all the things we know by other senses. "If any man be in Christ, — *in Christ*, — what does that mean, if not something far more than a mere external or even intellectual presence, — *in him* as in an element, an air of life, a vital and inspiring ether, a flood of light? whosoever is thus in Christ "is a new creature. Old things are passed away; behold, all things are become new." Sin is hateful. Transgressions are repented of and renounced. There is a new principle of living, which is the love of God. Wonderful things are written of it, by them that know. It makes men willing to suffer, willing to die. For "every one that loveth is born of God," and cannot really die. "His seed remaineth in him." "He that loveth not, knoweth not God, for God is love; and he that loveth dwelleth in God, and God in him." "And hereby we know that he dwelleth in us, by the spirit which he hath given us."

All this is but the waking up, quickening into active and conscious life, of a germ or faculty formed in us by our Maker; the calling up of a vitality which sin had deadened. Doubtless there is a difference in degrees of the natural endowment, in different persons. But in every man it exists, and in every man there is enough to make a Christian of. In this also, it follows the analogy of the other faculties, in sane and common cases. The power is of God; the use is by man.

Nor is it to be overlooked that for the training of this spiritual power there is an appointed tuition. We are sent to that school. The "selfsame spirit" that is the quickener and teacher, in order to deal naturally with us, and give regularity to the spiritual life, will have a language, rich and varied, to express to the inward sense the invisible things, by things that are seen and heard. Images, forms, books, rituals, ministries, become symbols and vehicles of the hidden reality. These are never to be thrust out of their place by a false spiritualism; never to be thrust into the place of the Divine substances they body forth by a materialistic superstition. Then they become idols, or a cant, like all unreal speech and ceremony; but in themselves they are the beautiful and fitting language to us of what we are by-and-by to see face to face, and know as we are known, the veil taken away.

Indeed, the spiritual world is so much greater than this, that it is probable all outward things are only signs of its realities, expressions of its facts. Very likely there is no form in nature, that has not its spiritual counterpart. However this may be, we know that we have a special language to teach us spiritual discernment. We have forms of worship, ordinances of consecration and communion, a Bible. Through these we are to read, with the spirit of sincerity for our lamp, the spiritual sense. To stop with the form or letter itself is like only noticing the grammar and the rhetoric of composition, regardless of what it conveys. We spell out our heavenly lesson under a higher and holier influence. God makes all life his interpreter.

> "The Spirit breathes upon the Word,
> And brings the truth to light."

In Judaism, in Christendom, that word does not profit which is not mixed with faith in them that hear it.

We may wonder that this spiritual light, or faith-faculty, was not given to us perfect and mature. The knowledge of truth and of heaven is a good: why should not a God of goodness, who holds this very thing supreme, confer it on us, without this slow, stumbling process of acquirement? Why not rend away the veil at once, and compel us to believe?

But compulsory belief would not be faith. Besides, no other desirable attainment is given us on these terms, — no knowledge of the stars, or the earth, or coins, or shells, or plants. And by going down a little way, we find a part, at least, of the reason. In the whole Divine Economy of Man, we see the enlargement of his powers reckoned a greater good than the bare increase of his possessions. The wisdom to use, to assimilate, and to set things into their relations, is more than the owning of them. It is no unusual thing to see a man surrounded by wealth that he has got together by one kind of faculty without the other faculty which can turn it to account in solid help, in true beauty, in culture, in the enriching and adorning of his own manhood. This is sometimes called success in business; but you would not call it so. So it is not uncommon to see a man who has piled up stores of information in his memory, but is as helpless as before, for want of the faculty that transmutes knowledge into personal force. This may be called learning, but not by learned men. In each case, how much better would a power of another sort be, — more mind and less money, in the one, — more wisdom if less knowledge, in the other. One sits there in his furniture and estates, a subaltern, mortified for his awkwardness, or else despised because he is not mortified: — the other carries about a load of the names of all substances in earth and air at his tongue's end, yet none the less at the mercy of all the hard weather of life.

So, even in religion, the first good will not be a formal or literal acquaintance with the objects. They must, as it were, enter into us, and become a part of us. We must know them by sympathy. Like must beget like, in the appreciative and responsive action of our own nature. Graciously God refuses to let us have spiritual things, save by the steady growth and ripening of a spiritual mind. In fact, otherwise we should not really *have* them. They might lie about us, like the items of a miser's property, but we should never own them. Possibly they might rather own us, enslave us in superstition, or some bondage to the letter. We should hold them only nominally, not really. It would be mortgage, and not freehold. Any mere passing of glories before the organs of sight would be a spectacle and nothing more, — the flitting images of the magic lamp, not "the powers of the world to come."

Hence, by a law that cannot be broken, spiritual knowledge is not poured irresistibly into the mind. We have to reach out for it, and work towards it, and strive after it, and little by little get the *feeling* of it, along with the *sight* of it. It is for our own sake. It is that the truth may really be ours, of us, our *life* and not our *furniture*. It is because otherwise it would be of no more service to us than bank-notes in the fingers of an infant, or a steam-engine in the hands of a savage. This is what Christ doubtless refers to, where, speaking of an extreme case, he tells the disciples not to cast their pearls before swine. The gross nature does not see that they are pearls.

That seen, there would be hope; and the patient Christ would wait, and labor, and invite to the last; for no Teacher was ever so encouraging. Yet there must be eyes willing to see. "He that hath ears to hear, let him hear."

The instruction and the encouragement are direct. Our Christian attainments are in our own hands, and yet are not less, for that, the gift and grace of God's spirit. Heaven is over us, and open to us. The Gospel is plain to the eye that reads in faith. All the world illustrates this Christian lesson. If the practised astronomic observer can see a star in the sky, where others see only the field of blue; if the worker in mosaic can detect distinctions of color where others see none; if the Esquimaux can distinguish a white fox in the snow; if the sailor sees the ship where the landsman sees no spot; — if thus, to a measurable keenness of vision, "the eye sees what it brings the power to see," then, much more, as we lift up the eyes of the spirit, in prayer and trust and charity, shall we behold the invisible, look on the things not seen and eternal, and, by purity of heart, "see God." "I am come," said Jesus, "that they which see not might see." Then, as in the higher walks of science the illuminated mind sometimes transcends the ordinary necessities of language, conquers defect, and leaps to its discoveries as by intuition, or translates the ideas of nature by a deeper familiarity with her signs, so it will be here. Outward things cannot destroy nor change that interior sight. It has been said that when the great English anatomist, Hunter, died, leaving the results of his life-long observations and his classification in unpublished manuscripts, his fraudulent brother-in-law, aiming to appropriate the system as his own, burnt the work and fancied his guilty secret safe. But the scholar had recorded his thoughts in another volume. When competent naturalists opened his museum of specimens, preserved in the Royal College of Surgeons, there, on the cases, they could read off, in the exact arrangement of his specimens, as clearly as in words, his whole theory of the animal kingdom. And if even the intellect rises to these noble freedoms and independencies, in its insight, how much more the spirit, which, because it dwelleth in Love, is born of God, and dwelleth in God, already, and forever.

And now, if this line of thought is just, you will not shrink from any lawful inferences from it; but will thankfully accept them, even if their practical application should be searching to the conscience.

1. See, then, first, that the waking of this spiritual power, in any individual heart, at the call of God's spirit, into a conscious and voluntary action, is the beginning of the Christian life. By man's creation, the germ of it was provided, and that was all nature did. Even what nature originally supplied, man has perverted. The germ was bent and hurt in its tenderness. Not only the individual but the Race has perverted it. Hereditary appetites have biased it. Bad passions have depraved it. God comes again, in Christ, to heal and quicken. For that act the New Testament has plain names: "being born again," "renewal," "regeneration," "conversion," "believing with the heart." It stands in rational analogy with all our living ways. To see, to feel, to begin to act, in the Spirit, — this is the essential of Christian discipleship, of the immortal life, on earth, in heaven.

2. One kind of exercise does not bring another kind of strength; one kind of effort another kind of attainment; but each its own. Muscular training does not furnish the mind, but the body. An eager acquisition of money does not refine the taste, nor liberalize the disposition; it only sharpens the eye to the main chance. Political ambition does not foster magnanimity, but cunning and calculation. So in every department of action and pursuit. And, by the same law, moral endeavors will produce moral vigor, but not spiritual,—for there is a difference. Uprightness in trade is a noble trait; it is worth more than it ever costs; and there is no Christian character without it. But honesty in business is, after all, a distinct thing from faith in God; there is not a village in Christendom where the two are not found in separate men. Honesty grows by honest dealing; faith grows by religious worship and experience. Veracity is established by telling the truth; but a spirit of prayer is awakened by going away in secret, and penitently, humbly conversing with God. The blessed submission that trusts heaven in every trouble and bereavement,—by the bed of pain, in loss of fortune, in the desertion of friends, at the new-made grave,—this is a spiritual grace, one of the "things of the Spirit," and it is no more to be gained by mere outward correctness of behaviour, or a compliance with all the decent rules of social morality, than fortitude is to be gained by frugality, or tender affections by a stout understanding. An inward sense of communion with Christ is a spiritual thing, and, a very practicable thing: it is the true Christian's peculiar privilege. But it cannot be found in the mere routine of an honorable, thrifty traffic, nor in the ex-

citements of society. It is found by coming to Christ, believing on him, thinking of him, loving him, being grateful to him, opening to him, as he stands at the door and knocks. The inward nature is made of organs like the outward. Each has eyes to see with, and hands to lay hold by. Christ came into the world to touch, restore, vitalize the benumbed and dying organs of the soul, — that they which see not might see; and every power, now paralyzed by sin, might leap back to life. If we would have this matchless and miraculous physician heal us, and make us spiritual beings, fit for a spiritual or heavenly society, we must be more than industrious, more than economical, more than amiable and temperate and respectable: though we must certainly be all these: "these ought ye to have done, and not to leave the other undone." We must, in all the powers of godliness, in devotion, in the love of God, in faith and hope and charity, go from strength to strength, — steadfast, always advancing, always abounding, in the work of the Lord.

3. The doctrine will remove, if we suffer it, many of those hinderances to our setting in earnest about the Christian life, which spring from a mistaken impression that the teachings of religion must first be encased in the formulas of reasoning, or seen through by the understanding, instead of humbly welcomed by faith. That mistake will only confuse, darken, and cripple the soul. Each power God hath given us, to its own place, for its own office! Thus only can we gain God's blessing, or do his will. If we put the heart where the brain belongs, we shall be children, and not men, in understanding. If we put the reason where faith belongs, we shall fail of our highest glory, miss the heavenly

peace, be ungrateful to God and to Christ, and stay ignorant of the first wisdom. Of the pure light of Heaven, gained by prayer and by doing the will, we can never have too much; but by trying to put our own tapers instead of it, we destroy the very temple we were exploring. The excess of candles in the illumination of the Church of San Spirito, at Florence, consumed the building. So our pride of human opinion quenches that Holy Spirit itself, of which all sanctuaries are but the shrine. "Spiritual things are spiritually discerned." "With the heart man believeth unto righteousness." In a life so solemn and so tempted as this, we need another guide than reason. The cross of this intellectual self-renunciation will ever be to the Jews a stumbling-block, and to the Greeks foolishness; but to them which believe, the power of God, and the wisdom of God unto salvation.

There is a servile deference paid even by Christians to incompetent judges of Christianity. They abjectly look to men of the world, to scholars, to statesmen, for testimonials to the everlasting and self-evidencing verities of heaven! And if they can gather up, from the writings or speeches of these men, some patronizing notices of religion, some incidental compliment to the civilizing influence of Christianity, or to the literary beauties of the Bible, or to the æsthetic proprieties of worship, or to the moral sublimity of the character or Gospel of Christ, they forthwith proclaim these tributes as lending some great confirmation to the truth of God! So we persist in asking, not "Is it true? true to our souls?" or, "Has the Lord said it?" but, "What say the learned men, the influential men, the eloquent men? Have any of the rulers or of the Pharisees believed on him?" Shame upon these time-serving concessions, as unmanly as they are fallacious. Go back to the hovels, rather, and take the witnessing of the illiterate souls whose hearts, waiting there in poverty, or pain, or under the shadow of some great affliction, the Lord himself hath opened! "I thank thee, O Father, Lord of heaven and earth, that thou hast hid these things from the wise and prudent, and hast revealed them unto babes!"

4. As the faculty of faith grows and strengthens by its own holy exercise, so it is lost by whatever sensualizes or materializes our life. While the spiritual energy in us becomes feeble, the world around us will grow hurtful and react against us. Travellers say that in the countries liable to earthquakes, before the earthquake comes, some subtle influence in the air weakens the nervous energy of the human system, and, by abating the power of resistance, predisposes the mind for terror. It is the same cause that produces the evil without us and within us. The same moral disorder infects our powers and makes nature herself our enemy, instead of our friend. Each separate deed we do bears its part. Every gross indulgence, or hour of selfish vanity, dims the sight. Darker and darker every day the chambers of the soul become. Weaker and weaker the energies for all noble, heavenly action. Grosser and more grovelling the desires. Narrower and narrower the limits of the inmost life. Character is lost. The soul dies, in trespasses and transgressions, — the second death. This is the fearful retribution: not always executed speedily, but inevitably: not arbitrarily nor angrily, but because the things of the Spirit of God are and must be spiritually discerned.

5. Hence we are responsible not only for what we do but for what we see. More than we often think, these eyes of the soul are in our power. Say what we will of the obscurities of Revelation, and the mysteries of Providence, truly spiritual and believing men and women go on reading both, deeper and deeper, clearer and clearer, all their lives, till at last, no longer through a glass darkly,—the veil taken away,—they see as they are seen, know as they are known, stand face to face with the Saviour they have so long and so trustingly followed, and have "open vision for the written word." If we do not behold the constellation of splendid truths that radiate their evangelic light from the Gospel, it is because blindness is in the dim pupils of our eyes, unused or abused. Just as fast as we will let it, the day will dawn and the day-star arise in our hearts. By living out all the goodness we know, in the daily beauty of holiness, we shall behold life's grand proportions. By walking with Christ you shall wear his likeness. Nay,—for he is a living Christ,—you shall have him formed within you, not only the hope, but the present possession, of glory. And because you know him spiritually, in the purity and love of his life and cross, men will also take knowledge of you, that you have been with him, and are with him now, and shall be his people forever.

6. Thus, while spiritual discernment is a power by itself, and works according to its own conditions, and is lost or deadened by its own wrongs, its results, when it is rightly and generously unfolded, belong to the whole breadth of character, the whole range and beauty and honor of human life.

When the faith-faculty is alive and at its principled

work, it will reach out in its supremacy into all those other parts of man, and all the real interests of society, to hallow, guide, and bless them. It will not stay confined to the closet, nor the sanctuary, nor the Sabbath, nor the conference, nor the chamber of the heart, where it began, and where it still gets nourishment, but it will mingle itself in business and company, in bargains and visitings, in the merchant's traffic, and the student's books, and the mechanic's handicraft, and the farmer's husbandry, and the Christian woman's housekeeping, — making all these to be no more drudgery, but cheerful, dignified, and sacred services of religious love and joy.

A man's religion is not then a part of him, but is a quality of the whole of him. Having its own life-spring and stream, it fertilizes the whole field of his being. It makes his business safer, his scholarship wiser, his manhood manlier, his joy healthier, his strength stronger. It is the crown of his enterprise and the charm of his affections, the humility of his learning and the glory of his life. Faith works by love. And because it has the sight of things not seen and eternal, it is the splendor, the transfiguration, and the sanctity of things that are seen and temporal.

SERMON IV.

THREE DISPENSATIONS IN HISTORY AND IN THE SOUL.

ABRAHAM BELIEVED GOD, AND IT WAS ACCOUNTED TO HIM FOR RIGHTEOUSNESS. THE LAW WAS GIVEN BY MOSES; BUT GRACE AND TRUTH CAME BY JESUS CHRIST. — Gal. iii. 6; John i. 17.

THE spiritual growth of mankind has proceeded through three great stages. Each of these has been marked by the evolution of one predominating element, or salient principle of religious action. On examination, we shall be able to discover an impressive correspondence between these successive epochs in the history of humanity at large, and the process of life in a well-disciplined, Christianized individual. This analogy is so thickly set with points of interest, as well as so fruitful of practical suggestions touching right religious ideas, and right living, that I shall let it fix the form, and be the subject of the discourse. That subject is: *The threefold discipline of our spiritual experience, as compared with the threefold order in the expanding nurture of the human family.*

The three Biblical Dispensations are types of three great principles of conduct, or rather three schools of religious culture, under which we must pass as persons, just as the race has passed in history, before we can be built up into the symmetrical stature of a Christian maturity.

I. First, was the dispensation of natural religious feeling. The race was in childhood. It acted from impulse. It obeyed no written code of moral regulations, but, so far as its life was right, it either followed some free religious instincts, or else depended on direct intimations from the Deity, directing or forbidding each specific deed. The man chosen as the representative of this period was Abraham. The record of it is the book of Genesis. That writing is the first grand chapter in the biography of man; and its very literary structure — so dramatic in contents, and so lyrical in expression, so careless in the rules of art, so abounding in personal details and graphic groupings of incident, so like a child's story in its sublime simplicity — answers to the spontaneous period it pictures. "The patriarchal age" we call it. The term itself intimates rude, unorganized politics; the head of each family being the legislator for his tribe. But, in the absence of systematic statutes, every man, by a liberty so large as to burst often into license, was likely to do very much what was right in his own eyes. If he had strong passions, he would be a sensualist, like Shechem, or a petty tyrant, like Laban. If he were constitutionally gentle, he would be an inoffensive shepherd, like Lot. Such were the first two brothers. Cain's jealousy made him a murderer; Abel was peaceable, kept sheep, and the only voice he lifted up against outrage was when his blood cried from the ground. Some of these nomadic people, having devout temperaments, "called upon the name of the Lord," we are told, like Enoch and Noah. Others were bloated giants, mighty men in animal propensities, gross and licentious, given to promiscuous marriages; so that presently God saw that the wickedness was so great, and the imaginations of men's hearts were so evil, that he must wash the unclean earth with a deluge. But there was no permanent restraining power; no fixed standard of judicial command; and so, when the flood dried, the tide of sin set in again, streaked only with some veins of nobleness. On the plains of Shinar pride fancied it could build a tower that should overtop the All-seeing Providence; and it had to be humbled by a confusion of tongues, scattering the builders. Even Noah, a just man for his times, so pure in *that* comparison, that he was carried over on the waves from a drowned generation, to install a new one, had scarcely seen the many-colored splendors of the promise in the rainbow, before he was drunken of overmuch wine. Abraham himself, so full of trust that his trust finally saved him, strong enough in the power of it to lay his son on an altar, at an earlier age stained his tongue with a cowardly falsehood, calling his wife his sister for safety's sake, — first pattern of the politicians of mere expediency, — and was rebuked for it by Pharaoh, who had seen less of the heavenly visions than he. Sodom, with its indescribable pollutions, was not far from Beth-el, — house of God. Jacob received a revelation from opened heavens; yet he overreached his brother to appropriate the family blessing, and defrauded his father-in-law. Throughout the whole of this patriarchal era, reaching from Adam to Joseph, and covering, by the common computation, twenty-three hundred years, there were beautiful virtues flowering into the light by the spontaneous energy of nature, but poisoned in many spots by the slime of sensuality. The human stock threw out its forms of life with a certain negligence, as the prodigal force of nature does her forests — as a boy swings his limbs in the open air. There were heroic acts; but they were dispersed over intervals, with dismal contrasts of meanness and cowardice between. There were ardent prayers; but foul passions often met and put to flight the descending hosts of the angels of God. Character needed a stanch vertebral column to secure its uprightness. No permanent sanction lent impregnability to good impulses. Even the saint, whose spirit rose nearest to heaven, walked on the verge of some abyss of shame. For though Abraham believed, Moses had not yet legislated, nor Christ died.

Corresponding, now, to this impulsive religious age of the race is the natural state of the individual. It is the condition we are born into, and multitudes never pass beyond it, because they are never renewed, or made Christian. Morally they are children all their lives. Bad dispositions mix with good; one moment holy aspirations, the next a flagrant immorality. What is wanting is a second birth of spiritual conviction. Conduct is not brought to the bar of a governmental examination, and judged by an unbending principle. Temptation is too much for this feeble, capricious piety. Nature, true enough, is always interesting; and spontaneous products may be beautiful. But man, with his free agency, beset before and behind by evil, is not like a lily growing under God's sun and dew, with no sin to deform its grace or stain its coloring; he is not like the innocent architecture of a cloud, shaped by the fantastic caprices of the summer wind; nor yet like the aimless statuary of the sea-shore, sculptured by the pliant chisel of the wave. He has to contend, struggle, resist. He is tried, enticed, besieged. Satan creeps anew with every new-born child into the Eden of the heart, and flaming swords are presently planted on its gates, proclaiming — no return *that way* to innocence. The natural religion, of which modern mystics are so fond, and modern peripatetics prattle, is not enough for him. It might possibly answer in the woods, unless this feeble pantheism should substitute artistic ecstasy for worship, and moonlight for the sun, that flashes down the glories of revelations; or in some solitary cell, though even there monk and hermit have often found the snare of impure imaginations spread too cunningly for it. But let the boy go to the shop, and the girl to school; let the young man travel to the city, and the young woman lend her ears to the flatteries of that silver-tongued sorceress, Society; and all this natural piety is like a silken thread held over a blazing furnace. We may put ourselves at ease, fancy we shall fare well enough under so kind a Father; come out comfortably at last; there is such tender pity in the skies. But the dispelling of that delusion will be the sharp word out of the throne of judgment, "Depart from me, I never knew you." No Babel of refuge will be built to the top. No friendly intervention will avert the perdition of the Sodom in the heart. No Tamar of custom will cajole with her coquetry the ancient and everlasting justice. No thrifty leagues of a low commercial instinct, postponing conscience to the arithmetic of traffic, — no corrupt political majorities, subscribing patriotic manifestoes as stock for party or private dividends, though they be as eleven against one, and though they piously profess to be sons of Israel by church subscriptions, — shall buy national prosperity by their brother Joseph's blood.

There is often a vague assumption that certain principles of natural right, evolved and compacted by ethical science, might save our social state. But, remember that society, without Christ, in its philosophy, its literature, its art, its morals, obeyed a law of deterioration and decay. Without him, it would have been sinking still. Instead of the Christian justice that hangs its balances over our seats of lawful trade to-day, we should have not even Punic faith, but something more treacherous than that — not even the hesitating Roman honesty, but a zone of restraint more dissolute than the Corinthian, and principles looser than the Spartan's. Instead of a respected merchant, or steady mechanic, going out to his business to-morrow, amid a public order that Christ has organized, might have been seen a barbarian with the concentrated falsity of a hundred Arabs, waking into a world convulsed with perpetual anarchy, or skulking away to transact his base affairs in a worse than Circassian mart. We may baptize the interesting displays of our intermittent virtue with a Christian name; but they may yet contain no quality of Christ's peculiar sanctity. They may leave human life quite untouched by that unrivalled glory, however bright their transient beam. They are not redolent of the New Testament. Their uprightness does not bear the sanction of the Sermon on the Mount. Their slender rectitude is not the principle that treats men justly because they are God's children, which was the law of Christ's great honesty. Their kindness is not the sweet charity of the beatitudes. Their moderation is not guarded by those majestic warders, reverence for God, and a Saviour's love. Nor is their worship, if they adore at all, fervent with the prayers of Olivet and Gethsemane.

And as the first dispensation ended in a slavery in Egypt, or broods darkly over Pagan nations waiting to be brought nigh by the blood of Christ to this hour, so the lawless motions of every self-guided will must end in a servitude to some Pharaoh in the members that cries aloud for emancipation — a settled alienation from the household of the good.

II. Next after this impulsive or spontaneous period, which is the period of Childhood, comes the legal or judicial, — a second stage in the history of the religious consciousness. Moses, the lawgiver, is its representative. From this crisis, the chief significance of the world's religious experience is concentrated, for some sixteen hundred years, in Judæa, and human progress runs on through the channel of Hebrew nationality. Other families have wandered off into hopeless idolatries. The religion of instinct has found its appropriate termination in a degraded Egyptian priesthood, mixing civil despotism with the incantations of an impure mythology.

And now, God calls up Moses *out* of this miserable oppression into the summit of Sinai, and appoints him the head of the second august human epoch. A period of laws, after instinct, begins. Instinct must be curbed, for it has done mischief enough. Impulse must be subjected to principle, for it has proved itself insufficient alone. There must be positive command, controlling wayward inclinations. "Thou shalt," and "Thou shalt not," are the watchwords. It is an age of obedience. Ceremonies and ordinances are set up to bring the wild will under discipline. And the better to secure exact obedience, a visible system of formal observances is announced, — so many sacrifices every day, and so many meat-offerings, drink-offerings, cattle, doves, fruits, cakes, for every sacrifice. To withstand the surrounding seductions of nations still steeped in the vices of their natural propensities, a scheme of coercive restraints comes in. The people must have multiplied festivals, jubilees, national gatherings, regularly kept, and by Divine appointment. To draw them, there is a gorgeous temple with an imposing altar, a tabernacle, a covenant, a shekinah lighted from heaven, a priesthood clad in splendid garments, and all the superb apparatus of a magnificent ritual. Even the daily habits, materials of common dress, qualities of food and kinds of flesh, are all to be regulated in detail by specific statutes. Law reaches down to determine the most minute particulars, — the cleansing of houses, the shape of the beard, the sowing of the field, — all having reference to neighboring idolatrous usages, of which these twelve tribes must, by all means, be kept clear. And for the breach of every law, from greatest to least, there must be penalty. That part of human nature that terror and dread appeal to is addressed. On the transgressor woe is denounced. There is a Mount Ebal, full of menacing curses, as well as a Gerizim pledged to blessings. Smoke, earthquakes, thunders and lightnings, marshalling their awful pageant about Sinai when the law was given, only prefigured punishments that should always torment the disobedient. And, accordingly, down through all the Hebrew fortunes, while prophets were set to admonish and call back the rebellious, the great staple of Israelitish history was, the Divine chastisement that followed violations of law, and the prosperity that rewarded its observance. Sieges and campaigns, conquests and captivities, judges and kings, Joshua, Gideon, and Ezra, David, Saul, and

Rehoboam, — all were of less consequence, as events, or as individuals, than as instruments of that mighty, organized power lying behind them, — Moses and the law.

So with all of us; there comes a time, when we feel that we cannot act by inclination, but must follow law. The principle of duty is that law. Babyhood is past, and its instincts suffice us no longer. To do as we like, would still be pleasant; but it is dangerous and false. We become stewards, and *must* give account of our stewardship. Life has put its harness upon us, and we must work in it. Passions have sprung up, and conflicts have commenced within us, that make impulse an unsafe guide. We feel a meaning in that hard word, *must*. We are free to do as we will, and yet we feel somehow bound under God's necessity. It begins to be evident that as sure as a stone falls or fire burns, sin will bring trouble; indulgence, pain; impiety, remorse; dissipation, disease; dishonesty, infamy. The spendthrift *must* be pinched, the fraudulent bargainer lose his soul though he gain the world, and the false professor be spiritually damned. Here are laws, — laws of the Almighty's ordaining, — laws that bring retribution. If we would live peaceably, we must come under them and obey.

Very often it happens that by obeying a law, we acquire superiority to it. Voluntarily submitting to certain rules for a time, our virtue is strengthened and finally becomes independent of them, so that it can go alone. The inebriate binds himself by a pledge, and thus regains his freedom. The disciple appoints specific hours for praying, and by that means gains the devout spirit which breathes a perpetual aspiration, at last inaugurating a silent converse of the soul with heaven, as natural as the pulse in the veins. The methodical division of time for business is only a form of law, coercing industry and efficiency. Many a man has to spur his sluggishness by definite tasks; and many more would bring nothing to pass, but for fixed methods and seasons. Without a morning and evening sacrifice, forgetful worldliness would render poor service to God; and memories, like Martha, so careful and troubled about many things, would fail of Mary's one thing needful. The laying apart of exact sums for charity has been all that stood between some men and the doom of avarice; benevolence had to be put out to school, and philanthropy be drilled into promptitude like a cadet. Let us not despise law, for every day practical proofs are scattered before us, that it is a schoolmaster to lead us to Christ.

Even fear, though fastidious nerves are apt to discredit it as a lower sentiment, has its office in disciplining thoughtless and stubborn wills, breaking down pride and prompting insensibility, till it is ready to hand us over to motives of a nobler order. There is a meaning in a tradition of an ancient German prince, who, in early life, was bidden by an oracle to search out an inscription on a ruined wall which should prefigure his mortal fate. He found the Latin words, signifying *after six*. Supposing they revealed the number of days he was to live, he gave himself for the six days following to his hitherto neglected soul, preparing himself to die. But finding death did not come, he was still held to his sober resolutions by supposing six weeks were the interpretation; and then he prolonged his holy life to six months, and six years. On the first day of the seventh year, by reason of the excellent manhood into which he had thus formed his character, he had gained the confidence of the people, and he found the fulfilment of the ambiguous prophecy by being chosen Emperor of Germany. Here is a figure of common experience. We may conceive it to have been a more "spiritual" process, that the prince should have been drawn to piety, by loving goodness for its own sake. But it was the timid dread of dying that drew him, and the royal benefactions of a truly Christian monarch justified the agent. Christian biography is crowded with instances of first awakenings by fear. It is remarkable that Luther, whose great soul, illumined afterwards by the text, "The just shall live by faith," became the modern apostle of the doctrine of Grace as opposed to justification by legality, was first aroused from utter indifference by two terrors, the violent death of his friend Alexis, and the thunderbolt that struck close by him on his way from Mansfeldt to the University. Have you never known a fever, or an accident, or the incipient symptoms of a consumption to be the determining cause that bent the whole current of a life from earthward to heavenward? Have you never known that a mere dread of punishment or pain, of hell or disgrace, has stopped the erring feet of lust, silenced profanity, driven back the Sabbath-breaker? God is not ashamed to take into the sublime economy of his purposes these stimulants to virtue; and let not us, in our puerile conceit, venture to pronounce them unworthy. Outgrow them if you will, and can; but take care that you are not found, after all, *below*, instead of *above* the plane of their influence.

For be assured, though we have read the New Testament, named the name of Jesus, and quite looked down on the Jew, some of us have not yet climbed up so far as to Moses and his Jewish law. In the Bible's older

Testament there are needed examples for us yet. Not all of us have learned that majestic, unchangeable fact, that God is Sovereign; nor those related facts that, if we will perpetrate the wrong, we must suffer the penalty; that we cannot dodge the consequences of what we do; that indolence must sap our strength; that selfishness must end in wretchedness; that falsehood is a mint coining counterfeits that must return upon our hands; that hypocrisy to-day is disgrace to-morrow. This is law, everlasting, unrepealable law; and our poor attempts to resist or nullify it, avail not so much as a puff of mortal breath against the gulf stream in the Atlantic. Blessed will it be for our peace, when we accept it, and bow to it, turning it into a law of liberty.

Remember that the grandest examples of sainthood, or spiritual life, that the ages have seen, have been souls that recognized this truth, — the firm, Puritanical element in all valiant piety; and without it mere amiable religious feeling will be quite sure to degenerate into sentimentality. We need to stand compassed about with the terrible splendors of the Mount, and with something of the sombre apparatus of Hebrew commandments, to keep us from falling off into some impious, Gentile idolatries of the senses. Holy places, and holy days, and solemn assemblies, still dispense sanctity. Our appetites have to be hedged about with almost as many scruples of regimen for Christian moderation's sake, as the Jew's for his monotheism. "We wish," says some one, "that it was not so difficult to be good. We wish that we could be self-indulgent, and yet be good for all that; that we could idle off our time, and yet be wise for all that." The worldling wishes he could combine his worldliness now with a heaven hereafter; the voluptuary, that he could have "the clear eye and steady hand of the temperate"; the vain, ambitious, capricious woman, that she could exhibit the serenity that comes of prayer. But Sinai stands unmoved, at the outset of every life-journey through the wilderness; and at the further end, beyond the river, Ebal with its curses, and Gerizim with its blessings. "Whatsoever a man soweth, that shall he also reap."

III. But there is a Third Dispensation, profounder and richer than that of statutes; and, at the head of it, One greater than Moses. The period of literal commandments was insufficient; humanity outgrew it. It became a dead profession, a school of foolish questions, a shelter of hideous hypocrisies. Lo! the enlarging soul of the race asks a freer, more sincere, more vital nurture, and it comes. If the simple religious instincts of Abraham had been accepted for righteousness; if the law had been given by Moses; grace and truth enter in by Jesus Christ; grace for the heart, truth for the understanding; favor for man's stumbling feet, and light for his eyes. Christ does not abrogate law, but by his own life and sacrifice first satisfies its conditions. He says expressly, "Think not that I came to destroy Moses, but to fulfil." The cross does not unbind the cords of accountability, but tightens and strengthens them rather. The Gospel affords no solvent to disintegrate the commandments; it only lets "the violated law speak out its thunders" in the tones of pity. Divine laws never looked so sacred as when they took sanctity from the redemption of the crucified.

Witness now a new light, "lighting every man that cometh into the world." It is the deliverance of the heart. It is the purifying of the life. It is the sanctification of the spirit. The law, by which no man living can be justified, because no man ever yet kept it inviolate; which makes no allowance for imperfect obedience, and yet never was perfectly obeyed,—which, therefore, is a rule of universal condemnation when standing alone,—this stern, unrelenting law gives place to a Gospel,—gladder tidings,—a voice that comes not to condemn but to save; a ministry of mercy, asking only a penitent spirit that it may offer forgiveness, and only an inward faith changing the motives that it may confer eternal life.

Law and prophets, then, are not annulled; what they lacked is supplied. They are absorbed by Evangelists. The Gospel takes up all their contents, recasts them, and quickens them with the vitality of a fresh inspiration. Moses remains, but only as a servant to Christ. The decalogue still stands; but the cross stands on a higher pedestal, invested with a purer glory. Humble Calvary is the seat of a loftier power than towering Horeb. We must still be under discipline; but the lawgiver is lost in the Redeemer. What *was* a task is transfigured into a choice. The drudgery of obedience is beautified into the privilege of reconciliation. Love has cast out fear. Man no longer cowers before his Sovereign with terror, but pours out his praises to a Father. The soul is released from the bondage of a thrall into the liberty of a child. Out of the plodding routine of mechanical sacrifice it ascends into spiritual joy, where the handwriting of ordinances is done away; the Great High Priest has ascended once for all into the heavens, and suffering is willingly borne because it makes the disciple like the Lord.

Thus the word spoken by the third epoch of religious

culture is not, "Act thy nature out and follow thy lawless impulses," — nor yet, "Do this circle of outward works, and then come and claim salvation for thy merits," — but, believe, first, and then out of thy faith do the righteous works which thou then canst not but do. Repent of thy short comings, and be forgiven. Lean on Christ, thy Saviour. Love God, thy Father. Help men, thy brethren. And come, inherit thine immortal kingdom!

Now, at last, if it only keeps on in the path divinely marked for it, the soul emerges into that wide fellowship of Christ, — that open hospitality of spiritual freedom, where the impulse of nature is only guided, not stifled, by law; where law is ripened and fulfilled into faith. The highest victory of goodness is union with God. That union comes only by a mediator. For reconciliation between finite and infinite, there must be a Reconciler combining both. The way to peace lies by Calvary. Humanity realizes its complete proportions only by inward membership with him who fills all the veins of his living body with his blood, and the chambers of his church with the glory of his presence to-day. "Believe in the Lord Jesus Christ, and thou shalt be saved."

For, observe, by all means, this striking condition pertaining to the doctrine; that neither of these three stages, whether of the general or the personal progress, denies, or cuts off, its predecessor. Nature prepares the way for law, — making the heart restless, by an unsatisfying experiment, without it. Abraham saw more glorious ages coming than his own, and the promise given to him and his seed, Emmanuel accomplished. The law disciplined wayward, uncultured man, making him ready for the church that was to descend "like a bride out of heaven." Every ordinance in its ritual was a type; every statute was a prophecy. All Judaism was prospective. Moses looked forward to the Messiah. So, in the heart of childhood, there are expectations, vague and yet brilliant, of the responsible second stage of manhood; it is too thoughtless yet to look beyond, to the age of mature Christian holiness. But see, again, when that second age of stern command and strict obedience comes, it grows sober and reflective. It feels heavily that it is not sufficient to itself. It must look longingly forward for the consolations of the cross. Nature does not comprehend law, nor law gospel; Abraham Moses, nor Moses Messiah; but the Son of God understands all, and the Gospel, in its majestic orbit, while embracing law and nature, transcends them both.

Remember, also, for its practical fruit's sake, this fact, that each stage requires fidelity in the preceding. You must have been true to the better impulses of youth, that you may be, to the best advantage, a servant of the law of maturity. You must be faithfully obedient to duty, before you are fit to be a subject of grace. Do not imagine you can glide over into the favor of Heaven, without first keeping the commandment. It is a strait gate, and a narrow way that leads to life. I must be a cheerful servant before I can know the joy of adoption, and cry, "Abba, Father." Willing to be constrained by the positive precept, I may hope, by-and-by, for the freedom of a child and heir. Many things that I would rather not do, — irksome to the sluggish will, hard to the love of ease, offensive to pride, bitter to selfish pleasure, — I must do, before I can ascend to that sublime self-mastery with Christ, where I shall *desire* to do only what I ought. You have seen a seabird, which in rising from the waves has to run some way with difficulty upon the water, striking the surface laboriously with its pinions; but when it has once lifted itself into the upper air, it balances its flight with a calm motion, and, enfranchised into the freedom of the sky, the slow beat of its wings is imperceptible. It is by pain and toil *under* the commandments, that the soul gets the liberty of its faculties; but when it has been taken up out of itself by love and trust, it moves in harmony with God. The law was our schoolmaster to bring us unto Christ, that we might "be justified by faith." But "after that faith is come, we are no longer under a schoolmaster." "All things are yours, and ye are Christ's, and Christ is God's." No longer at Gerizim, nor yet at Jerusalem, but everywhere, we may worship the Father!

You have seen the religionist of mere feeling. That impulsive temperament is doubtless capable of good services to the Master. But, to that end, the Master must have the reforming of it. That unsteady purpose must be made steadfast through a thoughtful imitation of the constancy, that said, "Behold, I go up to Jerusalem to be crucified." That fluctuating wing of worship, must be poised by some influence from those hills, where whole nights were not too long for a Redeemer's prayers. That inexpert swimmer in the sea of life, now rising, now sinking, and now noiselessly splashing the waters, must be schooled by sober experience to glide onward with a firmer and stiller stroke. Ardor must be matched with consistency. You are not to be carried to heaven by a fitful religion, periodically raised from the dead at seasons of social exhilaration; not by a religion alive at church, but stagnant in the streets and in the marketplaces; not by a religion kindling at some favored hour of sentimental meditation, only to sink and flicker in the drudgery of common work. It is to little purpose that we read and circulate and preach the Bible, except all our reading and all our living gain thereby a more biblical tone. And it is quite futile that our breasts glow with some fugitive feeling in the house of God, unless that feeling dedicates our common dwellings to be all houses of God.

So have you seen the religious legalist. In business, in the streets, in sanctuaries, at home, you have seen him. In business, measuring off his righteousness by some sealed measure of public usage, as mechanically as his merchandise, and making a label or a dye-stuff his cunning proxy to tell the lie that some judicial penalty had frightened from his tongue; disowning no patent obligation, but cheating the customer, or oppressing the weak, in secret. In the street, wearing an outside of genial manners, with a frosty temper under it, or a cloak of propriety with a heart of sin; in the sanctuary, purchasing, with formal professions, one day, the privilege of an untroubled self-seeking the other six, or possibly opening the pew door and the prayer-book here to-day, with the same hand that will wrong a neighbor to-morrow; and, at home, practising that reluctant virtue that would hardly give conjugal affection but for the marriage-bond, and that, by being exported to another continent, would find a Parisian atmosphere a solvent of all its scruples. Not descending, at present, to the depth of depravity, he certainly never rises to a pure piety. Whatever respectable or admirable traits you see in him, you miss that distinctive mark which every eye takes knowledge of as a spiritual consecration.

Engraft, now, on that "wild olive" stock the sweet juices of Christian love, drawn from their original stock in Bethlehem, "of the seed of David, and the root of Jesse"; soften that hard integrity by Christian charity; in place of duty done from sheer compulsion put duty done from a willing, eager, and believing heart. Do this, and thou shalt live.

Abraham, Moses, Christ; impulse, discipline, faith; nature, law, gospel; instinct, obedience, grace; Mamre, Sinai, Calvary; this is that divine order, — not bound by rigid rules of chronological succession, but having the free play and various intershadings of a moral growth, — to which we are to conform our lives. When the "*Thus saith the Lord*" shall have controlled our impatient will, our hearts will be ready to say, "Our Father, who art in heaven!" Seek, first, after that indwelling goodness that has its fountain in the centre of the soul, and good works will be the constant stream. Be children of light. Live by the spirit, not the letter; by faith, not by fear. For you are called to be disciples of Jesus. Henceforth the Christian is to be known, and to be saved, not by the hand so much as by the heart; not by a righteousness that is legal, but spiritual. Let not your piety be the occasional piety of Rabbinical Sabbaths, with ghastly intervals of worldliness between, like isolated springs in a desert of sand; but a piety, whose perennial influence, like the river that keeps the meadows always green, shall penetrate and fertilize the whole soil and open field of your being, and thus make glad the city of your God. No rich, nor beautiful, nor accepted life can be lived by us, except Christ be its inspiration. Hope will not reach up to immortality, except it climb by the cross. Let not your lives be dead shapes of outward decency, — the carved and gilded wood of an ark and a tabernacle deserted by the Spirit, — but vital branches, filled with leaping and vigorous currents of holy feeling, on the living vine! "For if any man have not the spirit of Christ, he is none of his."

SERMON V.

THE FEELING AND CRY OF SIN.*

GOD BE MERCIFUL TO ME A SINNER! — Luke xviii. 13.

By contrast with the arrogant and egotistical boast of the Pharisee, and on the score of its natural modesty, this prayer of the Publican wins the respect of all classes of people. But to enter into the anxious and burdened feeling out of which such a cry of sorrow must have sprung, and to make that feeling our own, is not so much a matter of course. This requires something of those more earnest exercises of the interior life, and that deeper discipline, which involve the very presence and power of the renewing Spirit.

This man, standing here before God, afar off from his fellow-men, the very image of depression, not so much as his eyes lifted, pronounces himself a sinner. And this expression of conscious unworthiness is not made as a piece of information to heaven or earth. It is simply the irrepressible confession of sincerity, pressed out of the soul by a longing for forgiveness; — short, because so terribly sincere. The straitened spirit in its anguish has no room for prolix particulars. The very sound of the words, the downcast look, the withdrawn

* Preached at the beginning of Lent, 1859.

position, the agonized gesture, as well as the character Christ puts upon these things, betray the reality of his repentance. The thing they expose to us is human sin,—its self-conviction, its wretchedness, its way of relief. It is with this disease of the moral nature as it is with some sorts of physical disorder; the sight of it is repulsive and forbidding, till the malady is acknowledged in our own body. Then for the first time, when the pain throbs along our nerves, we are willing to contemplate it without impatience. It is a spectacle of ugliness and humiliation, from which men are eager to turn away their eyes, till they feel its hurt and peril pressing into the organs of their own frames. The prosperous and self-satisfied and unawakened say, Why talk to *us* of sin?

One reason why, is that it is a fact pervading the world. Another is, that it is the greatest of evils, and the malignant source of all evils that exist, being the sting of death itself. Another, that it is, or will be, incomparably the greatest of miseries, a misery that only a knowledge and a feeling of sin like the publican's can prevent. Still another reason is, that Christ and his religion continually refer to it, having it for their express object to take man out from its control and give him the mastery over it. So that it has come about, as the divine order for us, taken as we are, that a quickened individual conviction of sin is the first step in passing into a new and Christian life.

An individual conviction. After all, what probably goes far to make all human discoursing about sin both unwelcome and ineffectual, is that so much of it is a rebuke of man by man rather than the humble confession of a common wrong. We must acknowledge, also, that in our public and formal treatment of it, we are apt to fall into cool, customary, unfelt language. That is, there is too much of the Pharisaic method in our judgment and speech about the world's depravity; too much vagueness, and verbal repetition, and tacit complacency; not enough of the sadness and sincere solemnity of the publican. Let us at least try to feel what we say, and put ourselves in with those that we rebuke, not to make out a bad case against mankind, but to help each other into God's way of delivering us from the bad case we are actually in. Observe, in all his intercourse with men, Christ displayed the utmost tenderness to those who had found out that they were sinners, — all that ran and knelt to him in penitence. His woes and threatenings and judgments were for those that were sinners without confessing it.

The sinning man is here presented to us as having given personal offence to his Maker. He implores forgiveness of the Father he has offended. All our evil, in act, or word, or wish, or thought, is a direct wrong against the God of all goodness and purity, himself. When we offend, it is not merely ourselves, not merely other men, not merely public opinion and social conventions, that we offend. Ah, this notion that there is no other iniquity for man than a transgression of the natural laws of his own constitution, and that no hurt is inflicted but on his own or some human sensibility, is not at all the doctrine of Christ or of the Bible. There is grief with God himself. A wound is given to the infinite and loving heart. A jar is sent not only through the air of this world, and across the chords of humanity, but up to the ear of heaven and into the Spirit of parental tenderness on high. Man is responsible to something beyond his own organization. Remorse is not merely the after-thought of a mistaken self-interest, the reconsideration of a hasty policy. Doubtless the wrong is double, and the suffering is on both sides. "He that sinneth against me wrongeth his own soul." But mark the first clause,—"Sinneth *against me*." As the blessing of truth is alike to heaven and earth, giving health and light, so are the curse and the pain of sin felt all along the immortal and sympathetic ranks of being. As godliness is profitable both to the life that now is and the life that is to come, so is wickedness a blight and a sorrow. And of both of these lives, and of all the worlds, God is a judge who must be just, and a ruler who must uphold the right, as well as a feeling Father who sorrows and pities. Those who have the dimmest sense of God have the dullest perception of what is opposite to God. Pantheism knows nothing of sin. As prayer is something more than a placid meditation on the beauty of the world or a gallery of art, Christian faith something more than confidence in our own powers to accomplish what we undertake, and religion something more than the tranquil balance of cultivated faculties, so is sin a personal affront, whose bitter consequences only the forgiveness of God himself can remove, and toward which, with the publican, we must implore him to be merciful. It does not read, "Nature be merciful," nor "Laws of my constitution be merciful," nor "Society be merciful," nor, "I will be merciful to myself," but, "God be merciful;"—nor yet, "God be merciful to sin in general," but "*to me* a sinner."

Men of the ripest attainments, deepest experience, and clearest insight in the Christian life, have been those who have gone through this sharp conflict; not men of easy views of the Divine requirements; not men too fastidious to accept the stringent action of God's law; not men disposed to palliate their own faults, or to narrow down or reason away the irreconcilable opposition between a principle of self-seeking and the principle of holy obedience. Indeed, in proportion as the religious character grows positive and fervent, the soul grows sensitive; and while charity for others is larger and kindlier, for the very reason that the heart has so heavy a record to return of its own weaknesses and errors, at the same time a strict personal doctrine of sin seems more reasonable and right; for sin itself is only more and more dreadful. Conscience, stricken with shame, confesses to the reproof; while the soul, rising in aspiration, and gathering itself into closer communion with the purity of the heart of Christ, repudiates with intenser disgust every unhallowed inclination.

We may contrive many plausible coverings and apologies; for the sophistry of sin is as old as its pride. We may maintain that we are no worse than our neighbors. One man extenuates his guilt; another denies it altogether, and counts the charge of it an insult, not remembering who brings the charge with most searching severity and with the most fearful authority. We may admit the offence, but plead the violence of the temptation, the treacherous opportunity, the customs of society, the necessities of business. The first man that sinned cried, "The woman tempted me, and I did eat," and the tens of thousands of his descendants who sinned yesterday protested that they did not sin willingly; they only did not see how they should "get along in the world" without doing as they did. But whose world? and "get along" *towards* what? Or, we sometimes think it quite hard that an amiable disposition, popular manners, punctual payments, and an occasional almsgiving, are not suffered to stand for our excusing, if our Father in Heaven is forgotten or profaned. Yet all the while we know these to be poor, pitiful pretences, which never wholly satisfy the minds that make them. Deeper down, in some spot of your nature which the gracious Spirit has not yet permitted to be hardened and perverted utterly, is there not another verdict, rendered at another plea? a voice that is ready sometimes to cry, "God be merciful to me a sinner"?

So profoundly rooted is this religious instinct, — the feeling that any thorough and effectual religious life must be born through the pains of penitence, — that you will probably have heard some persons deploring their feeble sense of sin. They say they are not pierced, or borne down, as they know they ought to be, with a keen and overwhelming conviction of their alienation and transgression. This is one of the common and most sincere confessions in the beginnings of religious concern. Men under moral conviction at once lament that they are insensible to their bad state, and yet show a lively sense of it in this very regret. They grieve because their grief is so small, and their condition contradicts itself. It seems like a tangled knot in the mind. Is not the true explanation of it simply that there is a conflict, or an inequality, between the moral judgment and the spiritual emotions? Conscience pronounces it our duty to realize and acknowledge our ingratitude and disobedience; it says *ought*. But habit has made the heart dead. The feelings do not come up properly to their part of the work. An apathy is on the soul; legalism holds her in its bondage; and till the subduing sight of the cross unseals the fountains of holy emotion, there is only self-accusation, but no peace. Repentance has stung the conscience, but has not reached, renewed, and comforted the heart.

The three scriptural words that are most frequently employed to express the special effect of Christianity all convey the meaning that the soul is somehow, in every case, if left to itself, out of its right line of life, on a wrong course, looking the wrong way. These are Redemption, Salvation, Reconciliation. Redemption; but why redeemed, except the soul has involved itself so helplessly in a false state, that this divine force must be interposed for its rescue? Salvation; but saved *from what*, if not from a peril and a misery incurred by a wicked will, and escaped only by the new principle of faith that comes of Christ? Reconciliation; but why reconciled, except there has been alienation; and where the Father of goodness on the one side and his child on the other are estranged, where is it possible the occasion of alienation should be but in some perversity of the child? In the same way, the words conversion, renewal, regeneration, repentance, words made familiar as the household speech of the church, unless we utterly discharge them of all honest meaning, impress it upon us that every one of us is out of his innocent subjection to God's will, — sinning.

The whole machinery of heathen worship has been a device for ending man's controversy with his Maker. Under Christianity, the same idea only takes a more refined shape and a higher sanction. The heart comes to Christ because it carries its burden of sin to every other system, philosophy, and teacher, only to bring it back heavier and more galling than before.

The world over, in its serious hours the heart longs, sighs, groans, and travails with sorrows that cannot be uttered, to be delivered from the bondage of sin and death. The Scripture has no other doctrine of the matter, on any of its pages; and scarcely one page where this is not. Read the burning confessions of the fifty-first Psalm, and of many another before and after it, where the fire of remorse, which is only the lurid reflection of sin, almost visibly scorches the Psalmist's heart; read the terrible descriptions of that state of man without his Redeemer written by Paul to the Romans; or the tragic picture of Paul's own fearful struggles with the law of his members; or the awful prophecies of a society forgetting its Lord, given in Jude. Recall the narratives of depravity in Scripture history, and the denunciations upon it by prophets, and the thrilling exhortations against it by apostles. Remember that the Bible begins with the first inroad of sin, and finishes with warnings of its punishments. Above all, remember that the first word of the new dispensation was "Repent," and its consummation was the cross built on Calvary to assure forgiveness to "repentance toward God and faith toward our Lord Jesus Christ;" and you will hardly need to multiply these convincing tokens that all the ministrations of our religion to the human soul presuppose that we all have sinned, are sinners still. If any of you are disposed to complain that there is too much preaching against sin, apply your criticism to the Bible. The Christ whom we preach came to be a Saviour from sin, did he not? How much better to think and feel thoroughly what sin is now, than when the "space for repentance" is exchanged for the determinations of the judgment!

Suppose, then, any one of us to be conscious that he ought to have a more living sense of his evils, assured that by that way only can he hope to come to a strong and pure religious character, how is that penitential frame to be produced?

It must be by setting up a contrast: a contrast either between our own character and the character of God, or between our character as it is, and as it should be under the perfect Christian rule of duty and the inspiration of Christian faith.

To the character of God as expressed to us primarily in revelation, and less directly in nature and history, we ascribe the perfection of holiness. But this sentence is only a repetition of words; and what we want is to get beyond this stale formality. We are to quicken in ourselves the true, right feeling of the publican, by reviving and strengthening, in every possible way, the impression of our Father's goodness. Could we only once break through this deadening influence of regularity, where the very love of God is hidden in its own constancy; could we see and feel that we are indeed utterly, and always, and afresh every instant, at our Maker's disposal and dependent on his will,—every fibre of the body kept in place by his care, and every breath inspired by him, and the whole spirit subject and amenable to him; could we then begin to consider his patience and recount his gifts,—his patience with us from the cradle, and with the race from Eden,—his gifts, as many as the organs, inlets, faculties, tissues, powers, of all our complex being multiplied by all the seconds of our life; could we then rise from this to some worthy conception of his own Infinite Life,—boundless, fathomless, endless, yet all intensest life,—the majesty, the might, the dominion,—the purity, the pity, the wisdom, the love;—God forbearing with all this impious and disgusting folly, God enduring all this abhorrent selfishness, God upholding all these unprofitable and unthankful creatures, if so be that possibly something may yet be recovered of their self-destruction, and the well-beloved Son dying for that;—and could we at last put in contrast with Him our lives, so mean, so weak, so bad,—then should we not be ready to exclaim, with something more than a mere recitation of the memory, "Lord! what is man that thou art mindful of him? God be merciful to me a sinner!"

Turn to the Scriptures. Another line of contrast is presented in the express standard of character set before us there. You take any of those great summaries of obligation, which are gathered up here and there in the Scriptures like waymarks to the generations,—easiest for the mind to hold, and oftenest repeated: let it be the ten Hebrew commands, interpreting them not only in the letter but the spirit, from that first and awful one,—its rigor not superannuated by three thousand years, its vitality not outlawed because we have moved from the neighborhood of the Canaanites and our heathenism has changed its name and its garments,—which declares, "Thou shalt have no other gods before me,"—prohibiting all our idols, self, friends, family, fame, property,—down to that last of the ten, which cuts so closely into our daily and hidden habits when it says, "Thou shalt not covet *anything* that is thy neighbor's." Or let it be the preacher's short but difficult compendium,—"the conclusion of the whole matter,"—"Fear God, and keep his commandments, for this is the whole duty of man." Or let it be the prophet's persuasive generalization, putting it as so reasonable, but still keeping it so far beyond us,—"What doth the Lord thy God require of thee, but to do justly, love mercy, and walk humbly with thy God"? Or observe the wonderful blending of simplicity and power in the Beatitudes, pausing to think on what hearts, and what only, each "blessing" can descend. Or let it be the Saviour's double precept, more unattainable than all, "Thou shalt love the Lord thy God with *all* thy heart, and with *all* thy soul, and with *all* thy mind, and thy neighbor as thyself." Or listen to that grand and stirring roll-call of the disciple's duties in Paul's twelfth chapter to the Romans. Or, finally, ponder that plain, brief definition of the practical James: "Pure religion, before God and the Father, is this, to visit the fatherless and the widows in their affliction, and to keep himself unspotted from the world!"—weighing well the measure of that Christian cleanliness demanded in the latter clause,—"to keep himself unspotted from the world." Let any of these or all of them be the statutes of the law and the will of your God. Remember all are without abatement, without exception, without qualifying clause, or proviso, or partiality, or respect of persons, the unrepealable command of the righteous Ruler of all ages and all worlds,—not to be evaded, because he is Omniscient, and not to be broken, because the good of all would then be betrayed. And then, having these for the rule and requirement, let us lay them down, syllable after syllable, side by side, with our outer and inner life for a week, or a day,—and behold the contradiction.

Place them beside the spiritual indifference and the moral obliquities; the earth-bound attachments and the broken resolutions; the obstinate self-will and the swerving aspirations; the irritable temper and the inflated vanity; the cunning calculations of self-advancement and the impulsive fires of passion. Watch the conversation of a single company,—its direct or insinuated slander, its envious or conceited judgments, its delight in censure and in the discovery of weakness, ill-disguised by moral protestations,—its enormous preponderance of blame, its excesses of supply to admiration or to appetite. Consider what a thing actual full-toned justice would be in the transactions and speech of society; what a Christ-like mercy would do; and how the splendor of an absolutely spotless soul would shine among us. Think what it must be to love God with all the heart, and to walk humbly with him. Reflect how full the world is of those precautions, safeguards, defences, which argue, from experience, a constant expectation that men will do wrong, overreach and deceive, if they can. Let all this work of individual comparison be done honestly, fearlessly, faithfully, and with a prayer that even He who seeth in secret may be satisfied. And surely the argument will come to an end. It will break into the publican's prayer, "God be merciful to me a sinner!"

But let us not fail to take one step more. The actual impression of human sin which the Scriptures give, which the Saviour himself in this passage and elsewhere gives, is not made by specifying particular detailed acts of wrong, but by referring to the one great pervading sin of an unbelieving, unrepenting, unconsecrated heart. This is the fatal thing,—the depravity that is unto death. You notice, — and it seems to me a very striking fact, — that while the Pharisee enumerates his merits, what he thinks his positive and negative virtues, his abstinences and proprieties and almsgivings, the Publican does not pretend to enumerate his offences. Now, goodness that can be measured and counted off is not enough. Goodness is a principle, and that is measureless. Christ would show this publican as knowing that down underneath all particular sins there lies the one worse sin of a wrong soul, from which all the little ones spring and take their energy of mischief, — the parent-sin of Satanic self-love that brings the whole vile progeny forth. It is not so much *sins* as *sin* that we have to confess and deplore. Some acts of evil will ever remain to be renounced. But the state of sin, nothing but a Christian renewal or a regeneration from the Spirit of God in the cross of Christ will change that. A mere indifference to the right, a mere unfilial forgetfulness of God, the mere coldness of disregard to Christ's compassion, makes up that godless condition. The Father asks a filial spirit in his child; the Saviour asks a disciple's affection. We cannot veil that deep gulf which stretches always between him that serveth God and him that serveth him not with any brilliant mist of kindly instincts or graceful accomplishments. This is life eternal, — to know thee and thy Christ! "Thou shalt *love* thy God."

My friends, we all shrink from the Pharisaic reputation. Yet this must be true; — that if any of us are not penitent with the publican, the prodigal, the woman at the Redeemer's feet; if any of us are going on with habitual self-satisfaction, with no burning uneasiness, no bitter accusations, no sad shame within; if the days pass over us and bring no feeling with them that we are far from where we ought to be and might be, and far from what our Saviour has come to make us to be; if we have not frequent hours of sorrowful self-scrutiny; no solitary struggles with ourselves, and none of that secret pleading on our knees for forgiveness which is the only way any holy soul ever found to the kingdom of God,—we may be sure that, though we should lack the effrontery to stand up and repeat the very insolence of the Pharisee, yet we are with him in spirit, and shall go down to our houses to-day no more justified than he.

Finally, recall the truth, written in those common expectations of mankind which Paul well describes as a "certain fearful looking for of judgment" almost as clearly as in the volume of the Book,—that an irresistible power, mightier than any of our passions, and penetrating below our delusions, will dispel every mistake, bring all that is dark to light, and make every soul stand face to face with its sins. What wisdom in us to anticipate these disclosures and their retribution! How reasonable that, seizing on all helps towards reckoning the departures of our transgression, we should see what is the sin that most easily besets us!

No generalities here can adequately unveil our private hearts. Pursue this salutary search, therefore, in the secrecy of your several retirements. Dismiss all concealments; we may well dismiss them before the God who sees beneath them. Reject those too flattering constructions which pride and self-excuse are always so ready to suggest, to quiet the disturbances of conscience. Give penitence free way, for it cleanses while it burns. Rebuke the whisper that says, "Soul, take thine ease, eat, drink, and be merry." Plunge down into the darkest corners, — not only among sins of the tongue and the street, of society and business, of the house and the hand, of the market and the Church, but among sins of forbidden desires, of subtle indulgence, of the temper and the imagination, — sins that ally themselves, if they can, with noble impulses and warm affections, with the intellect and with honor. This will be a worthy sacrifice, an acceptable lenten service, — such a fast as God hath chosen. And it will be a new wonder, if, at the end of that solemn scrutiny, we do not all implore, with no need of exhortation from each other, "God be merciful to me a sinner!"

In the Castle of Despair, Christian found the key of promise in his bosom. And this is the promise: "If we confess our sins, He is faithful and just to forgive us our sins, and to cleanse us from all unrighteousness." "Who hath delivered us from the power of darkness, and hath translated us into the kingdom of his dear Son, in whom we have redemption through his blood, even the forgiveness of sins."

SERMON VI.

THE ECONOMY OF RENEWAL.

ARISE YE, AND DEPART; FOR THIS IS NOT YOUR REST.—Micah ii. 10.

THERE is no incongruity between the use of this solemn command as the Prophet wrote it, and the use to be made of it here. The arising and the departure, as the passage stands, referred to a visible residence; there was to be a literal change of place. But even there the act was required as part of a religious discipline, and for a divine purpose. The national condition that made such a migration necessary was one incident in a peculiar providential history. The outward removal was the result of an inward state,—a state of moral deterioration and danger. Domestic comfort must be abandoned for the sake of the spiritual safety, purity, and progress, of a corrupt, imperilled people. The call is made in the name and by the Spirit of the Lord God. In all these respects, the original bearing of the language agrees with the present application of it. There is no violence in transferring it from a Hebrew to a Christian age. The need that a self-absorbed heart should bestir itself and arise,—should go forth and follow God's call, should be moulded into a new form and born into a new life, through separation, travail, sacrifice, — is as independent of the differences of time and country as any attribute of humanity.

Indeed, this permanence of the essential realities of life through all social changes, wherever a human soul lives, sins, and suffers, furnishes the starting-point in this subject. The Maker of both man and the Gospel, fitting the one for the other, has laid a preparation in the constitution and the experience of every one of our hearts for all the great promises, ministries, and beliefs, of the Word. And so, if we make a reverential examination of the actual proceeding of human life, in its deeper currents, we shall find there a universal need, if not always a believing cry, for the power and the peace that come of the Christian change. Unless it is the emptiest of sentimental exclamations, the penitential prayer, "God be merciful to me a sinner," will be followed by an arising and departing, with new-born affections, energies that are not of the flesh but the Spirit, from the old and far country, for the Father's house.

First of all, the true growth of every really progressive character is made through a *succession* of decided departures out of positions, habits, estates of thought and feeling, which have once become familiar, into untried territories. Some of these points of transition belong to the common order of our lives. There is the passage from the comparatively irresponsible and dependent period of early childhood into the greater self-determination of youth, — a spot where the holy hand of our religion is as much wanted, to help the tempted heart through the sudden rush of responsibility, and through the strange sense of freedom, and through the restless irritation of ill-adjusted duty and privilege,—a spot where the tranquil influence of a spirit of faith in God is as manifest a blessing,—as at any later stage in the whole way. Within the safe enclosures of a guarded external innocence the moral purposes will not stay any longer. They would not be fulfilling the Creator's design, if they did. That is not their rest; they must arise and depart. And generally, at the moment, the young mind is eager enough to go; the leave-taking from the former securities is light-hearted and with few regrets. It is only they that look on, from places further along, who discover, underneath the merriment, the elements of pain and tragedy already at work. Youth must see its visions, and dream its dreams, and taste its awful liberty. The hour for that comes. Well and happy for it, blessed for it, if they are only visions of purity and honor, dreams of holier and nobler attainments, a liberty never to be sunk into the license of corruption, and by that way into the bondage of iniquity! Yet already there is judgment. The Past begins to bear its fruit. If father and mother have been heedless, passionate, worldly, or have taught one thing with their lips at the child's bedside now and then, and another with their life every day, no remonstrance afterward can retrieve that fault. Parental fear and love can then only send out their ineffectual entreaties after the receding and scarcely listening adventurer. Misdirected and robbed, where it ought to have been fortified and enriched, the young soul must nevertheless arise and depart. Or, if, on the other hand, the training has been Christian so far, still the old shelter, however gracious, would presently prove a prison-house. God must be served by an individual will. He bids each go, find his vineyard, bear his burden. Moral childhood is not our rest.

Again, later, there is a transition from youth into maturity. The dream is broken. That graceful, airy tent, which the uncommitted thought reared for itself at will, is dissolved. A more real habitation, of severer shape, supplants it. Or, rather, it is now a field of outdoor service. To remain at the less arduous post would be — at least, for more timid or indolent natures — the pleasanter way; to have occupations laid out, instead of laying them out, under the great Taskmaster's eye, ourselves; to have our comforts provided and our costs paid, with little strain of forecast and self-denial; to be receivers and observers rather than laborers and stewards; — all this might suit the sluggish and self-indulgent. But it is not our Maker's plan. Chilly as the future looks, the least enterprising must go to meet it. Hedged up and steep as the path lies, we must push into it, and clear it, and conquer it, step by step. And this, not because of any blind force of fate, or any drudging necessity of a mere worldly subsistence, but because it is the sacred calling wherewith our God calls us. The Eternal Spirit is very near. It is a miserable stupidity and ingratitude if we fail to see that all this change is of Him, and for Him, and must be religiously turned to his glory. That result the honors and applauses of men will avail nothing to secure. The young shepherd, David, going forth from his pastoral retirement, is found presently clad in the mantle of a king. But what then? Will the king be David the debauchee, with murder in his lustful heart; or David aspiring to build a temple to Jehovah? If the first, then the purple and the crown are no consolation in that hour of retributive agony which wrings from him the sobs and groans and bitter repentances of the Fifty-first Psalm.

In some vague, indefinite way, this decree of departure makes itself felt in all thoughtful souls. How many a young man, to whom the guilty resort is just as hospitable as to the rest, turns away with a sad face from the shows and the gayeties, because the shadow of a more earnest and holy reality has fallen upon him! You say he seems melancholy, and needs to have his spirits cheered; and you think the plummet of your Epicurean philosophy has sounded him. But he knows the Prodigal's country and the charmer's voice as well as you do. The old enchanters call, but he does not hear them. The light laugh rings, but if there is shame in it he does not follow it. That is not his rest. The spell of a deeper fascination holds him; the drawing of a mightier attraction leads him. The vulgar spectacle may shine in the streets, with music and dancing; but close by, in the temple, the sages are sitting, wisdom speaks, the veil before the ineffable and everlasting glory is lifted. He will stand and look and listen there. He will ask questions of Revelation and Eternity. Almost he can say, with that divine Child of twelve years old at Jerusalem, "Wist ye not that I must be about my Father's business?"

Beyond these earlier and successive departures, from one period of our age to another, made necessary by the inevitable movement of time, there are a great variety of other changes, having the same general purpose, and illustrating the same plan of God. With a dealing which our reluctance and disobedience sometimes make sharp and dreadful, now in warning and now in promise, but always tender, always affectionate, because always the dealing of our Father, they all invite us one way. They repeat, What doth the Lord thy God require of thee, amidst all this fluctuation and uncertainty, but to follow the holy commandment? They bid us arise and depart, because we have here no continuing city, that we may seek one to come.

Sometimes this dissolution of our former order of life is made unavoidable by conditions beyond our control. Sometimes it is only urged upon us by our sense of duty, and we make it rather than be openly false to God, or faithless to man, or traitors to our better selves. Sometimes it is attended by an outward alteration of fortune or dwelling-place, which only gives emphasis to the spiritual lesson. Sometimes it is wholly a shifting of the internal proportions and scenery of our being, and we have to find out where the Spirit would have us go only by the light he has set in conscience and in his Word. In one way or another, we have to learn respecting stage after stage, where we had thought to find a permanent repose, and to be able to lay aside our vigilance, dismiss our anxiety, relax our effort, and lie down to be happy,—that instead of that we must bestir ourselves once more, leave the dear delights behind us, arise and depart, for our rest is not yet.

So, for example, a particular line of employment is found to have furnished all of opportunity, or stimulus, or trial, that the great Former of our characters intended, and it is broken off. A particular place of residence has exhausted all its helps and ministries upon us, and we must take up the little parcels that we call our goods, and go to be schooled in some new neighborhood. A particular set of acquaintances, or kind of business, is found to be secretly undermining our principles, leading us to measure truth by favor, flattering our pride, or confirming our prejudices, or softening our courage in duty, or circumscribing our sympathies and judgments by the petty notions of a class and its fashions; and then we have to be taken off, and cast upon simpler, perhaps rougher, but more wholesome and righteous relationships. Old estates are sold and divided. Old resorts are cut off. Old houses are taken down. Our parents die, and the whole domestic framework, of which their venerable persons were the centre, crumbles to pieces over their graves. Perhaps in the close circle of our own household affections these affections are tempting us; our human love grows selfish and ungodly; kindred are made idols; our own flesh and blood stand between us and heaven, casting shadows and not light; wrong is transformed into an angel, and is only a more beguiling wrong. And therefore, in that mystery of bereavement which is often "past our finding out" only because we will not be still and look where the Almighty points, these circles are sundered: the little graves or the longer ones are opened and filled, and the windows are darkened, and the mourners go about the streets. The family flower fadeth. The strong faint, and the beautiful wither. Suddenly, "our tents are spoiled," and "our curtains in a moment." One by one we arise and depart, for this is not our rest.

In other cases, with less visible signals, but not less effectually, we are moved out of our moral and mental habitations. So long as we are in them, nothing seems more fixed than our opinions, tastes, and estimates.

But they may become too fixed. Opinion hardens into bigotry. Tastes grow fastidious and luxurious. Estimates of men and things stiffen into prejudices. And hence, by one process or another, we are mercifully led to give many of them up, or modify them. Events are ordered to that end. By convictions within that we cannot resist if we remain honest with God, or by forces without that we cannot resist if we remain honest with men, we are pushed over the boundaries of party, or sect, or a scheme of thought to which all our fibres were fastened. It is hard loosening them. It makes the sensibilities bleed, and the affections ache. But our progress, our piety, nay, our integrity, may depend upon it, and then it is an inexorable master that says, "Arise, and depart." Rest is an inferior consideration. There are vices of the intellect, and vices of social conformity, and vices of moral indolence, as well as vices of appetite; and they all require a rigorous correction. In this migratory state, we are meant to be kept moving. Every moral climate here is more or less tainted, and grows pestilential if we linger in it too long. It is just as the text says: "This is not your rest; — because it is polluted, it shall destroy you with a sore destruction." Pilgrims and foreigners, it is only in a heavenlier air that we are to be acclimated, and abide. The moment we come to consider our scheme of living satisfactory, our schedule of performances perfect, some unexpected revolution breaks in like a whirlwind to disturb this complacency, and set us into larger, perhaps plainer rooms, where we can drink in more light, and gain a deeper wisdom, if we will. If we have been living by the average morality, we must be led out where we can catch sight of a loftier and more absolute standard. If we have been content with artificial rules, we must learn to walk by faith. If we have counted it enough to do as others do, or to escape the reproach of law and of public opinion, we must look with more searching and humble eyes to the original law and will of God. Or, if we have taken our own instincts or reasonings for our religion, then the cross must shine out in the sky where we worship, and we must kneel and be penitent and confess at the foot of it, and henceforth "conquer" both self and the world "by that."

Secondly, these turns of the inner life will often be painful, demanding something more than a natural or stoic courage. This is implied in the language. We imagine ourselves in a state of rest. It may be sinful. It may be false and foolish. But use has made it easy. Familiarity has deadened conscience, or stifled its protest. The senses spread their couch, and deck it, and make it fragrant, and think to lie luxuriously upon it. Avarice builds greater barns to bestow its fruits and its goods, and says, "Soul, take thine ease." Conceit desires no improvement. Religious indifference wishes only to be let alone. But no! Pain comes. The insensible heart must be startled. The earthly and the divine fight together within us, and we suffer under the conflict. Fearful controversies — as of our will against the God of Right, as of ourselves against ourselves — must vex the patience, and agitate the soul. As the mind goes up to vow an independent allegiance to the Spirit of the Lord, many seductive solicitations are plied to quiet it back into its ignoble rest again. The former habits, taking up the terms of honor, say, "Do not leave us; never break the old friendship." Degrading associates say, "Do not set yourselves up to be better than your equals; the average virtue is virtuous enough; anything but pretension and hypocrisy!" and at that shallow sophistry false modesty is terrified. Nevertheless, the secret soul knows the voice of the Tempter — knows the voice of its Lord: "Arise, depart!"

Comfort says, "Stay where you are; build here on the plain. Why try the unknown? Why tempt the dangers of the steeps? Here is much goods for many years; eat, drink, and be merry." But the patient mountain stands there, a rough stairway from the plain to the sky, and, with all its cliffs and thorns, it offers a more irresistible invitation. Arise! Duty lies there, and only pleasure here.

Sometimes, as many of you need not be told by me or by anybody, this separation from familiar evil is a struggle as between life and death, shaking the whole soul, and tearing its shrinking quick in torture. It is like the sword that pierceth to the dividing asunder of the joints and marrow. And yet, such is the power of the conviction of the spirit of truth when humility has once begun its holy and honest work within us, how many even go out to meet that saving sorrow! Indeed, when the heart has slept too long in the lap of indulgence, there often creeps upon it, I believe, an undefined feeling that before long this rest must be ended: the foreshadow of some darker angel cast across the path. And if the ear of our sympathy were quicker and finer than it is, we should doubtless often overhear, in the tones that breathe around us, the sadness and the prayer of an unsatisfied spirit striving against the evil in it! Blessed is the mind that springs with alacrity and thanksgiving to its better ministry!

For, thirdly, all true souls, really touched with the Spirit, and consecrated to the fellowship of Christian obedience, will be ready for this sacrifice. Not all equally ready. The bonds of past practice and attachment hang unequal weights about our necks. But what awakened soul will not willingly be drifted away from the accustomed repose, if it is thereby brought nearer to the righteousness and charity of Christ? This, in fact, is the test of the sincerity of faith: the willingness to give up all that has been precious but not holy, and launch out upon the future, trusting only to the Unseen Hand,—like the Patriarch, of whom that beautiful thing is written, that when he was called to go out into a place which he should after receive, he obeyed, and went out, not knowing whither he went, dwelling in the land of "promise," and looking for a city which hath foundations, whose builder and maker is God. Great difficulties will threaten every such obedient foot,—the wilderness before, the bondage to evil behind; but God is mightier than they,—a pillar of fire for the night, and of bright cloud by day: "Greater he that is for us than they that are against us." Outside our private battle, society exposes gigantic wrongs to be redressed: but the right which is to redress them is sure, and the prophetic ear of hope hears the sound of its footsteps from afar. There are changed faces, disappointed companions, an angry class or denomination forsaken, sneers, imputations, false charges, and criticisms,—such feeble weapons of the modern world's inquisitions as betray the cowardice of persecution, without its positive creed or its power. But these are not a terror to him who hears the voice say, "Awake, arise, and Christ shall give thee light!"

So, through familiar analogies, we are led to see how the sacred provision is made, in our fallen but still aspiring nature, for that one only radical and complete transformation which changes the governing motive of life, — the "regeneration" of the Gospel. We catch sight of a solemn and beautiful economy of spiritual renewal.

It has been said that no period of our life becomes quite intelligible and clear to us till we quit it for the next: not childhood, till we have left it; not youth, till it has departed; not life itself as a whole, till it verges to its close. There is certainly truth here; and there is a much larger and more sacred truth connected with it. Retrospect is not all our outlook. Our best wisdom is not gained from what is behind us, but from what is above. The deficiencies of knowledge find at once a cause and a compensation in the immeasurable certainties of faith. "I know," said the Apostle, "in whom I have believed." Our great want is to look up, with just that assurance. For that we have to be moved and dislodged. For that we have to change our state, our mind, our heart. As there are arms to take the reluctant child up and carry him to his good, so God lifts us along. We are born that we may be born again. We live that we may have life everlasting.

Once more, when the heart is really made new, and is filled with all the holy life of its Lord, it matters nothing what the outward place or scenery may be. Then there is no restless thirst for novelty, no contempt or complaint of commonplace task-work. Then, even in the new country, the old and familiar has to be taken back. There is much in common between the *forms* of the old life and the forms of the new. The same people have to be met, and served, and endured. The same body has to be fed, clothed, exercised, kept under. The same crosses of temper, self-disgust, baffled aspiration, have to be borne. No emigration transports us out of the reach of mortal annoyance and infirmity. If the old duties look small, the old labors irksome, and the old places incapable of religious grandeur, it is probably a sign that the new heart is not really in us, but only some specious and vain imagination instead. It is rest we are seeking, then — and that is not for us here. We are breaking from Providence. After his high communion in the temple, Jesus, the Lord of souls, went back to Nazareth, content with the companionships of his childhood for eighteen years more, cheerful with a village reputation, and subject to Joseph and Mary.

To this, then, we are brought, that there is one migration of the soul more complete and adventurous than all besides: that which takes it over from every kind of self-direction into a pure self-renunciation to the Spirit of God; — one "going forth" more decisive and sublime than all journeys or discoveries — from the miserable effort to satisfy ourselves into the liberty of the sons of God; one central and all-transforming change — that which refashions us, by a new principle of life, from the likeness of sinful men into the likeness of God's Son. All other transitions touch us at certain points or parts of our nature: this transfuses another spirit through the whole; old things pass away, because the old evil is gone; and all things are new.

Here enters the regenerate soul upon a new country, which, after all, turns out to be its native land.

Coming to himself, arising and going to his Father from his famine, the Prodigal finds himself at home — a home now such as it never was before. •Except ye be converted and become as little children, ye cannot enter into the kingdom of heaven. But childlikeness is not childishness. If we try to keep the irresponsibleness of childhood, its innocence is gone. That would be only staying in our shelter of careless impulse and unconsecrated custom, till the shelter is a "sore destruction." The man that refuses to renounce himself for Christ on the plea that he stays as he was made, mistakes the apathy of an underling for the freedom of God's child. He does *not* stay as he was made; for he was made to be a disciple, growing in goodness, and renewed day by day. If he is not *that*, day by day his depravity is debasing him. "Seekest thou the highest and greatest," says Schiller, — "the plants can teach it to thee. What they are involuntarily, that be thou voluntarily;" which is well enough for poetry. But what if the plant should find itself, some morning, with a twisted stalk, bruised stem, blighted leaves, and a disordered sap running in all its veins? Man can never take his Gospel from the flowers. If he gives up to the nature in him, he is a great deal worse than their deadliest poison. If by the grace given in Christ, and welcomed by holy faith, he is born again and brings his earthly nature under, by so much is he nobler than all their beauty. Immortal, and made alive with the very life of God, he can say, in the grandeur of his humility, "It is no more I that live, but Christ liveth in me."

And now, having thus traced the steps of this great truth, of a necessary change in character from the sluggish, selfish, sinning state, till Christ is formed there, and having done it rather in the language and by the method of common discourse, it only remains to remind you — if it has not occurred to more than one of you already — that for all this doctrine, and more than we have been able to convey, there is a statement far more strong and complete, more clear and convincing, of simpler speech and sublimer authority, in the Gospel of the New Testament. There you find again and again, repeated in as many forms as the heart and customs of men could need it, from the lips of the Redeemer and his first disciples, that truth of which all this train of remark has been but a feeble echo, or exposition: "Except a man be born again, he cannot see the kingdom of God." There you find that to "arise" there must be repentance toward God and faith in the Lord Jesus Christ — since "it is God that worketh in us, both to will and to do." There you find that Lord to whom, with Peter, when you have arisen you must go, because he alone has the words and the gift of eternal life. There you see revealed what is to be *departed from*, — the "evil heart of unbelief," "the old man and his deeds," "corrupt according to the deceitful lusts." And there you behold the "rest" that is not here, but remaining "for the people of God," — the peace that is given not as the world gives.

And then all that is earthly can be freely sacrificed for this life divine. When we go out from one resting-place after another, it may feel at first as if it were an exile from all joy. But as the old roof drops away, the Almighty arms will close us round — and lo! another house, not built with hands, begins already to reveal its spiritual symmetry, its fairer form and eternal strength, around us. Though father or mother forsake us, the Lord will take us up. If you are disheartened at your trivial fruits and slow advances, you will remember that even the great Saints and Prophets who have done most have been conscious of leaving the vast work of good unfinished, — dying, one after another, "without the sight" of their desired achievement, — still declaring that "they seek a country." Then our own death itself is no more terrible. We cease gazing backward to the Eden behind, but look steadily to the heaven above. We lose sight of the earthly gardens of ease and pleasure from which our infirmity expelled us, in expecting the immortality to which we are called. Forgetting the things that are behind, we reach forth to those that are before, — willing to arise and depart, that we may be found risen indeed into newness of life.

SERMON VII.

NAMES AND ELEMENTS OF THE GREAT CHANGE.

CONVERSION. — Acts xv. 3.

THIS word is now separated from its connections, because it better serves the use I intend to make of it standing alone than with any additions. Excluding every other matter, I wish, with the help of your attention, to inquire what is the Christian doctrine of the soul's "conversion." The Christian doctrine: let us give emphasis to the word Christian. For, if we were to enter on this inquiry through the forms of human opinion upon it, following the method of theological speculations, criticising all the theories and dogmas that men's philosophies and fancies have invented and fought about, we should be quite sure to have a very long, a very dull, and a very unprofitable discussion. But if, on the other hand, we could only catch the truth as it comes fresh, direct, and radiant, out of the heart of the New Testament, we should be sure of something clear, simple, attractive, and of unspeakable practical value.

You will hardly need to be persuaded that Christ himself, by his own lips and through his Apostles, tells us precisely what is to be believed about conversion, as the truth. Even before that Divine Ministry which has changed and saved the world had opened, the Forerunner of the Messiah came preaching repentance and a new life. The wilderness in which the voice of the Baptist cried was the wilderness of sin, — the desolation in the human heart. When the Son of God, who had been thus announced, himself appeared, he did not unsay what John had said. He took up the same penetrating, stirring strain. He confirmed John's message, — expanded it, — gave it greater consistency, breadth, life, power. Being the whole world's master, he gave it a universal sweep, applicable to all nations, ages, and souls. "Repent, and through faith in me be converted," was the epitome of his preaching. He came from heaven into the world because mankind needed just that change. He found them gross, sensual, false, proud, frivolous, hypocritical, bigoted: he would make them pure, spiritual, upright, meek, thoughtful, sincere, charitable. That is conversion. He found the ascendant principle in the world's life, ruling everything with its iron hand and cruel breath, to be selfish passion: he would make that ruling principle to be disinterested love. This would be conversion. Above all, he found the great mass of men to be living as if there were no true God: he would make them to live in conscious communion and obedience with the one only living and forgiving Father; and to that end would show them the Father in himself, and die on the cross to touch men's hearts, and draw their faith to his gracious atonement. This would be conversion. And since this latter is the change that is *deepest down* in a man, — a change of his radical principle, his inmost motive, or that which makes character, — this conversion is the real one, — the primary, absolute, essential renewing. So that, state the Saviour's benign errand on earth in whatever language you will, you find that *turning*, *changing*, *making over*, was his central purpose; and that is literally conversion. You may trace this idea through all his parables and discourses. It was to clear a way into men's minds for the entrance of this renewing power that he astonished them with miracles and warned them with prophecies. When he cured so many kinds of maladies, he pointed inward to the sick heart, and said his chief design was to heal the disorder there, — conversion. When he raised the dead, he showed by that physical sign that the soul must be raised up to a new life, out of the death of trespasses and sins, — conversion. When he cast out demons, he signified that in all our breasts are the possessing devils of self-love, — avarice, lust, vanity, jealousy, anger, — which must be cast out before we can be his disciples; — conversion, again. Some of his last words on the cross were a recognition of a malefactor's conversion, and a blessing upon it. After his resurrection, on his walk to Emmaus, he sought to convert the slow-hearted and foolish men he talked with. At his ascension to the right hand of the Father, where he was before, he charged his disciples to go forth and convert the people, founding a church to be composed of converted souls. Still, we are taught, he liveth to make intercessions, and to be an advocate for the world's conversion. The Apostles did as they were bid; and if you read their history and letters with simplicity, you will see that the burden of their preaching also, like their Master's, was, "Repent and be converted." Christianity has not renounced its character, to this day. It still finds men needing to be changed, from bad to good, from self-will to devout submission, from unbelief to faith, from worldliness to holiness, from petulance and intemperance to a principled and sweet self-control, from gain to God; and so it still has to preach a new character, a changed heart, a different life. And precisely that is conversion.

Much has been done to confuse and perplex the subject by certain technical terms, which have come to be invested with artificial associations. I take four of these words, and suggest that each of them, after stripping off the human accretions, signifies something plain, evangelical, and vital to the matter; and that, in fact, by combining their significations, we get a complete view of this great spiritual necessity. These four words are Repentance, Reformation, Regeneration, Conversion.

The first, *Repentance*, taken as a translation of the compound Greek word used in the New Testament to express the same thing, points to an internal alteration, or a thinking differently from some former way of thinking. The modern word seems also to introduce a reference to pain. It means a changed mind, an altered ruling purpose, a new way of looking at things. Used as it is here, it means, of course, a new way of looking at the deepest and greatest thing, the central thing, the object of life, or our relation to God. This change of mind affects the whole judgment, intention, spirit, of our being. It implies a turning about in the direction, the drift, of a man's innermost life. If he regarded the world, before repentance, as a place merely to get the greatest amount of bodily pleasure in, after repentance he will regard it as the place to get the greatest amount of goodness in; he repents of his sensuality. If he looked upon it before as only a shop for making money, afterwards he will look upon it as a mission-field for cultivating righteousness; he repents of his sordidness. If he treated his position before as only a dressing-room for ostentation, he will afterwards treat it as a vineyard for honest and useful labor; he will repent of his vanity and idleness. If he esteemed men and women before only as beings made to promote his comfort, and advance his interests, he will afterwards esteem them as beings that he is to comfort, and whose interests he is to serve; he will repent of his cupidity and selfishness. And so through the whole circle of virtues and vices. His inmost purpose is changed. Literally, he *thinks the other way.*

But, then, consider that most of us do not live according to mere momentary impulses, but according to a pretty well established and uniform rule, or habit. We may not be conscious of having adopted such a rule at any particular time, but practically it is so. Even the most impulsive people have a settled method; and that is the simple but very dangerous method of acting as they happen to feel inclined at the moment. If you examine yourself carefully, or study human nature wisely, you will also find, probably, that with every individual this settled rule is one of two, — viz. self-gratification, or religious principle. I know there are some persons kind-hearted, sympathizing, helpful, by their natures, who are far from loyal to religious principle. But these amiable instincts, being natural, and not the result of discipline, or conscience, or faith, are really easier to their possessors, and give them more pleasure, than the opposite order of feelings would. So that these persons do not form a third class, as at first sight they seemed to; they belong, after all, to those whose main object is self-gratification.

We have, then, two great governing motives, — two states, by which mankind are broadly divided: that in which men really try faithfully to live by a righteous principle, rooted in God through Christ, on the one hand; and that in which they live carelessly, at the dictate of some form of worldly policy or self-gratification, on the other. Hence it follows that to be changed from the last of these to the first — which is a change of the state, or of the ruling affection — is the real repentance. That is indeed a thing of the mind, the inmost nature of the man; what constitutes character — what makes one a Christian, from having been not a Christian. This is the Evangelical, the radical, comprehensive repentance.

Furthermore, as this change of the mind, or of the inner man, affects one's views of the past, as well as of the present and future, it must of course be accompanied with a palpable sorrow that the past life has been what it has, and has not been what it so plainly ought to be. In a true repentance, this sorrow will be intense and bitter. A sincere and spiritual man cannot but loathe himself for having done those shameful, vicious, ungrateful things. Paul's vivid language of self-condemnation becomes actual and natural to us. We are disgusted with our spiritual meanness. Looking up to Christ and his redeeming love, we are smitten with the disgrace that we should so long have been wounding and insulting him. Looking to the Holy Spirit, so infinitely tender and forbearing, we feel that the first utterance of prayer must be a confession of unworthiness, — a cry for pardon and deliverance from a deserved ruin. And if this grief is not a mere dictate of selfish fear, or mercenary calculation, but a *spiritual* penitence because the pure God has been offended, and the crucified Christ wronged, then it is that godly sorrow, needing not to be repented of, or changed from, which purifies and brings peace and pardon to the heart. This is repentance.

The second of the four words is *Reformation.* To take the special force of this, you have only to separate it into its elements — re-formation. This takes us out from the interior process, signified by repentance, into the external part of the change. It is no less a change than the other; for whereas that gave a new spirit, this gives a new form. That was thinking, feeling, purposing, aiming another way: this is being formed another way. That breathed into the life a new principle: this clothes it in a different shape. That was a concern of the heart — the affections: this is a concern of conduct, or action. Taking the comparison of a tree, repentance would change the vital element, the nature of the circulating sap; reformation would show a different kind of fruit, as no longer thistle-down or thorns, but figs or grapes.

Reformation is just as essential as repentance. That is, it is just as essential that you should, up to your power, do the deeds of a good man or woman, as that you should take the resolution to be a good man or woman. If you are heartily sorry for misspent years, you will make it your business to spend your future years wisely. If you are called to renounce an undevout heart, the same Lord calls you to work with holy hands. In whatever the past has been irreligious and mean, the future must be sanctified and noble. Despising your selfishness, you must go on to generosity. Renouncing a paltry ambition, you must serve humanity and truth for their own immortal sake. The invisible energy that makes the acorn vital is nothing, unless you give it soil and air for growth and expansion into the fair proportions of the oak.

Thus, in fact, reformation becomes the *test* of repentance, proving its sincerity and its worth. We infer that a miser is penitent, when we see him giving liberally to the poor, or to spreading the Gospel. A sensualist may profess to have repented; but we are not sure, till we see him forsaking dissipation, and living temperately and chastely. A vain, frivolous girl deserves small confidence as repenting, till her whole appearance reveals a constant life hidden with Christ in God, and the dignity of a sober devotion to the welfare of others. It is not to be believed that a sullen or angry temper has been actually repented of, till the countenance loses its unhallowed fire, and the voice its asperity, and the words come gently, like his who when he was reviled reviled not again.

Now, obviously, reformation must be a much slower process than repentance. A thought may dart instantly through the mind; a feeling may flash across the heart like the lightning across a cloud; sorrow, the sincerest, may wring the soul during a single breath. And in a certain sense, the man may be thus changed, because the heart is changed, and the face is turned. But that building up of character which we call reformation, and which gives to repentance its value, is the patient work of a life.

After the beginning is a progress, patient, painstaking, unceasing. All is not over with the rising of the day-star, or the flush of dawn. The transport of a new sensation is not the great object of a Christian conversion. With some that will be more vivid than with others — partly on account of temperament, partly on account of the sharpness of the contrast between the old life and the new. With some it will be more sudden than with others. There is nothing in nature to prevent its coming sometimes, as it did to Paul, and many a strong and consistent believer since, like the instantaneous throwing open of a close, dark room to the sun. But there is everything to prevent its being transient, — i. e. if it is true, — its vanishing like the lightning, or fading in early clouds. It must endure; and not only endure, but grow. It must shine brighter and brighter unto the perfect day. Perhaps the first freshness will not be always felt in it. Nay, as the day grows fierce and long, and the toil heavy, the birds may stop singing, and there may be dust and heat. Resolute souls, counting the cost, will not faint, nor look back with longing to the morning. The day's work is better than the morning's hope; the sheaves of harvest are better than the seed-time. If the spiritual life has really sprung from its eternal source, and knows its resting-place in God, we shall not complain of the burden, nor forget the fountain, nor withhold our hand till the evening.

The third term is *Regeneration*. This brings into the doctrine a third element, as indispensable as either of the other two. Repentance, as we have seen, is an act of the individual himself, though an act that is internal, affecting the dispositions, or spirit. Reformation expresses an act without, — or rather a series of acts, — yet one that is equally the work of human agency. But regeneration is a term which shows us that in all this change, including both repentance and reformation, we are not acting of ourselves alone, but are moved, *are acted*, by the Holy Spirit. Regeneration, or being born again, is then something done for us. The second birth, like the first, is in some sense independent of personal agency. Our part in it is faith — yielding to it. *Be ye* born again, the Saviour says. Our part is the trust which lets the Spirit's influence into our hearts. Our part is to receive God's gift, — seconding it by a holy purpose. In all genuine renewing there is a power acting upon us from above, — God's power, whose energy is felt through Christ's redemption and the Comforter's presence. The task is too great for our damaged competency and our enfeebled faculties. The vivifying and gracious Spirit must breathe over and quicken our dulled and sluggish souls, as the genial gale of spring wakens the clover and wheat on the warm April furrow. Our spiritual renewing is from above. "No man can come unto me," said Jesus, "except the Father who hath sent me draw him." We are roused into this more glorious life, this resurrection from moral death, only by coming into contact, by faith, with him who comes to give life unto the race, — himself the light and life of the whole believing and living world. "Of mine own self," unassisted in this regeneration, "I can do nothing; but I can do all things through Christ strengthening me."

So we come to the last of the four terms in question, which is *Conversion*. This signifies the entire result, — the turning of the whole nature together from one state to its opposite. When repentance has changed the grand ruling affection within, when reformation has wrought a corresponding renewal of the outward life, and when both have been done, not in the imagination of any conceited mortal ability, but, as they can only be done, by self-renouncing and holy submission to the silent energy of the indwelling and inworking Spirit of the living God moulding us as he will, — then indeed is the soul created anew in Christ Jesus. Spiritually it is no more the same, but another. The *inspiring and regulating force* is different; for, instead of being the narrow and dark dominion of self-will, it is the free, large, upward-soaring love of the Father, kept warm and glowing in the love of man. The *substantial body of life* is different. Instead of the ferment of the passions, the ever-disappointing scramble of ambition, the strain of unrewarding competition, the strife of worldliness, there is the calm work of righteousness; everything is colored by the celestial tints of a heavenly hope; the secret influence of a divine communion spreads into the commonest drudgery; daily toil is elevated; the hands are sanctified; more and more, not by spasmodic, strange, or fantastic jerks, but by a steady growth, as orderly as "the blade, the ear, and the full corn in the ear," the Christian disciple is fashioned into the likeness of his Lord. The *influence from above* is different; for instead of being a mere preserving Providence, which is nominally recognized and practically disobeyed, it is the accepted and welcomed inspiration of the Holy One, helping our infirmities, encouraging our timidity, pardoning us in our penitence, urging us forward in our reformation, — Renewer, Quickener, Comforter, Sanctifier. Repentance, Reformation, Regeneration, are here united, consummated, and consolidated. This is the conversion that Christ proclaimed, that the cross provided, that the resurrection symbolized, that the Apostles preached, that has filled the ranks of the church, that we are told heaven is entered by, when it is said that "Except a man be born again he cannot see the kingdom of God."

Thus do we see that each of these four terms, which we are apt to employ indiscriminately, and half-indifferently, as if they all expressed some unreal or vague thing, stands for a distinct, intelligible, and most interesting fact in a Christian's experience. Each denotes a step in the way to eternal life. Through each every soul must pass which is to have strength, beauty, freedom, — which is to attain either the noble and fair proportions of Christian excellence here, or the believer's immortality.

Not one of the three first can be left out, if you would attain the blessedness of the last. Theological sects have often tried to put one for the whole, and so have blundered into the worst practical errors, narrowing the broad Gospel, and crippling the soul's progress.

We cannot, for instance, take repentance alone, and call that conversion. To change the mind, or feeling, or purpose, is the first thing; but it avails little if we do not press forward to reformation of the life. That would be the seed sown where there is no depth of earth. The beginning is right, and the promises are fair, but all ends some day in a miserable apostasy. Characters of that stamp are loud in pretension and profession, but soon fall into dismal, foul endings. This nas been no uncommon delusion, — repentance without reformation, — a flush of feeling without the patient labor of righteousness. Society has been often deformed, and the church humiliated, by these abortive conversions. Equally impotent is repentance without the regeneration by the Spirit; for what is it that a man, in his shortsightedness, thinks this way or that way, unless the Almighty author of all life and power works within him, both to will and to do?

So take reformation alone. Lacking repentance, it lacks the right motives. It is all outside work. It is form without spirit, body without life, a stream without a fountain, — which is not a stream very long. No doubt, you may keep up a temporary imitation of Christian improvement by other means, like policy, or pride, or love of esteem, or a cool temperament. But if it is not rooted in holy principle, in a conviction that all sin is hateful and impious, in a thorough turning of the heart to Christ, it will not stand sharp trials, nor will it yield the heavenly fruits. And without devout dependence on the Spirit, without prayer and faith, it is more uncertain and helpless than vegetation without the sun, or infancy without parental love.

So, again, regeneration cannot be without repentance and reformation. For God never compels our conversion. There is no spiritual coercion. Gracious and forbearing as our Father is, he does not save us against our will. No soul is forced into the kingdom of heaven. Nor can we ever be born again, except as we voluntarily open our breasts to receive the divine gift from on high, and freely yield our bodies and lives, servants of righteousness. The Saviour calls:

we must answer. The Spirit pleads: we must arise and come. Heaven throws wide its gates: we must enter in.

Laying aside all dogmatical prepossessions, then, do we not get a plain and effective doctrine from the study of these scriptural terms? Conversion is threefold. No one of the three elements can be omitted without weakening and damaging the whole. Repent, reform, receive and quench not the Spirit by which the new birth is given,—and ye shall enter into life.

Gathering up the practical points of the doctrine, we find them also to be three.

First, of this new life in the heart Christ himself is the immediate source. The knowledge of it, the power of it, the promise of its exceeding joy, all come by him. His words, his life, his cross, move us to repentance, stimulate us to reformation, baptize us in the waters of regeneration. The more intimately we enter into fellowship with his life, the more we bear his spiritual image, the more we are impelled by his heavenly affections, the more truly regenerate will our souls be. The New Testament always associates a true conversion with faith in his person. Look to his sufferings, and repent of the sins for which he bled. Look to his example, and be reformed into the character of which he is the pattern. Look to his perpetual and secret influence over the believer's heart,—the Comforter he promised to give after his ascension,—and be new-created by his Spirit. It is his own word, "I have come that they might have life."

Again, we see what is for us personally to do. It is, by the energy of an inward resolution, to renounce our state of indifference, to disown sin, to cast off the works of darkness, not to be satisfied with social respectability, to have a changed mind, a new purpose, a Christian aim; i. e. to repent. It is, by constant fidelity, by imitation of the perfect example, by effort, by all means of help and grace, to live righteously; i. e. to reform. It is, by childlike trust, by tractable affections, and above all by the prayer which kneels in daily adoration through the interceding Son, to welcome the renewing Spirit; i. e. to be regenerated from above.

And finally, we witness the beauty and the glory of the result. A consecrated life, — what spectacle of dignity or loveliness can all our visions of the good or the fair bring into comparison with that? It is the consummation of man's estate. It is the crown of humanity. It is the flower of all the world. Peace after storms; bursts of morning sunlight after murky tempests; spring verdure and blossoms after the cold trance of winter; resurrection after death; — all these but faintly image the peace, the sunlight, the vitality, the power of a Christian's heart, recreated in Christ Jesus. For, "if any man be in Christ, he is a new creature. Behold, old things are passed away, and all things are become new."

SERMON VIII.

PERMANENT REALITIES OF RELIGION, AND TIMES OF SPECIAL RELIGIOUS INTEREST.

SEEK YE THE LORD WHILE HE MAY BE FOUND, CALL YE UPON HIM WHILE HE IS NEAR. LET THE WICKED FORSAKE HIS WAY, AND THE UNRIGHTEOUS MAN HIS THOUGHTS: AND LET HIM RETURN UNTO THE LORD, AND HE WILL HAVE MERCY UPON HIM; AND TO OUR GOD, FOR HE WILL ABUNDANTLY PARDON. — Isaiah lv. 6, 7.

To a singular degree, the history of religion is also a history of the power of names. Once, names, if they are really names, had things corresponding to them; and the existence of the thing accounts for the name. So long as this correspondence continues, — the actual name standing clearly for the fact, and the same fact being always pointed to by the name, — so long all goes well; language fulfils its designed office as a sign of realities, and as a medium, or currency, for thought; men are mutually helped and enlightened by it; science finds it a safe instrument; instruction and debate become possible; knowledge is increased. So that, sometimes, hardly any better benefit can be conferred on a thing than to get a good, true name for it. Many a great cause has been signally advanced, has virtually conquered, when some genius in statesmanship, in reform, in letters, has penetrated to its core, and named it.

In other cases this natural relation is broken; either the thing is found without the name, or the name without the thing, or names are transposed and applied to the wrong objects. Then arise discussions that yield less light, and are farther from the heart of the matter; then come confusion and verbiage, and an unprofitable attention to the letter that killeth, rather than the spirit that giveth life. Then come the vexed interpretations of instruments, questions of a constitution with a party for each, an age of controversy, dogmatism, appeals to documents and lexicons, commentary upon commentary, — and then, sometimes, an age of mere cant, formality, and ventriloquism. We feel then what Dr. South calls, in the title of a celebrated sermon, "the fatal imposture and force of words." This process had begun so early in the Christian church as the time of Paul, who evidently had a lively sense of the evil, repeatedly warning Timothy against disputings and dotings about questions and strifes of words, which minister no edifying and are to no profit, but subvert the hearers; and so, it need not be added, it has continued to this day.

Religion is not wholly peculiar in this respect; other great human interests have had to suffer in the same way, for the error is not in a particular subject, but in human nature, — it is the resort of a superficial or less earnest mood, taking refuge from moral or intellectual dissatisfaction in phrases, or feeding emptiness of feeling on husks. Only you notice that where the interests involved are most palpable to sense, there the mere name has least control. Material commerce suffers comparatively little in that way; yet there are instances of it even there. Men have been kept from great enterprises, great gains, by the power of names alone; refusing to colonize fruitful lands, refusing to admit new discoveries of vast material productiveness, refusing to embark in prosperous ventures, for no other reason. So agriculture, manufactures, and trade have been kept back. Yet, generally, the plainer the profit the less hinderance from a name. When we come to the region of feeling, and of ideas, or of a welfare that is spiritual, the name will be relatively more effective, just because the thing is less palpable. And when you tell men to stop doing wrong, and begin to do right, to put off their hardness and selfishness, and live like children of God, to get them a new heart and a new spirit, some of them will tell you, perhaps, No, they shall not do that, because that would be a "Revival of Religion." We are to look beneath this term, "a Revival," to the reality it has been chosen to express.

I. "Seek ye the Lord while he may be found, call ye upon him while he is near. Let the wicked forsake his way, and the unrighteous man his thoughts: and let him return unto the Lord, and he will have mercy upon him; and to our God, for he will abundantly pardon."

Commonly those sentences, read as the text of a sermon, might convey no other than their direct meaning, — their simple contents; and certainly language was never written in a more direct or simple sense. Used so now,* they very likely associate with them the thought of a particular religious movement, acting through the community; and in their association with that movement, according to the view taken of it by

---

* April, 1858.

two classes of persons, meet a furtherance or a hinderance to their natural impression. Here are preached two duties,—repentance and reformation. Men are bidden, by one of the Lord's Prophets, by one of the great thinkers and reformers of history, as from the Lord himself, and for the sake of their own good, to come back from the way of iniquity to the way of religious integrity; to pass from a state of self-seeking to a seeking after God; to repent of sin, and be forgiven for it. Of course the ability is implied, goes with the duty, measures the obligation. If anybody is unable, the call is not for him; and if the disability is general, the whole message is void, and can only return to heaven; which, in the same passage with the text, God promises his "word" shall not do, but rather refresh the earth, like rain. But beyond this, to some persons the words will have more power now, to others less acceptance now, for the reason just given. We cannot well afford much time to a mere criticism on either side of a temporary attitude of a great truth; but it lies in the way, and it is a proper subject for unprejudiced examination. Instead, therefore, of taking up with a mere name, "Revival," which name may possibly have become unrelated to the essential thing, or been artificially colored by the accessories, let us, at the outset, try to look in on the substantial facts, which for Truth's sake we ought to see, and seeing to revere.

The first of them is that to have the feeling of God awakened, made alive, in any human heart, is a good. That is a very tame expression. It is the one good of life. It is so vast, and deep, and wide, and beautiful, and comforting, and satisfying a good, that no other good deserves to be mentioned in comparison. Like Him who comes to embody and open its glory on the world, it is "the desire of all nations." Whatever difficulties there may be in reaching it, whatever ignorance in seeking, whatever obstacles from passion, pride, or sense, or a fickle will, it is all that. And if it is all that for one person, it cannot be less for many. The more hearts it comes to, possesses, and fills, the greater the good. The sooner it comes, still the greater the good. Let the way be what it will,—we shall consider that presently,—the result is infinitely desirable: to have the habitual feeling of God, our Father, and of living as his affectionate, obedient child. "Seek ye the Lord."

Come to the second fact: this feeling is to be had because God is with us. He is not far off. He "may be found." His presence is perpetual, universal. Am I to stand here to urge the Omnipresence of God? We may be far off; he is not. He abides and follows after. He remains and accompanies. He besets us behind and before, goes with us, and waits for us where we are going, lays his invisible hand upon us,—and whither shall we flee from that presence? He dwells in all our houses, always has, always will; and when we are carried out of them not long hence, to be buried, he will continue there. He is in this house, but not less in any other houses, this moment. If we are getting ready an answer to his voice, "Go work to-day in my vineyard," he knows what the answer is, and how much it is worth. If we are silently apologizing, he weighs the excuse in as just a balance as if we did it aloud. If we are bracing up our pride, because it is uncomfortable to feel self-accused and we want to go on in the old, careless, indulgent way, this also he sees. If when we go away we turn aside the edge of his truth, so mercifully sharp, that searching "sword of the spirit," because it hurts our bosom sin, or threatens to cut into some pleasant, wicked habit,—if we turn it aside by raising foreign questions, or finding fault with other people's way of acting, or fitting the Divine word to some neighbor's conscience,—that is seen by him who sees the thoughts when most anxiously concealed. What a boundless blessing,—when we are so easily swayed by custom, so pliant to fashion, when we have so many tricks for deceiving each other and ourselves, and so often succeed, or are succeeded with, in that destructive business,—that there is One undeceivable, One always knowing us, One always true, to warn us from the most disguised and subtle sin! When we turn to Him, he is found. When we call on Him, he is near. This is the second fact, the second element in the reality of the case. And to feel this also, we shall agree, is an incomparable good.

The third fact is, that in very many of us the feeling has not been so, but fearfully otherwise. There is a Past, and it has its record. No man can read it for another; but there is one reader of it, a conscience, in our own breasts, that is far more to be dreaded than any person outside on earth. What is to be done about that Past? If there were no memory, and no law connecting past and present and future, we could dispose of it. As it is, we are aware of it, inevitably. We see it has been wrong, bad, foolish,—perhaps so self-absorbed and prayerless as to be properly called "without God in the world." The thought of Him, to some of us, has not been welcome, or, if we have made it tolerable, it has been only by trying to make Him such an one as ourselves, not like himself: lenient, not holy; indulgent, not consistent, — goodness yielding even in the high spirit of the Almighty. For a Past like this what will be the best? Will it not be forgiveness? Both an escape out of sin, and out of the burdened feeling of it? A free, relieved, joyful mind? Another part of the reality of a new life: the New Testament full of it: Christianity making it its peculiar truth: thousands and thousands in grateful confession, in song and praise, in volumes and in secret whispers, Christendom through, in all ages, telling of that reality. "To the Lord, for he will have mercy upon him, and to our God, for he will abundantly pardon."

The state of mind that leads to this is repentance, — a fourth great good. But the essence of repentance is sorrow, — sorrow for our sin. Sorrow is painful, and we shrink from pain; we avoid it. To those that have not felt the evil that repentance cures, — how dark and bitter a thing it is to be away from God, homeless, fatherless, an orphan, and made so by selfish ingratitude, — to those it will not seem a good. It is a good only to those who feel the evil it delivers them from, — the nobler peace it brings them to. We know there is one thing worse than pain: the painless disease that kills; the slow, insidious, fatal malady that eats away the springs and energies of life, without giving the warnings of bodily distress. To stop that, to heal that, we gladly go in search of pain. We tell the surgeon to hurt us that we may live. Physical vitality is often undermined unconsciously. To avert that process by a pang, by a period of needful and saving agony, we account a blessing. After the first stages of suffocation, the drowning, on their own testimony, pass into a state of insensibility to suffering, or even, as many maintain, of positive and exquisite pleasure. Adam Clarke, who went through it, says, in his autobiography, it was like being borne gently through the most luxurious tropical verdure,—the keenest enjoyment. And when this swift, easy passage to destruction is interrupted, and friendship applies restoratives, there are spasms, tortures; the sufferer begs to be let alone, to die. It is not otherwise with the spiritual sensibilities. It is their coming back from death to life that makes distress. But no wise man, only the demented man, regrets that distress. Paul, with his singular exactness of expression, says that the sorrow that is *unto life*, the price of living forever, needeth not to be repented of, not to be sorrowed for. The pain that rescues life is a good.

Another element to be taken into view is the sympathetic nature of man,—another good. So far as we have now gone, the religious work might proceed in the separate individual,—for he could, in a degree, though a fainter one, feel his relation to his God, feel the direct action of God's spirit, and the power of the love that forgives, alone. But nature has not constituted us for constant solitude: all our practical sentiments gain something by being shared. In some natures they gain immensely, and can do little without it. In others they are quickened, revived. Christianity, whose entire principle is love, has always been prompt to avail itself of this natural helper. Every meeting for devotion is an example of it. Every house built for a congregation of worshippers is a monument to it.

The living church itself, the repository of Christian

truth and life, is a collective Body, a social institution. Man's social nature is at the basis of it. Some men seek such sympathetic encouragements on one day of the week; others find a still farther assistance by pausing in their business and turning aside for instruction or refreshment from the midst of temptation. It is not a matter of uniform demand, nor of canonical regulation. If we are free beings, and natural, sometimes we shall ask more, sometimes be satisfied with less. It is not because God is ever more merciful, or righteousness ever less sacred. It results from the liberal and spontaneous character of this sympathetic part of our nature. We are not tied up to ceremonial rule; please Heaven, we will not be entangled again with any such yoke of bondage. From causes we cannot wholly explain, the motions of men's hearts are unequal. Every idea that has been alive, and really stirred the world, has kindled and animated its servants by the interaction of numbers and the familiar stimulus of society. Everybody knows this force needs to be guarded and limited; everybody, who really knows anything about men, knows it is one of the beneficent appointments of the Maker of men.

Added to this, grafted directly upon it, is the power of social prayer. And certainly no one who has had any knowledge in himself of what this achieves, what answers it brings, doubts that it is a good. There is much in all prayer that passes our understanding. It is the meeting-point of the seen and unseen. It is the border-land between earth and Heaven. It is the contact and communion of finite beings with the Infinite. What wonder any analysis of ours should fail to unwind all its mysteries and explain all its divine economy? It is enough that wherever religious Wisdom has opened its lips to teach anything, it has taught this; enough that the great body of believing men since Christ, if we may not say since the beginning, have proved it; that all Revelation, calmly, as by prophetic, unanxious, assured authority, promises especial blessings to it; enough that Christ, by his example and by his lessons, enjoins it: "If two of you on earth shall agree as touching anything that they shall ask, it shall be done for them." "For where two or three are gathered together in my name, there am I in the midst of them."

Christ made his religion public; he instituted and practised social prayer. In our sensitive anxiety to make religion private, let us take care not to make it so very private that it shall be both invisible and impalpable, depriving it of all those immense accessions of power, provided for in human nature, which come of our social constitution. With many among us, it has long been the favorite and the noble teaching, that religion — which is surely the name of our intercourse with Heaven — should not stay in sanctuaries and Sabbaths, but go out into the highways and markets. At last she has gone there, and lifted up her voice by the way, "in the places of the paths," in the midst of toil and of merchandise. If now she is bidden, by these same persons, to go back into sanctuary and Sabbath, as the proper sphere of her dignity, or to "move on" elsewhere, what shall she conclude but that she is not very cordially wanted anywhere?

I have thus mentioned four or five of the chief, controlling ideas, or facts rather, which must be active wherever there is a real, living interest in Christian

Truth; wherever there is a general, practical obedience to the animating words of the text. There is no one of them, I am very sure, which any of us, in a moment of deliberate thought, would not pronounce a solid, unquestionable good, even though his will should hold back, or his life stumble, or his heart be cold. When we strip away all superficial matters, — the traditional language, the adventitious impressions, the bad names given by opposition, the real blemishes left by folly or presumption, — these are what remain, as the elements of a true religious movement in a community: the feeling of God; a conviction of his direct presence and action on the soul; a new sense of the want of relief from transgression, — of being lifted out of that lost, orphaned state, and forgiven, and taken home, — with the supply of that relief in Christ the crucified, "the Lamb of God that taketh away the sins of the world;" the activity of the social sympathies, and their enlistment in the highest of all our possible acts, communion with God, seeking both greater nearness to Him, and spiritual blessings for ourselves and each other from Him.

Methods are all secondary. Whatever way leads to that result is a royal way, honorable, justified, blessed. I rejoice, yea, and as Paul said, will rejoice, in every road that has that end. To make religious verities realities, — to get the whole subject out of this dim or fantastic nebulous haze where it hangs before so many, to bring it near from its distance, and clear from its obscurity, and bright from its vagueness, and strong from its weakness, — this appears to me the one thing needed. For when religion is once real, it will be all-commanding and all-attracting. Let me pay homage to and make room for all sincere measures that lead to that!

II. As to measures in operation at any particular time, we shall be certain to hear criticisms and objections. The whole subject of religion is one on which those that have convictions are sensitive, and those that have none are free-spoken. The individualism of Protestants, the jealousy of Sectarists, the frigidity of Rationalists, all have their protests. Passions too may be provoked to a louder remonstrance than all. Let us not forget, whichever side we take, that the same underlying, all-essential and eternal realities remain, and remain unchanged. Still, for us, the voice of Infinite Goodness will say, "Seek ye the Lord; seek him now; repent; forsake the wicked way; believe; work; be faithful unto death." The threefold question will return, and keep returning: Is it possible to love our Father too soon? to love him too well? to love him too long? And that other threefold question: Is not the Gospel true? Have you received it, in its practical power, into your faith? Is there any reason why you should not take it, believe it, give thanks for it, to-day?

1. Protests are made against religious excitements. Excitements are of different kinds and degrees. Excitements that come from without are to be suspected. Excitements that are due to the senses are full of peril. Excitements which necessarily, by a law of nature, must be followed by a reaction into *apathy*, are hurtful. These statements are past question, and need not be oracularly put forth every day as discoveries. Indifference so stolid that man, made to love God and

goodness with all his heart, cannot abide in it, but has to be excited out of it, is also suspicious. A coolness so complacent that it must be broken up by a wrench of repentance, is also full of peril. Your worldly unbelief is hurtful. We have to set off exposures and dangers against each other, in this world, and find the safe way, or the way of salvation, by coming as quickly as we can to our Guide. We shall probably estimate the harm of religious fervor very much according to our relative estimate of the importance of religion itself. Men are least apprehensive of too much feeling where they love most; and some who have little fear of excess in pleasure-seeking, in a gay season, in social brilliancy, in business, counting all days or nights and all companies and all energies suitable for them, appear to be nervously afraid if a few unusual hours in a week are given up to devotion; to converse with our Maker; to counsels for the object for which Christ gave his life; to the free unlocking of those grand, commanding affections and aspirations in us, through which all principles of justice and mercy for men grow, and which more than anything else determine duty; to that life which is to go on when all of this world has vanished from us, and go on to eternity. Meantime, we see a general religious movement working about us, differing, I should think all of us must confess, from many that have gone before, in its freedom from fanaticism, in the general quietness of its operation and calmness of its temper.

2. It is inquired, fairly enough, whether the phraseology of special religious movements imputes caprice to the Supreme Being, — coming and going to the Ever-present, varying moods to the Unchangeable, de-

grees of nearness to Him who is closer than the air, nay, always in us, the life of our life, — every power and breath and consciousness dependent on his being there. A fair enough question *of phraseology*, and to be thoughtfully regarded. But even when the language is mistaken, we shall not surely so grossly or wantonly misconstrue one another, as to suppose that the error reaches in from language to thought, and that, in their actual *conceptions* of Him, any class of Christians contemplate God as local, or itinerant, or fickle. If anything in sectarian misrepresentation were incredible, we should say it is incredible that any person, most of all any preacher, with any sense of professional responsibility, or even of the common responsibility of veracity, and with competent information for public speech, should allege of any considerable portion of his fellow-Christians, in this age, and in this land, that they disbelieve in the Omnipresence of God. The truth is, every call to repentance that now fills the air presupposes the liveliest and the firmest faith in that omnipresence. It says, "Seek, ask, pray," everywhere, continually, to all alike. It *never* says, You may not seek, you must not ask, it is useless to pray. Of course, the belief that the Almighty Spirit is everywhere and always present, is universal. There is no exception. To affirm the contrary of any order of Christian people is a wicked absurdity, known as denominational bigotry in the church, but in the world as slander.

Beyond this, and notwithstanding this, it is true, there is a frequent fault of expression, chiefly for the reason that language, which is the medium of finite natures, is inadequate to contain and convey the facts of an Infinite Being, or even, very accurately, our highest views of him. So there is weakness; there is ambiguity; and not seldom there is, in all of us alike probably, carelessness. We have to shape our images according to human models, a good deal; and so we humanize the Deity, — we represent him under the figures of human life. All religious expression has done so from the first. The Bible habitually does so; ordinary speech does, — especially as it grows earnestly poetic, or earnestly practical. The fervent feeling takes the first graphic term that comes, which is apt to be very human; — reverence would gain by more care. But it is plain enough, to all but blinded and angry partisans, that when men speak of the Holy Spirit as *here* in distinction from *there*, as present and absent, as near or far, they mean something actual; they mean just what the Wise and Holy Scripture means, when, in it, the pious Patriarch says, "Behold, the Lord *was* in this place, and I knew it not;" what Moses and the Prophets mean when they say the Lord "passed by," or "came from Teman;" what the text means when it says, "Seek ye the Lord, *while* he may be found, — *while* he is near;" — because, let critical nicety and captious philology prescribe what rules they will, the fact is that there *are* times when God is more easily found, his gift of life more readily gained, and when if not gained it is missed altogether, so that there *is* a "now," and an "accepted time;" what the Apostle James means when he says, "*Draw nigh* to God, and he will draw nigh to you;" nay, what the Son of God himself, who alone "knoweth the Father," and "saith true," means, when he declares, "The kingdom of God *is come nigh* unto you." Do you imagine these teachers, because they used these words, believed the God they loved and worshipped to be only occasionally present anywhere? An unworthy and an ignorant cavil.

3. There are indiscretions, we hear. No doubt of it. The question is, whether the indiscretions are so many, and so glaring, as to overbalance the palpable and lasting good that comes of engaging many people heartily in the new conviction that they have a spiritual, immortal capacity, and owe their lives to their Creator. When we have governments without indiscretion, families without indiscretion, colleges without indiscretion, manners, trade, navigation, over any sort of sea, without it, we shall have an administration of Christianity without indiscretion. But, remember, the greatest indiscretion we can possibly fall into about religion is to let it alone.

4. It is said, the eager demonstrations that attend strong religious movements disgust the "cultivated and refined." Men have even been found saying this who are not usually over-forward to appear as the advocates or patrons of these particular classes, — who have generally found in them, in fact, only a spirit of selfish aristocracy and a conservative anti-Christ, but now, all at once, by "sudden conversion," are jealous for their scruples. Doubtless, there is such a thing as a high Christian expediency. Thought is to be taken for the weak conscience, for the fastidious taste, and even, I think, sometimes for the narrow prejudice. Christianity is broad enough, generous enough, strong enough, for that. Paul expounds that law in the fourteenth chapter to the Romans, and acts upon it wherever he becomes "all things to all men that he might

gain the more." Religion wants the intrusion of no impertinent appointments, and no bad manners. That complete Apostolic gentleman, just referred to, knew very well the need of the precept, when he directed the Corinthians that "all things should be done decently and in order;" yet he was certainly the central and animating figure in many a scene quite as "excited" and "exciting" as any witnessed this year among us. Christian wisdom will deprecate any violations of true dignity or decorum, will carefully forestall them, — the ranting appeal, the rude phrase, the distasteful arithmetic definiteness, the publicity and prematurity in computing converts, the vulgar interruptions. Our God is a "lover of concord" in forms and sounds and seasons and colors and ceremonials, as in the temper and disposition of men, and "he hath made everything beautiful in his time." But nothing is so "beautiful" in his sight as the heart that trusts and loves him. He has made the laws of fitness and of grace to be steadfast and sacred; but he tells us that all the outward graces of propriety and art are but dim symbols of the clustering group of spiritual graces that his own immediate Spirit makes to bud and unfold and yield their ripened fruitage, in the believing soul of man: that to hasten now, in the accepted time, to present our bodies a "living sacrifice," is a most "reasonable service;" and that all the "fitness he requireth" is to "feel our need of him."

We have to remember that the "cultivated and refined" are to be considered, just because culture and refinement are a positive good, and because every human being is to be considered. Christianity says, "Honor all men." But something, in turn, must be asked of these well-bred persons, and something must be expected of intelligence. Among other things, it is expected intelligence will consider the variety of adaptations, the limits of occasion, the pressures of emotion, the fallibility of human understandings, the adventitious disfigurements that attach to the noblest works, and consider how gloriously, blessedly true it is, that while there are "diversities of operation" there is "the same spirit," and while there are "differences of administration," there is "the same Lord."

If, when the actual blemishes are put away, or only a few are left, and these so insignificant as not to be appreciable beside the grand earnestness overshadowing them, — as in these days generally happens, — if then, still, the cultivated and refined are repelled from a large blessing or duty by a trivial indiscretion, that will be something for the cultivated and refined to look to. A positive, aggressive Faith, like the Gospel of Christ, has too much to do to stop and smooth away every little human roughness from its rugged reformations. Prophets that are full of the preaching of repentance and a new kingdom will sometimes wear camel's hair instead of broadcloth, and a leathern girdle instead of fine linen, and we must get used to it as we can. There is such a thing as an overweening pride in the knowledge of this world, which shuts the spiritual sense. There is a disproportionate zeal for the advantages and splendors of a material civilization, which hides the loftier glory of the skies. "Not many wise, not many mighty." "They have *their* reward." In that day of simple, spiritual revelation, when the secrets of all hearts shall be revealed, all earthly distinctions levelled, and all ranks and badges forgotten, the question shall not be, Who was highest, who lowest? who richest or who most beautiful? who cultivated alone, or refined alone? But, Who loved God and man, who honored the right, who was loyal to truth, who lived and walked in the spirit, who had faith in the Lord Jesus Christ, and out of that faith, as towards Christ himself, did minister to those hungry, athirst, naked, strangers, sick, in prison? So, many that are here first shall be last, and the last first. It was when the Saviour had placed the favored children of light and opportunity below the infamous idolaters, Chorazin and Bethsaida below Tyre and Sidon, proud Capernaum below perished Sodom, that he calmly lifted up his eyes to heaven and adored the wondrous, equalizing mystery: "I thank thee, O Father, Lord of Heaven and Earth, that thou hast hid these things from the wise and prudent, and hast revealed them unto babes."

By some inwrought principle of a free being, any unusually vivid, searching truth that meets him alters his position. Truth turns aside for no man; he is instantly obliged to take some attitude towards it; it not only measures, but it places him. So it comes about, that the waking up into extraordinary activity of a social religious sentiment separates, inevitably, those whose natures are in opposite relations to it. Put any great moral idea into any community, and it will instantly divide asunder the receivers and rejecters. The very touch of a forcible, reformatory, innovating, reviving influence or doctrine, is a universal power of discrimination; it polarizes all minds; it sends each "to his own place." The ultimation of that dividing process by the one radical and decisive question will be the Last Judgment; and this dividing process no amiability, no diplomacy, no caution nor compromise nor legitimate charity, can wholly prevent. We are to avoid that result where we honestly can; but neither honesty, nor candor, nor prudence, can escape it always: Christ found it so, and declared it. "It must needs be that offences come." "I am come to send fire on the earth, and what will I if it be already kindled?" It was a fire of love, but the terrible transmutation of mortal selfishness turned it to hate. "I came not to send peace, but a sword;" "separating child from parent, brother from brother, making a man's foes to be those of his own household." Yet none the less was his spirit peaceful, his aim reconciliation, the church he was to found a Brotherhood. Sin is the base magician that so turns the truth of God into a lie, and the compassion of Christ into a strife. But truth cannot keep itself back, Christ cease to be preached, zeal refrain from running and urging men to be saved, according to the Great Commission. Right and wrong cannot really be reconciled, nor take each other's seats. Light and darkness cannot mix, nor both retire. Blessing and cursing cannot mean the same thing, if they do come from the same mouth. Gerizim and Ebal cannot wheel on to each other's bases, nor sink their peaks into the plain.

So the outbreak of uncommon religious earnestness will probably stir up, in some quarters, the worst elements of human nature. The scoffers, if there are any, will redouble their ribaldry. The jesters, who, in their sad struggle between God's purpose for them and their own folly, make life a ghastly burlesque, will discover material for caricature or scurrility. If there is a clerical banterer anywhere, who seasons his generous exhortations to rectitude, for flagging appetites, with slurs and sneers, he will find the temptations to special smartness too much for him, and intermix, in unusual proportions, raillery with religion, low comedy with lessons in virtue, irreverence with maxims of moral progress. All this will not seriously interrupt the Almighty, nor hinder Truth, nor affright the deeper intuitions of man. More probably it will serve to expose the exigences of a Christless theology, show how a denying habit vulgarizes at last both intellectual self-respect and a chaste heart, and, by making the excess of offence disgusting, correct its own damage.

5. It is said a social religious interest is made dependent on "machinery," is "manufactured." Distinguish again between two kinds of machinery. In its own place, machinery is held very far from being an evil. Kept to its use, nobody objects. If brought in to do what can be done, at last, only by the free, unforced choice of the spiritual nature, it is mischievous utterly. If it is thrust out of its sphere, to obstruct or to dishonor the higher motions of the conscience and the affections, it is still a mischief. If by machinery you only signify outward means to achieve an inward result, or visible measures to arrest and engage voluntary attention to a great truth, you will not willingly discredit it. All moral and spiritual improvements are carried forward by such means. Every institution is such a means; the meeting-house; the vestry; the stated assembly; the order of exercises in worship; personal appeals to man's religious sensibility; the serious letter you write to a friend in temptation; ordinances; pictures on church walls; the bells that

shake the air. You do not stigmatize these as "machinery," and for the reason that they are fit, and are familiar. What other instruments are fit will be a matter of individual construction; there is no law, no code; only let it be a generous construction. It does seem strange that a wide-spread spirit of religious inquiry and resolve, appearing simultaneously in all parts of a vast country, not suggested by a priesthood, but often encountering clerical opposition, proceeding almost wholly by unpremeditated operation, having simple and unlettered prayers for its chief utterance and aliment, — thus as purely spontaneous, or rather bearing as many traces of a divine origin, as any authenticated reformation, — that this should be held up to reprobation as the article of a crafty "manufacture." You might as well say that the forests of Mt. Washington, or the freshets of the rivers, or the American Revolution, were got up by manufacture. When you hear men speaking, and see them laboring, unpaid, often unthanked, with sincerity in every look and tone, to persuade their fellows to accept some blessing, simply because it is a blessing, whether your tastes accord or not, you are not apt to suppose they are acted by machinery, nor engaged in a manufacture. What shall be thought of the knowledge of affairs, the insight into human nature, the scientific reading of phenomena, that come to that impotent conclusion? It will be happy for us, brethren, I think, if we are not all painfully reminded of those words of sorrow and dread, which speak of a "despite to the Spirit of grace," and a "quenching" of it, and of the woe pronounced on words uttered against the Holy Ghost out of a state wilfully wedded to self and to past opinion.

6. It is the character of vivid experiences, we are told, to be temporary, — which is partly true and partly not. The vividness may be temporary, and the feeling, or still better the principle which the feeling helps to warm and foster, may be permanent. That depends on the individual's fidelity, or fixedness of purpose. If he lets it go, he has shame and self-contempt for his portion; if he consistently holds fast the principle, as we would fain believe, and must believe by the facts in a large preponderance of cases, then he thanks God for the unspeakable peace to the end of his earthly days and forever.

Distinguish also between the proper transientness of one process, and the proper permanency of another. To come out of insensibility — and it will not be denied some persons are in that state — is transient; to remain interested, and go on, and live accordingly, is permanent. To object to the former that it is transient, would be just as unreasonable as to object to the latter that it is permanent. It is in the nature of the thing, and cannot be otherwise. As has been well observed, the object of waking up is to be awake; and we do not object to the means of waking, that the person is not expected to be waking up all the time. The questions are: "Is he asleep, and is it better to be awake?" Perhaps he will not be the less likely to keep awake, because he awakes suddenly. We do not criticise the morning bell which rouses us to our work, that it does not ring all day. One thing is wanted to open our faculties, and another to keep them at their task. The first will avail little without the other; but you never discredit the first because it does not do the work of the other. Conversion is the opening of the spiritual faculty, or sight, to Christ, the Light of the world.

Plentiful analogies occur for this variation of movement in the other chief interests of man, and in nature herself, whose order is indisputable. In the business of legislation, there is a certain period — a few weeks of the year — when legislators devote a special attention to the State and the Statutes. They hold meetings from day to day, and are engaged, sometimes excited, in adjusting the claims of the people. After they adjourn and separate, the government, thus revived and reinforced, goes on; the statutes quietly do their work; the results are permanent, and nobody wonders that the assemblies are not in session all the year. In education, special seasons are set apart for waking up the intellectual faculty, and getting it in working order; lessons, libraries, lectures, apparatus, machinery, fulfil this office; and the rest of life is spent in putting what has been gained of mental life or power to practical use. Our men of science hold a "protracted meeting" of several days every year. If any new enterprise, like a new facility for travel across the country, is to be achieved, you hear of special meetings, measures, till the community are "waked up," as we say, to the importance of the undertaking. Nobody is afraid of a reaction. The demonstrations of feeling cease, or are changed. There is still interest, and still feeling. Only the proportions or methods of expression are altered. Preparation gives place to the work, and leads to it. Waking up is followed by organization, regularity of labor. It is according to human nature. It is according to the best philosophy of human life. We are not always alike; yet this does not necessarily imply any abatement of real energy. We are creatures of many moods, faculties, and members; a liberal interpretation of man and society and truth bids us believe that God in his great plan has room for all. In the stated and gracious succession into which the Church has distributed the Christian year, respect is paid to the same principle in the alternation of Fasts and Feasts, each with its appropriate emotions. The natural year itself is reviving. All around us, in ten thousand signs of new and exuberant animation, over all the fields and hillsides and meadows, it is budding and blossoming into verdure and beauty. Among the branches of trees, in the choirs and orchestras of woods and orchards, on the banks of loosened streams, you will hear the voices of this "time of refreshing from the presence of the Lord." The feet of spring are beautiful upon the mountains, and these glad or growing creatures of God break forth into the singing of their unconscious revival hymns. Nor will any censures hold against these marvellous and divine renewings, because after they are complete, and leaf and fruit stand in their finished glory, spring passes into summer, and the grand maturity comes on in a more silent strength.

Nay, our Lord and Redeemer himself had *one* advent; the wilderness of the world bloomed but once *for his coming;* the isles of the south awake once, at his call; he rises once from the dead. Yet he liveth evermore, and the soul that is risen indeed with him, and is awake to his righteousness, walks with him, and hath an eternal life abiding within.

Ever since the church was founded, it has had its times of peculiar demonstrative activity. During the intervals it may not always have had less power than in those days of its waking and reawaking; but it certainly had greater power *for* them. Church history opens, in the second chapter of the Acts of the Apostles, with an account of a notable revival, — a Pentecostal outpouring of the Spirit. In the patristic period Christianity was revived in many countries, sometimes on new fields, planting its heavenly seed on fresh earthly soil, but sometimes on itself, putting new life into the old forms, new blood into the old body. So in the Catholic ages Christianity was often revived through the missionaries and the mystics. It was revived through Luther and Huss. It was revived through Wycliffe, through the Anglican Fathers, through the pious Puritans, through the Wesleys and their fiery-hearted friends. The Holy Spirit has roused, directed, blessed believers, and thus borne forward the Kingdom of Heaven among men. If there is any class, any sect, any community, any single soul that may take the posture of consistent, clear, thorough objection, it seems to me it is only that one which is sure it does not need more faith and righteousness than it has; and that one can object only for itself; and finally that one, in its poor complacency, will need reviving most of all.

The appeal to personal experience is instructive. Looking back at the beginnings of their efforts, most Christians see that the first strong impression was unexpected, had a certain mystery in it; many will remember that it had a marked character. The man "came to himself," all at once perhaps. Why not? Some new event, at the Spirit's touch, let in, in a moment, a light not seen before, as when the shutters of a dark room are thrown open to the sun. That "faith in the Lord Jesus Christ," out of which all just works and noble dispositions will proceed, is awakened. To pretend that they have thus proceeded already, or that the building of character is done, or that the soul is safe without further exertions, would be absurd, and worse.

7. The virtue of liberality is implicated, as has more than once been already implied, — and the more so as the spirit of the religious interest abroad is itself singularly liberal, comparatively free from dogmatic debates or denunciations, from sectarian exclusiveness, from narrow definitions or inclosures. There may be those who do not see how to join in these public acts, and honestly believe that, for them, this is not the best way to promote the religion of Christ. If they therefore despise, or misjudge, or misrepresent their differing brethren, ascribing to them other doctrines than they teach, or errors they do not commit, they only transfer the disrepute of bigotry from those they abuse to themselves, whom they abuse worst of all.

No man, it seems to me, who looks largely over the facts and the phenomena of the Christian World, can dare to insist that all mankind shall take one *outward* path to Heaven. If he does, it will be a dangerous symptom that he is not quite in it himself. The inward path must be essentially the same for all. There is but one Door. "By me," Christ said, "enter in;" "I am the door." But the ways that lead to the door, with slighter or greater divergence from each other, reach out, at last, over all the intellectual territory of the great continent of humanity. Who shall say his alone leads to the Door? Who shall not rejoice to believe that through them all pilgrims are pressing on, sincerely, patiently, humbly, with hope, with faith, that they may enter? "Now, when the pilgrims were come up to the Gate, there was written over it, in letters of gold, 'Blessed are they that do his commandments, that they may have right to the tree of Life, and may enter in through the gates into the city.'" "And now abideth faith, hope, charity. But the greatest of these is charity." Read the twelfth and thirteenth chapters of Paul's First Epistle to the Corinthians, and you will see that he was before any modern theologian in setting the grace of Christian Love above any "gifts" of healing, of tongues, of interpretation, of miracle, of prophecy, — actual as they were.

As with the ways, so with the agents. They are various as the materials of the universe, the forms of being, the motions of the mind. God has honored both the obscurest and the weakest instruments, and highly exalted them, and made them "confound the mighty." If many have been led to trust and serve him by great Christian eloquence, others by broken petitions, or stammering remonstrances, or a single word, — as when John Bunyan, dissolute and hardened, overheard a poor unlettered woman praying in secret, and was turned by it to pray himself, — or as when young Malcom, at Brown University, was kindly told by one of his teachers to "make one honest effort for his soul's sake," went to his room, and locked it, and thought of that expression, — "one honest effort," — till he came out the new man whose name is now revered and beloved by hundreds, thankful for his fidelity. If some by vast events, held up before the eyes of nations, in the tempest, the fire, and the earthquake, others by the still small voice, — as when an eminent modern apostle, lately gone up from the world,* was first really touched, as he afterwards said, by hearing the president of the college where he studied, in one of the daily prayers, repeat that tender prophecy of Isaiah, "A bruised reed shall he not break and the smoking flax shall he not quench." Some by terrible things, seen or heard, like John Newton by a storm at sea, like Chief Justice Hale by seeing a companion fall dead in the intoxication of a convivial entertainment, or like the Christian Emperor who was awakened to Christian sensibility by thinking of the miseries he had caused in his battles; but others by some sweet memory or meditation, like Sarah Martin, the devout philanthropist, who first had the Christian love kindled in her heart by the remorse that followed the telling of a childish falsehood; or like a young American scholar, who never believed in the God of Revelation, till one day, when he was hearing a recitation on the Copernican system of astronomy, suddenly he saw him the Builder of the solar order, balancing the stars in his wisdom, and saw him forever after. Sometimes the Spirit makes even the least congenial scenes his ministers, as when a young man I knew of, just entering a place of revelry, an hour after midnight, heard the clock strike one. It brought instantly to his mind words he had once read.

> "The bell strikes one, — we take no note of time
> But from its loss. If heard aright,
> It is the knell of my departed hours.
> Where are they?"

And that course of sober thinking, beginning with

---

* Dr. Taylor.

the bell's note, ran on till it condensed into the Christian purpose that controlled the rest of his life. These are facts. We all feel them, as we hear them, to be reasonable, natural, beneficent. Who shall doubt that in all the sights and sounds we meet God sets signals for us to seek him? As soon should we be at liberty to doubt His presence in the world, to blot out the majesty of His religion from our life, to unbind its laws of responsibility from our consciences, to reject its immortal consolation from our sorrows.

From these suggestions, I am obliged to believe that — laying all particular mistakes and local extravagances out of view — the occurrence of special seasons of religious interest rests on principles as indisputable, as close to science, as natural, as any known to us; — the supremacy of the religious element in man; the immediateness of the Divine Spirit; the unity of an ascendant, governing motive in the soul; the possibility, at least, of a direct transition from one to another, or a change of mind (μετάνοια) leading to a newness of life (παλιγγενεσία); the social susceptibility to impression; the spiritual suggestiveness of common objects to a spiritual mind.

The theology of a real revival is a very simple matter. It is in three words. It is Christ's "Come unto me." "Come to Christ," — that you find is the prevalent watchword, call, creed. That is the theology. If you choose to distribute it, you find it contains these principal truths: the gracious activity of the Spirit of God; the indifference, unbelief, sin, of men; the merciful and all-sufficient approach of God to men in the Person of Christ, the Redeemer, with overture, invitations, inspirations, sacrifice, — everything to draw men to a new and holy life and save them, — in Him whose name is "the only name given under Heaven, among men, whereby they can be saved." The entire movement emphasizes the efficiency of means, and so discredits any notion that could put the Divine Grace into contradiction with human freedom. Its one question is precisely Christ's question: "What shall it profit a man, if he gain the whole world and lose his own soul?" Undoubtedly, denominational interpretations modify this comprehensive theology; but they are everywhere subordinate. Does it betray a very cordial sympathy with the Saviour's own purpose, when differences are so far forgotten, and hearts are taken up into the glowing, harmonizing air of devotion, to interpose a polemical discussion? Will a practical and ardent zeal for the Saviour's own "love of souls" take just then the direction of a controversial commentary on opinions?

But the harm is not great. If here and there some thin, discordant note is heard, it is soon lost in the resounding praises that arise from the dwellings and churches of a nation. The mighty sweep of holy feeling, impelled by the hand of Heaven, bears down the expostulations of a fastidious brain. The wind bloweth where it listeth. Men, and women, and young children, having in them the peace and joy of God, are not to be much disturbed. Already, their acclamations ascend, from the north and the south, from the east and the west, from the city and the village, from the lonely chamber and the great congregation. In the stately sanctuary you catch their majestic melodies in the ancient "Gloria in Excelsis," sung with grander trust. In unnumbered companies that gather in plainer courts, — places of every worldly use turned to temples by sudden, solemn, and glad dedications,—you hear "Worthy the Lamb that was slain!" In closets and secret chambers, where God alone listens, he hears the broken confession,—"This only I know, that whereas I was blind, now I see." "Nothing shall be able to separate me from this love of God, which passeth knowledge."

III. If now we return to the positive teaching of the text, we shall see that it contains for us, for all men, three things, with results.

First, The presence of the Spirit. On that fact depends all the good, all the joy, all the glory of mankind. On the feeling and confession of it depends all high and strong excellence. Man's greatest and most blessed hour is when he wakes into the living consciousness of this, becomes aware of his spiritual relations and his immortal destiny, ceases to live in himself and for himself, stretches his thought and affection to the Infinite and Holy One that inhabiteth eternity, and then, through him, to all souls of men having the same Father, however weak, dark, erring, sinning. That is the one great good, for every human soul. It is possible for all; God is always "near," never afar. The "now" is for us; the "while" is for us. These are human conditions. The will is free. For us there are "times" and "seasons," and, as every day of life in all its interests shows, if we fail then we may fail utterly. But in his own unchanging compassion, the Holy Spirit always "may be found." To the prophet God had not been manifest, outwardly, in the Christ. Now, in him God has come. "Come unto me." "Whosoever will, let him come."

Secondly, there is, for men, a possible absence from God; not of God from men, but of men from God. So our speech feebly and falteringly shapes the truth. God may be near to us and we not near to him. An unfelt presence is no life nor comfort. It is a silent form near us in the dark. Sin is that distance. Moral disagreement is a thicker and higher barrier than mountains, or the stellar spaces. To be indifferent, where trust and love should be, is absence; and that, remember, is no single deed, — it is a state; God is not "found" in it, not "sought."

The third thing is an act of man's, accepting the ceaseless act and offer of the Spirit, co-working with it, to bring these two together; God's presence, man's practical consciousness of it; seeking and finding. It is the opening of the spiritual sense. It is the renunciation of that proud self-will that has kept it shut. It is the changing of the soul's state. It is regeneration. It is a new creature. It is a different heart. There is another motive, and so another life. It is of God himself, in man. Acceptance in the one of grace in the other. Faith answers to the promise. How swiftly the homeward way is passed over! Penitent affection is eager, and the Father is waiting. There are conditions, favorable and unfavorable. There is an accepted time, a day of salvation; a "financial crisis," if you please; which is sometimes suggested as the whole explanation of ten times ten thousand better hearts! Only remember, behind the "financial crisis" there is the Eternal Spirit, working, inviting. Yes, a "financial crisis," — in other words, enough of the "husks that the swine did eat;" an hour of thought, a broken constitution, an opened grave; but how much better if it is the joy of youth, the still persuasion of prosperity, and the bounding pulse of grateful health, or the manly voice of Christian invitation, "the goodness that leadeth to repentance"! You may suggest that people meet to pray because they have leisure, "nothing else to do." But it is a new thing in the world, if idleness alone, with all the modern appliances for filling up vacant hours in great cities, should crowd strong, shrewd men into plain rooms, to entreat spiritual blessings on themselves and one another, with every token of urgent sincerity in look and tone. There is no shorter way of explaining that, I think, judging it by its fruits, than to say, our God is in it. Manifold, mysterious, merciful are these calls and ways of God. He has made the universe wide enough, and the human soul various enough, for them all.

The result will be twofold; the two parts of character. Character may have yet scarcely begun to be formed. That is a labor remaining. But there has been planted the forming principle. "The wicked will forsake his way, and the unrighteous man his thoughts."

There will be a harmony of the affections with the Divine Spirit. There will be the hidden life, ever nourished by prayer, ever making prayer more real. Its deep peace is indestructible, passing knowledge, not given by the world's wealth, not taken away by the world's robberies or reproaches. This is piety. It is the habitual and ever-growing consciousness of dwelling with the Father in Heaven. It is the power of being forgiven. "Unto the Lord, for he will have mercy upon him." It is the wonderful admission to a yet more intimate and personal endearment: "And to *our* God, for he will abundantly pardon."

There will be a life consecrated to righteousness; morality; only a morality warmed, expanded, deepened, by the spirit of Christ, the love of God. Not a drudging bondage to the legalist's commandments; not a frigid compliance with the literalist's rule. Every beneficent and generous duty will take its place of honor, but more as privilege than as duty. Religion will be the natural inspiration of conduct, not because it is some volatile and graceful sentiment, nor the mere instinct of happy lovers and fond mothers, but the grounded principle of Right, — law eternal underneath it, a Personal Maker above it; the fruit of a profound experience; the offspring of law and love reconciled in the Gospel; the steadfast righteousness in Christ, to which the Law, as a schoolmaster, had led. No task will be too heavy, no sacrifice too bitter, no human being too base or ugly or far away, for the zeal of this convert and disciple, made an heir of Heaven and the brother of the race. Every slave's oppression, every wronged sufferer, every unjust practice in business, every impurity in society, every onesidedness in education, every falsehood in institutions, will be his solemn and intense concern, for he follows Him who gave his life for the least. "Right feeling, right thinking, right acting, right being," will all be his, more and more, because "the law of the spirit of life in Christ Jesus hath made him free from the law of sin and death."

Of all the instances of awakening religious life lately reported, none carry such power of impression as those where the new feeling of obligation to God has been attended, from the very beginning, with a new feeling of duty to man; where the reform of practice has kept pace with the growth of faith; or more even than this, where the convert has felt that he could not go a step in religious regeneration without first putting himself right, wherever he was wrong, with his neighbors. Hear a parable, yet a true story, — one of a class that might be told here all night. Not fifteen furlongs from where we are, and not long ago, a certain man, who had repeatedly and openly avowed himself a disbeliever in Christianity, in worship, and in the very being of a God, — of active powers, large intelligence, and an average conscience, — began to see the truth he had so long kept covered up. He began to believe himself mistaken, and to think that God, and the law of God, and Revelation, and the Future Life, might be realities, after all. It was borne in strongly, irresistibly; he hardly knew how, except as he did know and see that it was through the sympathies and intercessions of some about him that he loved and trusted. He was troubled to agony. Such inward revolutions as that do not come about without straining the sensitive parts of the soul, breaking up the frozen fountains of penitence and self-reproach, and shaking the whole nature with pain. Dealing quite honestly with himself, he went into solitude and prayed. He prayed only this, that if there was a God, he might know and believe in Him. He prayed rather into the wide heavens than to a Heavenly Father. But, after this first and single act towards his Maker, he said: "I know little yet of religion; there is evidently something here I never dreamed of yet; but if I am going to pray to God, I must settle my difficulties with my fellow-man. There is my former partner in business, whom I quarrelled with a year ago, and whom I have been hating ever since; the first thing for me to do now is to go and confess my wrong, and be at peace with him. No more prayers, till that is done; no falsities left behind; no sins reserved; a clean beginning or no religion." He went to his partner, and was forgiven, and forgave. He went to his God, and was sure he was forgiven there; and then he went on, into a sound, consistent, spiritual life. Old things passed away, and all things became new. This is Christianity. It is Christ's spirit of sincerity, courage, truth, faith. We do not often see a more literal compliance with the Saviour's own direction: "If thou bringest thy gift to the altar, and there rememberest that thy brother hath aught against thee, leave there thy gift before the altar, and go thy way: first be reconciled to thy brother, and *then come and offer thy gift.*" Let us remember the latter clause, no less than the first. It was coming to the altar, to the prayer, that first made this man feel compelled to go to his offended brother. It was going there that made him ready to go back to worship: here, as everywhere, faith and works proceeding together, each helping the other: repentance toward God quickening the conscience; conscience, obeyed, opening the temple-door of devotion.

God grant to his church ever new, deeper, more genuine revivals of pure and undefiled religion! May he pour out his spirit upon all flesh, in other Pentecosts, on every barren place, every cold church, every unprofitable heart! As the rain cometh down from heaven, and returneth not thither, but watereth the earth and maketh it bring forth and bud, so may the living word be, that goeth forth out of his mouth! Again, and again, the voice of one crying in these wildernesses of passion, and care, and sin, "Repent!" Again, and again, may the Son of Man come in power and great glory! Till, in all of us, and all around us, and all over the earth, "instead of the thorn shall come up the fir-tree, and instead of the briar the myrtle-tree, to be to the Lord for an everlasting sign that shall not be cut off."

SERMON IX.

PEACE BY POWER.

THE MOUNTAINS SHALL BRING PEACE. — Ps. lxxii. 3.

WHAT is to be noticed in this metaphor is, that it proposes an unusual view of the conditions of peace. In itself a mere image in the mind of a poet, reflected there in a study of natural scenery, it is hardly less the declaration of a principle of moral and spiritual life, carried out into the material world for an illustration.

" The mountains shall bring peace." Commonly, we expect impressions of tranquillity in the lowlier places of a landscape, where the objects are so minute as to stir no effort in the mind, and the place is so level as to lift it in no upward movement. Enclosed valleys, with limits easily reached by the eye and restraining rather than tempting any bold imagination, smooth and flower-sprinkled plains, or green meadows and still waters, — these are thought to represent the moods of repose, and perhaps to produce them. Instead of this, but with a sense of real effects quite as true, the writer of this Hebrew ode finds the peaceful in the grand, — rest in greatness. If we have ever felt that the sight of high hills, with strong outlines and broad reaches, recruited us, that there was intellectual refreshment in a wide horizon, we shall have all that is necessary to make the figure a fit introduction to our doctrine and its argument.

This doctrine is, *that the quiet of the human soul is to be honestly found, not in descending to its lower or less forcible states, but in the freedom of its highest qualities, and through its stronger exercises:* or, *that Christian peace is an attainment of the spiritual energies, and not a mere acquiescence in inferiority.*

The positive results of this conviction, in awakening action and giving a healthy inspiration to the will, as well as our liability to leave it for less invigorating notions, will lead me first to put forward some general illustrations of it, and then to connect it with the personal concerns of character.

When the Saviour speaks of the ultimate result of his religion, in the single heart or in the world, he calls it Peace: "Peace I leave with you; my peace I give unto you." But as soon as you look into the spirit and relations of his words, you see that in this peace there is something quite peculiar. It is no wonder he emphasizes the pronoun, and says, "*My* peace." It is a peace obtained by the drops of blood and the cross; Gethsemane and Calvary; by a life in which there was no place to lay the head. It is not a mere constitutional, negative, nor any superficial peace; it is not what we call pleasure, nor a happy temperament, nor gratified sensibilities, nor satiated appetites. It is something deeper and stronger. It is an attainment; it is a victory; it is tribulation overcome. It is the mightiest powers of our nature balanced, reconciled, and harmonized at last, through we know not what struggles and sufferings, till, by the perfect sway of one supreme principle of faith, there are the equipoise and serenity that pass all understanding.

So long as mankind put up their first prayers for happiness, they need to learn that power of character is before happiness, and indispensable to any joy that is Christian. We are to be suspicious of effeminate contentments. Christianity has to suffer cruelly, not only from its open deniers, and its merely nominal adherents, but from the needless imbecilities of its sincere disciples, — if moral weakness can ever be called very sincere. Plenty of infirmities will remain, at our best; but we are not to make room for them, and domesticate them, by the vicious theory that it is enough to subside into a nerveless placidity, imagining that God is indulgent instead of kind, finding food for our complacency in the fondness of Heaven, and substituting a harmless routine of easy virtues for the originality and valor of a great-hearted faith. One of our most insidious temptations is to mistake a comfortable deadening of aspiration for Christian assurance; and of the two possible sorts of satisfaction, viz. raising the soul to its objects, and quenching its nobler desires, accepting the last. Some people think if they are calm, at ease, and especially if their serenity has a pensive or sentimental color, no matter about their strength. But no man who is not as strong as he can be, and making himself stronger in a piety that is muscular and adventurous, is really righteous. Our religion to-day wants red blood and thick sinews. It wants the spirit of the hills in it. Bodily health and genius are commonly reckoned as gifts, and blessings only in that meaning; but in another sense they are both duties, as the parables of the steward and the talents prove. And it is so with all the greater attributes of the soul.

We are apt to keep up in the mind — tacitly, at least

— a faithless alternative between goodness and greatness: the fallacy being that these two do not bear to each other any relation of comparison, since each is an element of the other. Their righteousness is the greatest thing in the really great; and by just so much as goodness lacks greatness, or strong qualities, it comes short of being divinely good. As surely as God meant each spirit of his children to be a completely-developed instance, with all the capacities fulfilled, there can be no feeble saints; their feebleness is just so much abridgment of their saintliness. Nor is there any comfort in this for gifted sinners. They naturally make the mental and social traits their first standard of judgment, and have their little sneer accordingly; but the infirmity of the irreligious is always really deeper than that of the good, since it is infirmity at that inmost point of man, where he was made to be strongest, where he was to touch God and eternity, and where disease debilitates the whole constitution with the deadliest certainty.

Taking a little further assistance from the image of the text, the three obvious attributes of mountains are elevation, magnitude, permanency. They are measured by their height; their most obvious impression on the eye is that of size, or majesty; and among the mutabilities of the globe they are the most enduring, being described as ancient, lasting, and even everlasting. Out of these three several characters, in their natural combination, and only rounded a little into the curves of time and weather, comes, as the Psalmist felt, and as most of us have felt in looking at them, an influence of peace. It will be no harm if we transfer this simple analysis in its terms to our subject. In just such attributes of strength human character, also, is to find its moral balance, its real peace, viz. in its aspiration, its largeness, its constancy. Man is high with his devotional affections, his prayers; wide with his practical principles, and steadfast with his convictions. Or, he is high with his spirit, wide with his will, and steadfast with his reason. With these three properly adjusted, you will have a general effect of serenity; because such a man will live in a certain equipoise within himself, centred and completed according to the grand designs of his Creator, as a creature belonging both to the world and heaven. He reaches up into the infinite mystery that broods like a sea of conscious life above him. He reaches out, in all liberal fellowships, to mankind, with a love that cannot narrow into hatred nor be fretted into war; and he rests firmly on eternal foundations. And thus, on all sides, — God-ward, and man-ward, and self-ward, — so far as man can, he resides in the securities of a well-defended peace; he is castled in the kingdom of his own tranquillity, safe from the changes of the time, and from the fear of change to come. He is "set fast like the mountains, being girded with power."

And the same causes that make him strong in this empire of rest within himself ordain him to exert unconsciously the same influence on others, rendering him a natural peacemaker in society; for, as has been said, "mountains are to the body of the earth what muscular action is to the body of man."

Spiritual serenity, then, is spiritual strength. It comes in by no softness of sentiment, but by thorough work. It comes by a faith that emboldens and energizes the whole soul, a penitence that searches and strains it, and often a secret fight of afflictions. Christianity is a robust religion. It was planted in the world by a race of heroes. Its great starts forward, into new continents and epochs, have been made through martyrdoms. The blood of sacrifice has watered its roots. Men of easy systems wonder and cavil at all this sacrifice and crucifixion, and call it a "blood-theology;" but they sneer at the highest glory of earth and heaven, which is voluntary sacrifice for love, — much as you hear languid fops criticise the fanaticism of the Puritans, that conquered for them, out of the jaws of the wilderness, the inheritance where they lounge and sprinkle rose-water. As the mountains bring peace, the sublimity of the Christian ideas tranquillizes. That Faith insists that we shall be brave men, in order to be peaceable men; that the people of God shall work, even as the Father worked, to obtain the rest that remaineth for them; that they shall strive, through a strait gate and a narrow way, to enter in where are pleasures forevermore. Those three mountain-attributes must appertain to their piety: height of spirit, reaching in worship toward the throne of God; amplitude of affection, in whose abounding charity all the landscapes of the earth shall lodge; and constancy in all the integrities and purities of a consecrated life. Then will be the peace that passeth all understanding, the peace of the Son of God.

In their natural organization, both men and mountains have roots. Of both, the deepest or primary formations often appear at the summit. These huge telluric pyramids are not mere masses laid in dead weight upon the surface of the earth; but are the protrusion of its own energies, organized parts of itself, discoveries or features of its internal forces, and so the springing expression of its passion and power.

Take any one of these three traits just mentioned

away, and, besides what other ruin you make, you most disastrously disturb the peace. Take away the aspiring faith, rob yourself of religion, and then all those implanted instincts of other worlds, which were meant for faith to guide and satisfy, become the haunting terrors of superstition. Shorn of its high commerce with the Unseen, the degraded mind shrinks with fear from what its providential intuitions warn it *must yet be*, and trembles to die because it has not found what makes it sacred and lofty to live. There is no peace there, but the misery of weakness. Take away the large confidence of a round-about and generous humanity: you mar all peace again by that littleness, for other men will be either hated, or suspected, or envied, or feared. Take away the constancy: you have vacillation, uncertainty, yieldings, capitulations, and whatever brings confusion and pain, with total loss of peace. On whichever side you enfeeble man, you unbalance and torture him.

Proceed to some examples, in other regions of life, how peace depends on power, how the gentler traits are upheld by the braver, and all noble joy comes of energy.

In literary expression, the effect of pathos is finest in thinkers habitually severe. What saves sentiment from sentimentality is the feeling of a firm intellectual fibre through the emotion. The lighter mental movements are most sure of respect where they adorn some massive argument; and imagination never sets its embellishments of style with such decisive impression as when it plays from a brain of great logical consistency.

If it should be supposed that this is a mere effect of contrast, as much to the honor of the lighter term in the comparison as the weightier, and so profitless to my doctrine, observe that if either style is carried quite through a given mind, or even through a single performance, unrelieved by the other, the result in one case will be well-nigh contemptible, but in the other never quite so bad. You never hold a string of fancies, however brilliant, in such esteem as a hard process of reasoning. We can better spare the beauty than the force, the ornament than the bones, and all the ornament than any one of the bones. Indeed, that which is beauty when it clothes strength, or crowns resistance, or graces grandeur, if it comes to constitute the total substance of an object, is beauty no longer, but in its characterlessness sinks to prettiness. Without the presence of some strong trait, a fair face is a sort of incarnate satire.

It appears to be owing to this principle of proportions that works lying in the sphere of the lighter literature, and the arts, require to be sustained with uncommon intellectual pith and dignity, to deliver them even into respectability. No writing of good sense, however prosaic, is so insufferable as commonplace poetry, where weakness publishes itself in the finery of measure and rhyme. No dryness of real reason is so cheap as a florid mediocrity. Unwonted decoration or sweetness, in humanity or nature, surfeits and sickens. There is no garden of summer flowers on earth that can satisfy the sight of an intelligent race like Atlas or the Jura; and, in his more earnest moods, no man can long for a tropical Eden, or a vale of Tempe, as for the soaring sweeps of mountain-side, whose wedges widen down into the central widths of the world.

We are able to cite, to the same purpose, the familiar fact that persons who have been in the strain and peril of some moral or civil revolution, wounded with real weapons, and compacted by times of terror, if they have benignant qualities, impress us in that way far more than is possible for men of softer discipline. Their past soldiership clears our confidence of all suspicions of a mere effeminate amiability, or cowardly conciliation. It is not only that they have been tried, and therefore can be trusted, but the very battles where they were brave give a loftier import to their sympathies, and to their kindness a certain authority. Tenderness is doubly tender where we know a rugged and aggressive temper has been subdued to it by that rule over the spirit which is mightier than the taking of cities. The gentleness of heroes, the love of warriors, smiles among sunburnt scars, the piteous tears of the Northmen's gods, — these are the irresistible pleaders. So the arms of the fierce Scotch family of Douglas bore the inscription, "Tender and True."

Even of mountains themselves, those eloquent peace-prophets of nature, the calmness is deeper when we know that their preparation has been through violence, — their walls upheaved by monster forces, their braces fixed by earthquakes, their breasts swelled with inner fire, their tops torn by hurricanes, or grated by the grinding drifts of deluge, or bitten and sawed by the teeth of glacier and avalanche, rock and ice.

Let me put it to your private experience. It is familiar how bereavements, which are the storms of the soul, prepare the way for religious tranquillity. I suppose that in every parish church in the land the majority of trusting disciples were made so under the rough handling of some kind of pain. They had to march, weeping, blinded, through the dry valley of Baca, to find it at last "a well" of living water, and, going from strength to strength, to appear in Zion before God. Resignation is rest; and, to know it, the heart has to be torn by terrible separations, — writhing at the new-made grave, heavy among the ruins of fortune, broken over disappointed plans, or unreturned affections. It is humiliating, but real. Tempests must sweep our sky, before the air is still and the summer sunshine calls up the noiseless energies of life. Ask the ministers, the Church records, the secret thanksgivings that rise around the communion-table. They will tell you, as One greater than they told you long before, that crosses bring calmness, that afflictions yield afterwards the *peaceable* fruits of righteousness, that the rough, sharp mountains, hard to climb, bring peace; and that the Sabbath temple, the Lord's great House of Rest, into which the toilsome nations flow to praise, is built upon their top.

In the solemn portrait-galleries of history, the serenest faces are the saddest, — where peace has not been inherited, but conquered. We have this union of power and tenderness eminently in such as Luther; the bravest heart of all his age; fronting the pride and wrath of Europe and ready to smite it in the face; fearless of men and devils, because so fearful of God, with his "rugged sterling strength and sense" in all he did, — lightning on his lips and thunderbolts in his hands, and his "smiting idiomatic phrases cleaving to the heart of the matter," — yet, as was further well said of him, "a most gentle heart withal, full of pity and love, as indeed the valiant heart ever is," — weeping at the death-bed of his little Margaret, making music with his flute, and with such "breathings of affection, soft as a child's or mother's," in his wild soul, that it was thought "to a slight observer he might have seemed a timid, weak man,—affectionate, shrinking tenderness the chief distinction of him."

Doubtless these fierce strengths need to be both balanced and mastered, to produce tranquillity. Loosen the natural attractions, and the soul becomes like a universe of uncentralized, plunging planets. Yet the very vehemence of the fury, and the magnificence of the misery wrought by unchecked passions, furnish a measure of their power for good, and inform us what imperial powers dwell kindly together in a true human soul,—just as the splinters that fly from a wheel shattered by centrifugal excess betray the momentum of the engine more vividly than all its beneficent regularity. This is the baleful energy and sublimity of crime. Yet, even in characters of such enormous evil, there is acknowledged to be a sort of fascination, like the beauty of basilisks,—the romance of villany. We are never wholly rid of the idea that strength of any sort is a good. That is precisely the secret of success in the scriptural and Miltonic character of Satan, who exerts his attraction, not so much by his baseness as in spite of that, through the marvellous and kingly splendor of that arch-angelic intellect, that was ruined but not obscured, and had all its royal might apostatized and turned over to rebellion. It is only when the power is kept in symmetry with love, and thus in the sanctity of divine order, that the spirit goes forth in its real majesty, and has its description in that radiant image of Scripture,—"clear as the sun, fair as the moon, and terrible as an army with banners."

May I not press this point a little further, and expect your agreement when I say that we begin to have fresh hope of a character, that it will be something and do something, when, after debility or effeminacy, it is roused even to an irregular activity, and manifests the vigor of a manly will, though it should be in ways not the most profitable; just as sometimes, after a monotonous mist in the air, or the dull dripping of a drizzly day, we begin to have a heightened respect, as it were, for the weather, if a roll of thunder peals through the fog, giving us a reassurance, if not a positive comfort, in that reverberating affirmation, that we are still girt about, not only with the softness and forbearances, but with the awful energies of creation; that the eternal elements are at work, and that the whole scene of things is not to be liquefied into a loquacious patter of drops, or dissolve away into lassitude in sultry vapors. Nor are these effects mere fugitive or fanciful associations. The positive use of the majesty is at least as great and as sustaining as that of the gentleness, to a reverential mind. For not all the genial fruits that the showers encourage on the farms are a nobler offering to the God who is a spirit, than when the awe-struck mind answers, with the old Psalmist, to the voice out of the cloudy tabernacle, "Verily, God thundereth marvellously, — and divideth the flames of fire, and shaketh the wilderness!" — or, with the Patriarch Job, "Canst thou thunder with a voice like him? Lo, these are parts of his ways; but the thunder of his power who can understand?"

Again, in the great pacifications of empires, the same rule prevails. Alienated kingdoms are not restored to one another, any more than they are safely upheld within themselves, by those amiable and unfortified instincts which merely recoil from blood; nor by multitudes of weaker well-wishers to the general welfare among the citizens. It takes the strongest heads to bring peace. Diplomacy has to summon her stoutest, clearest-sighted, and farthest-sighted ministers. Through the laborious disentanglement of political subtleties, and the firmest confronting of thought against thought, the robust encounter of strong reasons, the friendly courtesies of neighboring states are preserved; the finest logical abilities of statesmen wrestle together for the restoration of concord. A treaty that settles the line across a disputed territory tasks the best brains of two nations; and sometimes, for want of such wits, a spark of war is fanned into a flame, and continents are shaken, or oceans reddened. All the soft-hearted dispositions of a whole people cannot provide national tranquillity like two or three powerful natures in the right place,—the mountains of the moral scenery. These are the "broadstones of honor," and the public amity reposes on them. We can well understand how travellers should say that, among all the exquisite openings along the Rhine, there is no more perfect aspect of peace than looks from the solid masonry of the Ehrenbreitstein castle, the impregnable Gibraltar of the North, with its silent battlements four hundred feet from the rock in the sky, with its vast magazine equal to sustaining eight thousand men on a ten years' siege, and its well sunk to the river-bed, never to fail till the Alpine fountains are dry. The most intrepid are most pacific. Magnanimity makes no quarrels. Indeed, the very seed-field of anarchy is a populace all of whom are too restless to keep order, and none of them wise and strong enough to rule.

In this very Psalm that contains my text you have a real instance. The Poem itself, in its first application, is a loyal lyric to an oriental prince, — a patriotic celebration of some sovereign both victorious and fatherly; terrible on the field, but very gracious in his home government. So the poet alternately celebrates the two sets of regal attributes. Now the king is a fighter, breaking in pieces the oppressor with vengeance; but in the next verse he is saving the children of the needy whom his sword has emancipated. Now he is exalted, as having dominion from sea to sea, a monarch moving in arms, the wilderness bowing to him, his enemies licking the dust, tributary chiefs and satraps waiting at his palace-door. Yet, in the same strain, and because the spear and throne are the badge and seat of so much power, he is shown looking compassionately after the troubles of the poor, counting precious the blood of the victims of wrong, and binding up their bruises like a sister of charity. In one line his glory shines with the splendor and constancy of the sun; and in the antistrophe it is said all nations shall call him blessed, or happy. Here everybody fears him; but presently his mercy comes down upon the people "like rain upon the mown grass," making "abundance of peace so long as the moon endureth." Obviously, in the poet's mind, so far from suggesting any contradiction, these attributes were thought to have a natural relation, the power being the source of the peace.

Or if, as some interpreters have done, we take the Psalm as a prophetic anthem to the Messiah, then we shall only pass on to a better and even the highest personal illustration of the same thing; where the greatness and the mercy blend in complete divine unity, —

a perfect peace; where the "Lion of the tribe of Judah" is also the "Lamb of God;" where the wielder of a power that compasses heaven and earth is meek and lowly, — the world's eternal conqueror its crucified victim,—where the strength that might have marshalled legions of angels is only employed to send out his infinite affection on a wider sweep, and with a mightier salvation.

Hence we come to discover in what order of persons we are to look for the noblest charity and the real consolation. We want our consolers to be, not only the subjects of pain, but its conquerors through their suffering. The more masculine your pity, the more it moves and melts. We never value greatly the tears of easy weepers, and even of those of mothers and lovers the power and the preciousness are proportioned to the frugality. Very weak people cannot know what charity is; and on a hot provocation all their professed liberality sours back into bigotry, and their kindness curdles into hate.

Writes Henry More: "Those that endeavor after so still, so silent and demure a condition of mind that they would have the sense of nothing there but peace and rest, — what do they effect but a clear day shining upon a barren heath? Neither sheep nor shepherd is to be seen there, but only a waste solitude, and one uniform parchedness and vacuity."

And when we speak of comfort, we are directed up to the Comforter. Paul speaks of the fruits of that Paraclete, or Holy Spirit, as "love, joy, peace, long-suffering, gentleness, goodness, faith, meekness, temperance;" mostly, you say, the softer graces. But he is there writing to contentious and boisterous Galatians.

What is the *whole* doctrine of that Spirit, in the New Testament and in Paul? They represent Him as not only Comforter, but also, and first, Rebuker, Renewer, and Sanctifier. He shall reprove the world. He shall tear up false confidences. He shall plant the stripes and wake the agonies of repentance, that he may be a true healer. He shall rend the guilty shelters of pride and self-complacency to pieces. He shall search secrets, divide joints and marrow, — so close and sharp is his work, — toss the heart with self-accusing, and then rebuild the whole character and church on clear, stout, rocky foundations. And this shall be his comforting. This will be the preparation of a peace that cannot be moved, — deep, genuine, strong, healthy, lasting, — a repentance that needeth never to be repented of.

Yes, all our peace is in God, who is not only the strongest, but Almighty. As the mountains are round about Jerusalem, the capital and throne of the nation, so the Lord is round about his people.

It is at the close of that superb hymn to Omnipotence, in the twenty-ninth Psalm, that we hear the subdued twofold benediction, — "The Lord will give strength unto his people; the Lord will bless his people with peace."

His presence is safety precisely because it is power, — the love invincible, — the compassion omnipotent. He in whose pavilion we can hide, in the shadow of whose wings we can utterly trust, must be the Father, and the Father of an Infinite Majesty; who himself setteth fast the mountains, being girded with power; who rideth upon the high places of the earth and breaketh the cedars; before whom the mountains themselves are moved and the everlasting hills skip like lambs, — Lebanon and Sirion like a young unicorn, and the seven thunders uttering their voices. He is our Father. He is our Infinite Clemency. He is the good and gentle Shepherd. And when work has made ready for rest, and discipline has ripened faith, and the energies of life have found their sabbath, and power has broken down the middle-wall of partition and made us one, He it is who then, in his Son, becomes "our peace," reconciling us thus to himself, and leading us then, at last, where we could not come before, in the green meadows, by the still waters.

Let me turn this train of thought now, as briefly as possible, to direct personal applications.

1. We learn from it never to be afraid of rugged and even painful experiences. Even if happiness were our highest end, which with noble natures it never can be, the rough handling of repentance and sorrow will be our shortest way. It is not among the children of indulgence or idleness that you find the most contented households, or the serenest souls, but with them that take up crosses cheerfully, and fear none of those things that they shall suffer, and never cry "Peace, peace," when there is no peace, nor seek it where it is not to be found. It is only truth, in its two-edged strength, that makes the arm strong; and only loftiness and largeness and firmness that give peace.

> "Great souls snatch vigor from the stormy air,
> While weaker natures suffer and despair;
> Grief not the languor but the action brings,
> And spreads the horizon but to nerve the wings."

2. We have also a rule for "strengthening the brethren." Influences of power, of course, whether in inspiration or sustenance, cannot go out except from vigorous hearts. And if we think to make up for the lack of these by abounding in gentle sympathies, we have seen

that vacillating and feeble people cannot be very effectual even as sons of consolation. We would all rather be spoken to of submission by heroes and prophets,— the men of iron arms, clad in camel's hair, their muscles fed on wild honey, or by the women of St. Barbara's endurance. As we would comfort one another, we must try, with the apostle's earnestness, to "endure hardness as good soldiers of Jesus Christ."

3. We see, further, of how sterling worth is a form of religious belief which holds fast the stringent as well as the soothing doctrines of Christ's evangelical teaching. Any theological system runs fast to feebleness, and secretly loosens its grasp, which deals in the unmingled imagery of caresses and indulgences. Just as a creed of rigid legality, a dispensation of threats and judgments, is bloodless, so a creed of indiscriminate compassion is nerveless. The order of the universe is poised between justice and mercy; and it is not kindness, but the bitterest cruelty, which would unsettle that order, by giving us a Deity too doting to punish, and too fond to judge. If we have a Father who is simply fond, we have one that cannot forgive, and whom it is not possible for a very intelligent being to love, but only to flatter and despise; and when we worship a deified fondness, it is likely that our self-direction will be only a fondling of our favorite sins. The Gospel is able to encourage us, just because its promises beam forth from such a tremendous background of equity and prohibition. Its reconciliations must be no mock deliverances, or rhetorical reliefs, or *quasi* salvation, but realities. Our God must be the God who hates iniquity, and destroys pride, and brings down the oppressor, and breaks in pieces those that lift themselves against him,—a God who

makes the natural penalties of guilt the exact measure of his grace in pardoning, and who rules in righteousness precisely to this very end, that he may be a Father of forgiveness.

4. We learn the way of making our own eternal life secure. The New Testament speaks continually to us of salvation. How little they interpret that term by Christ himself who find nothing in it but a timid appeal to calculating, sordid self-love! By salvation he means such safety as lies in a sturdy and athletic power of character, will, heart, conscience, and intellect, got by daring to attempt great virtues, and by incessant intrepidity. Hence he stirs the great deeps of human nature, moves its most magnificent affections, requires the travail of a new birth, prophesies warfare, will have his disciples consent to crucifixion sooner than deny him, and let the dead bury their dead rather than look back. He offers a new yoke to the weary who pray for rest, and says that yoke shall rest them. He holds up no lower standard than to be perfect as the Father in heaven is perfect, and impartial as the God of sun and rain. He says, Give up houses and lands for duty, false friendships for principle, fame for truth, the whole world for God. So he strikes boldly in among the grander verities of the soul. He would build broadly and loftily. He sets up, as the chief apostle, the manliest person of his age, — the embodiment of all that is indomitable, generous, shrewd, witty, patient, independent, modest. He wins confidence by the very immensity of his demands. Men speak of Christianity as honoring the passive virtues, like poverty of spirit. But it does this for the very reason that, by a profounder understanding of human nature, and a sharper

insight into facts, it knows that in the consistency of those virtues with the active ones is the hardest stress on men's individuality; and so it is original in proposing the tests of Christian manhood just where they are most decisive,—in faith, in the taking of crosses, in a free consent to be inspired, and thus be saved by the Divine Spirit acting down into humanity from heaven, in the Redeemer's life and love.

5. My final remark grows out of all that has gone before; and it is that we disturb the true spiritual order, and invert God's plan for us, whenever we go in search of peace first, and not holiness; when we pray most heartily for the quiet of repose, instead of the honors of toil, and the noble pains of sacrifice. "First pure, then peaceable:" that is the clearly-pronounced order and everlasting law of a disciple's way.

SERMON X.

THE CLOUD AND THE VOICE.

AND THEY FEARED AS THEY ENTERED INTO THE CLOUD. — Luke ix. 34.

THIS scene of the Transfiguration lies on the borderland between the material world and the spiritual, and belongs partly to both. The simplest truth taught by it is that both these worlds are real. At present, we know the one through our senses, and the other, if we take knowledge of it at all, through inward perceptions of the soul. If any of us live chiefly in the senses, — if our interests, habits, and tastes lie chiefly on that side, or if the exercises of our minds cling principally to the material aspect of things, — then the discernment of the other great reality grows dim. When anything is told us of it, even in the Scriptures, it sounds like a fable. Openly or secretly, we question its authority. The spiritual discernment, or faculty of faith, has not been used, — perhaps not even opened; and then, though we should stand around the Son of Man, who came to show how these two worlds are one and open into one another, — though the Prophets should come, clothed in light, and a voice speak out of the excellent glory, — we should only say it was a meteor, or it thundered. It would take more than a Bible, more than a miracle to convince us. No matter how merciful or wonderful the work,—"Neither would they be persuaded though one rose from the dead." And so it turned out where the wonder-working Saviour stood. He healed men's miseries;—they that were dead sat up and spake. Some believed; some doubted.

Three men, the three who seem to have been the best prepared to enter into the higher meaning of the Christian life, and were therefore admitted whenever the Saviour's divine power was more mysteriously manifest,—John, Peter, and James,—were called up to witness this immortal interview, where the two great Prophets of the elder and preparatory covenant were to meet, in transfigured forms, with the Messiah of the Fulfilment, and there, in the serenity and splendor of the Mount, to converse together of "the decease which he should accomplish at Jerusalem;" a theme vast and solemn enough even for that august audience. Moses the Lawgiver, Elijah the Reformer, Jesus the Redeemer! In the whole representation of what took place, you see things that in themselves are quite beyond natural observation, exhibited by natural objects and appearances,—as a mountain, human bodies, light, sound.

This fact has sufficient religious importance to justify us in dwelling a moment upon it. Setting aside notions purely Pagan, and keeping in the line of the nominal belief in one God, there are three distinctly marked stages in the progress of opinion about the natural world, with a fourth to come.

The first of these is where the natural world is regarded as divine only as to what appears to be extraordinary or exceptional in it. Thunders, tempests, earthquakes, eclipses, famines, pestilences, are thought to betray a divine presence. Or, in human affairs, sudden accidents, unexpected deliverances, strange coincidences. God is a God of occasional interference, not of constant regulation and animation. Not all our daily affairs and the regular processes of creation are subject to his watchfulness, and charged with his indwelling spirit; but nature is liable to arbitrary visitations from without. The religious sentiment feeds on the marvellous. There is a piety of surprises and alarms, — intermittent, spasmodic. God is not in the order of nature, its laws, its silent, beneficent growths and noiseless motions, but in its loud jars and grotesque anomalies. You will hear much there of special providences: it is not Providence at all, but intrusion, improvisation, perturbation. Of course this will be a God of violence and of terror. And the name of this first view will be Superstition. The supernatural is, then, strange, frightful.

The second is exactly opposite to this. It is where the attention is turned wholly to the law-side of nature, and does not see that there is a personal will acting freely anywhere within nature or about it. It is so bent on getting rid of exceptions that it forgets the Maker. It mistakes uniformity for self-acting mechanics. Virtually it denies the spiritual world, with all its nobler, varied and glorified forms of life. There are men so absorbed in the regular processes of the universe as to be insensible both to its Original and to its holy object. Prudence is substituted for piety. The nearest approach to penitence is regret for a miscalculation. Self-reliance is put for devout trust; a little knowledge, which vanishes away, for faith and hope and charity, which abide. The future is all dark, without promise or resurrection. The name of this is scepticism. The supernatural is denied.

The third, which is unquestionably a great advance on the other two, is where God is believed to be *over* both the natural and the spiritual world, but only *in* the spiritual. These two worlds are driven wide apart. Thus the only religious purpose answered by nature is to furnish a convenient supply of figures and illustrations for religious discourse. In those who have a lively admiration for external beauty there will grow up a sort of fanciful, poetical, sentimental piety; in those who distrust and despise the material world, asceticism. Christianity and creation are sundered, though God joined them together. It is a kind of half-belief. The supernatural is essentially unreal; and the evidence of miracle, where it is introduced into theology, has a materialistic cast, as if the high and self-attesting truths of Christianity and the soul were actually dependent on proofs addressed to the senses.

But there is a fourth condition,—or will be yet,—where the natural and the spiritual are seen and felt to be parts of one plan, under one Creator. The laws of the one are recognized to be exactly harmonious, nay, identical, with the laws of the other. There is not only a resemblance, but a correspondence; the things of nature being found to be the things of the spirit of man, good and evil; and *all* the things of nature having their counterpart in the spiritual world, whether life or death, health or disease, clouds or sunshine, serpents or doves. Christ's instructions are full of these things; and they are not accidental comparisons, but are meant to bring

God's works together into the closest unity. So says the Apostle Paul in a passage which commentators have only partially and superficially comprehended: "The invisible things of Him, from the creation of the world, are clearly seen, being understood by the things that are made." He is the God of the insect as much as of the archangel. In the original design of the Creative mind, each was meant for the other, — everything in nature, great or small, star or starfish, to meet and answer to something in man. This at present may be Christian mysticism. But it will be Christian faith. All the strong tendencies of true science, as well as of Revelation, are bearing in this direction. They tell us that when God formed the lowest living creature, already man, with brain and heart and immortality, was in his thought. In every department of knowledge and thought, unity is the reigning idea. All interdepend; all belong to each other; all serve each other. And this is the Christian doctrine. Revelation is to find each of its great practical truths confirmed in the universe. The sovereignty of God; his personal and free presence to every part and particle; the disorder of sin, or disobedience to law; the remedy for that, or reconciliation; the necessity of a second or spiritual birth to restore and complete the natural man, — have dim types in nature. And, above all, — what now concerns us most, — there is hinted the reality of a revelation of what is unseen and eternal, through appropriate and pre-adapted forms that are seen and temporal, in connection with the ministry of the Son of God and Son of Man, as a mediator belonging both to earth and heaven, or rather as having both these belonging to him. In this view, the Christian miracles become not only credible, but what we should have a right to expect; such breakings through of the spiritual upon the ordinary world as a mediator's ministry would probably bring with it, and the only rational explanation of the beginnings of Christian history.

As to this Revelation, then, the first of these four views I have mentioned — superstition — is ignorant of it; the second — scepticism — rejects it; the third misinterprets it; the fourth — faith — finds it full of blessed meaning, and brimming at every point with a heavenly inspiration.

In the light of this principle, let us return to the scene of our Lord's transfiguration. There we see, in perhaps the most striking spectacle ever beheld by man, the forms and substances of the visible world employed to bring out and make manifest the bright realities of heaven. To a few quickened eyes and elevated spirits, and through them to the Christian multitudes and ages, for a demonstration never to be forgotten, the gates of the unseen Home were to be opened; the curtain of the hidden glory to be lifted; the sublime forms of the great religious masters of antiquity, long since withdrawn from the flesh into the tabernacle of their eternal worship, were to be revealed. They were to come in shapes like those of their mortality, indicating some mysterious and transcendent correspondence between the perishable and the celestial bodies. Above all, in the centre of all, was to be seen, for once, the glorified appearance of the Redeemer, not marred or mortal any more; and the wonderful words spoken were to be of the suffering that was to be borne for the remission of the sins of mankind. Once this was to be. One glimpse within the veil was to leave its inextinguishable light on the records of the believer's faith and hope. Never call it an unpractical testimony. Whatever gives these erring and fainting hearts of ours a livelier sense of the Spirit, — whatever inspires them with new courage, or bows them in a deeper adoration, — whatever enlarges or exalts them, — that is most intensely practical. If, in the realms of knowledge, those are really the most practical truths, and most vital to the ultimate progress and welfare of the race, which at their first discovery seem most remote from uses because of their very comprehensiveness, the general principles, the pure and vast ideas that seem to lie only among the skies of speculation, but are afterwards brought down to serve in the drudgeries of men, — so there may be found to have been a grander utility to the world in the awful and removed disclosures of Tabor, or Hermon, than in the repetition of any catalogue of prudent virtues, or any table of a law.

Come nearer to the special part of this scene given in the words of the text. As the disciples looked on with wonder upon these radiant persons, a cloud swept in between them and their trusted Master, and they were left alone. They *felt* alone, cut off from their safe protection. "And they feared as they entered into the cloud."

With a natural cloud the facts we associate are obscurity, dimness, a degree of mystery, a *hiding of the light*, — sometimes very mercifully softening and tempering what would be more dazzling than the delicate organ of sight could bear — yet a body so attenuated, transparent, and movable, that we feel the darkness is transient. It may pass away from the face of the sun; it may be touched by his beams, transfigured to the eye, and made almost like another sun in splendor. Such, under the laws of light and air and water and attraction, are the properties of the cloud in nature.

Now, in that succession of special disclosures of the Divine Presence and care for man, of which the Bible is the completest record and Christ the perfect incarnation, it is striking to see how each principal act of Revelation is covered with a cloud, — a palpable veil of mystery. In the book of Job, supposed to be the oldest piece of writing, there is a statement, — an anticipation of what has just now, after thousands of years, come to be the settled conclusion of studies in science, — that in the very process of creative power the whole planet lay enfolded in a garment of cloud, — "thick darkness a swaddling-band for it." The earliest covenant of God's mercy for his children, it is written, had its token in a rainbow of the cloud. At the emancipation of the chosen people, the beginning of the history in which Christianity was to be born, a cloud led the tribes, which was "light by night" to them, but was "darkness" to the pursuing Egyptians. Throughout all their long march to the Land of Promise, this cloud was not only a guide, but a special sign of Jehovah, and they saw his glory in it. At Sinai, through all the giving of the Law and the founding of the Hebrew commonwealth, which was the inauguration of the first dispensation, it is said a cloud covered the Mount. In the ark of the tabernacle, in the holy of holies, in the Shekinah, which was the lineal antecedent of the temple and the church, the symbol of the Lord's perpetual watchfulness was a cloud over the mercy-seat; and at great crises in the religious history we are told of a cloud filling the sanctuary. Isaiah prefigures the flocking in of the Gentile nations into the true fold, and the worship of a universal assembly, under the same image. All the devout Jewish poetry preserves these allusions, and finds in the clouds a fit dwelling, or chariot, or pavilion for the Most High. In the New Testament, the highest and clearest manifestations of the Son of God robe themselves in this mystery, — as at the transfiguration, the ascension, and the predicted judgment. "As they beheld, a cloud received him up out of their sight." "They shall see the Son of Man coming in a cloud, with power and great glory; every eye shall see him, — men's hearts failing them for fear, and the powers of heaven shaken." The Apocalypse repeats these representations. From the beginning to the end you see the persistent and remarkable reappearance of this symbol. Considering how these different books of the Bible were produced, and what a variety of authors, periods, countries, stages of literary culture, they proceed from, this is more than a coincidence, — it is design. It discloses a general truth. As men are brought near to the very sight and feeling of their Lord, an obscurity overshadows them; there is a shrinking; reverence hides the face; the angels even, admitted to the brightest day, veil their eyes with their wings; no sight is clear enough, no faith is bold enough, not to need the screen. "They feared as they entered into the cloud."

Instead of looking farther away from us, let us see if the great truth lying under all these forms does not come very near, to strengthen or to comfort us, in our own familiar experience. The loftiest visions of heaven have much to do with our lowliest and commonest duties. There is one lesson for the privileged disciples and for us.

1. Most of our deepest acquaintance with religious

truth comes by a discipline of some severity. To pass out of a life of indifference and self-indulgence into one of purity and prayer requires a painful effort. If you can look back to any time when your life took a new starting-point, or rose to a higher aim, you will remember there was some hard conflict connected with it. Suffering is not only the consequence of sin, but the instrument of recovery. It is a means of penitence, and so a minister to the only real peace. The source of the trial may be without or within: in disasters of fortune, defeats of pride, failures of ambition, companionships which cross and torture our temper, disordered and aching bodies, secret adversaries fighting with conscience, or bereavement by death, putting such a look on the world that it never can be again what it was before,—quenching joys never to be rekindled. It is under some shadow, through some cloud, that most of us have to approach our Master, and enter into the brightness of his communion. The Christian's path, as he enters on it, is very apt to run by ruins or graves,—ruins of desire, or graves of those not less dear because their beauty was mortal, and their strength was frail. Think as we may of this humiliating necessity, it will not be easy to trace the secret workings of Christian power, or to examine the records of the visible church of believers, and deny it. Nay, Christ himself announced it plainly beforehand: "Whoever would be my disciple must take up a cross to come after me." The question in the mind of any one of you *may* be, whether it is true or not. But the real question is only whether your life has yet been wide and deep enough to find it out, or whether you have it yet to learn.

2. The second point on this practical side of the doc-

trine is that it is when we are *entering into* this cloud, — having only the dark side of it before us, and its damp and chilly folds closing around us, — that we are afraid.

The purpose of the cloud is to shut out all that we are not meant to see. It is also a kind of background for the heavenly vision. There must be a bitterness in the draught that heals us. This is only one way of expressing the exact and eternal contradiction of right and wrong. The true life is born by a painful travail. The all-giving Father does not begrudge us joy; but when we were created with the capacity of immortal growth and infinite bliss, we took with it the capacity of a fall,—and we fell. The very knowledge of our highest good is overcast. So that when the merciful Lord brings us on the way towards himself and his glory, we do not know what is before us. The trials that result in our regeneration are dark as we go into them. They are trials for faith. Is it all black vapor? Are there horrid, fiendish shapes? Are there possibly bright forms of heavenly helpers? Will deadly blows be struck at our hearts in the dark? Or, will voices of promise and blessing speak? It is so with the coming of a physical disorder. The struggle is at the appearance of the first fatal symptoms. The sufferer fears them. Afterwards, as the malady wears on, very often angels come and minister about the happy bed. It is so with the early agonies of penitence; with the first crash of our breaking, long-cherished plans; with the announcement that those we love must die. The alleviations, the illuminations, are not yet. Fear is a sign of weakness and dependence, perhaps of conscious wrong and remorse. And in the best of the disciples there will be enough of this sense of shortcoming and estrangement to make the entrance into the cloud dreadful. Either the fear of guilt, or the fear of reverence, will bow the most self-confident down. The time that brings the clear warning of some advancing sorrow is a day of clouds and darkness. We shudder and start back, and ask bitterly if this cup cannot be removed, and cry that we cannot, cannot bear it; and then we go into a secret conflict with ourselves, or our fate, and it is indeed a valley of the shadow of death. Like the solitary Patriarch, in an agony that no human soul can share, we wrestle there till the day breaketh, or else till it is hopeless despair and the second death. When mothers look into the faces of their children and listen to their breathing, and then first realize that another and stronger arm than theirs is drawing the little darling frame irresistibly away; when some definite sensation in the body tells that all remedy is fruitless, and it is only a matter of a little longer or shorter postponement, and the keepers of that house tremble, and its windows are darkened; when the roused conscience is first stirred by the conviction that all thus far has been horribly ungrateful and hollow and ungodly, — then it is *entering into the cloud*, and it is *fear*. The heart sinks. The mind wavers. The reason is blinded. The universe is a riddle. Providence seems gone. The sun is hid. Faith has not laid her hand yet on the clew. We see no way out, and no morning beyond. It is darkness, and nothing but darkness, — before and around and above. Are there some that do not know this? We cannot even pray that they may never know it, — because so are we made that only by knowing it can we know what comes after.

3. For, thirdly, there comes, as the Evangelist writes,

"a voice out of the cloud," which is sufficient, if we will hearken to it, to guide us through the dark, into the light, where the sun is never dim. Nay, it will infuse light through all the cloud itself; and that, instead of a cavern of blackness breathing deadly night-winds, becomes a pillar of fire, a token that our Leader is near, a luminous temple of peace and rest. If we are not buried in the cloud, and lost there, by a faithless and obstinate impenitence, then we shall be permitted, after patience and through faith, to behold this transfiguration. For the voice says, "This is my beloved Son, hear him." Hear him, and he will scatter the cloud from about you with the breath of his mouth. Hear him to believe, and you will be willing to let the cloud remain all God's time, for even the night will be light about you. Hear him to obey him, and you are sure that the upward path he has appointed shall be brighter and brighter, till the light of the moon shall be as the sun, and the light of the sun sevenfold. Hear him to love him, and, in cloud or sun, health or sick chamber, in a glad house or sitting by the gravestone, living or dying, you will never be afraid again, because perfect love casteth out fear.

So it is, as many of you will bear witness, that in the Christian life it is only the *clouds before* that are terrible; when they are passed through, or when faith looks up in the midst of them, and hears the voice, they put on garments of light,—their receding forms are beautiful; or, if they follow, it is only as luminous witnesses what God's discipline has done for us,—moving and ethereal monuments of a pain that was merciful.

Many thousands have found this to be wonderfully true; the heavenly hand leading them forcibly just where they dreaded to go, and so bringing them, by a way they knew not, to the mount of his glory and his peace. There may be other clouds yet before us. But they also, forbidding as they will look at first, if we bend to hear the Divine voice speaking in them, will roll away behind us like the rest, and dissolve in sunshine. So that the voice says, Be of good courage; only believe; *only believe;* fear none of those things that thou shalt suffer, — pain, or affliction, or separation; I will be with thee; my rod and staff shall comfort thee; open thy heart to me, and then my truth shall irradiate all thy soul as the unhindered sunbeams fill the spaces of the air, and there shall be no dark corner left. In the world ye shall have tribulation; but I have overcome the world. Only live in love and purity and trust. Then all heaven is above you. More than that, the very heavens are come down. You have nothing left to fear. Christ walks with you. "The Lord shall be thine everlasting light, and thy God thy glory."

The end of this line of thought must be with the end of earth and the earthly life. One of two sorts of deathbed every one of us here is daily preparing. At one of them, the cloud will be heavy and thick and cold; nay, it will not be cloud only, but night, — the sun gone down; and there will be no voice from the Christ of the Resurrection speaking in it, bringing life and immortality to light. Whether conscience is then awake and afraid, and the restlessness and alarm show that judgment is begun, or whether long recklessness and self-conceit have created an insensibility whose calmness is more frightful than any fear, — it will be dark: dark to the dying, and dark to the surviving. *They* will try, in the desperation of a partial fondness, to glean up from your waste of life the memory of some better fragments of amiability, or outside virtue, to relieve the dreary retrospect, — hardly to brighten the prospect. So die the foolish and the faithless; and it is death indeed.

The other is the departure of the Christian believer and workman: not to be described, because there is in it something of that spiritual and mysterious grandeur which never went into any speech of man. Yet it is a mortal transfiguration begun. Whatever the aspect physical disorder and emaciation may wear, the cloud has another side turned to the unfading sun. There is no distressing attempt to palliate, or to excuse, or to flatter. The mourners may weep; but it is as those weep who hold a cross in their hands, and are sure that the terms of forgiveness have been fulfilled. The dying one may groan; but it is as the most human lips of the Divine One groaned, praying, "Not as I will, but as thou wilt." We need not ask that our friends should die in transport. Yet if their trust is in the crucified and transfigured One, it is a bright cloud that receives them up out of our sight. The voice speaks out of it. And on the other side of it is the wide spiritual tabernacle, that has no need of the sun, or the moon, or the stars, — where worship, before the throne of God and the Lamb, John and Peter and James and Moses and Elias, and "a multitude that no man can number"!

SERMON XI.

CHRISTIAN LONELINESS.

I HAVE TRODDEN THE WINE-PRESS ALONE. — Is. lxiii. 3.

LIKE much of the most impressive language, both in the Bible and in general writing, this sentence affects us rather by what it dimly suggests than by what it directly expresses. Nor is this a mere secondary or accidental property of language. It is one of the prime uses affixed to it by the Author of all language. In a similar way, you have noticed how the commonest objects take on attributes and exercise influences not at all accounted for by their material substance. The house where you were born speaks to you; and it says what cannot be explained by the wood and mortar and iron that compose the structure, nor by the shape into which architecture has fashioned them. Its language is eloquent with the immaterial voice, the unwritten poetry, and the fleeting images that cluster about those two lyric names, Home and Childhood. The Bible that your mother gave you borrows its beauty from no skill of the book-maker's art, and it has sent in a nameless significance upon your heart before you open its leaves. So it is that all language possesses itself of a spiritual character, and works effects like a living soul. And this is pre-eminently true of words addressed to the religious nature, such as hymns, parables, prophecies.

The text is one of the most remarkable examples. "I have trodden the wine-press alone." Taken literally, this is a sentence quite barren to us, or even worse. Difference of climate and customs has taken all literal interest out of it. Yet under the law of suggestion referred to, it becomes forcible and significant. We may have never seen a wine-press, nor even be anxious to inquire who the person is that is speaking. And yet every one of us probably takes an impression, and the same impression, from those words. What is the figure they summon up before us all? Probably that of a man left to solitary toil, deserted but not faithless, having a heavy burden to bear, and bearing it uncheered by social sympathy, — a hard and bitter work to do, yet nobly doing it alone. From this image our minds pass unconsciously over to the solitude of our spiritual strifes and inward sufferings. We instantly and universally recognize in him who "trod the wine-press alone" a representative of all our internal work.

My position is this: that, for a religious purpose, and as a part of God's spiritual discipline with us, our deepest experiences must be passed through in solitude. We must suffer alone, we must get wisdom alone, we must be renewed in the inmost spirit of our minds alone, we must resist temptation alone, we must meditate alone and pray alone, and we must pass through the valley of the shadow of death alone. Some degree of solitude is a necessary condition of all these great acts. We cannot expect companionship in them; we must not lean too much upon human sympathy in them. It is a fact of our constitution. Some strengthening results will be found, I hope, in veins of thought opening out of this truth.

It was a distorted perception of that truth that gave what value they had to the old systems of monasticism, or religious retirement. These ancient practices our modern times have, for the most part, reversed. If a man is much alone now, it must be rather by a direct effort to that end than by popular habits. Some such effort will be salutary to his virtue. This sweeping tendency to social agglomeration, wholesome as it is within bounds, will be all the more wholesome for being occasionally resisted. If its direct action is to harmonize the many, and combine scattered forces, the effect of an independent superiority to it will be to emancipate the individual judgment, and make solid the personal character. Social habits may soften asperities; but it needs solitude to settle our principles. Social habits may make us good-natured; but to get certainty for our ideas, or assurance for our faith, we must be alone. The stronger traits, the more rugged and manly virtues, powers of endurance, energies for moral enterprise, are never developed except in such balanced spirits as have been thrown back much upon solitude and themselves. The friction of society may smooth down individual peculiarities, but there are such things as a smoothness that is insipid, and a compliance that is so accommodating as to be cowardly. If constant intercourse with others neutralizes our prejudices, it may also undermine our simplicity, coax our kindly sentiments into vicious compromises, and tempt our integrity out of its self-possession into disgraceful bargains. If we learn amiability in the mixed company, so do we learn what stanch and steadfast convictions are by standing alone. If we form delightful connections in the one, so do we gain the nobler faculty of thinking for ourselves, acting for ourselves, and believing for ourselves, in the other.

At a period when the activities of associate enterprise threaten Christian individuality with so many perils,—in a place where the personal sense of right is beleaguered and solicited by so many plausibilities,—among customs where majorities take the place of single-headed tyrants, and the bribe of promotion bewilders the clear-sightedness of faith,—let us look to our integrity. It is useless to talk of character, at all, if we are to go on measuring ourselves by one another, and asking our neighbors how far it will do to go in breasting the current, or anxiously querying with ourselves how many friends, or favors, or votes, or offices,—how large a piece of "the world,"—we shall have to lose by taking sides with Christ, instead of striking out boldly, and committing ourselves unreservedly, in faith, to his cause. If we are set, in earnest, on escaping from delusions and sins, we cannot afford to wait for the multitude. If we would walk with clean steps, we must gird ourselves for a solitary march; if we would find God, and be his children, and have the great reward of his presence, we must "enter into the closet, and shut the door, and pray to the Father who is in secret."

I do not forget the obvious arguments for association, nor the often quoted benefits of a union of minds. Let them stand for their undoubted worth. It is clear that Christian faith wins some of its noblest victories only in social revivals. But let it be also remembered that a concentration of the individual will upon its own chosen purpose, such as a man never gets except by isolating himself, is a matter of as much moment to the success of every good interest in the world as the contact of numbers. Who would not prize more highly the solemn determination of a single independent mind, taken and weighed and perfected in solitude, unswayed by public dictation, and incorrupt from the hot breath of crowds, than the longest subscription-list to a set of written or concocted measures, or the enthusiastic "resolutions" of the loudest caucus? Let it be further remembered, that if combinations of masses are promotive of good causes, they are also mighty facilities for bad ones. If they create, they can destroy; if societies are agencies potent to bless the world with reformations, mobs may also confound it with new mischiefs. And the grandest regulator of their shifting play is in those firm convictions that strike their roots in the soil of lonely meditation.

Providence will doubtless amply vindicate itself for making men gregarious; and our multiplying methods of intercommunication leave no stimulus to that side of our nature unsupplied. There are two extremes; and at times we are moved to say, O, if we were as ready to deliberate as to combine, — to study and reflect, as to organize societies, — to live righteously and pray to God in secret, as to hide our individuality in fraternities and escape the responsibility of our free will in public meetings, — we might hope for a speedier advent of the Kingdom of Heaven.

This truth may enter more readily if we remember that the higher intellectual qualities — those that are more intimately related to the moral, and thus have the largest agency in forming character — depend on solitude for their most successful cultivation. Judgment, imagination, clearness and consistency of thought, breadth of vision, whatever constitutes the originality and natural force of the mind, — these are all nurtured in lonely studies. The stream may sparkle and widen in the hot glare of public engagements, but the perennial springs whence all its waters are supplied must be up among the cool and shaded heights of solitude. The biography of nearly all those master-intellects that have left a deep mark on human affairs brings testimony that at some period of their lives they were cast much apart from men, and made to rely on their own resources, and on the powers unseen and eternal. One of the most remarkable of them all, the life of a leader in English literature, contains this testimony, in his own words: "If, after the model of the Emperor Marcus Aurelius, I should return thanks to Providence for all the blessings of my early situation, one of the very first I should recall, as chiefly worthy to be commemorated, would be that I lived in solitude." A very appreciative critic of art, a man who studies the beautiful through the eyes of his heart as well as through his scientific understanding, has said that he always chooses to walk through galleries of great works unaccompanied; for the reason that conversation belittles every subject, enfeebles the judgment, and fritters admiration away. In the lives of all the strong thinkers that have rendered great services to science, by discovery, by original combinations, by concentrated force, there has been a preparation of solitary study, a youth given to the habit of retirement. Can you find a single exception? So, emphatically, of those best persons, who by the combined weight of intellectual and moral attributes have been the signal reformers or builders of institutions. Affecting society far and wide, they did not gather their best power in social resorts, but alone with Heaven: Paul, three years in Arabia; Luther, in his cell; Alfred, in the Island of Nobles. Mahomet, Columbus, Washington, — their youth was apart from men; their career was baptized and initiated in the air of retirement. And of the great Lord of all the divine ministry to the world must begin with forty days in the wilderness.

If being alone is tributary to intellectual greatness it is still more so to the proper symmetry and health of the moral principles. Every soul that has had any moral experience whatever must know that the best elements in his composition are those derived from passages in his life where no second could keep his soul company, — where he must be alone; disappointments that he must suffer alone; difficulties that he must face alone; reflections where he must look to his own soul and his God alone. Two conditions have affixed themselves to the history of moral reformers and heroes: they have first been overshadowed by the great ideas for the redemption of humanity which have filled their souls, in solitary thinking; and when they have gone out on their beneficent errands, they have had to work alone,—confront apathy and opposition unsupported by the sympathies of any multitude. Is it not inevitable to infer that this very separation from outward props has lent them inward victory? Superiority to slavish customs, single-hearted allegiance to the invisible Right, — the mind that makes and the sensitive conscience that respects moral discriminations, — these are fruits of treading the wine-press alone.

Still more strictly does this rule hold of the deeper emotions. And as these are the most spiritual motions within us, they prove how close the kindred is between solitude and spirituality of character. The loftiest of all our possible emotions is religious reverence, expressing itself in worship, or prayer. This communion with Heaven is inseparably associated with secrecy. It has been ever since worship took its Christian ordination from him who said, "Enter into thy closet;" ever since the Lord God spoke with Adam alone in the garden, in the cool of the day.

Nature has herself given a broad hint of this truth, in making it absolutely impossible for us to express to any mortal the deepest feeling. She indicates our duty by making even some inferior kinds of veneration too deep for utterance, — "too deep" sometimes even "for" the utterance of "tears." Just when she discloses to our perceptions any of her grandest pictures, she shuts our lips. Whenever she stirs our sense of the sublime, she sternly tells us, "My children, be dumb!" When we are most profoundly moved in any way, she thus prisons our hearts in a practical solitude, at least, and we feel the utter helplessness of our tongues. If we are so presumptuous as to speak, we feel instantly rebuked for the foolishness of our babbling. The less imposing, the smaller and lighter aspects of nature, permit us to be sociable; but when her more majestic voice sounds, our impertinent ones must be still. A lively company may talk and jest as they float among the winding threads of a picturesque harbor, — shut in by the limitations of that narrow scenery; but, if they have souls within them, they will grow thoughtful and be silent as they sail out upon the infinite sea, amidst the boundless simplicity of the waves and the sky. Or they may chatter and laugh together in the variegated and blooming valley; but when they go up among the everlasting hills of God, and stand on those solemn pillars of his arch, an invisible Hand will seem to draw them apart from one another, and fill them with a wonder that cannot be uttered. They may prattle the gossip of the drawing-room in gardens of sunshine, but the roll of celestial thunder will hush their empty levity with awe. It is because the grandeurs of creation take us nearest to the Creator.

So, whenever the uplifted soul approaches God in its sincerest devotion, it must go alone; if other souls bend around, in unity of spirit, yet the communion of each with the Father is solitary, and each must be accepted not for another, but by itself. It must bear its own single burden to the mercy-seat. "Hast thou faith, have it to thyself before God." The prayer must rise from a heart leaning on no earthly arm, — even as it goes up to a Spirit of whom it is written that "He is God alone," and that He "alone doeth great wonders."

Impatience of solitude is a bad religious sign. Whoever dreads to be alone has reason to dread the hereafter. If he is afraid of being left to himself, how shall he dare to meet the searching of his Judge? It becomes quite indispensable to the wholesomeness of a man's spirit, that he should escape from crowds. As much moral peril as physical lurks in the air and poisons the breath of dense communities. Too much company scatters the sublimity of the human will; it intoxicates the sober reason; it flatters pride; it debauches the conscience; it puts our independence under a base apprenticeship to the popular caprice;

it sets our steadiest purposes whiffling in every wind. And so it happens that the mind whose habit is to dwell habitually in mixed assemblages of men is overtaken, by and by, with a humiliating sense of having squandered itself. That is the foretaste of its after retribution. And remember *this*, that if your sensibility fails to be thus mortified for its immodesties, it is for the alarming reason that the defection from truth has been so wide that the simplicity of the soul has been lost amidst the necromancy of the senses; dissipation has luxuriated into satisfaction; remorse has been gossipped out of being, and perpetual publicity, after drenching the character in exposure, has left it too soft in fibre for resistance, — too shameless for self-reproach.

Yes: something must have gone terribly wrong with us, if we are afraid to be shut up with none but God. They are not valiant souls that are frightened to find themselves in the unfamiliar and strong hands of his Truth, shaking their false proprieties, oversetting their timid hiding-places, and tearing open dangerous concealments. It is a stern safety; and to shuffle ourselves out of it into the superficial intimacies where we are more at home is not the way to maturity of spiritual life. It is the way of evasion. There is no escape from the law that makes the work of regeneration into higher spiritual states personal, reserved, separate. There is no social salvation excusing the individual. Society is a great interest, but it can never shift responsibility from you and me. Men must go into the kingdom of heaven, if they go at all, just as they go into any grand experience, — be born again just as they are born into the life that now is, — one by one, and each for himself. The fight with the adversary is a single combat, after all. What earnest men want is not flatteries and pageants, but the simple and steady verities that they can stand on for eternity.

Nay, this is demanded from us in mere fidelity to Truth herself; for when we begin to esteem her for the multitudes she fascinates, when we begin to count up her adherents and ask whether she draws large audiences, we have already broken from the true loyalty. Next to the sordidness of wedding Truth for her dowry, which Stillingfleet satirizes, is that of choosing her because all the world admires her. We need to remember — we of this public age, we of these supple times — that very often the living energy of an idea is not proved till it is *voted down*. For when it rises again, a resurrection-power is born with it. So the finest qualities of persons are not developed, sometimes, till they are crowded out of favor, and banished into a minority. Good men have very often to be ridiculed and thwarted, all their lives through, and their vindicator never comes till their coffin comes. Where conscience counts her ten that are willing to save a city, popular compliance has counted her ten thousand willing to ruin it, and be ruined with it. But, then, principle does not *count* men; she *weighs* them. If numbers tested truth, there never was a time, since history began, when falsehood would not have been on the throne, and right in exile or at the block. We have got to do Christ's work, in the world and for the world, without anticipating the world's verdict, or we shall never do it at all.

A Christian loneliness, the solitude that has Christ in it, renews man's strength. It fortifies his resolution. It establishes his peace. It clears away the dust of the earth's day-delusions and the damps of its night-sorrows. It enables us to look abroad with an untroubled eye on the future. It makes the mind populous with beautiful imagery from regions of the invisible. It sends the thoughts on cheerful pilgrimages to all the holy shrines of the Bible and the universe. It lets in happy memories through the open door of our affections to console our misery, and blessed promises to animate our faith. The Father is with us.

"I have trodden the wine-press alone." Human suffering, in all its forms, is solitary. Tenderest sympathies may flock abundantly and graciously to visit it and minister to it. But there is something in it that their kindest offices cannot reach; something appointed by Providence to be left alone; and it is well. Bear holy witness, all you who have been purified by heavenly discipline, and found your light afflictions turning to an exceeding weight of glory, and the sadness of your countenance prophesying crowns of life, — bear witness that it is well! Grief is of many kinds, but all grief that is really terrible sends the soul into speechless, secret solitude. Human love may reach out ready hands, eager to help and to soothe; but it cannot reach down to that lowest centre of anguish where the pang throbs in intensest pain. So true is it that the heart knoweth its own bitterness, that not only the stranger, but the friend, cannot intermeddle with its distress. Here is a healthful group of confiding friends; so long as they are glad and well, every shade of happy feeling may be mutually communicated and shared. But let sickness stretch one of them in wasting fever, and, as the dark mystery of disease closes round the clouded senses, there rises up a silent wall of impenetrable loneliness between the sufferer and the watchers. There are experiences busy in that failing frame that cannot be told, thoughts that cannot possibly pass over from one to the other. I have seen a sick child that was so frank by nature that concealment was all impossible to her, and yet, when the solemn spell of dissolution was coming slowly down upon the features, no entreaties of affection, not the longings of trusted parents and loving sisters, could draw out from that august silence one whisper of the struggle where life and death were wrestling for the mastery.

> "She saw a hand we could not see,
> She heard a voice we could not hear,
> It beckoned her away."

Even the little child must tread the wine-press alone. By some it has been believed that the young spirit has a consciousness of this, and feels "that if he should be summoned to travel into God's presence, no gentle nurse will be allowed to lead him by the hand, nor mother to carry him in her arms, nor little sister to share his trepidations. King and priest, warrior and maiden, philosopher and child, all must walk those mighty galleries alone." It is always so; no cries of friendship can break the sacred stillness of the dying, or bring back more than some short syllable of exclamation. Let faith believe that this significant reserve in the depths of a great experience is meant to chasten our patience, to bid us wait with calmer hope our resurrection.

Bereavements—I need hardly tell you what the truly bereaved know so well, and what none but they can understand at all—must be borne, after all attempts at participation, essentially alone. And the falling away of those nearest to us, whether by the coldness of changed love away from ourselves, or through disgrace away from honor, must most emphatically be suffered alone. The world's mightiest tasks of reformation and regeneration have to be wrought out when lookers-on refuse their friendship, and the workers in them stand misunderstood, misinterpreted, reviled, persecuted, alone. All the deliverers of mankind from wrong and sin must be men of sorrows and solitude, following the Saviour who had not where to lay his head. Even of that divine Redeemer, who laid down his life for our sanctification, how often do we read that he went away alone to be strengthened; that when night came he was alone; that he went apart to pray! What loneliness in his spirit at the supper — let the table, as often as it is spread before us, refresh our remembrance — when he said, "All ye shall be offended because of me this night;" and on the cross, when he prayed in agony that the Father "might not forsake him"!

"I have trodden the wine-press alone." Alone we must go, brethren, and be prepared to go by prayer and faith, through all the deeper and more solemn exigencies of our life; alone through besetting temptation, and the loss of what is most precious; alone through the defection of friends and through personal discouragement; alone to the judgments of the Most High; alone from thence to reap as each hath sown.

Take, then, to close and seal the truth we have pondered, these two convictions:

Solitude is a means of spiritual education. Seek it; ordain it; cherish it; value it not for its own sake, but for faith's sake and Christ's sake; sanctify your life by the prayers it will then inspire. Do not take these thoughts as mere secondary suggestions about the outside of religion. They have to do with its very core and spirit,—its spiritualities, its devotions, its regenerating power on the soul. In order to let the great truths and influences of religion do their work upon us, we must put ourselves in the range and sweep of their action; we must — so to speak — give them a chance at our inner life. The street is no such place; the crowd is no such place. Enter into thy closet.

Couple with this truth another: that as you draw yourself apart from the noise of men, you draw near to God. Enter into thy closet, and when thou hast shut the door, *pray*. Pray to thy Father which is "in secret." When human companionships forsake thee, the Lord will take thee up. Herein, precisely, lies the unfathomed meaning of that Eternal word of Christ, "All ye," mortal friends, "shall be scattered every man to his own, and shall leave me alone;"— alone from men, and "yet not alone" from Heaven, because "the Father is with me." Absent and distant from the world; nearer and nearer to God! So it shall be in all the wine-press and trial of your faith. Even in the valley of the shadow of death, though alone in the former sense, in the latter compassed about with brightness, and fearing no evil, his rod and his staff shall comfort you.

SERMON XII.

SAINTHOOD IN CÆSAR'S HOUSEHOLD.

THE SAINTS THAT ARE OF CÆSAR'S HOUSEHOLD. — Phil. iv. 22.

THIS incidental allusion informs us that already, in Paul's day, there were Christian disciples in the Pagan palace of the world. Jesus was confessed, it seems, not only "before men," but before emperors, — men that, in irresponsible power and savage cruelty, had almost lost the nature of men.

Faith has won its grandest conquests on straitened and sorrowful fields. If the strength and joy of believing are proportioned to the weight of the crosses borne for it, — and such a rule as that does appear to have place in the spiritual economy, — then it is in some such post of perplexity as a Cæsar's household, some age of persecution or close corner of peril, that we must look for the bravest witnesses to truth. So keenly has this been felt by some adventurous souls, that they have positively longed for fiercer onsets of trial than our common and easy fortunes bring, giving their religious constancy a chance to prove itself invincible. Sir Thomas Browne, with his unbounded veneration, had an appetite so hungry for this stimulus to trust, that he says, in one of the passages of his Treatise on the Religion of a Physician, "I bless myself and am thankful that I lived not in the days of miracles, and that I never saw Christ nor his disciples; for then my faith would have been thrust upon me, and I could not have enjoyed that greater blessing promised to all that see not and yet believe." He envies the old Hebrews their title to the only bold and noble faith, since they lived before the Saviour's coming, and gathered their confidence out of mystical types and obscure prophecies. Modern society does not abound in instances of such enthusiasm for believing. More persons seem to be asking what is the minimum of faith that can be made to serve for safety, — how much knowledge will release them from here, and divine indulgence there, — than how affluent a measure they may be privileged to keep in reserve. We eulogize virtues that flourish only in a favoring soil and climate. We palliate and excuse the deficiency, when honesty is missing in the household of Cæsar, — in seats of power or wealth or folly, in office or at court, in Washington or in Paris. We forget that the current piety of the Church, of society, and of the market sinks and dwindles inevitably, unless it is replenished by the energy of those valiant examples which will dare to bear testimony and be true in the very palaces of power and fashion and mammon.

Of the line of Roman Cæsars, — that race standing apart, of whom it has been well said, by a scholar competent to speak, that there met in them "all the heights and depths which belong to man, all the contrasts of glory and meanness, the extremities of what is highest and lowest in human possibility," — the personage whom Paul speaks of here as having saints in his household was the sixth from the founder. Nero was a prince that as far surpassed others in infamy as

Augustus did in royalty; a man who, if every soul beside himself in his household had been a saint, concentrated inhumanity and pollution enough in his person to have darkened all their virtue by the blackness of his unnatural crimes; a man that expended more ingenuity in contriving new modes of dishonoring humanity than most Christians have in serving it, and who earned the reputation of introducing into history, as facts, crimes so enormous, and combinations of wickedness so revolting, that but for him they would have been held too fabulous for the wildest fancy; a man that hunted up and down his vast domains to find some fresh species of murder, with exquisite and aggravated accompaniments enough to season it to his monstrous appetite, with the same eagerness that gluttons search out a fresh delicacy for a sated palate; a man that tried three different ways of butchering his own mother, and at last despatched her by a vulgar execution, in a petulant rage at being baffled so often; and who added the tyrant's caprice to the incendiary's, by undertaking at once to throw off the suspicion of his own agency in the diabolic conflagration of his capital, and to comfort his bloodthirsty temper, by imputing the fire to the innocent Christians; who tortured his Christian subjects by unheard-of torments, dressing them in the skins of wild animals to provoke dogs to tear them to pieces, or wrapping their bodies in clothing smeared with pitch, and then setting them on fire to light up the Roman night with their burning; a man, in short, that wrought so awful an impression of his attributes of superhuman atrocity on the minds of the believers of that age, that a common rumor went abroad among them, after his horrible death, that he would return again alive to vex the world anew, and to be the Antichrist of prophecy.

In the household of such a man and such a Cæsar it was that the Apostle, himself now a voluntary prisoner at Rome, awaiting his trial and probably his martyrdom, found "saints," — saints that he mentions with special honor, when he sends their message in his letter to the friends at Philippi. There, and then, if nowhere else or since, we can all feel that it was something heroic to be a saint. By contrast with so dark a depravity, and in the teeth of so relentless a spite, "professing Christ" had a meaning; to be called a Christian cost sacrifices that deserved the name. Saintship shone, then, with a palpable glory; and no man could fail of seeing whence the light came. The followers of the Crucified, and the lovers of the world, were separate companies of souls; the sword and the lions pronounced the distinction between them with emphasis. No wonder Paul thanks God that even then the faith of the *Roman* Christians was spoken of in all the world.

Across the chasm of almost eighteen hundred years, beyond an ocean that is narrowed now by the Christian civilization which those saints installed, we are speaking of it, — thanking God, too, I hope, for his own wondrous providence in his Church, — thanking Paul's pen that has left us this bright trace of a precious martyrology, — thanking these saints of Cæsar's household themselves, for the mighty arms of faith which they reach over to us, to encourage our confidence, to shame our unbelief, to reinspire our too sluggish zeal.

Possibly it may be found that there is just as real and deep a distinction now as then, between him who serveth God and loveth the Lord Jesus Christ in sincerity, and him who serveth and loveth not. Possibly it may appear that the glory of an actual saintship, the veritably faithful spirit, is just as pure and lustrous now as then. Possibly we may see that yet there are saints in Cæsars' households, and that there is as good cause to venerate and to multiply them, as when the gladiators waited in the ring, and beasts licked up their blood from the sand.

For, the substance of all sainthood that has vitality enough to survive in households of Cæsar is this, — that its virtue is so built on interior foundations, and its religious faith so rooted in the spiritual source and Divine Master of its life, that no outward opposition avails to break it down, or even to interrupt its worship. You see, at once, how this carries the spirit of it out of the first age, and beyond Nero's palace; how possible it is, and how much wanted also, wherever an adverse influence frowns on Christian purity, or hinders Christian fidelity, and therefore how the subject is reduced at once to a practical study. For that bad influence may proceed from things not held in much suspicion; — from a false social standard; from a set of surrounding associations hostile to holiness; from a dominant worldliness in a nation, or a city, or a college, or a literal household; from an inhuman course of legislation; from maxims of pretended honor really barbarous; from customs of evasion and apology, or of self-indulgence and sensual excess, of profaneness and cruelty, that creep in among loosened principles, as well as from courts and tyrants' thrones.

There are three or four special traits essential to this sainthood in Cæsar's household, — whoever the Cæsar may be, and wherever his house may stand. The first of these, we shall agree, is courage. Christianity has not only room, but favor, for every noble sentiment in human nature; and so she offers even to the veteran soldier, and to the enthusiastic youth, a field for all his bravery grander than any of his battles, in the resistance of moral invasion. Accordingly, we find that, very soon, Christianity seized on some of those rough warriors that never quailed themselves, but had terrified and conquered the world. Mention is incidentally made of one convert who was "a centurion of the band called the Italian band," and some of these believers about the person of Nero must probably have been guards of his palace. On one of the early Christian monuments at Rome there is an epitaph of a young military officer, saying that he deemed himself "to have lived long enough when he shed his blood for Christ." But Christ's religion courts no consideration from armies. Its courage is of another kind,—the courage that bears wrong, but will not commit it,—that saves life, rather than destroys it. It is a courage that springs from an unspotted conscience, and wins the triumphs of generous good-will; the courage that goes into and out of all companies, counting-houses, caucuses, and churches, with an uprightness not to be bent, whether you bring threats, or sneers, or golden baits to tempt it; a courage that lifts up an unblenched face in the most formidable array of difficulties, satisfied to stand on the platform of the New Testament, and on God's side, to listen to the encouragement of the beatitudes and to hold to the breastplate of righteousness. And, as I suppose it really takes about as much unadulterated fortitude, if all things are brought into the account, for a young girl, to-day, to maintain a truthful and devout conversation,—that is, to be a Christian,—as it did for St. Agnes; or for a student to carry an undefiled soul through an apprenticeship or a university, as it did for Vigilius to go by night from his post in the palace to hear an epistle read from one Paul of Tarsus, when it was whispered about Rome that the Apostle had sent a letter to his brethren there;—so wherever such a Christian courage in duty is, there will be saints of Cæsar's household.

And if there are, a second of their qualities, always attending the highest kind of courage, but very difficult to be united with its counterfeits, you will find to be modesty. It does not appear that these devout persons in Rome set themselves up to revolutionize religion, or to be patterns of perfection. They did not call themselves saints; Paul called them so. They did not boast of their religion; there was too much solemn sincerity in it. They did not lurk about the temples of idolatry, to mock its soothsayers, and to disseminate self-righteous slanders about its priesthood. They knew the joy of their own believing, and the blessedness of their communion with Jesus; and cared more for fellowship with the Redeemer than for admiration from the citizens. That was their Christian modesty. Disjoined from their fortitude, it might have degenerated into timidity. And that is often our danger. There are some persons — we all know such — of diffident dispositions, that err in not mixing enough boldness of resistance with their good nature or amiability. They remain inefficient disciples, because they shrink from the public notice of taking up the cross. This is to turn one of the most beautiful of Christian graces, "the ornament of a meek and quiet spirit," into a deformity and an offence;

it robs the Master of the testimony that is his due, and it glides easily into a selfish and sluggish indifference. It sometimes happens that there are individuals among us placed in a very literal resemblance to those that were saints in the household of Cæsar. In a state of society like ours, nominally Christian, but often more careful to render unto Cæsar the things that are Cæsar's than unto God the things that are God's, there will occasionally be instances of single believers in large groups or communities of practical unbelievers. While the main current of speech, feeling, and habit runs one way, and that to self-pleasing, some one living a higher life, having a spiritual aim, pledged secretly to the law of Christ, and devoutly desiring above all things to take up the cross and come after him, is sorely perplexed with the trial of a petty and cowardly persecution from those that ought rather, if not perverse in their depravity, to revere the better heart as a heavenly presence amongst them. And then this very trait of modesty, a virtue in its place, threatens to become a traitor, to intimidate the trembling purpose and draw back the soul from God to folly. This is the position of all threatened minorities. They will get strength for the fiery trial by going back to see how the inmates of a palace full of gluttony, licentiousness, and all royal vices, held their allegiance fast.

But to imitate that successful blending of modesty and courage, they will want a third quality, namely, independence. The question of duty once settled, all gates but that which leads to acting it out must be shut. And beyond that point, all arguments from custom, from the general expectation, from popular applause, from public or private gratification, are impertinent; as much so as for the little band to hesitate whether they should lose caste by going out one day fifty miles from the capital, as far as Appii Forum, to meet the despised prisoner who was conducted in from an Eastern province as an accused insurrectionist, after he had made Felix tremble, and half persuaded Agrippa. Remember, they were living in the centre of the great world's energy and splendor, as well as of its corruption, and in the very focus of its intelligence, as well as under its hottest hatred. Independence was a virtue quite indispensable to them; but not a whit more so than to us. For, every day, Providence, through our own instincts, pushes us into some crisis of moral peril, where, if we do not act simply of ourselves, and take our direction at first hand from the Spirit, our integrity itself is gone.

And superadded to independence and modesty and courage is constancy There must have been a great many days when it would have been easy, and very convenient, for these valiant saints in Cæsar's household to slip round into the old comfortable heathenism again. Inducements were not wanting. For the ignorant there was personal safety. For the cultivated, Seneca was alive, competent to commend the Pagan philosophy in its purest aspects and its Stoic severity, and professing himself ambitious, Jerome said, to be to Heathendom what Paul was to the Church. But they held fast. They might be hunted out in their obscure retreats, and might see their teachers slaughtered, as good Stephen once was, the moment the benediction had passed his lips; but they gathered again, the next evening, and other hands, willing to be mangled by the same martyrdom, broke to them the bread of life. The Emperor might send them out to build his baths; they raised no civil rebellion, but, while they bent to their slavery, knelt and prayed to the Father. Arrows might pierce their bodies; but, as you see in the picture of Sebastian, they believed that angels would draw all the pain of the weapons out, and the Lord Jesus receive their spirits. Extermination itself would not alarm them; Diocletian afterwards fancied he had killed the last, and set up a column to show that the whole Christian sect was extinct. But faith is prophetic; and although they could not foresee what actually happened, that their sculptured images should one day crowd the Pantheon, and the temple reared to a heathen goddess be dedicated to the mother of their Christ, they did foresee that they should all stand, with white robes, and palms in their hands, and songs on their lips, before God, in another temple, to go no more out.

God is asking constancy of *us*. You do not need that I should remind you what ever-besetting and fearful tempters are waylaying your steadfastness. If you swerve from Christian consistency; if you go from prayers here to profanity and passion in the paltry annoyances of the week; if you purpose, and will not perform; if you talk of heaven, and live only for self; if you profess Christianity at church, only to dishonor it by your daily infidelity,—then it wants no judgment out of yourself to tell you, that you belong not to the saints of Cæsar's household, but among its sinners.

Our Nero is self-love. The senses are the Cæsars of all ages. Fashion is a Rome that commissions its legions and spreads its silent empire wider than the Prætorian eagles. The reigning temper of the world is the imperishable persecutor and tyrant of the faithful soul. And so, in all our New England, in every home and street, seminary and dwelling, there are chances for the reappearing of saints in Cæsar's household. Wherever a fearless man deems any bribe to do wrong, whether it come in cunning insinuations or open bids, and whether it offer him promotion, better wages, a larger house, more luxuries or leisure, or easier tasks, — deems it all an insult to his clean heart, and so spurns it instantly away, as a disgrace that would soil his spirit more than the dirt of any drudgery would his hand; wherever an incorruptible merchant refuses to conform to popular deceptions, at the risk of losing trade, or exercises as unsleeping a vigilance over every stroke of his pen, and every branch of every transaction, when no eye but God's looks down on his desk, as if the whole board of the public exchange were watching him, or scorns to take up subterfuges which commercial customs may wink at and excuse, and does it because God's eye is the guide of his life; wherever a righteous mechanic refuses to let down his performance to the variable standard of thoroughness or shabbiness extant in his class; wherever an honest statesman stands above his party, the moment his party cast their principles into a lottery, and will not put on the robe of office so long as it hides in its folds the hypocrite's curse; wherever a consistent theologian keeps a conscience as well as a pulpit, and will not compromise his exhortations and prayers by the bigotry of a sect or the reverence of a salary; wherever a self-commanding woman is greater than the extravagant edicts of the fashion-makers, and dares to be a rebel against wasteful and ambitious competitions or a society speaking polite lies; wherever young and joyous persons fear God too wisely, and venerate duty too sacredly, to scoff at religion, or laugh at temperance, or tolerate impure companions, under any tempting; wherever a disciple of Christ is not ashamed to own and praise that holy Lord, by whom only he has forgiveness, though unbelieving associates taunt and ridicule his constancy; — there you behold "saints of the household of Cæsar," of Roman firmness but of Christian holiness, the true succession of immortal confessors to the truth, the moral Apostolical lineage of Christ's unterrified witnesses, and heirs of his kingdom.

Most of our knowledge of these old Roman Christians comes by the way of the Catacombs, — that subterranean passage, reaching out many miles, from Rome to Ostia, stamped, on all its walls, with the sculptured and pictured symbols of early Christian ideas and the funereal inscriptions of the men that lived in and died for them, preserving in the silent burial of fourteen hundred years these traces of martyrs and confessors, but uncovered at last by the enterprise of discovery, and made to rehearse the lost history of the first struggles of our religion in the capital of the world. There you may read what it was to be a saint in the household, or even in the city, of the Cæsars. You may see how prayers that could not be stifled went up from caverns, with no doubts that they should find their way to the ear of God through the rocky roof, sooner than the shrieks and incense from the shining heathen temples above. There you will see how Providence, honoring humble instruments, as his method is, used the vulgar sand-diggers that excavated the Campagna, after they were converted to the new doctrine, to act as guides to their brethren of the young Church, providing a hiding-place for it in the scene of their former labors. You behold the long tiers, or alcoves, of the graves of those who, having died in faith, inherit the promises. No symbols of hateful passion, no tokens of revenge for the wrongs they smarted under, no wails of heathenish despair, no signs of bloody altars; — but, instead, the tokens of peace, hope, and joy; pictures of love; legends of reconciliation; a monogram of the Saviour; a lamb; a branch of palm; a cross; some epitaph commemorating a "friend of all men," "an enemy of none," "one meek and lowly," those that "sleep in Jesus," or others "borne away by angels." Everywhere you see traces and proofs of that heavenly temper, that pure and prayerful spirit, that disinterested and self-denying piety, that influence from on high, which you know was never the product of the Roman nature, never caught from Roman philosophers, never fostered by the Roman armies, never ordained by Roman law, never inspired by Roman mythology, — the gift of God in the Gospel of Jesus Christ, the heritage of his Church, the new creation, the regeneration of the Holy Spirit.

In the sixteenth century, the Catacombs, which formed both the church and the cemetery of the early Roman Christians, were thrown open to the light. Notice now the change that passes on the outward position of these sacred memorials. The monumental stones, the coverings of graves, the decaying bones even, are removed from their dark chambers, and lifted into the day. They are placed in royal collections of costly treasures; they are sent all over Europe as precious gifts to princes; they stand in honored niches in great museums of art; and even on the splendid walls of the Vatican travellers find these plain tablets, with their rude inscriptions scratched by unlettered gravers in the dark, — with their badly spelt epitaphs, simple as the Sermon on the Mount, — they find these ranged in showy publicity along vast galleries, beside the pompous eulogies and exquisite sculptures of more artificial days, — relics of a troubled, lowly past, venerated, nay, worshipped now, by a prosperous and perverted present. The Church that hid underground in sackcloth and ashes, scourged by the Cæsars, has risen out of dens and caves into the world's homage, conquered its enemies, and sits on Cæsar's throne.

Is there not a twofold change, — one within exactly the reverse of that without, — an increase of danger keeping pace with the increase of power? The change from outward poverty and inward strength to material prosperity with spiritual starvation, is no such progress as Christians can pray for. When one reads these simple and joyous words that were written in the Catacombs by the saints of Cæsar's time, he feels himself borne back into the fresh morning air of faith, — into the original purity of Gospel life, — among brave, upright, and steadfast souls, incapable of being shaken by imperial, commercial, political, or social intimidation, — very near to the Divine Master who was tempted in all points as we are, yet without sin. Ascend from the humble Roman Church of the second century into the arrogant pretensions and inconsistencies of our own, — from the Christianity of the damp pit, where self-denial would rather face crucifixion than take all the bribes of comfort, up into the Christianity of the popular and outside appearance which satisfies so many to-day.

We have nothing to fear from caverns or palaces, — from emperors or popes. Yet there is something to learn from the noble faith of believers that could lay down their life for Christ, and something to fear from the hollow sins of hypocrites who waste life for worldly welfare. Human nature is the same, though the great seats of power are shifted from the Tiber westward, and the currents of thought and habit flow in altered channels. We have our probation daily, amidst the conflicts, interests, exposures, enterprises, of a New England community, — not the wickedest on the planet, but wicked enough to need all our vigilance, purity, example, and prayers; and enough like Cæsar's household to make us aspire to be saints, righteous souls, within it. But whatever we do, or fail to do, outside ourselves, be it our first care to save our own hearts from destruction. Within us lies an empire to be lost or redeemed. What personal relation each soul has with God, — that is a question not to stand unsettled any longer. For over every passing moment impends the whole arch of eternity. The God who calls us to regeneration, calls us to judgment. Cæsar may wear the crown, and saints bear the cross, on earth; but into the household of heaven can enter nothing that is defiled, or maketh a lie, and "crowns of *life*" are only for the "faithful *unto death*."

SERMON XIII.

DIVINE REWARDS.

THEN CAME TO HIM THE MOTHER OF ZEBEDEE'S CHILDREN WITH HER SONS, WORSHIPPING HIM, AND DESIRING HIM, GRANT THAT THESE MY TWO SONS MAY SIT, THE ONE ON THY RIGHT HAND, AND THE OTHER ON THE LEFT, IN THY KINGDOM. BUT JESUS ANSWERED AND SAID, YE KNOW NOT WHAT YE ASK. ARE YE ABLE TO DRINK OF THE CUP THAT I SHALL DRINK OF, AND TO BE BAPTIZED WITH THE BAPTISM THAT I AM BAPTIZED WITH? THEY SAY UNTO HIM, WE ARE ABLE. AND HE SAITH UNTO THEM, YE SHALL DRINK, INDEED, OF MY CUP, AND BE BAPTIZED WITH THE BAPTISM THAT I AM BAPTIZED WITH; BUT TO SIT ON MY RIGHT HAND AND ON MY LEFT IS NOT MINE TO GIVE. — Matthew xx. 20 - 23.

WITH a dim perception of his objects, and a feeble feeling of his divinity, but with sincerity, these two disciples had attached themselves to Christ's company and his fortunes. Something in that wonderful person and ministry — they hardly yet know what it is — has drawn them honestly to him, and the attachment grows with a growing intimacy every day. But presently there creeps in a thought for their private position, which is the first form of selfishness; and then a thought for their national ambition and revenge, — damaging the whole-heartedness and beauty of their devotion.

They are loyal to the great and good Master they have found; but they are not yet Christlike enough to forget that his imperial ascendency will probably bring with it their own promotion. They really mean to be true to his interests; but they are not so far spiritualized as not to be thinking that they can at the same time serve his interests and advance their own. They are following, but following half unconsciously for a personal reward.

Christ's answer is not for these seekers of office only, nor for place-hunters in our day only, but for all men who would think of being Christians for a compensation, in whatever form we give that compensation shape,—in a secular civilization, in public prosperity, in agreeable society, in our neighbor's confidence, votes, trade, esteem, or in personal happiness. He says, You may drink of my cup, which will often be bitter; you may be baptized with my baptism, which may be one of fire and blood: but you are not to think of honors and rewards: those are all of so different a sort and are to come in ways so different from those you dream of now, that if I were to tell you what they are you would only marvel and doubt. Wait! think nothing about sitting on my right and my left, in my new kingdom, which is even far newer and stranger than you imagine. Follow on in my path. Do all the daily work of a disciple. Take up my cross and learn what its great redemption means. Warm and enlarge your hearts with my Holy Spirit. Be concerned about your service and sacrifice, not about the recompense.

This introduces the doctrine of Divine Rewards. For what reason is Christ to be sought? Out of what motive is his will to be done? Is it because he has the power to make us miserable, and the power to make us happy? and so is it for the hope of getting payment or for the fear of getting punished, — which are only opposite sides of one and the same principle, — or is it from another reason altogether: viz. out of the affection, the reverence, the trust, and the gratitude, due to his divinity and awakened in us by his goodness? As the answer to these questions affects the very motive out of which men begin and pursue a religious life, or refuse to do so, the subject is of course abundantly practical. Is not one of the main reasons why Christian faith exercises such an imperfect power among men, that they misapprehend the sort of advantage they may expect to get from it?

There appear to be three principal desires which direct attention to religious truth. The first of these, and the lowest in the order of moral purity, is a want of personal comfort. Those actuated by this motive have heard that religion makes life happier, — eases its burdens, lightens its labors, heals its pain, and, generally, gratifies the sensibilities. That is, on the whole, it will be a pleasanter thing to live with some religious emotion and protection than without. The idea that this pleasure will be of a higher character than sensual or worldly pleasure is not entirely forgotten; but it is secondary. Comfort first, nobleness afterwards. And so this class, deciding that they will get more happiness from religion than by any other process, go in search of a religion.

The second want is that of moral guidance, or a rule to act by, and is of a much higher grade than the first. Persons under this motive, having got clear of a supreme concern for comfort, look out on life as a school for training in right exercises, and for the practice of the virtues. They are conscious of being under the weight of a tremendous law, or command, which they must obey. Their interpretation of Christianity is summed up in the maxim to keep the commandment. But the world is a perplexed scene, they find. One way of doing right seems to conflict with another way. The paths cross and recross each other. It is a tangled labyrinth. A thousand questions of casuistry come up. The problems are hard to solve. Too much is thrown on a short-sighted intellect and an infirm heart. Besides, duty as duty, by compulsion, is not inspiring, but drudgery. God's law, even if known, can never be perfectly kept, but is broken somewhere by fallen man continually. From sheer inability to do the right thing, at the right time, in the right way, such persons go to religion to help out their deficiencies; but they go to it rather reluctantly, as to a rule, — not as an inspiration, nor for love of it.

The third want is of a different character. It has no regard to selfish satisfaction whatever, whether by agreeable emotions, or the complacencies of good performance, or exemption from the fear of penalty for bad performance. It is, so to speak, a want of giving and loving, — of giving to the Lord what the soul feels belongs to him, — affection and gratitude: a want of loving, and of rendering all the hearty service that love inspires. It is a spiritual aspiration. It would pour out freely and forever the spontaneous tribute of a glad and self-forgetful spirit. It does not stop to inquire so much about the pleasure to be got out of piety, nor about the commands that apply to conduct. It springs straight up by an impulse whose proper name is faith, and puts the whole heart into the keeping of the Holy One, to let him have it, and mould it and fashion it as he will. Meditating on the divine excellence and mercy and sacrifice, it feels that he is the irresistible object of a devotion uncalculating and unlimited, which it would be impossible to keep back. It ceases to calculate and hardly even prays to be made happy. It is the desire of a harmonious and affectionate union with God in the reconciling and forgiving Spirit of the Saviour.

Here are three motives sending men to religion. After their simple statement, no man needs to be informed which is the loftiest and best. Not that each of them is necessarily free from any intermixture with the others. They may be blended in different degrees. But one of them is likely, in every case, to predominate strongly over the other two; and so each of them is represented among us by a distinct class of persons, with specimens that all of us have seen, — the religionists of self-gratification, the religionists of moral obedience, and the religionists of spiritual aspiration and affection, or of faith.

Next, be reminded that these three different wants spring up from different places, or faculties, in our nature.

The first comes from a mixture of natural instinct and shrewdness, which we commonly call by the suspicious name of self-interest. When that feeling turns to religion, it acts in different constitutions in various ways, from the hypocrite who puts on the profession of Christianity and goes through its ceremonies merely as a means of advancement or social currency in a Christian community, up to the sincere and aching sufferer, who applies to the New Testament, precisely as he would to a medical adviser, to be rid of pain. Between these are many degrees of character: the dishonest formalist, deserving nothing but disgust, — the bereaved mourner, or the victim of misfortune, or treachery, or disease, who carries an agonized and dissatisfied heart to the Bible for a cure, and is to be met in a spirit of tender compassion. But none the less is it a serious question for every one of us, how far self-interest, in any of its shapes, is at the bottom of our religious pretensions; because just so far as it is, these pretensions are hollow, — we are on the wrong road, and are estranged from the large and beautiful soul of our Lord, whose greatest work is sacrifice, and whose name is Love.

The second want comes from the region of the conscience. Conscience exacts obedience. It refers to a law. It speaks of the irreconcilable opposition between what is right and what is wrong. It is the seat of morality, and governs all our moral action. It is the noble faculty that rules by divine right over the appetites, and even the understanding. All honor to obedience simply as obedience; to duty as duty; to men and women who try to find out God's command and keep it! They are not far from the kingdom of heaven, and keeping on shall surely come there. Among the nobilities and glories of religious character, this is next to the very highest, and second only to the life of love. No man can be a complete or Christian man who slights conscience. It is what regulates most of our human intercourse and social relationships. It girds up business and amusements, commerce and personal habits, with mighty restraints, checking all manner of excess, forbidding fraud, and instigating many righteous deeds. Its demands are just, and it has a right to be satisfied. Nor can those be mistaken who go to the Saviour to satisfy it. For it can be thoroughly enlightened, and kept quick-sighted, nowhere but in him. Yet this need not make us confound the religion of conscience, which is somewhat legal and rigid alone, with the religion of spiritual aspiration and affection, — of Christ's faith.

The want of this third kind originates, not in the understanding, nor the passions, nor the conscience, but in the soul and the soul's peculiar activity, — especially, as was said, in its love, its trust, and its gratitude. These do not so much send us out in search of a religion; for love, trust, gratitude, directed to the soul's Saviour, constitute the Christian religion. They are the thing itself, in its divinest purity and dignity. Filial love, trust, gratitude, rising to the Father, are greater than anything a servant in the bondage of the law can know, and more glorious than the fairest form of self-interest. They are the peculiar brightness and power of the Christian style of religion. They exalt the faith of Jesus over every other principle. They bind the heart in generous and immortal fellowship with him who is the Light and Life.

It becomes evident enough how out of these three fountains flow three sorts of religious life, as distinct from one another as their sources are. One we may call the religion of calculation, the second the religion of duty, the third the religion of holy love. This last is pre-eminently the religion of Christ. It is what we find in the New Testament. It is our gospel. Here the willing and affectionate heart, touched by grace, and springing freely up to the Father, adores no longer a judge, but a friend; not a lawgiver merely, but a redeemer. It takes up all the law, but looks at it in the light of love. It keeps the commandments, but from another motive, — not *as* commandments, but as the will of Him whom it delights to honor, and in whose bosom it longs forever to dwell.

We have now prepared ground from which we can look more clearly at the rewards God promises to those that diligently seek him. They depend, in each case, on the motive and spirit in which we serve him.

First of all, then, religion will never yield its true rewards to those that seek it *for the sake* of its rewards. It deals very frankly with us, having no concern to make proselytes under false pretences. It is willing we should understand that those who court it for anything else than its Giver's sake will meet perpetual disappointment. Whatever else they may get, it will not be Christian peace. Men may carry their selfishness into their religion, or rather into certain religious formalities and observances, as into everything else. But they will bring away only what they take in. If you espouse the Christian cause only to better your social position, or your business prospects, you will find you have grasped a phantom. You only provide an accumulated fund of shame, against the hour when the secrets of all hearts shall be laid open. Under the pretence of seeking God, you have only put on a mask, and gone on seeking and serving yourself. God has never engaged to be a "rewarder" of such; for it is not *Him* that they seek.

But suppose you rise a step above this covetousness for outward gain, and enter on what is called a religious life for a better kind of comfort, — as, for example, to obtain relief for sorrow, or the satisfaction of self-approval. No man can say that in such cases God may not lead the soul on, through this half-selfish state, into serving him for some more disinterested affection. His compassion is boundless; the very contact of the mind with him in any way is hallowing; and he is willing to save to the uttermost the weary and stricken hearts that lift their eyes from earth to heaven. But just so long and just to the same extent as their motive is personal comfort, they will fail of any glorious reward. I have known persons to be so haunted and scourged by some great grief or suffering, that they were ready to try any new prescription, to get rid of the aching. They begin at the wrong point, with a wrong idea, and cannot succeed. What they need first of all is a renunciation of the worldly and selfish heart they are still carrying in their bosoms, and because it is offensive to the pure God; what they need is repentance and a renewed life inwardly; what they need is the change that will put them at once into thorough reconciliation by faith with the spirit of Christ, fixing their chief interest to a new centre. Gaining this, regardless of comfort, and willing to suffer on, even, if that should be the Divine purpose, so entire is their subjection of unworthy self to the blessed Hand,—saying, with the great-hearted patriarch, "Though he slay me, yet will I trust in him,"—comfort will come fast enough of itself; and precisely because they did not ask nor think of rewards,—knowing, in fact, that, sinners as they were, they deserved none, and if they had done their very best had done only what was their duty to do,—the most splendid of all rewards will suddenly appear.

There is a deeper meaning than we sometimes seize

in that saying, that God will reward every man "*according* to his works,"—not merely in proportion to his works, and in some way or other, but in one way, and that way according to his works, in the line of his works, in the kind of them,—love for love, purity for purity, faith for faith,—heaven, which is perfect holiness, for holiness. Precisely in that temper Paul said, "What is my reward, then, for preaching the gospel? Verily, that when I preach the gospel, I may make the gospel of Christ without charge." So Christ puts the disinterested spirit at the very centre and core of the whole message: Drink of my cup, be baptized with my baptism,—no matter where you sit, on thrones or footstools! Do good and lend, hoping for nothing again, and your reward shall be great; for ye shall be the children of the Highest.

In this honorable quality, man's Christian service is not disconnected from his best acts in other lines of life. The higher sentiments answer with Antipater of Macedon, who, being presented with a work on happiness, replied that he had no time to study happiness. Those memorable and inspired deeds that waken the world's delight, and live on its tongue, are never done for a price. All heroic achievements, the sublime sacrifices of man for man, of ease for right, of life for love, of self for country, stand clear of calculation for reward. The moment history has to say of a man, "He did it for pay, and took his wages,—he played the hero by bargain," that moment she strikes him from her catalogue of heroes, and kindles her enthusiasm at other fountains. The friendship that gives blood and breath for a friend, the martyrdom that is borne cheerfully for faith, the patriotism that faces death or crucifixions of feeling worse than death, — these and all of the same high race of magnanimities spring from uncalculating affections. So our instincts demand, and so the facts testify. In these august enterprises of the soul, all thought of recompense and even of obligation, is gone. Moral revolutions are not brought to market. Oppressed peoples are not set free for a consideration. Terrible wrongs are not righted with an eye to the main chance. A state is never made illustrious by its office-seekers. A church will never "arise and shine, the glory of the Lord being risen upon it," through the agency of those who are ambitious to enjoy its dignities and administer its affairs, — whether Hildebrands and Gregorys, or village popes and parish demagogues. And in the quiet joys of every-day life, and the graces of household devotion, the delicious charm and the beauty never lie in the computed service, but in the willing offering for love's dear sake alone.

If these are the nobilities of man elsewhere, we need not hesitate to recognize them as legitimate in our Christianity. Indeed, it is Christianity that interprets and sanctions them. When we go down into its deeps, through the words of Jesus, or through the lives and confessions of its strongest believers, or through a profound experience, we come to the same discovery. Man is meant to live his best life, not because he must, not because he shall smart and ache if he does not, nor yet because he shall be made happy, — he, in his little selfish paradise of personal comfort, if he does. Christ's gospel holds another language, offers a more inspiring doctrine, reads man's deeper soul by a heavenlier lamp. Its central idea is self-sacrifice. Its everlasting symbol is a cross. Its universal sentiment is love. All its apparatus of punishments and rewards, threats and promises, — which are certainly very real and very frequent, — is to educate us up to that mark, at last. If we are far below it, the law as law must come in to train us up to it. Command, obligation, duty, must rule and discipline us in that elementary stage. The law is our schoolmaster to lead us on to Christ, just as in earthly schools the scholar is taught, by coercion, to live and learn from higher motives. In the framework of a compulsory discipline, he grows up to seek knowledge for its own sake and to study from love of it, which is the highest result of any education. Duties, Christ teaches, must be done as duties, work as work, till in the regenerate spirit of his own self-forgetful devotion we do them spontaneously, or do them even as he died for us, for love.

Here, too, we shall find the peculiar and distinctive ministry which the Christian Revelation brings. Precisely what the world wanted was a being near, visible, palpable, — good enough, gracious and divine enough, to inspire an affection or a faith of such mighty energy as to breathe in this new motive, and start the moral life of men from a new point. And this came in Christ, our living, suffering Lord. The unseen Jehovah had done much for his people; but in the distant deific Providence man had not seen yet that last and crowning proof of mercy, a willingness to suffer for the beloved's sake. In Christ, in all his humiliation, and most of all at Gethsemane and Calvary, that is embodied. And whosoever has in him the grateful and believing sense of it, is a new creature. He lives again. He lives forever. It is the regeneration. It is the Life Eternal.

No more to sit on the right hand or the left of kingly power and splendor; no more for outward reward, no more for fear, no more as a servant obeying the rigorous and literal commandment; but as the loving child, with filial discipleship, he lives for God. All the weighty and striking words of the New Testament and its new and divine philosophy are fulfilled in him. He walks with Christ, rooted and built up in him. He has put on the Lord Jesus. Christ is verily formed within him, a new creation, a spiritual, personal life,—which is the life of self-forgetful, of more than obedient, of trusting love.

Nor can it be said, to derogate from the virtuous character of this unsordid fidelity, that it is merely impulsive, and partakes of the fitfulness and uncertainty of impulse. To be spontaneous, and to be impulsive, are not the same thing. The acts of the maturest, most rational, most thoroughly disciplined saint may be just as spontaneous and just as natural as the simplest instincts of the child. It only requires that the inward life shall be so full, so harmonized, and so holy, that its acts shall proceed, as it were, unconsciously from it, by a choice so constant and ready that the mind does not seem even to choose. In fact, this is probably the highest result of religious discipline. Friction ceases. Effort is lost in free allegiance. Only it is now not instinct only, as in infancy, but the instinct of the convicted soul and principled conscience, of the man "born again of the Spirit" into the kingdom of Christ. It differs from the spontaneity of childhood, just as the purity of the man from the purity of the child. It has been tried by temptation, and had its fight with the world. There has been the struggle of passion and the warfare with evil. Between this and that lie all the conflict and trial and agony and experience of the converted heart and the developed life. They differ as Peter the consistent apostle, fervent and self-renouncing, from Peter the natural man, hot and self-asserting. Command has been obeyed. Law has done its work. But now constraint is swallowed up in the Christlike eagerness of doing good because it is good, and all things for the Father's glory.

The same principle must be applied to the desire of going to heaven as a motive to religious endeavor. Just so far forth as I desire to go to heaven for the sake of any personal pleasures to be enjoyed there, because it is a place where there is more ease, or an endless round of festivities and happy excitements, so far I degrade the true conception of heaven and prepare a certain disappointment for myself. But if we hope for the next life as a scene of larger spiritual freedom, nobler opportunities, and an escape from all sin and meanness, we are right to long for our immortality. The kingdom of Heaven is a state of spiritual purity, not meat and drink. This is the sense in which Christ always holds out to us the promise of a hereafter. "Set your affections on things above," he says, i. e. noble, exalted, disinterested, divine things, — eternal truth, a Christlike life, God's love, angelic holiness, — not easy, comfortable, pleasant, good-tasting things. When he says, "Your reward shall be great in heaven," he is speaking of disinterested conduct, and he means that its whole consciousness and feeling shall be lofty and serene as heaven, — and he assures the spiritually minded who have faith in him that they shall have eternal life. But he nowhere offers us heaven as a price for good behavior, as foolish parents, or rather wicked parents, hire their children to obey with sweetmeats and toys. It is in no such sense as this that he engages to be a rewarder of them that seek him. The very passage just quoted discredits such a thought; for it says, "If ye love them that love you, what reward have ye?" There must be spontaneous service. The heart must go into it, uncalculating and ungrudging. You must love your enemies, do good to them that hate you, and bless them that curse you, and lend hoping for nothing again. Then you will be children of the Highest; and, precisely because you expected no reward at all, verily your reward shall be great.

There is a striking legend of saintly old Bishop Ivo, who walked with God, and saw through the self-seeking religionists of his time, and longed for larger faith. He describes himself as meeting, one day, a figure in the form of woman, of a sad, earnest aspect, like some prophetess of God, who carried a vessel of fire in one hand, and of water in the other. He asked her what these things were for. She answered, The fire is to burn up Paradise, and the water is to quench Hell,—that men may henceforth serve their Maker, not from the selfish hope of the one, nor for the selfish fear of the other, but for love of himself alone. God does not consume Paradise, nor quench Hell. He keeps the fountains of sweet and living waters leaping and flowing in the one; he keeps the awful fires of the other burning. But surely all this promise and penalty do not mean that we are to stop in their discipline, and calculate the price of our obedience. O no! Not while the glorious voice of the Apostle rings out over the centuries, "The love of Christ constraineth me: I count all things loss for the excellency of the knowledge of him." Not while the Saviour says to the aspiring heart of the world, "Be ye perfect, even as your Father in heaven is perfect," "hoping for nothing again."

So we come up at last to those acts of the true religion — our Christian religion — which are done in the faith of the heart; and here we reach the highest view of the Divine rewards, simply because God has made these to be their own reward. The reward is in doing them; in the inevitable feeling that goes along with them, far enough from being set about as the end, but interwoven with them by the gracious bounty that ever surprises faithful souls. With all these true acts and emotions of the really spiritually-minded man, it is precisely as it is with any of those acts of common life that the heart goes most into. You cannot speak of any rewards for the love that is the bond of a true marriage, without insulting those to whom you speak. You cannot connect the notion of compensation, pay, with the affection that twines a child's arms about the mother's neck, or that keeps her waiting, in vigils that outwatch the patient stars, over the child's pain or sin, without profaning that affection. You cannot associate the prospect of a reward with the heroic humanity which keeps the friendly vessels hanging close, many days and nights, in the frightful companionship of a common peril, to take off the passengers of the imperilled and sinking ship; nor with any generous and brave rescue or sacrifice. Now, to any spiritual estimate, the services of daily piety are as full of the charm and fascination and glory of self-forgetting devotion as any of these. Christ is nearer than wife or husband. The

Father in heaven is more real, and infinitely holier and tenderer, than the human mother. All fellow-souls in moral misery or sin need help more urgently than the shipwrecked company. And so, if our piety is real, like Christ's piety, it must be just as self-oblivious, as hearty, as spontaneous and free, as that. And then it will have a more unspeakable, glorious, infinite reward.

These, then, are the Divine Rewards. They are rewards in kind. They are large just according to the spirituality of our lives, the zeal of our worship, the strength of our faith. They are interior, not visible. They are incidental, not sought. They are of nobleness, rather than of happiness. Sometimes "the Rewarder of them that diligently seek him" will reward the true Christian soul by giving him a strengthening and encouraging consciousness of harmony with the divine will; sometimes by taking him out from under the power of temptation, or a straitened self-accusation, and setting his feet in a large place; sometimes by redoubling his spiritual energy and quickening his Christian activity, breathing a prompter zeal into all the secret forces of his being, through the unseen agencies of the Holy Spirit; sometimes by giving him a blessed sense of renunciation, of having given up all to Him to whom all of right belongs, together with an exalted sense of liberty from all limitations of appetite and ambition; sometimes by affording us greater satisfaction in our appointed struggles and our every-day drudgery, and sometimes, too, by granting us — provided we do not ask it too eagerly, as if it were better for us than toil — an inward peace, or rest from care and from strife and from fear, passing all understanding, — such as the world never gave.

I have read of a devoted sister of charity who, year after year, attended a division of the army of France in every campaign, to care for the wounded and watch with the sick. Her energy, courage, gentleness, and presence of mind saved many lives, and gained her the reverence and admiration of officers and men. On the field of slaughter and agony, her impartial, Christlike compassion made no distinction between her own people and the enemy; and three foreign empires — Russia, Austria, and Prussia — conferred upon her crosses of honor. From her own nation it was contrary to the rules of her order that she should receive any badge or decoration, as a reward for her services. But the gratitude of the generous soldiers found out a way to remunerate her as beautiful as it was appropriate. Knowing well whence her lofty pleasures sprang, they petitioned and obtained for her, from the minister of war, the privilege of pardoning, every year, two criminals condemned to death. This is what I mean by rewards *in kind.* It gives us, I think, some feeble conception of what may be the noble joy and the sp recompense of heaven.

> "For when the power of imparting good
> Is equal to the will, the human soul
> Requires no other heaven."

"If we love one another, God dwelleth in us."

But, O greater mystery yet, which faith must still accept or die, — for God leads us to himself through ways that we know not, — he rewards us sometimes, in his deepest love, only by setting us to the performance of larger and harder tasks; only by beckoning us on to steeper heights, with sharper rocks, where we must climb; only by handing down to us grander opportunities of endurance; only by calling us on and up, with his own animating voice, to some more splendid because more grievous sacrifices. These also, to the truly brave and truly consecrated heart, are rewards. On the heads of some of his children God sets special sufferings as crowns of honor, as signs what great things he has yet in reserve for them, because he will make these crosses ladders of light whereby they shall ascend nearer to himself. And to all that are truly his, when he would give his greatest reward, he gives himself, the Holy Spirit, in his Son. Or, if we will have it set in music, we shall find it in a brave and lofty hymn of Francis Xavier:

"My God, I love thee, not because
I hope for heaven thereby;
Nor because they who love thee not
Must burn eternally.

"Thou, O my Jesus, thou didst me
Upon the cross embrace; —
For me didst bear the nails and spear,
And manifold disgrace;
And griefs and torments numberless,
And sweat of agony, —
E'en death itself, — and all for one
Who was thine enemy!

"Then why, O blessed Jesus Christ,
Shall I not love thee well,
Not for the sake of winning heaven —
Or of escaping hell, —
Not with the hope of gaining aught,
Not seeking a reward,
But as thyself hast lovéd me,
O ever-loving Lord!"

It is well to seek salvation; — that old phraseology is not mistaken. Only we must remember salvation is not a thrifty, self-promoting concern, by which we just graze and enter the gates of Eden, and get somehow landed in a place of comfort, where there is no hard work. Christian salvation is a spiritual state, here or hereafter, where nobler and heartier service can be done for God and man. That is a weighty saying of St. Augustine: "God counts among the reprobate not only those who have received their comfort on earth, but those who grieve because they have not." It is right to exhort men to make sure their calling and election in heaven. Only, we must remember, heaven is not a spot to lie down in, and there, on our couches, tuning our harps, to think how much misery we have personally escaped. The Christian heaven is an exalted society of self-sacrificing spirits, bound together in mutual fellowship by their common consecration to Him who is above them, where each accepted soul will go from strength to strength, run and not be weary, toil and not faint, aspire and not be baffled, do good and not be misinterpreted, and will be assimilated in ever closer and closer affinity to Him who is its Light and Life, in whom whosoever liveth and believeth shall never die.

Let us fearlessly carry our standard beyond the old line of our inferior moods. And if any of us find we are asking for a religion that shall make us comfortable, or put us at ease, be sure we are asking, out of a false spirit, what no reverential prayer should dare to petition, — what cannot be, — and are no longer in a posture to receive the Master's gifts, nor the favor of our God. For of our Christian religion the badge is a cross, — even as self-forgetfulness is the spirit, love is the motive, disinterestedness is the principle, faith is the inmost spring, "Believe on the Lord Jesus Christ" the first lesson and the last.

SERMON XIV.

THE SECRET OF THE NEW NAME.

TO HIM THAT OVERCOMETH WILL I GIVE A WHITE STONE, AND IN THE STONE A NEW NAME WRITTEN, WHICH NO MAN KNOWETH SAVING HE THAT RECEIVETH IT. — Rev. ii. 17.

THE Book which is the grand interpreter of man's inward nature and relations makes repeated references to the sacred power of names. In the Biblical view, to give anything a name is to perform an act of religion. What is it? It is to apply to some individual object, having God for its maker, that sign by which it shall be known, separated from other things, and called: and surely that ought to be done reverently, as in the presence of Him from whom all things came, and to whom all things are known. In the original design, it cannot be doubted that God meant there should be some special correspondence between the qualities of each thing and the name it bears. This gives to names their highest significance, makes them descriptions or pictures, and in a manner judgments, of the object they are applied to. And when we think of the moral consequences that may be involved, it is not strange that in the Divine history of the creation such prominence is given to that critical and privileged hour when "the Lord brought every beast of the field and every fowl of the air to Adam, to see what he would call them: and whatsoever Adam called every living creature, that was the name thereof." To every discoverer, explorer, inventor, and original mind in science, the same privilege and trust and duty have been committed, in a degree, ever since.

When we rise to the plane of human life, this same sanctity of names becomes more evident yet. Because then they come to stand not only for individual existences, but for conscious beings. They discriminate not things, but persons, with will, conscience, purpose, accountableness, and every other attribute of personality. They mark off soul from soul, among the infinite ranks and gradations of the immortal family, on earth and in heaven, that no man can number. It must be for this high reason that the first and characteristic ordinance of the Christian Church — Baptism — is associated with the giving to the person of his proper name, —his Christian name, we say. It means the recognition before the Father, the Son, the Holy Ghost, — all of these august and separate *names* to be spoken there,— the recognition of the child's personal being, yet as belonging to the social body or Family in the Church. The old Church-catechisms tacitly assume the same truth. If you ask those who profoundly comprehend the spirit beneath their letter, they will tell you that first question — "What is your name?" — is put to the candidate, on his way to the Lord's table, and put even when the name is well known to the questioner, to point to the fact of separate, responsible life; because the Head of the Church asks a personal relation to each member by name, and would appeal to the inmost soul of the young disciple, making him think who he is, whose he is, and how he shall answer for himself when he is called again at the Judgment; "singling that special child out from all the millions," — making him stand alone, and "confess that he is a person," with a life's work to do that none can do for him, a person whom Christ died to redeem. This is what they will tell you, to explain that question. Christ himself once very tenderly and strikingly affirms his intimate personal remembrance and regard for every such member, even the least and the weakest, where he says that he, the Good Shepherd, calls every one of his own by their names. What the organs or modes of communication shall be in the spiritual world, is beyond us. But, if we we were in the habit of connecting, in our common thoughts, the life we are living now with the life that we live after death, as much as the spiritual laws allow us, and as much as simple Christianity teaches us and all holy comfort entreats us to do, then we should account it nothing unnatural that our Christian names should attend our identities everywhere; and that, at our final awaking hereafter, love and sympathy should call us by the same names that were so dear and so definite on earth, — the same, perhaps, and yet "new" names, because so modified, in the language of the skies, that each shall betray the quality or character of the life that has been lived in the body, — the name a judgment.

If we ascend still higher, from the human to the Divine, the power of names is more signally manifested yet. Him whom no eye hath seen, nor ear heard, nor hand touched, we yet know by his wonderful and Almighty name, — our God. It is striking that the Scriptures everywhere speak of the "name" of the Lord as of the Lord himself. His name is his glory, his presence, his power, his wisdom, his person, — and it is the only outward sign, or bond, of personal communication between him and us who are allowed to make no image of him. How impressive, too, that when his great manifestation is to be made in humanity, it is declared that the eternal *word* is made flesh. That is the *uttered* Divinity, — the God pronounced, communicated to man, through the incarnation. And when we breathe the universal prayer of childhood and age, taught us by the Saviour, we entreat first of all, "Hallowed be thy *name!*" In the dawn of Hebrew history, by the voices of prophecy, God gave his people a memorial *name*, by which he should be known forever, — Jehovah, — a seal upon his covenant with them, a name of promise, pointing to a deliverance to come, a Saviour, a Messiah; and that mighty name stood, on the lips and in the mind of the chosen tribes, through centuries of trial and expectation, an impregnable defence, an inexhaustible hope, an unfailing herald of redemption to come. After the Redeemer appeared, the universal command to Christendom was that its prayers should be lifted to the Father "in the name" of Christ.

So we arrive at the point of the text: "To him that overcometh," saith that Faithful and True Witness, the First and the Last, "will I give to eat of the hidden manna, and will give him a white stone, and in the stone a new name written, which no man knoweth saving he that receiveth it." I suppose most readers feel that, besides what the understanding clearly grasps in this sentence, there goes along a certain mystery of suggestion, an influence not defined, making up a part of the beauty, and indeed a part of the power, of the promise. It leads us to expect more than we can exactly shape, and so stimulates wonder as well as faith. This is often true of the higher utterances, the raised expression of poetic or prophetic states, where more comes to the soul than precise phrases can carry. Much of the associative impression of sacred language is of this sort; another more open part of our nature than the reason is addressed and moved, especially where the imagination is made an active vehicle of the spiritual message, as in the Apocalypse, where the text occurs. The hearts of children are often lifted we know, to reverence and holy moods, by passages they cannot analyze nor interpret; and before the infinite truths told us here from heaven the strongest intellects are little more than children.

The likeliest explanation of the writer's figure is found by a reference to an ancient custom connected with the public games. The victor, "he that overcometh," among other honors was presented with a white stone — *tessera* — with his name inscribed on it. Such a stone was often of two parts, each bearing a portion of the name, and was thus used as a talisman or secret token between friends or families. None but the two parts made for each other completed the device. Each, whenever presented, in whatever part of the world, would instantly match into its place, and constitute the bearer's passport to kindness and favor with the kindred of its fellow's owner. One of the Roman poets (Plautus) alludes to such a tally where the name of a Deity was engraved, as well as those of the parties pledged. The original cause or incidents of the alliance were the secrets hidden by the emblem, hidden to all but the holders. And the rights of hospitality, secured by this badge, seem to be the occasion of that other allusion in the same verse to the "hidden manna," thus filling out the metaphor.

This much we find hinted to us, at least, by way of verbal interpretation; and it is enough. The spiritual truth which the veil of figure covers can hardly be mistaken. He that overcometh — every victorious soul prevailing by faith and by righteousness in the long and patient battle of life — shall have secret satisfactions springing up in his heart, known only between himself and his Lord. They will not consist in outward applauses, in visible successes, in any worldly compensations whatever. The chief of them all will be the silent assurances of His personal affection, who is the purest, highest, holiest. The testimony of his friendship will be the best reward. The token of his favor will be the inestimable good. So much light does advancing excellence always cast on old forms of truth, a deeper life ever illuminating even familiar oracles, that the very name of the Christ shall have a new meaning. It shall be a new name. It shall have a personal charm and preciousness to each several believer. None shall know it as he knoweth it that receiveth it. No man *ever* knows the meaning of our deeper experiences, or of the words that express them, as we know them ourselves. Just as the Almighty said to the great Jewish leader and lawgiver, when he declared to him his memorial-name, "By that name thy fathers did not know me," though they had used that name for hundreds of years, — meaning that in their less luminous state and backward education they did not comprehend or realize what the name contained, — so, to each growing nature of man the significance of every sacred word gains depth and clearness at every step of his way. What was dark to unbelief is bright to faith. What was perplexing to the beginner in Christian living is simple and radiant if he perseveres. The very name of the Source and Spring of the world's only perfect spiritual illumination, Christ, has no attraction and no interest to those whose daily habit is alien from him. But let any walk in his way, adopt his spirit, be joined to his society, and then another feeling shall invest that name, give it beauty, and open its gracious meaning, and make it a name above every name, — a new name, to which every knee must bow, — known only to him that receiveth it.

Let us divide, and state in their order, the principal points of Christian truth which seem to start, for our practical instruction and encouragement, out of this mystical promise of the Apocalypse.

I. The first of these is the strict and private individuality of all real religious experience. When the profounder feelings of some persons begin to be stirred, as their penitence for a misspent life, or their conviction of the hollowness of all mere external virtue, they become uneasy at the strength and solemnity of their emotions. They run out to dilute their conscience in mixtures with society. They are afraid of themselves, and of those sober self-questionings that are their best friends. Instead of letting the wholesome process of conviction go on with thoroughness, in solitude, till they fathom their hearts, and find out their evil, and rouse from their danger, they are frightened to find themselves in the strong and unfamiliar hands of religious repentance, and retreat into positions more genial, but less honest and less brave.

We cannot come right with God and his truth till we are able to confront the facts in our own breasts, and accept their rebuke. Sooner or later, some monitory Providence comes and searches us, and shows that the path to God's right hand is in great part a lonely one. For such souls as have undertaken the higher life with Christ in earnest, it is enough that the Infinite and Unchangeable One shall be on their side, and comprehend their struggle, and call each one of them by His own name, at the end of the conflict, and give "to him that overcometh" that token of secret recognition which he "knoweth that receiveth it."

II. A second characteristic of that true inward life which the text implies is that its rewards are not such as can be described beforehand. No man knoweth them saving he that receiveth them. They remain to come out, and be felt unexpectedly in their place. The very result the religion of Christ undertakes to achieve in men's hearts is disinterested devotion. The instant the idea of a literal compensation is brought forward, therefore, the essential doctrine is denied. Virtue under pay is no longer virtue. Stipulated wages and heart's love are distinct motives. The principle of implicit submission to the Infinite Goodness, or of an eager reception of heavenly favor through a grateful faith, is a totally separate thing from the notion of earning a self-satisfied heaven by a quantum of deserts, and of establishing a claim on a Divine creditor by a square account with his demands. It is not strange to find thoughtful and wise persons, as they go farther into life and deeper into acquaintance with themselves and other men, gradually giving up as preposterous the idea of anybody's really being saved by his merits, or a Christless salvation; — i. e. of being such a keeper of the perfect law of God as to be lifted into a fellowship with its author, and justified in claiming eternal happiness as a fair equivalent. Arrogance itself recoils from an insolence so audacious. If we are never to feel ourselves friends and co-workers and children with God till we have bought that place by legal conformity, we must give up the whole hope. It is another relation altogether. Obedience itself, or the constant prayer and effort for it, springs from a different root. It is a penitent, dependent, spontaneous movement of the unselfish soul, towards the Almighty love, for its own sake. Faith is not hired. Why, even in all the loftier and purer human relationships, affection scorns the calculations of self-interest. There is not a tie of holy friendship on earth but feels itself insulted by the suggestion of a price. That preacher aggrieves the finest natures he speaks to, and practically wrongs the whole spirit of the Gospel he professes to administer, who appeals to people to believe in God, and follow the Crucified, only for the sake of winning a paradise of comfort, or of escaping a pit full of pain. Doubtless, the scriptural language considers all the mixed conditions of human want, and condescends to stimulate our low and impoverished aspirations by promises of rest and joy. But read on, — read all; ponder and compare; see where its celestial philosophy culminates, — and you find that it does not leave the disciple till it points him to Love as the fulfilling of the law; till it carries him up above offers of hire to a self-forgetful passion for excellence; till it fastens the supreme appeal on the voluntary sufferings of One who gave himself freely for us; till it makes the cross the symbol of its spirit. Heaven has no element of idle or exclusive privilege in it. The disciple shall not have places pledged on the right hand or left, but drink of the Master's cup, be "near and like his Lord." This personal nearness and assimilation will be enough. Then we shall be able to take up, and repeat, and pray ourselves, this prayer of Bradwardine, — a brave believer of ages ago, — kneeling there in the twilight of a darker time, but closer, I think, than most of our modern piety to Olivet and Gethsemane: "Thyself, my God, I love, for thyself, and above all things. Thyself for thyself, and not for aught else, I will always and in all things seek: — with my heart and all my strength, with groaning and weeping, — with continual labor and grief. What, therefore, wilt thou give me as my final end? If thou givest me not thyself, thou givest me nothing. Thou dost not then reward, but torture me. If thou deniest me thyself, and that forever, whatever else thou givest me, shall I not always languish, mourn, and weep, because I remain ever empty? Grant therefore, O my gracious God, that in the present life I may ever love thyself for thyself, above all things; and in the future world may I find thee and hold thee forever." "To him that overcometh shall be given a white stone, and in the stone a new name written, which no man knoweth saving he that receiveth it."

III. Another branch of the same great truth, and one that we of these times need much to realize, is that a Christian piety is to be prized for its secret intrinsic quality, rather than for its quotable results. No man knoweth it like him that hath it. Its hidden testimonies are worth more than its public demonstrations. Those who look for the latter will be perpetually discovering disappointments; and then, if their faith leans on the visible return, faith fails with the failing harvest. Some things must be held as settled, whether they gain many converts or few. The moment we begin to measure the actual power or blessedness of our convictions by counting the number of their disciples, we have inflicted the grossest affront on the spirit of truth. This constant reference to outward responses and results vitiates the very essence and spirit of righteousness, as it does of every pure and sacred feeling. Being religious for effect spoils the effect, — like being honest for effect, or humble for effect, or affectionate or chaste for effect. It runs straight to a base hypocrisy, and not only abolishes its own influence, but begets a general scepticism of sincerity which blights every high interest, and unsettles virtue itself. Faith must dwell in her own sanctuary, see by her own light, feed on her own secret and immortal manna, be content with her own joy, cling to the white stone with the ineffable name, and wait for her spiritual justification and victory. It is when religion begins to think more of keeping the people safe, civilization progressive, and the public decent, by its forms and professions, than of keeping the heart clean and holy by its silent intercourse with God, that it ceases to be religion, and degenerates into a policy. The grandest testimony to Christianity is a soul penetrated and hallowed by its light. No influence like real conviction. No plea like consistency. Society will come right when its members have overcome in their private warfare, and are inwardly at one with Christ. The people will be safe when individual worldliness is dislodged, and the searching Spirit of God finds the hidden doors of the heart open. Institutions will be vital enough, and "broad" enough, and full enough, when this personal soul, and that one, and each one, has given its affection and its trust to the Head and Former of the Fold.

There is encouragement, as well as trial, in this sharp demand on the individual. The promise goes with the command. True, it makes it hard to commend the real satisfactions of a Christian life to those that will not try them. That can never be very effectually done. Literal descriptions of the delights of believing inspire no adequate emotion. Language itself is too feeble a medium. After you have exhausted the rhetoric of jubilant encomium, the untouched hearer says, "If that is all, the poets and painters of this world's joy match your kingdom of heaven." The sense is wanting which can appreciate or even comprehend what you say. Far better serve these dim but large and moving symbols of Scripture, like the image of the text, stirring hope but never bounding it: the white stone with the new name which no man knoweth saving he that receiveth it. What Jeremy Taylor says of mysticism is true, in some degree, of all deep Christian spirituality, — that whereas, in other sciences, the terms must be known first, and then the rules and conclusions, here the experience must first be obtained before we can so much as know what it is. But then, on the other hand, the end is not dependent on language, nor on mortal tuition. It comes by the simple and ever-waiting gift of God, like the light in the sky, to every willing and believing heart. Formularies are not its vehicles. Terms are not necessary to it. Articles and rules do not monopolize it. If thou believest with all thine heart, thou mayest be baptized into the full, deep peace of a disciple. He that doeth righteousness, in every nation, is accepted. Understanding shall grow with growing earnestness of purpose. And he that tries heartily to do Christ's will shall know of the doctrine; know it more and more; know it deeper and deeper; know all that he needs.

To selfish, earth-bound hearts no secrets are revealed. No tokens of personal remembrance, no signs of secret favor, come from the Master. True redemption is our deliverance from that restless selfishness, and our return to union with God So far the old mystics were right. No mastery among men, no conquests of self-promotion, no prosperous economy, no career of politic success, contains a joy so exquisite, and so full, as that pledge of friendship from the love and power and wisdom that fill the throne of Eternity. If any reply that it has a strange, unpractical sound, the believer can only take up his Master's repeated saying, with its undertone of mournful compassion, appeal and lamentation together, "He that hath ears to hear let him hear." Treatises on the laws of sound would not bear in the music upon our finer sense, if heavenly anthems were to float down upon us through the midnight air. As I write these sentences an illustration comes to me through the outward senses. A stately company of sorrowful mounted soldiers are bearing out the lifeless form of their commander to burial. His horse, saddled but riderless, walks alone behind the hearse. Rising and falling on the waves of the solemn Sunday evening wind come, from the blended instruments, the melodious measures of that wonderful, weeping, supplicating dirge, — the Dead March in Saul, — swelling slowly through the streets, winding over field and river, penetrating the silent chambers of the sick and dying, hush-ing even the children's talk in a hundred homes, till all the sympathizing elements and features of the scene — the still trees and waters, the drooping clouds, the fading sunset — seem to join the funeral procession, and weep with them that weep. But withdraw yourself a moment from that august impression, where death is made so real, — look along the crowded groups that gather to gaze and listen. On some subdued faces the moving power has visibly descended, and they wait, perhaps they worship, in this awful sanctuary of grief, — amidst these irresistible harmonies. But others prattle and gossip and jest, even there. Levity must have its laugh, and the frivolous must trifle, and irreverence see only the glitter of the uniforms and the sable plumes, — even where the faithful tomb is unveiling its bosom to take this new treasure to its trust, and Life and Death are lifting together the curtains of the "illustrious morn." O yes! It is ever so, and ever must be. There are shut souls, that having eyes will not see, and having ears will not hear, though the vision be open, and the voice as the voice of many waters, and of a great thunder, and of harpers harping with their harps. None the less do the Eternal Truth and the Eternal Way stand fast, and offer themselves in mercy inexhaustible to the needy heart of "whosoever will." Christ is that Truth. Personal union with him is that Way. To know him thus in the first faint feeling of grateful trust is the beginning of discipleship. To know him finally, in the fulness of his mediation and Lordship, by his "New Name," will be glory and honor and immortality. Then will be the joy of recognition, — the Great Friend seen no longer as "through a glass, darkly," but "face to face." And then, not as the believing little child, who asked, when dying, that her Testament might be buried in her hand, that she might hold it up on coming into the Saviour's presence, lest otherwise he might not know her in the great multitude, but as the victorious seer of Patmos expected, — we shall receive from himself the token of an immaterial covenant, the "New Name," written not in the outward letter, but in the secret testimony and intuition of the Word that is from the beginning and Everlasting.

IV. It has been implied all along, as a chief doctrine lying at the very heart of this passage, as it lies at the heart of the Gospel itself, that the special character and privilege of the Christian rest in a personal and conscious union between him and his living Redeemer. We vex our ingenuity straining after comprehensive definitions of the distinctive thing in Christianity. They are all superficial and irrelevant compared with this. How uniform and majestic the testimony that rises from all the lands and ages of faith to this simple truth, — that it is not rules of conduct, not systems of ethics, not patterns of propriety, not eloquent expositions, that inspire the believing and faithful heart with its immortal energy and peace, — but the simple, secret assurance of being at one with the Lord Jesus, and resting in his Almighty friendship! Where is the fiery furnace deep enough to burn despair into our souls, if we can see walking with us through the fire the form of the Son of God? What, then, is the tribulation, or famine, or sword, or nakedness, that shall separate us from the love of God in Christ Jesus our Lord? The mystery of that unity where He who is one with God yet cried, "Not as I will, but as Thou wilt," is not for us to understand. Yet the prayer of promise, "They shall be with me where I am," is for us to lay hold of, and breathe again and again, when we are aching and alone and troubled. So the believers have found. When the brilliant, amiable, and accomplished young Italian woman, Olympia Morata, whose learning and loveliness graced the splendid epoch of Leo X., had become the persecuted victim of Romish tyranny for honoring Christ above a polluted priesthood, then poverty, sickness, desolation, exile, tried their worst upon her constancy. After she who had been the delicate nursling of courts and letters had fled across the stony fields of Bavaria, with literally bare and bleeding feet, the strength of the frail body failing, she bent under the roughness of fortune, and quietly lay down to die. To one of her noble friends in Italy she wrote, "Let the word of God be the rule of thy life, the lamp upon thy path, and thou wilt not stumble." As the purple flood of life ebbed in her thin, white frame, she said, "I desire to die, because I know *the secret* of death. The cunning mechanism is near to its dissolution. I desire to die, that I may be with Jesus Christ, and find in him eternal life. Do not be disturbed at my death, for I shall conquer in the end; I *desire* to depart and be with Christ." *With Christ!* So, the world over, and through all ages, in the first century or the last, the true heart of faith answers, in its final and glorified hour, to the prayer of Jesus, "With me, where I am."

And the same devotion to God's will that is the solace of distress is the inspiration of labor. We have not ascended to the loftiest and worthiest motive of all well-doing till we have reached this mark. You and I, in this little day of life, and with these poor powers, can verily do something to further the purposes and glory of the ineffable Name. Could that thought penetrate our common avocations, business, hospitality, trades, studies, to what a height of sacred dignity would it lift them, and of what dross and meanness, and selfish grossness, and besotted care, would it purge them clean!

We have, in our present state, a visible institution or household, which is meant to stand as the image and the threshold of the future society or family of those who are with Christ and in him. We call it, as Christ called it, the Church. It is the company of men and women, not presuming to have yet attained, but knowing in whom they have believed. There are many reasons for a sincere soul's belonging to it; and one of the best of these is, that a divine wisdom has so fitted it to our wants, that it is found that in its ordinances and its communion the heart has a special sense of being near to the Master, and strengthened by him. On the ground of this reasonable and affecting privilege, it throws wide open its hospitable arms, and bids all that think it good to be Christ's and Christlike, to come in. To the busy, tempted, world-beset man it offers guidance, and a memorial of him whom all the kingdoms of the world could not bend from right. To the anxious, suffering, loving, dependent, or fashion-urged woman, it offers the better part that nothing can take away, and the bliss of sins forgiven. To the dying it gives the bread and cup, the nutriment of that life which the body cannot imprison nor death detain. To thoughtful, prayerful, right-hearted youth it extends just the guidance, protection, encouragement, that youth needs.

The only condition the New Testament requires is a heart desiring it, and a sincere and settled faith in him who founded it. Baptism really seals the infant as the proper future subject of it. There is no mystery to puzzle a child's understanding, for it speaks only of love, sacrifice, a Saviour; and these are the very realities that we all have to become like little children to comprehend. The reckless, the selfish, the false, the profane, or those of ungoverned temper, will have no fitness for it; for there is too little in common between its hallowed meaning and them. But all who have been taught to love the Lord Jesus Christ in sincerity, and have yielded to the Shepherd's call, shall be placed like the lambs in his bosom, — that they may not stray neglected outside the blessed home-fold, but be sheltered and guarded within its endearing and loving enclosure. Tender hands can grasp the "white stone" that hath the new name written in it.

Nor are we without witnesses how, in answer to faith and prayer, to baptismal vows and the motherly call of the Church, bright and clear discernments of spiritual things, such as all of us might covet, sometimes shine out in the soul of childhood. I knew of a disciple of Christ whose whole earthly life was measured by nine short years. In her sickness she said to one of the family, "When I am dead, I wish my pastor might preach a sermon to children, to persuade them to love Jesus Christ, to obey their parents, and think more about heaven. I have been thinking I should like to have him preach from the text about the prophet Elisha and the child of the Shunamite, — 'Is it well with the child? and she answered, It is well.' The prophet will come to see you after I am gone, and when he says,

'How is it with the child?' you may say, 'It is well.' I am sure it will be well with me then, for I shall be in heaven, singing the praises of my Lord." — "Father, I will that they also whom thou hast given me be with me where I am." When the children in the Temple cried, "Hosanna to the Son of David," Jesus said, "Out of the mouth of babes and sucklings thou hast perfected praise."

Rejoice not, then, in any outward or selfish success, — not even that the spirits are subject unto you, but that your names are written in heaven, with the name of your Saviour. Seats of honor, on the right hand and the left, are not promised, — but to drink of the Master's cup, and to be baptized with the same baptism. Patiently and persistently, again and again, by all figures and comparisons, now by this image and now by that, Christ strives to bear up the minds of his followers above every material and earthly impression, to the realization of the blessed and unspeakable fellowship between the believing heart and himself: showing us the water of such secret satisfaction that he who tastes it never thirsts again; meat to eat that the world knows nothing of; the single inward eye lighting the whole body; the Shepherd calling his own sheep by name, — *by name*, — leading them out, and they knowing his voice.

Here is the conclusion. The satisfactions of a Christian life, however generous and humane, are secret and personal, as its burdens of repentance and conflict are. They must be tried, to be known. Whoever waits to know them by description waits in vain. He mistakes the law of the heavenly mind and the condition of the heavenly gift. Christ grants them to those only who give themselves to Him for their life. That life must be begun by each soul alone. Penitence, duty, faith, prayer, bear their own witness, and bring their own confirmations. We must trust ourselves to them, or they will not bless us. It is a personal experience. Each name has to stand clear in the Book of Life, written by him whose memorial Name is above every name. Only they whose names are found there shall be able to interpret the glory of his own.

SERMON XV.

CHRIST'S VICTORY OVER THE WORLD'S TRIBULATION.

IN THE WORLD YE SHALL HAVE TRIBULATION; BUT BE OF GOOD CHEER; I HAVE OVERCOME THE WORLD. John xvi. 33.

It is worth our thought, how small that audience must be that would assemble, life through, to listen to a Gospel that said nothing to sufferers, nothing to sorrow. How tiresome would be that monotony of superficial satisfaction! How the poor, weak hearts, aching and staggering under crosses, would refuse to come to a comforter that never wept, nor remembered that his followers must weep. Even those human companions who are ignorant of grief sometimes grow insupportably wearisome to our heavier moods. Their perpetual gale of hilarity grates upon our sensibilities, as unsympathizing as the east wind.

How much more unsatisfying a pretended Saviour, that was not himself a sufferer, or a worship which touched us only in our happier hours, but never went down into the depths of our darkness, with its grand condescension, to raise us in its holy arms, with the lifting up of its promises and the inspiration of its anthems, giving the garments of praise for the spirit of heaviness, and good cheer for tribulation!

A religion that should address itself only to persons in a state of comfort would be like a system of navigation that should calculate only for sailing in clear weather. The hours when a voyager needs the aids of science most are those when the night and the cloud have conspired to wipe out all waymarks from earth and sky, and robbed the rudder of its meaning; when the tempest shrieks over a sea with no north, no port, no light. Very little honor belongs, it is true, to that view of Christianity which represents it as suited to no seasons but funereal and gloomy ones. It is meant for the whole of our life, and sooner or later there comes from the common human heart in us a cry that nothing else will answer, and nothing else will still.

Christ confronts the fearful fact. He conceals nothing, disguises nothing, treats nothing timidly. He acknowledges the humiliating necessity for discipline. He frankly prophesies it. "In the world ye shall have tribulation." We have all known foolish parents that were willing to entice their children into acts of disagreeable submission, by promising there should be nothing disagreeable in them; so defrauding childhood both by a deception and a disappointment. The perfect Father never deals in that way with the hearts he would mould to his will. And so, when his Son is revealing that will, you see his sublime candor. The medicine, he says, must have a bitter taste; take it, nevertheless. Ye must be chastened; it is enough that the Lord loveth whom he chasteneth. Persecuted and reviled ye must be; blessed are ye, and rejoice if it is for the Son of Man's sake, who took persecution and reviling and pain for you.

It is no mere happiness of the jester and the trifler

that God desires for you. It is not the empty merriment of a convivial company, nor the physical composure of healthy nerves, nor the complacency of self-satisfaction. It is none of these. If it were, they might be had, perhaps, on cheaper terms, with no costly ritual of sacrifice. It is not "cheer" merely, observe, but "*good* cheer." It is a holy joy. It is "that peace which the world cannot give;" and which, as faith knows, the Saviour sufficiently describes when he calls it "*My* peace." To have his peace, you must first drink of his cup, be baptized with his baptism, take up his cross.

Woes, famines, and pestilences, in the spirit if not the flesh, are but the beginning of sorrows; see that ye be not troubled. The sun of your inward world shall be darkened, the moon not give her light, the stars fall from that heaven; but it is because the Son of Man cometh with power and glory in your soul. "Ye shall have tribulation;" for it is through much tribulation that any soul entereth into the kingdom of heaven. But "be of good cheer."

The "cheer" thus offered, then, does not forget trouble, but presupposes it. Christ does not undertake to give us happiness here unmixed, nor to give it by administering moral anodynes to blunt the sense of pain. He means rather to show us the ultimate joy to be gained by the suffering. He treats it as a necessity to our spiritual education; and so bids our fortitude face it, our submission accept it, our faith endure it, our Christian principle draw strength from it. There are three points: —

I. The necessity of suffering. "Ye must have tribulation."

II. The power and manner of Christ's victory. "I have overcome."

III. How it is a victory for us. "Be of good cheer."

I. Wherein this necessity that we should be troubled consists is a part of the insoluble problem of evil. It is one of the mortifying proofs what stubborn and unteachable pupils of the Divine Master we are, that no way could be found of bringing us to our immortality but through such a system of checks and penalties. We must be baffled, smitten, scourged; we must ache, and weep, and die; we must suffer the stripes of misfortune, of disease, of mortified ambition, of bleeding affections, of mortal separation. The very word "tribulation" suggests this. It predicts the result, as well as describes the process. The flail (*tribulum*) in the hand of the thresher is to bruise the sheaves and break out the wheat from the straw. In every threshing-floor there is tribulation; and that is the world over. Blows of pain have to divide the spirit and flesh. The pure fruit of goodness does not come from us but by breaking off the worldly crust. John the Baptist shows us the Mighty One that came after him, holding the fan in his hand, sifting the chaff away, and thoroughly cleansing his floor. Suffering is our John the Baptist, clad in grim garments, with rough arms, a son of the wilderness, baptizing us in bitter tears, preaching repentance; and behind him comes the gracious, affectionate, healing Lord, gathering the wheat into the garner.

Let us not take so outward an understanding of the Saviour's meaning as to suppose he was referring wholly to sufferings that visit the soul from abroad. The worst troubler of the world is a wilful heart. No man ever found so dangerous an enemy as he bore in his own personality. Here is one of our most frequent and fatal misjudgments. We reckon those to be the only afflictions which befall us in the ordaining of Providence, or in what, for want of a more reverential name, we call fortune; forgetting that the essential circumstance of all real evil is that it has its root and nourishment in the bad soil of our own hearts. It was not the fruit Eve tasted that "brought death into our world, and all our woe," but the disobedient appetite that lusted after it, and the rebellious, selfish will that reached out and plucked it, and brought it to her lips. That tree of good and evil grows in every child's bosom. We carry the germs of our most disastrous calamities about with us, and whenever the earthly nature in us gets the mastery of the spiritual, some one of them bursts into a luxuriant and malignant growth. Vanity, emulation, love of money, envy, hatred, self-indulgence, — these prepare for us our most dreadful tribulations.

You dread the death of a friend; but you ought to dread with deeper apprehension the dying out of spiritual aspirations from his heart. I am overcome by the loss of a child; but I know, if the New Testament is true, I ought to grieve more heartily when some new sin has defiled my conscience, and dropped a deeper veil between my soul and the God of my life. Tears and sighs mark all our way as we carry out our dear ones to burial; but there are no graves so mournful as those that Mammon digs for our uprightness, and sloth for our holier energies, and the world's flattery for our single-mindedness. When faith in Christ ceases in any of our souls, there is infinitely more cause for private or public lamentation than when the most honored citizen passes out of his body, or a terrible accident plunges a hundred lives into visible destruction. And yet, so far from rising into these spiritual judgments of our gains and losses, how often we let some petty outward calamity — an unsuccessful plan, a bad venture, a bankruptcy — wring from us heavier groans than the sacrifice of all our sympathy with Heaven! There are shops where the ruin of a bale of merchandise is more deplored than a falsehood or a profane oath, as if what we call "goods" were our literal good; where a spoilt fabric or broken bargain awakens louder lamentations than a tarnish on character or a sinking of principle, and where a reduced income is harder to bear than a guilty mind.

We can all conceive of a state of society so thoroughly Christian in its customs and its estimates, that the tokens of extreme sorrow which we now see misapplied to the funerals of those who sleep in Jesus only to reign with him in his glory, should be transferred to signalize our shame when we are conquered by temptation, or corrupted into crime.

If we learn to look on moral losses — inroads upon purity, swervings from holiness — as the real tribulations, the bitterest bereavements, we realize how in sympathy with our own weak nature the whole creation groaneth and travaileth in pain, waiting for deliverance by Him who overcometh the world.

In connection with this truth we are to look for another, viz. that which reconciles to our feeling the apparent severity of this law, that through suffering we must be perfected. One might think, indeed, that to be perfected, or spiritually completed, in any way, would be honor and bliss enough, let whatever purifying anguish come, as the instrument. And so I have known many and many an earnest, convicted soul, thinking no more of the pain, counting that the least of its evils, to entreat, "Pray for me, that by any means, at all cost, through any agony, I may only be purified, and these hateful, horrid fires of passion and iniquity be burnt out of me." That is a real feeling when the deepest passage of life comes,—let our lighter and easier moods call it sentiment, or fanaticism, or whatsoever in their mad, blind foolishness they will. It is, in its time, the most real of realities. And it is so simply because our first need, and our first good,—unclean, fallen, lost souls as we all alike are before the perfect purity of God,—is to be made whole again. And this healing can come only by some painful reviving of the deadened sensibility, just as the lost vitality of the drowning and of many morbid bodies is brought back only through a physical torture that is terrible. If we were in a wholesome, orderly, or sinless state, all this would be different. Doubtless, our Father would not then plunge us into gratuitous pains of sacrifice. But we are in another condition,—down under disorder, diseased, broken, dying of the sin our own bad will and guilty indulgence have gendered. And how to raise us out of that is the problem. The Redeemer alone has solved it. He has shown us, in his own cross, what by our own natural experience in other things we had perhaps begun to see already, that recovery comes by inward suffering, by penitential tears, by sorrow. Still, as at first, through much tribulation we must enter into the kingdom of heaven. To that end even our glorious Leader, the Captain of our salvation, is "made perfect," not in the infinite and eternal perfection of his nature, but in the perfectness of his condescending incarnation and mediatorial sympathy,—made perfect "through suffering." Sublime mystery of God! Gracious wonder of our redemption! Why should we complain of the sorrow that we ourselves, by our disobedience, have created? of the sorrow that ends, not begins, our real misery? the sorrow that is as much the needed pathway and natural preparation of the joy of immortality with our Lord,—joy that no eye hath seen, nor ear heard, nor heart conceived,—as the night is the needed preparation of the morning, or hardship the natural path from the wilderness of the far country to the peace of the Father's house? Said Thomas Arnold, that pure and lofty soul still longing to be purified and ennobled, amidst the anguish of his last disorder, "I thank God for pain."

If we look deeply enough at both these two saddening facts, bereavement and sin, we shall find that, though they seem to wear different aspects as they meet our eyes in actual experience, yet the most sorrowful element in sorrow is sin, and what makes tribulation a necessary part of the world's discipline is the world's guilt. God knows I do not mean to lay on any sufferer the stupid cruelty of affirming that sufferings are distributed in the world according to relative degrees of merit, or that afflictions are always specific or measured penalties for particular crimes. But evidently, in the system we live in, the two are intertangled inseparably. Paul condenses the whole matter into few words: "The sting of death is sin." His conclusion follows legitimately: "Thanks be to God which giveth us the victory through our Lord Jesus Christ." Transgression is tribulation. Just to the degree that any soul gains freedom from iniquity, it gains a conquest over sorrow. If the sufferer had no sin in his heart, he would have a perfect mastery over all the damage that the world and its whole army of diseases and accidents and mortality could do to him.

Thus far, then, we see what it is that is to be overcome; what "the world" means; what its tribulations are.

II. The next question asks, How, by what means and what process, Christ has, as he declares, overcome the world and conquered suffering. The most comprehensive answer we can frame is this: In his own person he overcame it, by the divine fulness and richness of his life. This raised the spirit of Jesus, not above the reach of suffering, — for to that end came he into the world — but above fear, above agitation, above subjection to any other tribulation than that which came from his sympathy with the sorrows of man, and his redemptive sacrifice. It is written of the Lord that he is "afflicted in all the afflictions of his people." What, then, is the real triumph of Calvary? Is it not the triumph of that love wherewith he loved us before we loved him? What is the peace that tranquillizes the agonies of Gethsemane? Is it not the oneness of the Son with the Father? "God so loved the world." We cannot hurt God's holiness. We cannot crucify his love.

Then, having overcome the world in his own person, he furnishes to mankind a power by which they also can overcome, through his own identifying of himself in his divinity with human suffering and experience. He takes flesh and dwells among us as one of us, purposely that he may make us partakers of his victory. He undergoes the crucifixion, that by conforming himself to the law that requires suffering for sin, or pain for a broken commandment, he may release us from both the power and the penalty of sin, stimulating us also by this pledge of forgiveness, and reassuring us by the sacrificial proof that God is still just, while he justifies the sinner that repents and believes.

Revert now to the point just shown. Directly or indirectly, the source of sorrow is sin. When Christ, therefore, by all the glorious offices of his ministry and passion, breaks the power of that evil in the world, he provides an infinite assuaging for sorrow. When he vanquishes temptation, he prostrates pain. When he puts Satan behind him and plants the kingdom of righteousness, he subdues tribulation and leads captivity captive. In other ages, you know, the rude conceptions of the church have given an objective form to this great spiritual fact, and have represented the conflict in actual figures, — as a warfare between two mighty leaders, where the Redeemer wins. So Milton, in Paradise Lost. The imagery only shadows forth a spiritual truth, the supreme truth in the history of the universe. By all the influences and forces of his divine mission into the world, the Redeemer has overcome the world.

If we choose to divide this one comprehensive fact into its parts, we find four chief methods by which this mission of Jesus overcomes sin and delivers us. First, by the sympathetic force of a perfectly holy life, presenting to our contemplation the most animating of all conceivable spectacles, — the actual presence of a Being who is literally overcoming the world's evil, hour by hour, at every step, in practical contact with its vilest shapes; who carries from infancy to his crucifixion an immaculate conscience, — such a temper that when reviled he reviles not again, an incorruptible integrity, an inexhaustible charity, an uninterrupted prayer. Whatever of inspiration can visit men from this consummate glory and divine transfigurement of the earth, — a complete goodness, — that power stands to overcome the world's baser nature, in Christ. Secondly, by his message, — the supreme spiritual wisdom, light informing us, not the triumph incarnate in a living example now, but uttered in the word and preserved on the page, — the precept and the promise assured by infallible authority. Thirdly, by his death, the propitiation, gathering up the whole spiritual efficacy of his mediatorship, and concentrating it in the submission of his agony, the bloody sweat of the garden, the mysterious torture that rent the veil, and darkened the sky, and shook the earth, — the free offering of the blood of the Lamb of God for the sin of the world. Fourthly, by his resurrection, — bright demonstration that death has no command over the Giver of life, confirming the promise, "Because I live ye shall live also;" showing us our God in Christ ascending up on high, leading captivity captive, giving gifts unto men. Slain, indeed, for our offences, but raised again for our justification; and reigning forever as Lord of the heavens above, and head over all things, and in all things, to his church below!

But, after all our feeble attempts to analyze and explain it, be our words few or many, by argument or illustration, by paraphrase or definition, the chief part of the evidence must be left to the secret apprehension of the soul, touched by the Spirit. The most we can say of it is, that the soul and its Saviour are divinely fitted each to each; so that, in ways transcending all our knowledge, by powers moving in a holy mystery which faith rejoices to confess, sorrow feels herself at peace in her Lord, and is satisfied. By what means he hath opened her eyes, she does not know. This only she knows, that whereas she was blind, now she sees. There is light; there is strength; there is peace. What the world never gave is given. It is its own explanation; and henceforth neither death, nor things present, nor things to come, nor height of pride, nor depth of affliction, shall be able to separate her from this love.

III. The other inquiry is the practical one, on which both the others bear their whole weight,—How are we to be personally overcomers with him and by him? The answer is not mine, but his own. By believing on him: not with that heartless assent which never touches the practice nor moulds the affections, leaving the whole man in his business as Christless as a Pagan; but by believing on him in that all-controlling and all-compelling faith which draws practice after it, and regenerates the familiar dispositions of home and work, as well as the secret springs of piety in church and closet.

Brethren, even our saintliest saints only partially apprehend the joy and benefit of their position. We profess to believe Christ has overcome the world, and that we have a right to be of good cheer because he has overcome it, and then, straightway we go and act and speak as if the gloomy burden rested on us of overcoming it unaided, ourselves. The very consolation of his assurance is that he *has* overcome it. It is a fact wrought. It is a triumph accomplished. Yet look on the nominal Christians, catch the half-faithless and complaining tones of unreconciled mourners, read the despair on the cheerless faces of so many avowed disciples, and who would ever dream we were the heirs of a glorious liberty obtained, and the children of a day whose morning beams, as they mounted the sky, were the banners of an everlasting victory? Fellow-Christians, we have not yet to find out the secret of redeeming the world to God. God so loved the world that he gave his Son. He has baffled evil by his prayers, trodden it under the feet of his virtue, and rebuked it by his word, and nailed it to his cross. What is for us is to take with living gratitude the divinely-offered gift, to clothe ourselves in his purity, to lean our sorrows on his breast, to come unto him, — the Way, the Truth, the Life. Yes, fourfold as his saving offices for us are, — living as example, enlightening as teacher, dying as redeemer, rising as advocate and intercessor, — fourfold must our acceptance be, — following the guide, obeying the word, moved to penitence and faith by the cross, kindled to holy praise by the hopes of the resurrection.

Out of this vital and spiritual assimilation of our souls to his — the true motive and fountain of the noblest action — will come the consistent obedience. If the real fellowship of our affections is with him who has overcome the evil of the world by good, righteousness will be our cheerful and unfaltering aim. Every morning afresh we shall take the new day God has given us as a new occasion for sharing in the great spiritual conquest over evil. In trials of faith and wounds of love, in the weeping houses that renew the griefs of Bethany, in the dying of wife, child, mother, father, husband, sister, brother, in the public anguish that rends all the air with some loud cry of perishing hosts, when a foundering vessel goes down into the waters with its hundreds of shrieking victims, we shall be steadfast and immovable. We shall not lose our faith in God. We shall "be of good cheer," always abounding in the work of the Lord, forasmuch as we know in whom we have believed, and that our labor is not in vain in the Lord.

We must never forget that this is a victory which comes from no other source but one. So manifest is this, that if you were to take even an unsympathizing sceptic and lead him silently around to the scenes where believers, one with Christ by faith, are suffering and dying, — if you would conduct him through these successive wards in the great hospital of our mortality, simply leaving him to contrast the pain of faith with the pain of unbelief, — he would have to say, as the Pagans exclaimed in the midst of their persecutions, "See how these Christians die!" Put the most terrible tortures that flesh and blood can feel on the disciple, there will yet remain an overcoming of holy submission, of sweet serenity, of blessed triumph, which, as a simple human fact in the world, can be accounted for, even to the rational mind, by nothing else than the presence of Christ, — not by science, not by philosophy, not by accident, not by temperament, not by the bracing up of the will, nor by mortal courage. And this has been going on ever since the first Christian whose death is recorded cried, in the pangs and joy of his departure, "Lord Jesus, receive my spirit!" It is going on in ten thousand Christian dwellings, this blessed day of the Lord.

Place beside all the haughty and frigid boasts of the stoics the tender minglings of affection and resignation from Christian sorrow; contrast Dr. Arnold's tranquil words in the last hours, when every breath was fierce distress, with the letters and treatises of Seneca; see the yearning love of kindred, the meek humility, the loss of self, the confession of unworthiness, the patient waiting for release, the whispered promises of the New Testament, the lips too faint to speak still moving in prayer, the clear smile and upward look when the glories of the other world begin to shine out and take form as the veil grows thin, the calm parting with the best beloved, the visible light on the face when the name of the Saviour is spoken, — the simple phrases, — "Christ is all," — "Come, Lord Jesus," "Rock of ages, cleft for me," "I know in whom I have believed." Either there is reality here, a reality of which faith alone is witness, or there is no reality anywhere, — and nature, history, the world, and life, and thought, and time, and love, are all a delusion and a dream!

So have the true believers overcome. Have we not sometimes seen them? The long line of witnesses reaches down from the Saviour's time to ours. The last willing followers of the immortal train have just ascended from our side. We listen to their Elder's assurance, "These are they which came out of great tribulation, and have washed their robes and made them white in the blood of the Lamb! They are before the throne of God, and serve him day and night in his temple; and God shall wipe away all tears from their eyes." We listen again, and the eternal benediction still falls in peace from Heaven, — "In the world ye shall have tribulation; but be of good cheer, I have overcome the world."

How often, through the world's literature and history, have we heard some ambitious commander or emperor babbling, in his vain waking dreams, of a world's conquest! We turn from these poor visions of cruelty and blood to the meek army of the living God; from the false victories of force to the true victories of faith. Here, on a lowly bed, in an English village by the sea, — as I was lately reading, — fades out the earthly life of one of God's humblest but noblest servants. Worn with the patient care of deserted prisoners and malefactors in the town jail for twenty-four years of unthanked service, earning her bread with her hands, and putting songs of worship on the lips of these penitent criminals, — she is dying; and as the night falls some friend asks, "What shall I read?" The answer of the short breath is one firm syllable, "Praise!" To the question, "Are there no clouds?" "None; he never hides his face. It is our sins which form the cloud between us and him. He is all love, all light." And when the hour of her departure was fully come, "Thank God, thank God!" And there, — as I read again, — in his princely residence, surrounded with the insignia of power, but in equal weakness before God, expired a guileless statesman, nobleman by rank and character, calmly resigning back all his power into the Giver's hands, spending his last day of pain, like many hours of all his days before it, with the Bible and Prayer-book in his feeble hand, saying, at the end, "I have been the happiest of men, yet I feel that death will be gain to me, through Christ who died for me." Blessed be God for the manifold features of triumphant faith! — that he suffers his children to walk toward him through ways so various in their outward look; — Sarah

Martin from her cottage bed, Earl Spencer from his gorgeous couch, little children in their innocence, unpretending women in the quiet ministrations of faithful love, strong and useful and honored men, whom suffering households and institutions and churches mourn. All bending their faces towards the Everlasting Light, in one faith, one cheering hope, called by one Lord, who has overcome the world, and dieth no more!

"One army of the living God,
To his command we bow.
Part of the host have crossed the flood,
And part are crossing now."

The sun sets; the autumn fades; life hastens with us all. But we stand yet in our Master's vineyard. All the days of our appointed time let us labor righteously, and pray and wait, till our change come, that we may change only from virtue to virtue, from faith to faith, and thus from glory to glory!

SERMON XVI.

CHRISTIAN RESTING AND WAITING.

REST IN THE LORD, AND WAIT PATIENTLY FOR HIM. — Psalms xxxvii. 7.

It has been sometimes believed that the common distinction between active virtues and passive virtues is unreal. And the suspicion gains strength when one is arrested by some such tranquil, ponderous thought as this, out of the old Hebrew faith. Hebrew faith, and not Hebrew philosophy. For philosophy, Hebrew, Greek, German or Scotch, Oriental or Western, with all her wealth, never gave to the world so rich a piece of wisdom as this simple precept; never let in, by all her speculations and discoveries, so clear and steady a light on the dark problems of human destiny as shines in this artless confession of David's piety. David was a monarch and a sage; but his royalty blessed his people with no protection so secure and no campaign so profitable, his sagacity contrived no maxim so profound, as when he said, in his psalm, "Rest in the Lord, and wait patiently for him." It was a more illustrious honor to the great Israelite, we should say, to have uttered that divine truth to his audience, — an audience reaching from Jerusalem around the globe, and down history till sorrow ceases, — to have cast that unpretending word on the everlasting stream of spiritual life, to have added that imperishable tribute to mankind's stock of holy confidence, than to have carried victory over an hundred battle-fields against the Philistines, or even to have planned the Temple for Mount Zion. For he who communicates a spiritual impulse to human souls does a diviner work than the builders of empire or of temples made with hands.

One of our hardest lessons is to find out the wisdom of our hindrances; how we are to be put forward and upward by being put back and put down; encouraged by being rebuked; prospered by being baffled. When the company in the "Pilgrim's Progress" had to sit up watching all night at the house of Gaius, Great-heart kept them awake with this riddle, "He that would kill must first be overcome;" and the truth in it has been practically dug out, by trials that broke sleep, through many a hard fortune, in every Christian experience since. It needs wakeful watchers, spiritual eye-sight, to read that riddle of life, how defeat helps progress; how a compulsory standing still speeds us on; how humiliation exalts; how putting a cross on the shoulders lightens the burden of the race. But Christ has solved the wonder in his own cross, humbling himself, becoming obedient unto death, and in his humiliation having his judgment taken away.

Gradually, to believing eyes, the fact comes out. Standing still at the right time, in the right way, for the right purpose, is the surest advance. Waiting on God brings us to our journey's end faster than our feet. The failure of our favorite plans is often the richest success of the soul. Let the pressure of trouble drive you down from your heights of health and pride, and you will come upon the primary foundation, and grow strong out of the rock. Be exiled from the convivial fellowships of comfort and popularity, and you make new acquaintances with stronger friends, — Christian self-possession, and wholesome repentance, and a mastery of your moral forces, and faith in your Lord.

"Rest in the Lord, and wait patiently for him." It sounds at first like the lesson of a very easy master, a negative sort of duty; too tame for a spirited ambition. "Rest and wait!" you say; "no: give us a positive doctrine, and we will listen; give us a task worthy of our energies, and we will be up and doing; sound a bugle-note that calls to close contests, and we will follow; but no such effeminate, spiritless, quietistic creed as resting and waiting!" We must see, if we can, what force there is in this answer. Possibly, if we search deep enough, we shall find that where some of us fancy our religion ends, it is only feebly begun.

And first, as to the popular distinction just referred to, between active and passive goodness. Now, goodness in the spiritual representation of Christ is a certain interior disposition, a frame of the soul, where the first fixed choice is for righteousness, and the first fixed love is for God. Goodness, then, lies not so much in specific deeds as in the faithful heart; not so much even in special attainments as in that principle of a consecrated will which presides over all our doings and gettings; not so much in this or that act, or even series of acts, as in that pervading and supreme purpose or motive, which, having been appropriated from Christ himself, rules the general tenor and course of life into harmony with his spirit; not so much in outward manifestations, as in an internal aspiration, strong and constant, for newness of life, and fellowship with God by his Son. In other words, a Christian righteousness consists in being first, and doing afterwards; in a right spirit before there can be a right life; in a changed and reconciled heart, in order to a noble and beautiful conduct. We must be purified within, or no outward cleansing avails. We must do Christian works from a love of them, or else we never do them — Christian works — at all. We cannot make our hands serve Heaven profitably, while our faces are turned another way, looking after self-promotion or sensual comfort. It may be the whip of conscience, or the spur of threatened punishment, that stirs us out of our sluggishness; but till we begin to serve Christ because the love of him is superior to every other passion, we are not born again. Make the tree a good tree, or the fruit will not be good fruit.

Notice how this principle affects the common notion of passive and active goodness. If the principle is true, what is often called passive goodness is the necessary condition, nay, the interior fountain of active goodness. A man, that is, must be a silent believer in his heart before he can be a powerful Christian worker with his arms, or speaker with his lips. He must pray in his closet before he can honor his Maker in the multitude or shop, in pulpit or street. He must trust God secretly, or he will not glorify him publicly. He must stand reverently looking upward, ready to receive the Holy Spirit, before the Spirit works through his body, to will and do Heaven's business. That is, precisely, he must "rest" his soul "in the Lord," and "wait patiently" for his direction, or he is not his Lord's man, a disciple.

This is one way of exalting the passive virtues, so called, and at the same time of honoring our doctrine, and opening the text; i. e. by an analysis of the nature of real goodness. Another way is, by comparing the two classes of virtues, and observing what each requires to sustain it. If there is any such division founded in reality, submission would be likely to fall on the side of the passive graces. Take submission, then, — Christian submission; look for a test case. Suppose a providential loss of any of your heart's dearest ownerships, your fondest hope, your cherished plan of future welfare, your best friend, your brightest child. Remember that Christian submission is not stupid indifference, not proud self-command smothering sighs and stanching tears, not sullen stoicism playing a dreary game with fate. It is gentle, tender, mighty trust; it is as full of sensibility as of strength; it is willingness that God should take his own; it is that triumphant, "Not as I will, but as thou wilt," which could come from no other spot but Gethsemane; it is resting in the Lord, and waiting patiently for him.

We need not hesitate to say of such submission, that in all the compass of human graces and achievements there is not one that more tasks the stoutest energies of the soul; not one that brings into intenser action the most vigorous capacities of the spiritual life; not one that demands a more resolute gathering up of all the resolution left, and the bracing of a firm resistance against denial and despair. And yet, this celestial attainment, this submission, the mourner's glory and privilege, the compensation of patient suffering and crown of spiritual victories, — this resting in the Lord, and waiting patiently for him, is one of your passive, secondary, ignoble virtues!

Gentleness oı temper, and of speech, would be reckoned, probably, among the passive excellences. And no doubt there is such a thing as a constitutional amiability that has no very fragrant odor of Christian sanctity in it, because there is no valiant struggle spent in gaining it; such fortunate temperaments must enlarge their Christian proportions in other directions, and go on to perfection in other paths; because judgment is according to gifts. But do we not also know some persons that need all the weapons in the Christian armory, and all the watchfulness of the camp, to reach that plain achievement, the "soft answer" that "turneth away wrath"? Do we not know others, who so damage their public usefulness and philanthropic professions by petulant manners, vituperative eloquence, and an ungoverned appetite for immediate effects, that it would have seemed a profitable exchange for Christian symmetry and decency, if they could have given half of their out-door zeal for a grain of that "passive" grace that sweetens the temper, and softens the tongue, and handles even a doubtful reputation charitably, and makes him that "ruleth his own spirit" greater than he that electrifies an assembly, or "taketh a city"?

If we learn to measure the bravery of Christian acquirements rather by the inward effort they cost than by their display, if we estimate character more by the standard of Christ's beatitudes than by what we shortsightedly call "results," we shall find some of the sublimest fruits of faith among what are commonly called passive virtues: in the silent endurance that hides under the shadow of great afflictions; in the quiet loveliness of that forbearance which "suffereth long and is kind;" in the charity which is "not easily provoked;" in the forgiveness which can be buffeted for doing well and "take it patiently;" in the smile on the face of diseased and suffering persons, a transfiguration of the tortured features of pain brightening sick rooms more than the sun; in the unostentatious heroisms of the household, amidst the daily dripping of small cares; in the noiseless conquests of a love too reverential to complain; in resting in the Lord, and waiting patiently for him. Have you yourself never known the time when you found it a harder lesson to learn how to be still in your room, than to be busy in the world? Of masculine natures that is apt to be the special cross. And so that may be the point where faith and virtue need to rally their strength, if you would be a triumphant disciple. It is a fact which not all of us may have noticed, that of the nine beatitudes of our Lord, all, unless it be one, pronounce their blessing on what the world would call tame and passive traits,—from the "poor in spirit" to those who are reviled and persecuted without revenge. So does Christianity turn upside down the vulgar vanity of our ambition, and empty our worldliness of blessedness.

But the subject reaches on to wider applications yet. "Rest in the Lord, and wait patiently for him," is a counsel addressed to the habit and tendency of these times; and no time perhaps ever needed to listen to it more; a time whose veins are full of blood,—of a restless temper and a busy body; more eager to conquer the world by putting girdles of intelligence and bonds of travel about it, than to feel its dependence on Heaven; readier to run, to work, to build, to ask questions, to yoke the elements, than to kneel, to believe, to have patience, and to pray. It is not a character to be sweepingly condemned, nor to be bettered by complaint; not deserving petulant blame any more than complacent idolatry; but one of which it would be wise to see the tendencies, and wholesome to understand the weakness. To require the unquiet mind of such a generation to be still is like bidding a person of strong constitution and brisk blood go away by himself and think; and yet both have to be often done before to them or the people is shown the word of God. Indeed the dangers of an age, like those of an individual, often run parallel with its chief merits. Social action and material enterprise and aggressive discovery, which are the grand characteristics of modern society, bring along with them the hazard of an irreligious self-reliance, a scepticism about all that is invisible and impalpable to sense, and a feverish propensity to judge everything by its show and its returns. So the bulk of our enterprise outgrows its strength; and in the pride of all his pushing schemes, and marvellous machinery, man comes to esteem himself little less than a critic of Revelation and copartner with the Almighty, whom the Church of Christ ought to consider herself much beholden to if he condescends to say kind things of her, and whom God himself cannot fail to covet as an ally for so much business and motion, if indeed there is any other God than the science that perfects the engine, and the nature-power that turns the factory-wheel. As long as you preach to such a man about his stupendous capacity, and stimulate his arrogant activity, he hears. But tell him of the deeper things of God, of self-renunciation and repentance, of a cross and a consecration, of silent worship and solemn faith, of resting in the

Lord, and waiting patiently for him, — and you seem to clash against his glorious career of aggrandizement. All the more do we need this deeper and stiller element in our piety. We want not only to work, but to believe that God in Christ works, and with mightier forces than we; works through and by us, or without us, as he will; and that we are at best but inapt and incompetent instruments in his hands. "Be still, and know that I am God!" — let our loud march of audacious civilization hearken to that. Self-righteousness is farther from the kingdom of heaven than the publicans and sinners. Will-worship gets no answer to its prayers. The strength of all enterprise is in the faith of its managers. We lose salvation when we lose the awful sense that God is near, loving righteousness, hating iniquity, bringing good and evil to judgment. The strength of a community, the strength of New England to-day, is not in its enterprising, self-confident, profane or prayerless great men, but in the men, be they few or many, who while they are "diligent in business," and faithful in public spirit, "rest" secretly "in the Lord," and "wait patiently" every day "for him."

The farther we carry our study into the heart of the matter, the more we shall see that this waiting for the word and will of Heaven is no idle abstaining from labor, but in fact the highest result and crown of the best spiritual labor. Resting in the Lord, is not resting in indolence. It is a rest which is nobler than a mere cessation from employment, or a flinging down of weary and baffled powers to breathe on the nearest couch. It is the truest balance of all our spiritual powers; and how can that be but by incessant vigilance and toil? It is rest by being in harmony with

God's wise, pure will; and, for tempted men like you and me, with wild desires to quench, and passions to curb, and sins to be forgiven, how can that be save by warfare with the flesh, and daily sacrifices of the spirit? It is a rest that is earned, a peace that is conquered, a silent joy that comes by the godly sorrows of repentance, not to be repented of.

See, again, what besides righteous labor such a stillness supposes. To wait patiently for God is to hold the heart open for what God gives. Subjection, then, it implies. It is to expect his love; and so it implies the penitence that goes before pardon. It is to believe he will give and guide; and so it implies faith. It is to hold all insubordinate and hasty impulses in restraint; and so it implies self-renunciation. It is to ask for his coming; and so it implies prayer. It is to rejoice in his presence; and so it implies thanksgiving. Subjection, penitence, faith, self-renouncement, prayer, thanksgiving, — these are not elements of man's infirmity.

Having thus rather intimated than shown how the precept stretches its broad significance over our whole religious life, and expands into that duty which in fact is the sum and substance of all religion, viz. a vital trust and spiritual communion in God, I wish to give it an application to some of the prominent passages of actual Christian experience.

And first, there is both comfort and courage in it for those of us that yearn for a speedier advent of the Christian Kingdom, for the unity of a divided and discordant church, for the healing of the terrible breaches in Christian charity and Christian peace. There cannot be many Christian souls that have not sometimes been visited by such wishes; have not longed to witness a reconciling of hostile creeds, to live in a fellowship of regenerated sects, to hear a blending of all litanies, and all lives, in one great harmony of praise, ascending from one choir of the nations. "Rest in the Lord, and wait patiently for him." If it took four thousand years at the least, from man's first residence on it, to fit the world for the Messiah's feet, what wonder if it should need as many more to understand his message, and breathe in his love, and see the building of his Fold? Be content if you discern any signs of that great reconciliation; if any foretokenings of that fresh Baptism and of the Spirit descending again like a dove, shine out here and there on the cloudy theological sky; if you hear the voice of any Johns crying ever in the wilderness, "Prepare ye the way" for that second coming of the Son of Man! Be it enough for us to bear some trifling part, in some corner of the vineyard, in purging out some of the poisonous suspicions that cumber the ground, and then to die without the full harvest in sight. God does not die, nor change, nor retreat; wait patiently for him.

There are doubts of Providence that spring up from other quarters. What the inquisitive and perplexed intellect of man needs, as it stands dismayed at the ghastly spectacle of suffering, slavery, warring nations, starving families close by bloated wealth, virtue bought and sold as merchandise, government perverted into the trade of tyrants and their tools, patriots broken-hearted, and a thousand other forms of misery and crime, — what it needs is that calm assurance from the Bible, like the voice of Christ to the anger of the storm, or the demons of human hate, — "Rest in the Lord, and wait patiently for him." His work-day is Eternity.

His plan runs from the beginning of days to the end of years. Every sigh and groan of anguish comes up into remembrance before him, and every oppression and cruelty survives for Judgment. The burdens of humanity grow already lighter, not heavier. The justice of the Almighty is not foiled. The year of his redeemed shall come. There is a Future, and it belongs to Christianity; and there waits the redressing of every wrong. It is an inspiring lesson of faith the Scriptures teach us, when they show us the old Jewish prophets and kings bending forward as if to catch some note of the Bethlehem welcome, waiting to see their Messiah's day, and yet dying in faith "without the sight." There are two vivid scenes in the life of the great Hebrew Lawgiver, not often brought forward among the wonders of his mission, which are affecting disclosures of that indwelling faith, which was the hiding of all his power: one, where he stood on the top of the mountain, not afraid, with a tranquil expectation, amid thunders and lightnings, and clouds and darkness, waiting confidently for the Lord God to speak at the beginning of his great work; the other, when, at the end of his trials and his life, he went up to look off from the top of another mountain, over the Canaan he could not enter, and then walked firmly down, without murmuring, to die. To us the Lord God *always* speaks by his Son, if we will listen; and to us the whole Future is a Land of Promise, and every hour an outlook from Nebo, if only we have that unshaken faith that is ready to wait or to work, and asks only to be led.

Bring the same consolation into the discontent that hangs about your own private failures in duty, and the slowness of your advances in character. Loosen no nerve of resistance; slacken no effort to press on; suspend no prayer for the Spirit. Otherwise you do not rest *in* the Lord, but rest *from* Him, and instead of waiting, like the blind man, for the Saviour's coming, you wait for him to pass by. But inasmuch as the struggle is long, and you are mortal, and life without your Father is orphanage, keep very near to your Lord; rest in him, wait patiently for him. "With him is plenteous redemption." Leave all issues and results with him, saying reverently, as Luther did of his greater work, "Let the Lord God look to that." But wait with open eyes and willing feet. The splendor of noon may be in the sky, but if the eyes be shut it is quenched to them. Preserve an open soul, that the truth as fast as it rises may pour in. And since you know not on what errand of duty or sacrifice God will call you to go first, hold your lamp trimmed and burning as those that wait for the Bridegroom's voice.

In the midst of our own houses there are more secret sorrows than I need to name. Every life has its own. Perhaps there are erring, ungrateful, and ungracious children, with parents' hearts breaking and bleeding over them, and agonizing in daily prayers for their return. "Have faith in God;" every prayer pierces the Heaven of heavens; the Intercessor and Mediator pleads with it; and its answer is committed to some strong angel at the right hand of the Throne. There are anxieties, alienations, unavailing affections, crossed desires and hopes. There are memories running back from pews in this house of prayer to the graves of those that worship no more in earthly temples. Rest, mourners, in the Lord. Seek not the living among the dead. Seek ye first the kingdom of God, and all else shall be added. "Let us lie still beneath God's hand; for though his hand be heavy upon us, it is strong and safe beneath us too: and none can pluck us out of his hand." O, impatient griefs, and sorrows that have no hope, be still; and ye hopes that would outrun the wisdom of a healing Providence and a saving mercy, be still; all unreasonable and rebellious thoughts, be still: know that the Lord, he is God. Remember that "the darkness is God's as well as the light," and "if we cannot walk" and work therein, "we can" at least kneel down and "pray."

"Here," exclaimed John, in one of the visions of the Apocalypse, here "is the patience and faith of the saints." Patience and faith are one. Faithful waiting is one of the grand duties of the Christian life. Till the Resurrection, the whole creation, groaning and travailing together, waiteth for the manifestation of the sons of God. A disciple, at his private post, must wait for the lifting up of many folds of mystery, for deliverance from his last temptation. The Church waits to be "made whole," and to be made "one." The lovers of concord and friends of oppressed nations wait for the dawning of peaceful liberty on the hill-tops, for the fulfilment of prophecy, for the leopard to lie down with the kid. The tattooed savage of the Southern Islands waits, leaning his ear over the surf, to catch the sound of the Gospel. The Ethiopian and Arab and Chinaman and Nestorian wait, stretching out their hands unto God, that he, whom they ignorantly worship, may be declared to them. And God watches and hears, and counts every heathen's sighs and Christian's prayers!

Let our subject terminate, then, in these three rules of practice: —

Let it regulate Christians' judgments of one another. Our Maker has graciously diversified the forms of character that he will admit into his kingdom. Action is honorable, and so is contemplation. Not all the accepted saints are bustling men. If there are only, deep in the heart, a steadfast faith and a holy love, then a sincere piety may be grafted on the quiet temperament and the noiseless constitution, as well as on the men of much enterprise and speech. The heart is all. If there was a stirring Peter in the Apostolic band, so was there a meditative John. If in Christ's favorite household there was a moving Martha, so was there a contemplative Mary. There was service in both, and not the least in her who chose the stiller part. Nay, we are told that in the glorious ranks of celestial spirits there are some who only "stand and wait," and that "they also serve." Let us expand our charity by the measure of God's spiritual economy.

Again, let the subject save us from morbid discontents at our opportunities. Let us not suspect that Christ is to be served only where there is room for outward action,—only in the ministering mercy of hospitals, and the stir of fields and shops and public scenes. He may be served as faithfully sometimes on sick beds, in helplessness, in prison cells, and within the limitations of many a narrow circumstance. These compel us to stand still and hear God speak. To learn the limitations of our ability is wisdom, as well as the exercise of that ability. "Whatsoever thy hand findeth to do, do it with thy might," is one precept. "Be still and know that I am God," is another, carrying us up to the authority, and down into the depths of Christian peace. Paul singing praises at midnight in the prison was as majestic a figure as Paul eloquent before King Agrippa. Martyrs and confessors bore testimony as sublime in the long hours of dungeons as out in journeyings, or in fights with wild beasts in the amphitheatre. Many a man has been valiant in the use of his strength, but a coward when his muscular vigor abated, — showing that his courage was not of faith, but of the body. We are called to be disciples of a Master made perfect through suffering. The essence of Christianity is self-renunciation; and the discipline that brings us to feel our childlike dependence is the perfecting of our piety. Grief after grief brings us to joy. Broken in spirit, we are made whole; humbled, we are exalted. We gain the great victory through a succession of defeats. Bunyan's riddle is a true oracle. Presently after Saul was stopped in the city to hear the word of the Lord, we are told, he was led up into "the hill of God." So we are struck down that we may ascend into the mount; troubled, that we may have peace; worried into the rest of our Father's arms. We sin when we chafe against the providential conditions of our lot. Submission is brave achievement. There is no state where you may not win acceptance, because there is none where you may not give your affections, and "rest in the Lord, and wait patiently for Him." If we are obedient, in all the gentleness of faith, to the voice that says, "Be still, and know that I am God," then will Christ do more for us than Samuel for Saul, showing us his word, giving us "another heart," and anointing and crowning the least among us, not princes and captains of armies here, but "kings and priests unto God," because servants of himself.

And, finally, remember that it is in "the Lord" that

we must "rest," — and that it is for his Almighty Will that we must "wait." Any other rest will be guilty indolence; any other waiting will be faithless self-love. It must be a religious repose. It must be that holy and consecrated frame in which every subdued and submissive energy shall breathe the consistent prayer, "Thy will be done." This will be casting all our care on Him who careth for us. This will be the peace and joy of believing.

SERMON XVII.

THE ADVENT.

HE CAME UNTO HIS OWN, AND HIS OWN RECEIVED HIM NOT. BUT AS MANY AS RECEIVED HIM, TO THEM GAVE HE POWER TO BECOME THE SONS OF GOD, EVEN TO THEM THAT BELIEVE ON HIS NAME. — John i. 11, 12.

THESE expressions look backward. The verbs are in a past tense. They seem to point to a transaction that is done. The question springs up, Why should we go back with them? Christianity is here, as hospitably lodged as most other interests. We reckon our time by "the year of our Lord;" the very chronology of civilization dating forward and backward from his coming. His name is stamped on the seals that accredit the best authority, in thought, education, and empire. The symbol of his sacrifice surmounts the highest buildings men raise, in village or city. Even a great deal of modern infidelity insists on calling itself Christian. The Gospel is recognized; we are familiar with the letter of its lessons. What occasion is there for recalling its beginnings? Why take our places, even for an hour, with the Evangelist, and Philip, and Andrew, and Simon, by the shores of Galilee? Why celebrate the season of the Saviour's advent?

There is a reason why. Christ's coming into the world was not for a particular generation, nor for a particular country. The causes for his coming are in every heart in this place, — every heart that beats anywhere, with life, and love, and sorrow, and sin, in its blood. The wants he came to satisfy, the alienation he came to heal, the depravity he came to atone for, the unbelief he came to scatter, and the misery he came to bless, were not local, nor of one age. The need of that dayspring which broke when "the Word" was manifest was not Syrian, Roman, nor Grecian, not Jewish nor Ethnic. Humanity did not exist four thousand years or more with none of the elements and susceptibilities that Jesus would personally meet, and after an interruption of thirty years or thereabouts return to that condition. "He came to his own;" to a race that belonged to him "from the beginning;" since "in the beginning he was with God, and was God." His outward appearance, limited as to time and place, was necessary to give form and force to the inward work he was to do. Christ must be seen, must be historical, must enter into time and into space, though having all time and space in himself. It wanted all the signals and efficacy of his physical presence and suffering: the houseless head; the speech of which it was said that man never spake like it; the look that was like no human look, — now healing the sick, and now sending a storm through Peter's conscience, comforting timid women, and striking down the stout soldiers to the ground as by their own swords and staves. It wanted the body and the blood, the countenance that was marred more than the countenance of any man, the shape that had virtue in the hem of its garments and arose visibly to walk again after death had done its work, because death could have no power over it. All this was needed. As John relates it, the word must be "made flesh, and dwell among us."

Notwithstanding this, and indeed as a part of this truth, it is a low view of the Saviour which insulates his ministry within a brief section of the reigns of two earthly emperors. The true view makes his physical advent only a type of what goes on in each single disciple's soul. Any one of us without a Saviour is like the world without him: wandering, weak, lost. What the world had to do each of us has to do; to receive him, to prepare a place for him, to welcome his spirit, to obey him as the friendly Lord, and trust him as the Redeemer.

The text presents three things in connection: the Coming, the Reception, the Blessing. "He came unto his own, and his own received him not. But as many as received him, to them gave he power to become the sons of God, even to them that believe on his name."

I. The Coming. This had an object, a motive, and a method.

To find the object, we might go either to the direct declarations of Christ himself and his apostles, or to the actual state of the world when he appeared. Both would give us the same account. Men had lost sight of God. Some nations, rather, had lost it; others had never had it. All alike, if we except a small class of Hebrew believers like Simeon and Nathanael, lingering about the old Temple, and keeping their devout simplicity, Israelites in whom there was no guile, — all were destitute of it. Three kinds of selfishness had blinded them. Three rank roots had struck into the soil, sending up growths of superstition and sensuality which overshadowed all pure religion; self-admiration, self-will, self-indulgence: three forms of sin; three usurpers of the human soul. One, — self-admiration, perverts and makes a rebel of the intellect; another, — self-will, of the conscience; the other, — self-indulgence, of the passions. The whole head was sick; the whole heart faint; the whole practical direction unstrung. In this threefold treachery and corruption, the world had grown giddy, rapacious, and godless. Curiosity was all that was left as the highest aim in science; war, in enterprise; and a sensuous enthusiasm for the beautiful in art. Alexandria, Rome, and Athens represented these three ambitions. In losing his God, man had lost himself, as always happens. The Fall was complete. Faith in God and the dignity of man went down together. With divine worship fell human rights and liberties. The scholars and the priests mystified the people, the Epicureans tempted them, the Stoics flattered and despised them. Seneca, with his dainty doctrine that "the finding out of things useful is not work for a philosopher, but drudgery for slaves," stood for the world's idea of learning; Cæsar, for its idea of politics; Corinth, for its idea of pleasure. There were gods enough: one for every propensity. But they were either patrons to be purchased, or abstractions to be apostrophized, or demons to be propitiated. Religion, where it was not a voluntary deception, had degenerated into an incantation and a ceremony. The priest, if he was a pagan, was a juggler or a dupe; if he was a Jew, — read the twenty-third chapter of Matthew, and its eightfold woes on the hypocrites, to know what he was. There was intellect enough; but the amount of all that was, as Paul put it, that "the world by wisdom knew not God," and never would, till that "Logos," or Messiah, came, who was to the Jews a stumbling-block and to the Greeks foolishness, but, to them that believe, Christ, the power of God and the wisdom of God unto salvation. And the literatures of the nations confirm his saying. Leave out two names, nay, leave out not even Plato and Cicero, and nothing puts a gloomier aspect upon the Christless world than to take up and really read, as seeking spiritual satisfaction, the works of antiquity that are oftenest quoted in company with the Bible.

The object, then, of the Advent is plain. Men had lost sight of their God, their Father. Christ came to show him unto them. Manifestation was the purpose; revelation; the bodying forth of the Divine; to show God; to reveal the Father. Not first by a book: that would have reached not one in ten thousand, nor him in his heart. Not chiefly by oral instructions, which have to be certified to the understanding before they can inspire faith. Not by a mere creature-image of Deity, for that would have been only adding another to the old Pantheon of idolatries. This infinite goodness, this One Spirit of God, must come in a life. Christ must be the Son of the Father; must touch humanity and enter into it; must wear its flesh; must lift its load; must partake its experience; must be tempted with it; must be seen, nay, felt, suffering for it. This will complete the manifestation. This will be, not an education, not an inspiration, not a human self-elevation, which neither history nor logic hints at; but a coming of Heaven to earth; a theophany, or manifesting of God. This is perfect compassion, and effectual relief. This gets the sundered souls together. Even stolid and blinded eyes will now begin to behold their Lord. And when they not only see him, but see him in disinterested agony, giving the last gift, life itself, in the most torturing anguish of body and spirit that human death can bring, an ever-living God mysteriously passing through the valley of the shadow of death,—this will move and melt and convince of sin, and arouse to holiness, and release from the bondage of law, if anything. He who could do this must know how to reconcile Law and Love, how to legislate and forgive, how to be just and justify the sinner, and thus be able to atone and able to renew,—a Redeemer, such as all weak and wandering hearts like ours need. We cannot fathom the metaphysical composition of his incarnate being. But we can bow before him, and follow after him, and be grateful, and cry gladly and gratefully, with Thomas, "My Lord and my God!"

You see, then, the object. The Advent of the Messiah was not a movement to establish an original right of possession in men. He came to his own. It was not to create an original religious capacity. It was to open the way, and fill out all the conditions of salvation. It was to gain men's faith. It was to quicken them with trust and love. It was to acquire, not a legal title to their persons, but the free will offering of their hearts. Why that? Because the one needed thing,—a living goodness,—could be produced in the world in no other way. Because sin could not otherwise be conquered.

And in finding the object of the Advent, we begin to find also the motive and the method. There could be but one motive: "God so loved the world." The method: "The form of a servant," "born in a manger," "the death of the cross."

II. The Reception. This is man's part in the Advent; the coming was Christ's. It was for a few of the purer, simpler, more advanced spirits, of the age of his outward appearance, to welcome him: with what special illumination or help from on high, in that unspiritual time, and uncongenial people, we can never know. Here and there a stranger or foreigner clung to him. When it was told him, just before his crucifixion, that some Greeks were inquiring for him, Jesus seeing in that a promise that the self-sufficient *mind* of the world was feeling its way to him, cried, "The hour is come that the Son of Man should be glorified."

A true reception of Christ, for every man alike, is of three parts: belief, sympathy, service. These together make up the righteousness of faith, the great characteristic and criterion of a Christian.

There must be, first, a belief that he is what he says he is, the Only-begotten of the Father, Emmanuel, God with us, the Giver of Eternal Life, the Sender of the Comforter, the Everlasting and Almighty Head of his Church in heaven and earth, the Vine of which his followers are the branches, the Friend of the poor, the Foe of oppression, the Forgiver of sin. For any messenger, ambassador, prophet, the first condition of acceptance is that he be found to be what he claims to be: much more for the Saviour of mankind. He knows who he is, or not. If he does, he is all that these terms mean. If not, ignorance or deception would make him less than one of the honest soldiers that obeyed orders and led him away to the judgment-hall. The text makes this part of receiving him plain:

"As many as received him," i. e. it adds, they "that believe on his name."

But, again, there is no receiving the Saviour without sympathy. A plenipotentiary from one court to another, a bearer of despatches, a commercial agent, or a purely mental operator, does not need this. But the moment you include a moral purpose, spiritual influence, the kindling of any new life, there must be a common feeling; there must be assimilation. The interests must be felt as identical. Loyalty must bind the subject to his King. Enthusiasm must mount at the mention of the Leader's name. If the Saviour's purpose was to fill human breasts with love, we cannot be *his* without loving him.

"His own." There are two ways of belonging to another: unwilling and inevitable, or willing and hearty. You may belong to a nation by birth, and dislike it; to a family, from dependence or self-interest, and care for no welfare in it; to a university, and be out of harmony and out of temper with its administration. But so you cannot belong to the brotherhood that is the body of Christ. You must be in sympathy both with the brotherhood and its head. The legal ownership you cannot help; it brings no animation and no comfort. By your creation you are the Lord's, — his to be disposed of, to live or die, to be judged. The business of your new heart, "receiving Christ," is to change this reluctant belonging for the closer and grateful loyalty of affection; the legal bond for the gracious one of faith.

Yet there will be service too; only not the service of compulsion, but such service as they that love each other render without calling it service. "Lovest thou me? then feed my sheep;" "Inasmuch as ye have done it unto one of the least of these, ye have done it unto me." There is a cross to be taken up. There are the hungry, the sick, the ignorant, bondmen and prisoners, all around you. In them the Lord makes a new advent to your door and your heart, every winter, every week. For the illiterate and the educated alike there is always a field for good Samaritanism: somebody lying half-dead by the roadside. Christ will not be received by society, by governments, by us, till everybody within our reach is made, somehow, better by our faith in the Saviour of us all.

III. After the Coming and the Reception, is the Blessing. "To as many as received him, to them gave he power," and gives he power, "to become the sons of God." That is the sublime promise: have we ever thought, deeply, how much it means? Servants we were before, creatures of God, and, in the sense of owing life and comfort to his impartial providence, his children; but not in the full and glorious significance "the sons of God." They are the royal line. They are the heirs of immortality. They are the conquerors that overcome the world, and the sufferers that rejoice in the midst of affliction, and the lowly saints that come spotless and beautiful out of their great tribulation. Persecution perhaps has purified them. Ridicule perhaps has made their regeneration perfect. Temptation trampled down has brought angels to minister to them. Born now, not of the will of the flesh nor of the will of man, but of God, their immortal seed remaineth in them. They are the multitude whose praise no unbelieving tongue can join, whose joy no arrogant and unrepenting heart can understand.

It was thus that the moment Christ appeared, he became a judgment, or a judge. There was no visible bench, no formal sentence. He was even anxious to remove the impression that condemnation was his earthly errand. He said, "I came not to judge the world, but to save the world." Nevertheless the judgment comes, and by a law inwrought into all your souls. No one of you can ever be as if Christ had not appeared on the earth. To hear the name of Christ alters the relations of every human being to the highest facts, to God, to eternity. It was not so much any special saying; it was his character, his very nature, that was judicial. As soon as he was manifest, the whole world of men about him fell apart, and souls took their places on the right hand and the left. It was as if that divine presence located instantly every human life on earth. And so he added: "Though I came not into the world to judge it, though that is not my special mission here in the body, but to manifest God to you, yet afterwards, in the world to come, and in consequence of that manifestation, judgment will come, solemn, awful, inevitable, sudden as a thief in the night. The word that I speak unto you, that shall judge you."

The question, then, for the individual is this: Do we see Christ? Do we recognize and own our Lord? Whether he has come, where he is, whether he can be found, is not the matter we have to consider; nor whether we belong to him. He has come: he lives: he is visible to the eyes of faith: his life goes forth into the race forever, flowing into all hearts that will open to receive it, making them sons and kings and priests unto God.

"He came to his own, and his own received him

not." Can we let the passage go without a penitent conviction? See how pathos and rebuke are mingled in it! The sentence of a heavier condemnation never was written. Severity never spoke in a tenderer compassion. It is not weak complaint. It is not bitter sarcasm. It is not sentimentalism bewailing its own impotence. It is not tyranny exulting over its victim, and saying, "You would not give me your heart, and so I rejoice to see your heart crushed." It is another spirit, and has another sound. "He came to his own, and his own received him not." It is the sadness of parental affection repulsed. It is the sorrow of a heart that bleeds, not for itself, but for children lost, and knowing the misery before them as the children themselves cannot know it. It is one audible note of the unutterable pity of God for ungrateful souls.

And who are they? Men of the past only? Peasants and Pharisees of Palestine only? Students in the schools of the Scribes, and the Scribes that taught Hebrew learning only? Answer for yourselves. In a day that is coming, we must all answer for ourselves. Who are God's ungrateful children? "Last of all he sent his Son," saying, They have slighted my common mercies; they have ridiculed or criticised my mortal messengers: I gave them food from Heaven and fruitful seasons, and they feasted and drank and were merry and profane, and forgot me: I gave them friends, and they tempted them, misled them, dragged them down to their own level of denial, vanity, selfishness, and shame: they stoned my prophets: but "they will reverence my Son." "He came to his own; they received him not."

As was said at the beginning, it is the language of

narrative. But in what we have to do with the Eternal One, to whom there is no yesterday and no to-morrow, nothing old and nothing new, the past brings no excuses for the present. Time does not alter truth. There is no partiality for ages, nations, or persons. As John writes, there was an advent and a rejection: a bodily advent, a bodily crucifixion: the image and outer form of the Word that was from the beginning, the ever-living Emmanuel, the Christ that comes to-day. If he is rejected to-day, it is by the pride and fashion and self-indulgence of to-day. It is our compromising consciences, it is our well-dressed sensuality, it is our commercial cunning, it is our literary conceit, it is our making merchandise of men and of men's virtue, our covering up cruelty, and calling it patriotism; dishonesty, and calling it regular trade; hollowness and mutual flattery, and calling it good society; prayerless self-idolatry, and calling it a rational religion; — it is these things that prepare and build his cross, and crucify him afresh.

How to receive the Son of God: they that, in any sense, believe on his name will seek earnestly the full answer to that question. They will seek it through the giving up of the dearest preference that hurts the simplicity and humility of their faith. They will seek it in the New Testament, in Christian instruction, in prayer, in doing every hour all of God's will they know, in counting belief, not doubt, the glory and power and joy of man. Strong and ample minds will reverently bring their strength and amplitude, a free and noble offering to their Saviour's cause, yet not thinking it much to give Him who, knowing all that is in men, having all the science they are striving after, the wisdom of which their learning is but a broken alphabet, the Master of that world of Nature whose margin they are holding up dim lamps to explore, and commanding that spark of life at whose mysterious, silent secret, all their knowledge of phenomena stops short, and is dumb,— not much to give Him who, having power and honor like this, yet gave his own mortal life for them. The young will bring the freshness and dew of their youth. Life and lips will not give too much emphasis to that good confession. No energy of health, no affection of the heart, will be willingly excused.

And if you have sought elsewhere, but find something lacking yet, then candidly and cordially consider whether some further help may not possibly be held waiting for you, where thousands upon thousands of stronger minds and humbler hearts than any here have found it, at the foot of his cross, in the communion of his body and his blood, the sacraments of his presence, the memorials that he has come, the symbols of his sacrifice, the images of his bread of Truth, which whoso eateth never hungers, and of his spirit of Life which whoso drinketh never thirsts.

SERMON XVIII.

CHRIST OUR PROPHET, PRIEST, AND KING.*

THIS IS OF A TRUTH THAT PROPHET THAT SHOULD COME INTO THE WORLD. — John vi. 14.

THAT HE MIGHT BE A MERCIFUL AND FAITHFUL HIGH-PRIEST IN THINGS PERTAINING TO GOD, TO MAKE RECONCILIATION FOR THE SINS OF THE PEOPLE. — Hebrews ii. 17.

THEN PILATE SAID, ART THOU THE KING OF THE JEWS? JESUS ANSWERED, MY KINGDOM IS NOT OF THIS WORLD. — John xviii. 33, 36.

THE subject is so distinctly threefold that it may be properly introduced with these three sentences of Scripture. Jesus Christ is presented by them in three offices, different in kind, but neither of them inconsistent with the other two, and all of them together serving to manifest the completeness of his Messiahship, or his character as the spiritual Guide, the propitiatory Saviour, and the reigning Lord of men.

---

* This sermon was first preached in an extemporaneous form, Sunday before Easter, (April 17,) 1859. It was written out and repeated elsewhere, May 1. Early in that month an excellent article on the same subject, the authorship of which I do not know, but an article entirely independent of this discourse, and very likely in type when this was first delivered, appeared in the "American Theological Review." The lines at the end, and one sentence beside, are now borrowed from that paper.

Each of the statements stands for a class, with many other examples to be found in the Bible. Within each class the forms of expression vary, following the freedom of individual constitution and culture in the writers and speakers, or else suited to the special object, the argumentative connection, or the moral temperature and coloring, of the passage. But the agreement between them is substantial. They are all grounded in one absolute reality belonging to the Saviour's nature and ministry.

Thus there is one large class of declarations which place him before us as a prophet. In the Biblical sense, the prophet is a teacher. Prediction is one part of his office, but only one. As being the most surprising to common minds, it gives a name to the whole. But it is not the whole. The prophet predicts by virtue of that larger vision, or insight, which is a deep and general endowment of the prophetic soul, enabling him to look both before and after, over and beneath, inside and throughout the matter prophesied upon. He is related not so much to time or times, as to the eternal truth of God which is beyond time, and the same in all times, unchanged amidst the changeable. Hence his power of penetrating to the heart of a matter, reading its secret laws, and by that means knowing how it will act and come out in the future; a divine gift, an inspiration. He foretells to other men because he sees deeper than other men. He sees from the centre, and so takes in consequences and relations by detail in their just place, and their interior or heavenly order. Accordingly, the old Hebrew prophets were a race reformatory and agitating. They were far-sighted because they were deep-sighted. One of their names signifies this: *Seers.* By the same piercing wisdom they knew at once how men *would* act, and how they *ought* to act, and then what would be the consequences of their acting. This they stood up and told aloud. It demanded courage, as it always does. It made them the heroes of their age. They rebuked kings and people. They called the national customs and institutions to judgment. They not only knew the lower and craftier elements of human nature, which is the knowledge of human nature possessed by what are called "men of the world," but the loftier and more disinterested elements just as well. Acquainted with God, and gifted with internal admissions of his counsel, they could discern what retributions would come upon guilt, and what blessings upon the righteous. The report of what they saw was their message, — now terrible, then consolatory. Brave by their conscious nearness to God, and earnest because walking in his light, they kept nothing back shown them in the "Thus saith the Lord." Mere speech of this sort is heroic and sublime. What we call action is for others. Yet this is the soul's action. The organizing part of a reform may belong elsewhere. In the case of Moses, David, Samuel, and Gideon, the two were united: they were the prophets, both of legislation and empire. But Elijah, Miriam, Isaiah, Malachi, and many more only spoke; they roused and directed the active force of others; and thus, intermediately, they made revolutions boil and commonwealths grow.

Besides this, there may be other and different gifts of prophecy. But in the largest sense it is the communication of religious wisdom. And this, everywhere throughout the New Testament, Christ is exhibited to us as doing. His earthly ministry was greatly occupied with revelations of truth and expositions of duty; with openings of the secrets of Heaven and earth; with showing men their sins, and the way out of them; the possibilities of their nature, and the abuse of it; the judgment and the life to come. No reader of the New Testament need be told that the four Gospels are in great part records of these teachings or prophecies of Jesus. He knew all that was in man; and he came forth from God. This made him, not only one of the prophets, but that one Greatest of prophets that should come. The long line of ancient seers, whose highest errand it was to prepare the way for him, whose most glorious predictions foretold him, whose longing and aspiring souls had it for their grandest joy that they saw his day, culminated at last in his supreme and complete person, — the Light of the World. And accordingly his teachings, or prophesyings, had power and created effects, with which no others can bear any comparison. They were the words of God.

In another class of passages Christ is represented as a priest; indeed as the great High-Priest of the universe, as much above any mortal priesthood in power and dignity, as his nature transcends mortal limitations.

This name points us to a distinct office, and is traceable to a distinct fact. The prophet, we saw, communicates divine wisdom to men. The priest makes an offering for their sins. The próphet would enlighten and admonish men, to prevent their falling into transgression. The priest would reconcile and restore them after they have fallen into it. The prophet has to meet the want of ignorance; the priest, of repentance: both equally real.

The two are found standing side by side through all the Biblical periods. When religion became instituted in the Hebrew commonwealth, and entered into the national organization, or rather became its theocratic law, the two lines appeared in official representatives,—Moses rising as the head of prophets, and Aaron of priests. These were not arbitrary arrangements, but rooted in the necessities of history and the soul. And so things continued, till the external priesthood disappeared, being at once spiritually superseded and historically fulfilled by the one offering of the Redeemer: "who needeth not daily, as those high-priests, to offer up sacrifice, for this he did once when he offered up himself;" "who is made priest, not after the law of a carnal commandment, but after the power of an endless life;" who, "not by the blood of goats and of calves, but by his own blood, hath obtained eternal redemption for us;" and who hath, not every year, but "once," appeared "to put away sin by the sacrifice of himself." Says John, "Jesus Christ the Righteous is the propitiation for our sins, and not for ours only, but also for the sins of the whole world."

"By the sacrifice of himself:" this brings into view another part of the truth; that as all the old sacerdotal apparatus was to be now taken up and borne away, having its types, shadows, and significances realized in the Saviour, so under the general term "priest," in the evangelical usage, are included the several portions of the priestly work. Thus the New Testament abounds in the application of all manner of sacerdotal imagery to Christ. He makes the offering, and he is the offering itself. He is greeted on his first manifestation as the "Lamb of God that taketh away the sin of the world." From the first, his suffering and death, as the grand necessity of salvation, are foreshadowed to his followers, as they are able to bear it, in mysterious intimations. They form the clearer subject of the high and awful converse amidst the splendors of the Mount of Transfiguration. Every thorough reader feels that the account of them by the Evangelists is the central and vital thing, the heart of the Gospel record. Scarcely a page of the New Testament expressing the Christian consciousness of the Apostolic Church, and dealing with events coming after the crucifixion, fails to set them forth in their sacrificial character, and under an array of sacerdotal symbols. The Apostles preached it, wrote it, reasoned it, exulted in it, put it into their ascriptions and thanksgivings. It was the fire and ecstasy of their apostleship. Every place and utensil of the old altar service came in to help the redemptive impression. All that long, wonderful, providential Hebrew economy had prepared the moulds of thought and images of speech which are now taken up, spiritualized, and filled out. And the last voices we hear, as the sublime story of Revelation ends, and the apocalyptic visions of ages sweep away before us, are the voices of the mighty multitude, saying, "Worthy is the Lamb that was slain to receive power, and riches, and wisdom, and strength, and honor, and glory, and blessing."

In still another class of descriptions our Saviour is represented in royalty. A kingship pertains to him. He is the Ruler of an empire, the Leader of his people, a Prince of life and peace, the Captain of salvation, the Head of the tribes of the earth. In some rude and dim way all prophecy saw him in this imperial supremacy. That conception was local and national, and Christ himself had to expand and correct it by showing that his kingdom is not in the geography or the blood of Judaism, but in all the believing and loving hearts of men. Still, the idea is never abrogated nor forbidden. It is repeated rather, and certified. So before Pilate: "Art thou a king, then?" Jesus answered, assenting, "Thou sayest that I am a king!" But "my kingdom is not of this world," "not from hence." His apostles are always ascribing to him, in the abundance of their veneration and their trust, royal honors. They behold him "far above all principalities and powers," and "on his head many crowns." The truth which all these civic symbols only feebly shadow forth is the truth of his mighty protection, his magisterial elevation, and his personal guardianship over the spiritual organization of his Church. He was to be, as he is, the Lawgiver to the Society of Christendom, everywhere and forever, in his personal presence and in the principles that must govern the social progress and make man the brother of man.

From this glance at the positive representations of Christ's character let us turn back to ourselves. What can give the truths of religion a heartier welcome, than to find that they meet and satisfy wants that are waiting and perhaps aching in our own souls? Of the two indispensable methods of authenticating a revelation, — that which starts from external authority, and that which starts from these inner cravings that revelation supplies, — this latter is apt to seem the most natural. Only we are not to take our individual sense of need as measuring the real needs of mankind; and not to forget that many sacred wants of which we have not yet ourselves become conscious may begin to burn and cry within us, under some new experience yet to come. So that we cannot limit or deny, with respect to what lies beyond our wants; while yet in what really meets and fills them no other testimony is so valid.

The three several characters or offices of Christ already named have in them, we shall find, just this interior testimony: they are suited to deep, strong needs that spring up sooner or later in the sincere heart and earnest life of men. And there they offer their convincing proofs that he is what the Bible represents him, — the perfect Master of humanity, the Saviour of the soul, and Lord of the race.

Beyond question, one of our great, universal religious wants is knowledge of the truth. The moment we wake into life, or into the consciousness of life, the moment we begin to see what we are, and where we are, and what is given us to do, and what is put upon us to bear, then the souls within us begin to beg for light. Just as the intellect hungers for acquaintance with its own fields of action and laws of motion, and goes for that to its teachers, — to the prophets of science, and the prophets of art, and the prophets of society, who read nature deeply, and by their insight unfold her secrets, prognosticate her activities, or imitate her forms, — so the spiritual nature longs for its own illumination, — light upon itself, its path, its origin, its duty, its hereafter, its Maker. It says to whatever has God's wisdom in it, Prophesy to me! Darkness settles down on many questions; mysteries brood over each deeper sorrow of our life; we cannot wave them away with our hand nor scatter them with our breath. Veils hang across the path before us, so impalpable that our blind gropings cannot lift them. And as the things we wish to know lie beyond this world, or can only be interpreted from beyond it, we get only a partial satisfaction from the wisest of the mortal sages and all the human periods. Hence Christ came as a teacher. "This is that prophet that should come into the world." He opened his lips, we are told, wherever he came, and taught the people. They wondered at the gracious words which proceeded out of his mouth. Waysides and hills and common dwellings were the simple apparatus and open halls of his lessons. He unveiled the mysteries of the kingdom of heaven. Men wanted to know their parentage, and he taught them of the Father; their duties to each other, and he told them by parables and precepts; their destiny, and he uncovered the retributions and joys of their immortality. He laid bare the profound and vital meaning of all man's feeling, suffering, longing; of regeneration, and prayer, and charity; of spiritual unity, and worship, and the resurrection; of the relation of the spirit to the letter, of the new to the old; of the Father, and the Son, and the Comforter to each other. Men saw, and knew, and felt that the greatest of prophets was risen up among them.

But, as religious creatures, we have another want than that of religious knowledge, or of the impulse that knowledge gives. Already we have more knowledge than we have used. Hence this new want, wakened by a reproachful, insulted conscience: a heart penitent, convicted, shamed. How will a republication of legal requirements bring peace, when the misery is that we have broken those we had, and so have found out that "by the law is the knowledge of sin"?

Exactly, then, our second want is deliverance from

our evil, including both forgiveness for the past and strength now; — something to

> "Be of sin the double cure, —
> Cleanse us from its guilt and power."

Manifestly this cannot come from ourselves. It must come from Him whom our ingratitude has offended; from the Ruler whom our selfish wickedness has wronged. It must come from God.

Look closely at this want: for it is that vital spot in all humanity where sorrow is most keen, and where relief is most joyful. The sure result of evil is pain; of persistent sin is death. Hence the voluntary surrender to pain, pain even unto the body's death, is felt, and has been ever felt, to be the natural expression of a penitent soul. It is propitiation: not because God takes pleasure in his children's suffering, but because that is the soul's fitting tribute to the just majesty of goodness and the holy authority of Right. Government without penalty is gone, and all its blessed protections are dissolved. Hence the honest heart cries out in its shame and fear, "Let me suffer for my sin." Suffering for it there must be somewhere; transgression is a costly business; so it must always be and always look; right must stand at any rate; law must be sacred, or all is gone; and since nothing is so dear as life, and blood is the element of life, life itself must be surrendered, and "without the shedding of blood is no remission."

Take the next step. Just because this life is so dear, He who loves us infinitely, and to whom it is dearer than to us, will be willing to lay down for us his own. He will not even wait for our consent; but in the abundance of that unspeakable compassion, in the irresistible freedom of that goodness, he will do it beforehand, — only asking of us that we will believe he has done it, and, accepting our pardon, be drawn by that faith into the same self-sacrificing spirit. Herein is love indeed. Suffering for our peace! Sacrifice, not that our service may profit and pay him, but that our transgression of a Perfect Law may be pardoned, and the noble life of disinterested goodness may be begotten in ourselves. Before, we had seen God as Creator, Providence, Ruler, and all the motives to obedience furnished by those characters had been offered, and had failed. His servants, the prophets, had come, and come in vain. But now we see him in the new, more wondrous, and more gracious character of Sacrifice. The last proof of tenderness is given. Says Robertson, — and how truly! — "Is not the mystic yearning of love expressed in words most purely thus, 'Let me suffer for him'?" We want to feel that our God of infinite love feels that. Calvary is the full answer to that want. In the person of the Son he so comes down among us, and into us, as to suffer for us. We have a High-priest that can be touched with the feeling of our infirmities, — nay, takes those infirmities upon him, bears our sicknesses, is bruised for our iniquities, is delivered for our offences, dies that we may live. All the priestly offices are fulfilled. "Herein is love; not that we loved God, but that God loved us, and sent his Son to be the propitiation for our sins." The atonement by Christ becomes the inmost and grandest power of the world. It is the one peculiar, characteristic, crowning, glorious truth of the Gospel.

And then if you turn from what it does *for* us, as a redemption, to what it does *within* us, as an inspiration, the fruit of it is not less divine. For it appeals directly to what is noblest, most generous, most disinterested, in all the brave affections and aspirations of humanity. It rises up in harmony with, and surmounts with its grandeur, all the heroic and martyr sacrifices of mankind. Mechanical and mercantile conceptions of salvation vanish before it. Right becomes more venerable; love, more lovely; charity, more beautiful. It was of charity that the Saviour suffered. His cross teaches us, not that each one is to be looking out for a selfish salvation, but that self is to be forgotten in hearty consecration to him, and in free service to our brethren. It carries us clear of the belittling notions of escaping Hell as a punishment or earning Heaven as a reward. It makes the lofty sentiment of gratitude the mainspring of piety; faith, the pure inspiration of righteousness; love, the sacred secret of beneficence. We learn from the Redeemer, who gave himself for us, to give ourselves for one another. We take up that cross which signifies an atoning sacrifice, a voluntary, vicarious humiliation, a making of no reputation, and becoming poor, a taking of the form of a servant, and being made an offering for sin, for others' sake. Henceforth we abhor sin for itself, for our brethren's sake, for Christ's sake, and not merely for its penal consequences. We love goodness, and are loyal to it for itself; not merely for its wages. We not only "admire philanthropy," but we "love men," as those for whom Christ has been willing to die. We cease longing for rest, and begin to have joy in God, in the "spirit of liberty," and in the eternal life begun.

This is what is meant by Christ our Priest. This is that profound, penitential, sorrowing, unutterable want in human souls which the Redeemer meets, and which, because he meets it, makes the heart that is thus consciously set at liberty leap with gratitude and gladness to join the praises which give blessing, and honor, and glory to Christ. It will not be for any of us to say there is no need of a blessing so deep and a joy so great. You may say you have not yet felt the need of it; and that — O pity of God! — may be mournfully true. But close by you is a heart which feels that beside this want and its bitterness all the common griefs of mortality are trifles of the air: the want of reconciliation with the Father in heaven; the want of an assured forgiveness; the want of Christ and him crucified. Where that is once stirred and alive, — and the first object of the New Testament is to stir it and make it alive, because that is the only way to peace and power, — there you find a heart that only one word of earth or heaven can reach. You may tell it that its sorrow is all needless and irrational; that all we have to do in this world is "to do right," or as near it as we can; but it will only look back upon you with speechless wonder. Do right? What if, with the strongest of apostles, I do not "find how" to do right? What if the right seems to me too high and holy a thing, and too far off, that I should do it of myself? What if, all my life long, by doing or leaving undone, I have come all too terribly short even of the right I knew? Then let me have, what the blessed, merciful Gospel gives me, a Redeemer! Let me rest my heart upon the cross! Take not away my Lord!

"Rock of ages, cleft for me,
Let me hide myself in thee!
Let the water and the blood
From thy riven side which flowed,
Be of sin the double cure,
Cleanse me from its guilt and power!

"Not the labor of my hands
Can fulfil thy Law's demands;
Could my zeal no respite know,
Could my tears forever flow,
All for sin could not atone:
Thou must save, and thou alone!"

Another real want of men whose Christian sensibility has been made alive, is that of a conscious and friendly and loyal relationship to the Saviour now. If those who do feel and utter this want misinterpret by it the feeling of some others who have no such want, it is very evident that they do not mistake the almost universal and unbroken testimony of the Christian world, declared in ten thousand trusting and supplicating and thankful voices from age to age. We look to a Lord who knows his own, watches and remembers them from his merciful throne in the heavens, calls them by their names in the personal faithfulness of his affection, and lends them secret powers from his kingly fountain of power. The mediation did not end with the sacrifice and the earthly theophany. It is a living Lord that we worship. It is an abiding as well as royal Shepherd that we follow, significantly typified in the shepherd king of old. Again, fulfilling a far earlier type, he is the true Melchisedek,—as the argument of the Epistle to the Hebrews so beautifully proves,—blending the sacerdotal and the regal offices together; Prince while also he is Priest. Consult the inmost faith of the truly believing heart, which has once given all to Him who gave himself for us, and see what a bleak bereavement would fall like midnight upon it, if you were to sweep away from it this perpetual privilege of confiding, loyal, adoring fellowship with its ascended, crowned, and yet ever condescending King.

Observe then, also, how these several titles of majesty

not only apply separately, to affirm the cordial ascriptions of the Church to the Son of God, but how they mutually sustain and fill out one another's appropriate meaning. We need the Prophet, to give us the knowledge and arouse in us the feeling of what religious duty is. We need the Priest of Sacrifice, to restore and reconcile and pardon us when duty has been lost. We need, too, the holy and governing Head, to preside over and guide and intercede for and quicken us, till we come into the assembly of the Just, the Church of the First-born, — when the kingdoms of this world are all made the kingdoms of our Lord. In these three celestial characters of the Son we find the manifestation of what we are taught to believe are the three great attributes of God, — wisdom, love, power, — wisdom in the Teacher, love in the Sacrifice, power in the King. To the end of days, every redeemed soul confesses to the Master, "My faith looks up to thee!"

Christ gathers a community. He binds together a brotherhood. He is the "Prince of Peace," — a peace that he has made through the blood of his cross, breaking down or melting away the "walls of partition." Each individual believer rejoices in the social consolation. Indeed, every one of the three offices, with the three corresponding dispositions in us, — docility to the Teacher, faith in the Propitiator, loyalty to the Ruler, — becomes a theme of thanksgiving. No one of them depresses, disempowers, or restrains our energies. They all uplift, encourage, and liberate. They are full of animation, promise, gladness. The Teacher enlightens; and what more glorious or gladdening gift than light? The living Sacrifice rolls away the burdens of remorse, and sets us in a world where love is seen forever victorious, with the cross for its sign. The "Head over all things to his Church" inspires us with the felicity of a Divine friendship, opens to us the inviting doors of that kingdom which is not of this world, — embracing earth and heaven, the holy life here and the holy life everlasting.

It is not strange, then, that, from the beginning, these great names have been chosen by the highest souls in the Church and the deepest-sighted believers, like Chrysostom and Augustine and Aquinas, like Melancthon and Gerhard and Krummacher, to set forth the homage due to the Master. Only three centuries of Christian history had passed, when Eusebius, the early historian, spoke of it as the prevailing conception of the Messiah. "High-priests, kings, and prophets," he writes, "were anointed as types, so that they all had respect to the true Christ, the Logos full of God, who is the only High-priest of the whole, the only King of all creation, and the only Arch-prophet of the prophets of the Father."

It is the right of the Church to celebrate her Head. Let us come without misgiving or miserable reservations to our privilege, having apostles and confessors and the holy teachers of centuries, and the heart of Christendom, to join us. It is no speculative nor barren praise. No words nor work of ours, when the spiritual currents that flow through us and the laws of divine impression are laid open, will be found more practical. Every honest tribute to Christ quickens that life within which Christ alone kindles. To exalt him is to ennoble ourselves. To venerate the Prophet is to open the mind to his wisdom. To thrill with faith in the Heavenly Priest is to yield the heart to the power of his love. To behold the King's majesty is to let the will find joy in obedience. All life will be simpler for this reverence; the world more beautiful; religion more real. We shall come from the high mount of communion with Jesus inspired for a nobler week-day righteousness among men.

For, finally, we are not to forget another practical and immediate lesson. In such differing measure as their capacity renders possible, all disciples are to bear their own faithful and cheerful part in the same three offices of holy influence in which our Saviour has now been passing before us. Whoever lets his Christian light shine daily before men, in the humility and charity and beauty of holiness, teaches the heavenly wisdom. Whoever surrenders self to truth, to mankind, to Christ, enters into the grandeurs of disinterested sacrifice, and, with the Crucified, dies unto the world. And we know that whoever shall suffer thus with him "shall reign with him." In these immortal ways, as the Spirit signifies, the sons and daughters of men shall "prophesy," and the patient servants be made "kings and priests unto God."

Unto the Saviour, then, glorious Head over all things to his Church, and blessed Lord of each disciple's life, only Name under heaven given among men whereby we can be saved, faith shall bring us with unquestioning adoration.

"Live in me, Prophet, Priest, and King!
As Prophet, lead me in thy light!
As Priest, present my offering!
Lead and restrain me by thy might,
So that, as King, thou mayst fulfil
In me thy kingdom, all thy will!
Live, Christ, live thou in me!"

SERMON XIX.

THE CROSS A BURDEN OR A GLORY.*

AND AS THEY CAME OUT, THEY FOUND A MAN OF CYRENE, SIMON BY NAME; HIM THEY COMPELLED TO BEAR HIS CROSS. —Matthew xxvii. 32.

BUT GOD FORBID THAT I SHOULD GLORY, SAVE IN THE CROSS OF OUR LORD JESUS CHRIST.— Galatians vi. 14.

HERE are two kinds of suffering: two ways of bearing the cross. We are struck, first of all, with the contrast between the positions of these two men, the effects they have wrought, the impressions they have made, the memories they have left in the world.

One of them is a mere name on the reader's tongue; the other is a living power in the heart of Christendom. One is a vague, feeble, uninspiring form; the other is a clear, radiant person, standing erect close to the centre-point of the world's grandest revolution, and moving distinct and strong among the most vivid and hallowed realities of history. Why this difference?

As the executioners, the paid officers of the government, and the willing servants of the priests, after the judicial mockery was over, led the Lord of Life

*Good Friday, 1858.

away to the place of his crucifixion, they found their victim physically unable to bear the weight of the wood whereon he was to be nailed and to die. It was not unusual, in such cases, to require some substitute to take up and carry that burden. Simon the Cyrenian happened to be by the way, a convenient drudge for the cruel purposes of the men: a stranger, a mere looker-on at the spectacle, not worse, not better, so far as we know, than the crowd that usually follows a passing procession, or gazes at a public punishment. It does not appear that any sympathy had been kindled between him and the sufferer; that he had any glimpse of the meaning of the Messiah or of his message; that one touch of spiritual illumination from that "Light of the World" had reached him, nor that one thought of the glory of the august sacrifice that was preparing made the cross feel lighter to him. It must have been heavy, and it must have seemed hard, as many crosses seem. As far as appears, he was the reluctant, stolid instrument of an arbitrary command, compelled to a menial service by an insolent and overbearing police. So Simon bore the cross of Christ.

Some years after, — but, remember, long before the cross had come to be the badge of honor and of beauty it is now, or anything but a mark of criminal disgrace, as the gallows, the penitentiary, and the pillory are to us, — while the Crucified was yet a name of general reproach, ridiculed in courts, despised by the religious and respectable, scarcely known to learning and fashion, — to the Jews a stumbling-block, and to the Greeks foolishness, — Paul, convert and apostle, was writing to a little company of believers he had gathered at Galatia in that outcast name. He, too, had seen Christ, but not in the body; had come after him in another sense; had gone to his crucifixion in a reverent, tender, sympathizing faith; had bowed his whole believing spirit with his body under the burden; had been hunted, hated, impoverished, stripped, scourged, imprisoned, banished, for that Crucified One's sake. It was not compulsory with him, but voluntary. He did not do it like Simon, because he must, save as the necessity lay in his own willing conviction, the free choice and irrepressible love of his heart. So Paul bore the cross of Christ, and he said of it, God forbid that I should glory in any thing but that, boast of anything but that infamy, count anything gain but that loss, be proud of anything but that humiliation!

To-day, Simon is but an insignificant and buried unit in the vanished multitude of the Past. Paul is alive among us; preached and preaching; converting mankind to truth, influencing nations, forming the ages, a master-builder still in the Church.

These two men represent two different attitudes of the soul or states of feeling, — neither of them very uncommon, — before the divine facts. Corresponding to them are two ways of meeting the inevitable discipline of Providence, — two ways of dealing with that deep exercise of the conscience which makes the cross necessary, — two ways of interpreting the signification and power of the cross itself, the Saviour's suffering. Let us take each in its order; for there is a natural order among them.

I. First, there is the constant, ordinary discipline of human life. By discipline we commonly understand some degree of pain, because we have all found out that we cannot learn, nor grow, nor prevail, without that.

There must be some restraining of desire; some denial of propensity; some yoke on the passions; some sacrifice of the less for the greater, of the present for the future, of pleasure for right, of inclination for duty. In all this there is suffering. Life, whenever it is earnest, contains more or less of this sacrificial element. Owing to temperament, to external influence, to inherited tendencies, to various causes, some of which we can explain and more that we cannot explain, this ingredient of sorrow differs in amount, differs in form. The principal fact is that every individual experience has, soon or late, its painful side, its crucial hours, when there is darkness over all the land, and we cry out to know if God has forsaken us. For the time, longer or shorter, we taste only the bitter, and feel only the thorns. The separations of death, the distance between our aspiration and performance, unsatisfied ambition, laboring year after year in vain, affection returned by indifference, the symptoms of fatal disease, former energy prostrate, a friend alienated, a child depraved, an effort to do good construed into an impertinence, — unconquerable obstacles that we cannot measure and can scarcely speak of, heaped up against our best designs, — these are some of the most frequent shapes of the misery; but no list is full. The one essential thing is that the will is crossed, crucified. Character is everywhere put into this school of suffering.

Without any pretence of insight, we know, for we are very plainly told in two separate volumes — the volume of past experience and the volume of the Book — why this is. It is Paul's old warfare of the law of the flesh and the law of the spirit. It is the conflict of two necessary moral opposites, on the great scale of humanity.

There is a battle of Good and Evil, and these special miseries are the bruises of the blows that fill the air,—sometimes seeming to fall at random, and perplexing our reason, because we cannot rise to such height of vision as to take in the whole field at once. It is a mixed engagement; we are socially responsible; we suffer both with and for one another, all the time. Suffering is the tax we have to pay for the privilege of being free to choose. Only this is but half the account of the matter; and we are hopelessly, desperately puzzled, till we see running through all this sorrow, working freely in all its various griefs, and using every pain for a means of purity, the steady wisdom and all-controlling Love of God our Father. In other words, sin is in the world, and death by sin Evil has but one source. There is a Law, which is Love. The commandment is holy, just, and good. Evil comes of the chafing of our disobedient, finite, selfish will against that perfect will of God. But the distribution of its natural pains is clearly not simply according to personal deserving: it is for an end of good thoroughly foreseen only by the All-seeing. We are helpless to explain our cross; but we have it to bear.

Here are presented those two sorts of moral condition, two postures of the soul, indicated in the two men of the text. One takes his troubles bitterly, unwillingly, unthankfully. He dreads them when he sees them coming. He runs from them while there is space to run. He struggles against them as long as he can. And then, as their fearful, irresistible step presses on him and overtakes him, he is borne down. He is their victim, not their pupil. They conquer him, and are not conciliated as his friends. If they are little troubles, they fret his temper and disfigure his dignity; he complains sentimentally or curses profanely. If they are larger, he only yields in terror or sinks in stupor. Bereavement has then but two reliefs: either he must be so cool-blooded that his affliction is really tolerable, or so proud that he is ashamed to weep; these failing, selfish affection mourns without hope. He is afraid to die, because it was not for Christ and man that he lived. He hates the world he has abused. He blames the Providence he has thwarted. He satirizes the life he has spoiled and emptied. He calls it poor, a mockery,—calls the world hollow, men hypocrites. He suffers; no doubt of that. None knows it better than he. The sorrows have got hold upon him, and he aches under their hands. But there is no faith; no submission; no stronger heart, nor sweeter patience, nor gentler charity, nor growing hope. He suffers because he cannot help it; dull, hard, dark, comfortless pain. "Him they compelled to bear the cross."

The other, too, suffers. Agony is not abolished for him. The grand laws of mortal travail are not revoked for him. The nerves of believers are not callous, nor the sensibilities of saints deadened. For evils in them and evils around them they suffer. But they suffer as Paul suffered, turning tribulation into victory, drawing peace from pain. The sorrow laid on them they take up so cheerfully that it loses half its weight. They can put off the body without alarm, because they subdued it long ago to the spirit. They can be disappointed in their plans, because the Almighty has other servants. They can say, as Dr. Arnold wrote in his journal late on that last evening of his life while yet in perfect health, after alluding to other and more public aspirations,—aspirations for England and for the Church,—"Above all, let me mind my own personal work, — to keep myself pure and zealous and believing, laboring to do God's will, yet not anxious that it should be done by me rather than by others if God disapproves of my doing it." They can endure the departure of trusted things and even trusted persons, as by faith seeing the invisible which never departs. They can let their children, their mothers, the most beautiful and the most beloved die, not unsorrowing, but consenting, because they know that their Redeemer liveth. They can be crucified unto the world, because the world is already crucified unto them. They can lift their cross up, and glory in it.

So every common trouble — a sickness or a broken scheme, a bruised heart or a defeated will — comes with a cross which is like two crosses in its hands. Feel no God to be there, and it sorely wears you down, — down till you die under its weight. Take it up in Christ's name, bear it for his sake, and it is light, — lighter than air. It is a "changed cross." It lifts you up as you bear it.*

II. But as we carry our search inward and downward, we reach a trouble deeper, darker, than any of these I have named. If we really feel it at all, we feel that no other sorrow can be compared with it. Till we have felt it, all descriptions of it by others must sound extravagant, austere, unmeaning; but when it has once come in and taken hold of our souls then we say no language, no penitent's self-reproach, no prodigal's cry of unworthiness, not Augustine's burning confessions, not the hot anguish of the fifty-first Psalm, is overwrought or too earnest. For what words can tell too

---

* "Si crucem libenter portes, te portabit." — Thomas à Kempis.

strongly the wretchedness of feeling self-condemned? My friends, that is an actual feeling. That is one of the states of a human soul like yours and mine. We may be awkward and faulty in our attempts to define it. We may put the wrong name to it. We may use the words of systems, or of creeds, or of other people, when we ought to take the first plain word that leaps to our lips; and so men may say, That is not a true image; that does not show the thing as it is. No matter, so you only know the thing. We are not thinking about the artist's skill, nor about words, but about a pressing, personal fact. It *is* a fact; and therefore even common sense will accept it. It is a state where men are found; and science, which has to consider storms as well as light, pain as well as comfort, must look at it. It is an experience of the human soul; and therefore philosophy, to say nothing of faith, would have to take it into her studies. But all these, when they have done their best upon it, will be glad to send us back to the New Testament, and hand the problem over to the Great Reconciler. Ah, if it were *not* a fact, no such Great Reconciler would have come. There would have been no Good Friday, no Gethsemane, no Calvary, no Pascal Sacrifice, no "Lamb slain from the foundation of the world." Nay, there would have been no Church, no altar of communion, no anthem of affliction, no wailing Miserere, such as to-day prepares our adoration of the Redeemer. SAVIOUR would be a word without a meaning. There would be no cross for Simon to bear; none for Paul to glory in.

This, at least, we know: when that hour of a great conviction, that sense of a new and awful necessity, has come, it finds a secret voice of its own, broken perhaps with penitence, incoherent with remorse, humble with shame; but the same voice that has breathed itself into the confessions of prostrate congregations, into the litanies of the kneeling thousands of the Church. It says, I acknowledge my transgression, and my sin is ever before me. Lo, thou art my Father, and yet I am not thy filial child. Thou art Love itself, and I have not loved thee; Truth itself, and I have not been true to thee; Purity itself, and I have been unclean, — unclean before thee! All the affection of mother and of father, of sisters and brothers, of friends and lovers, gathered into one bright and beaming sun of tender and unchanging sympathy, would be only a shadow of thy kindness, for thy nature is infinite, and all that nature is mercy; yet to that I have been ungrateful, and against that have I been insensible. Verily, against thee, thee only have I sinned! Thou didst shape and fashion my body, and in thy book all my members were written; yet selfishness has been in my heart and reins, in my blood and my bones, in my nerves and my motions. I am "shapen in iniquity." Thou desirest truth in the inward parts; yet inwardly and outwardly, in myself and in society, in my business with the world and in my bosom, in tongue and deed, how often have I been false, — false to the best I knew, false to duty, false to thee! Nay, thou didst make and order the way of holiness to be the way of safety and peace and joy for me; and not even that would draw and keep me. Thou didst bid me, in eating and drinking, and in whatsoever I should do, do all for the glory of God; and I have lived for myself, for a paltry pleasure, for an empty admiration, for a passing breath of fame. Thou didst give thy dearly beloved and only begotten; and practically I have denied him.

He came down to the earth, and I would not let him lift me to heaven. He took my poor nature and infirmities, and was tempted with me, yet I would not become a partaker of the divine nature with him. He groaned and prayed in the olive shade, and did sweat great drops of blood, and died for me; and I would not live for him. O Lord, most merciful! O Saviour and Redeemer most pitiful! purge me, wash me, and I shall be clean! Forgive, spare, renew, recover me! I am not worthy to be called thy child! My God! my God!

Just here, then, appear to us again the two aspects of the Cross. Hard, loveless, unwilling, drudging duty: shall that be our way? A cross, indeed, but not Christ's cross. "Him they compelled to bear the cross." All life will be crucifixion, and all our consciences will be servile Cyrenians. It will be law, and nothing but law. We shall be eye-servants, not loving children. Existence will be a task, and not a privilege; our service will answer to an exacting homily, and not a hymn of praise. We shall work at it, or grind under it, in bondage to the commandment, not in the cheerful liberty of the sons of God with which Christ makes his people free. Lingering in the old Judaism and its legality, keeping a score of merits, weighing and gauging our own stock of virtues, bent in self-inspection till the energies are crippled and faith consumptive, we shall never get beyond "Thou shalt." If we see ourselves as we are, by the law itself, we shall be terrified, and work only from fear, and the world will be covered with gloom. If we flatter and deceive ourselves that we are as good as we need be, we shall stand still, and that is destruction. Our God will not be a Father, but a Judge. Christ, in his true character, as a disinterested, life-giving Propitiator, who takes the soul over from its condemnation to its freedom and acceptance, we shall not know at all. Here is exactly the point where so many of Paul's arguments, utterly unintelligible without this key, but clear as day with it, converge, and write their conclusion in letters of light. "By the deeds of the law shall no flesh be justified," — not Jewish law only, but Divine law everywhere, anywhere, in Rome, England, America, simply because the Divine law is always vastly greater and higher than human performance, and so always a broken law, — of course no man justified by its deeds. Our blessed Redeemer has taken all the misery and suffering and penalty of the broken law upon him, and sent the believer on his way joyous, unburdened, free. "The law made nothing perfect;" it only told what the perfect was, — did not inspire the motive, the love, to keep it. If kept at all, as law, it would be by fear, or a selfish seeking for safety from its penalty, not by self-forgetting loyalty. "If ye are led by the Spirit, ye are not under the law, but under grace." Law is compulsory; grace is free. Law is obligatory; the Gospel is attractive. Law is command; the covenant in Christ, which "the law cannot disannul," is promise. Law is terrible; the Spirit is animating, — pardon, peace, love, joy, gentleness, goodness, faith.

Yes: Law alone is a cross. Here stands the anxious conscience, troubled, discouraged, looking far up at the blazing standard, the commandment, and then looking back at its disordered and miserable self; no way of bringing the two together. It needs a Reconciler, who shall not lower the law, but keep it, honor it, magnify it, and at the same time lift up, forgive, reinvigorate man, and breathe a new life of the Holy Spirit into him.

It needs that mediator; another cross, not Simon's cross now, but Paul's. Man is in need, not of another commandment, but of a consistent pardon for not keeping and of a new affection impelling him to try to keep the old one. By the law was the knowledge of sin; what he wants is a way, a deliverance, a justification. "The law made nothing perfect," "but the bringing in of a better hope did."

Do we then make duty less important, less sacred? Infinitely more important, infinitely more sacred, because it is duty, not to a stern judge, but to a Father; not to one ready to condemn, but ready, through his own gracious atonement, to accept. "Do we make void the law? Nay, we establish the law." Law, conscience, the sense of duty, did great things for us; it pointed us to the right, it showed us our weakness; it disciplined us, and made us ready for a higher and a more spiritual relation. "The law was our schoolmaster to lead us to Christ," and "Christ is the end of the law for righteousness to every one that has this faith." Nor has it done with the disciple yet; only since Christ has died, it is transfigured into invitation, become "spiritual," "good."

The believer is not exempt then from work, nor from pain. He works with tenfold the legalist's earnestness; he may suffer with tenfold the moralist's pain. But he longs to work, and he is willing to suffer, in the joy of his thankful faith. Paul bore the cross no less than Simon; and it *was a cross*; no easy figure nor fanciful image of it. Yet it was a cross not laid on reluctant shoulders. He took it up, and lo! it grew light in his hands. He welcomed it, and it glowed with lustre, as if it were framed of the sunbeams of heaven. He embraced it in the arms of his trust; and then he could say, God forbid that I should glory in anything but that!

III. Thus, thirdly, the same spiritual contrast, the same principle of difference between compulsory and voluntary service opens to us two interpretations of the suffering of the Saviour himself. Neither the cross of Simon nor the cross of Paul was both literally and actually the cross of Christ. Simon's was literally; the same cross, but how different in fact! Paul's was not literally; but in kind, in moral sympathy, in religious purpose, in the unity of faith, only not in degree, as the disciple may resemble the Master,—the same. We pass up now above them both to the one cross original, supreme, all-sufficient, on which were laid the iniquities of us all, by which the world was redeemed, on which, as the Sufferer himself said, even as Moses lifted up the serpent in the wilderness, that whosoever looked might be healed, the Son of Man was lifted up, that he might draw all men unto himself.

We mistake utterly both the attraction and the power of that sacrifice, the moment we regard it as a reluctant compliance with necessity. Its charm was that it was chosen. Its power was that it was free. "No man taketh my life from me; I lay it down of myself. I have power to lay it down, and I have power to take it again!" The divine dignity of those words! as divine as the mercy.

Such, in kind, observe, is the wonderful transforming energy of the spirit, of the soul, of its affections, its charity, even in man. Outward things are pliant, plastic, completely subject to it. The plainest face, to eyes that love really looks through, has a kind of beauty in it, not of the features. A child's deformity comes to wear a grace in the mother's tender beholding. Prison walls are palaces to the martyr whose heart holds daily court there, for the King of kings. All measurements are reversed, all criticisms are reconsidered, all blemishes are beautified, when this transfiguring light of love touches them. That special sign of debasement, of mingled servility and crime, the slave's scourge, the cross, becomes glorious when the Son of God takes it up; there is goodness enough in him to exalt it. The pain of dying was joy to him, because the compassion of Heaven flowed down through the pierced and bleeding body. Then was the Son of Man glorified. The nails, and the thorns, and the spear, and the reed, and the rough soldiers' insulting hands were honorable to him and welcome, because they only signalized that sacrifice where self was forever crucified for love.

Yes; the freeness of the sacrifice was its efficacy. It was no device of perplexed counsels, no expedient for an emergency, no escape from a surprise. If we make it so in our poor systems, we put a compelled cross on the Lord of all our liberty. It was the way chosen from the beginning. God so loved the world. It was not the offering of the Father alone, nor of the Son alone, but of the Divine heart of God in them both, — a heart that was loving before the foundation of the world, and finding this overwhelming utterance at last. There, at Calvary, was set up the one immovable, unfailing, everlasting barrier against the tyranny and triumph of Evil. There the waves of hatred, oppression, envy, unbelief, scorn, sensuality, and every sin, break their force, — dashing in vain, and dying away against that planted cross; for its living roots are wound by God into the centre and core of the world. No wonder the sufferer was "amazed," as he went to the garden! No wonder, as the shining ones, prophets of the elder covenant, met him on the Mount of Transfiguration, this was the theme of their high communion, and they spoke together of "the decease which he should accomplish at Jerusalem." No wonder, as the hour drew on, sorrow and victory took their sway by turns in his feeling, for he was the son of Mary as well as the son of God. "Now," he said, "Now is the Son of Man glorified;" and then, with natural anguish, "My soul is exceeding sorrowful, even unto death," and in the dear craving for human sympathy that brings him down from Tabor and Zion so near to us in our mortal Gethsemane, "Tarry ye here and watch with me." Now it was the cry, "If it be possible, let this cup pass from me;" but immediately after, "Daughters of Jerusalem, weep not for me, but for yourselves and your children." Amidst the pangs of the crucifixion, now it was a prayer for himself, Son of Man; "My God! my God! why hast thou forsaken me?" and then a prayer for his murderers, out of the bosom of his own divinity, "Father, forgive them, for they know not what they do." And just in the measure that the spirit of his sacrifice is in us shall we be praising him that the path of his eager choice was the march to the Passover, to his Passion.

Doubtless there was a necessity. Sufferings like that, in all the Father's universe, are nowhere borne superfluously. Crosses are nowhere laid on, save as there is necessity. It is the necessity that comes of the inevitable conflict of right with wrong. It is the irreconcilable issue of the law of God and the disobedience of man.

The first must stand, have its way, be honored, be vindicated, be maintained. If Justice, blessed Justice, holy shield and safeguard of all our peace both human and divine, should falter, and falter up there in its very throne and fountain, the order of nature would be shaken into anarchy. But then, the goodness that encompasses all that necessity, wiser than the wit of human legislation, knows how to solve its hopeless problem; and the cross is its solution. It is freely borne; it is chosen; it is gloried in. He that gives himself, saying, "I and my Father are one," how shall he not move, and save, and atone? He that gives his Son, and is in him, reconciling the world unto himself, how shall he not forgive? Well might Paul, and the Church, and the Christian ages, and our grateful rejoicing eyes, looking up to that "miracle of time," "God's own sacrifice complete," glory in it.

Our Ruler is our Father. He is "just, and the justifier of him that believeth in Jesus." God forbid that we should not glory in this!

And if we glory in it, friends, in the only practical way, and with a living sympathy, we shall share in the spirit of that sacrifice. Daily self-denials, cheerfully undertaken, will lighten life of its gloom, and make the burdens of all about us easier. Pride will not join with the Pharisees, nor indifference with Pilate, nor luxury with Caiaphas, nor unbelieving learning with the scribes, nor cruelty and slavery to man with the soldiery, nor sensuality with the rabble, to crucify the Son of God afresh and put him to an open shame. False manners, false living, false speaking, will not deny him. Pretending to be Christians, we shall not, by coldness on the one hand, nor by bigotry toward brethren on the other, make the blood of this meek and holy "Lamb of God without blemish and without spot," to be an unholy thing. Hardship will not be a hopeless burden. Pain will not make us forget our patience. Trouble will not turn us away, ungrateful, from our Father's face. Repentance will not be compulsory. Faith will not be reluctant. Love will cast out fear. Nay, in all these things, we shall be conquerors, and more than conquerors, through Him who hath loved us and given himself for us, by whom the world is crucified unto us, and we unto the world, — that, being dead unto sin, we should live, new creatures, in the Spirit.

SERMON XX.

LIFE, SALVATION, AND COMFORT FOR MAN IN THE DIVINE TRINITY.

GO YE, THEREFORE, AND TEACH ALL NATIONS, BAPTIZING THEM IN THE NAME OF THE FATHER, AND OF THE SON, AND OF THE HOLY GHOST. — Matthew xxviii. 19.

THE Saviour spoke these words at a moment fitted above all others for a clear and full declaration of the fundamental article of Christian belief. It was at the end of his visible ministry on earth and his outward connection with his people. It was when he was commissioning his chosen disciples to their work, — a work which was to take up and bear on his own work through all the future ages. In every respect, it was the natural and fitting time for the decisive, explicit communication of the one essential characteristic truth of his religion. The "teaching Church" was then to be told what was to be taught. That central and sublime verity on which the whole matter of the Gospel rested was to be condensed into a brief, comprehensive, significant sentence. This is the last hour. It is the critical and awful meeting and commingling of two wondrous periods, — the period of the Incarnation, and of the everlasting age of the organized Christian commonwealth. Now, if ever, Christ will distinctly proclaim the doctrine of Christendom. We listen with breathless anxiety to hear what Christianity means. Under these solemn conditions, at this unparalleled crisis, it is remarkable that our Lord gives his Church three things necessary to its life, — a Ministry, an initiatory Ordinance, a Creed: — Go and teach, — baptize, — in the Triune name. What concerns us now is, not the order of Preachers, nor the Sacraments, but the Doctrine. We find here no recapitulation of moral and spiritual precepts, as the ethical view would lead us to expect; no array of what are sometimes called practical directions. We find something more grandly profound and more intensely practical. Our faith is summoned to the three persons of the one God: the Father, the Son, and the Holy Ghost. No hint is given that there is any difference of nature, dignity, duration, power, or glory between them. There is nothing in the situation, the relations, or the contents of the Divine formula to suggest that either of the three is less than the others, or less than God. The obvious, unforced, natural interpretation is that the Three are persons, and that the Persons are three. Each of them is elsewhere in the Scriptures referred to as God. Each of them is distinguished from the others by the personal pronouns. To each of them Divine attributes and Divine acts are ascribed, and to each Divine worship is offered. So, by a vast preponderance, the Church of Christ has received and held these words. So all the parts and powers and operations of the entire Gospel agree. The term *Trinity* is not applied to the doctrine in the Bible; but it is a definite and just description of what the Bible teaches; and there is no reason why it should not be adopted and used. It is sanctioned by the venerable and hallowed custom of Christian centuries, and of innumerable hosts of confessors, sages, and saints. There is an especial reason for using it if from its omission the inference should be anywhere drawn that the truth itself, which the term conveys, is denied. Calvin said he was willing that the name "Trinity" should be "buried and forgot," if only this could be the accepted faith of all,—that Father, Son, and Holy Spirit, each distinguished by a peculiar property, are one God. Equally willing ought we to be to take up and assert that name, if thereby we may render to this "accepted faith" any more unambiguous or unreserved honor.

Let the solemn and tender spirit of that parting scene where the doctrine was announced with such august authority be given to our unworthy attempt to reaffirm it! It ought to be the last of all subjects to be handled in a hard, technical, jejune, or merely dogmatic treatment. Still less should the sharp, fierce temper of dialectical ambition or partisan controversy intrude to embitter the discussion. How different might have been the result, for the interests of a true theology and an undefiled religion, if, in their arguments and expostulations for their Master's divinity, believers had always remembered the gentleness of his example! May that Lord of perfect love breathe a better influence over the studies, reasonings, and persuasions of those who seek to behold and publish his glory! No apprehension, however clear or deep, of the great reality of the Three-in-one can justify a defence with the unhallowed weapons of pride, denunciation, or dogmatism. We must remember there is also a threefold unity of the complete human goodness, as of the being of our God, and that of this charity is the perfect bond. If we break it, earnestness may plead in extenuation for us, but it never expunges the wrong. And with charity let us try to keep humility; — try to keep it the more, since one of the plainest offices of the special mystery of faith before us is to require and preserve this lowliness of the Christian mind. Where the arrogant, self-asserting intellect has to veil its face, presumption in judgment may well lie still. If in all the circle of sacred themes there is one where both the dryness of scholastic speculation and the acerbity of polemics should be laid aside, where the method should be spiritual, the tone devout, and all the thoughts penetrated and tempered with the fragrancy of holy affections, it surely is this.*

It may furnish an aid to this catholicity, as it certainly is an impressive testimony to the doctrine itself, that the Christian world has been so generally agreed in it. Truth is not determined by majorities; and yet it would be contrary to the laws of our constitution not to be affected by a testimony so vast, uniform, and sacred as that which is rendered by the common belief of Christian history and the Christian countries to the truth of the Trinity. There is something extremely painful, not to say irreverent, towards the Providence which has watched and led the true Christian Israel, in presuming that a tenet so emphatically and gladly received in all the ages and regions of Christendom as

---

* "So that we may rather experience the power of these mysteries of the Trinity in the heart than speak about them in lofty words." — TWESTEN.

almost literally to meet the terms of the test of Vincentius, — believed always, everywhere, and by all,* — is unfounded in revelation and truth. Such a conclusion puts an aspect of uncertainty over the mind of the Church scarcely consistent with any tolerable confidence in that great promise of the Master, that he would be with his own all days. We travel abroad through these converted lands, over the round world. We enter, at the call of the Sabbath morning light, the place of assembled worshippers: let it be the newly-planted conventicle on the edge of the Western forest, or the missionary station at the extremity of the Eastern continent; let it be the collection of northern mountaineers, or of the dwellers in southern valleys; let it be in the plain village meeting-house, or in the magnificent cathedrals of the old cities; let it be the crowded congregation of the metropolis, or the "two or three" that meet in faith in upper chambers, or in log-huts, or under palm-trees; let it be groups in dark and by-way alleys, companies of rescued vagrants, victims of persecution in caves of the rocks and hiding-places of the hills; let it be regenerate bands gathered to pray in any of the islands of the ocean, or thankful circles of believers confessing their dependence and beseeching pardon on ships' decks in the midst of the ocean. So we pass over the outstretched countries of both hemispheres: — it is well-nigh certain, — so certain that the rare and scattered exceptions drop out of the broad and general conclusion, — that the lowly petitions, the fervent supplications, the hearty confessions, the eager thanksgivings, or the grand peals of choral adoration,

* "Quod semper, quod ubique, quod ab omnibus."

which our ears shall hear will end in the uplifting ascription to the Father, the Son, and the Holy Ghost, the one ever-living and almighty God of all the earth. This is the voice of the unhesitating praise that embraces and hallows the globe. Or we stand still, and look backward, to see what teaching it has been that has achieved all the great results that we glory in, as constituting our Christian civilization; and we find that in simple, historical fact, this very doctrine appears in immediate and significant connection with nearly all. It is this, or at least that system of which this is a characteristic and inseparable element, which has reverently reared the majestic and humbler temples, has piled up the vast cruciform structures by the hands of generations which crumbled one after another as the slow toil proceeded, has written the ancient creeds and modern confessions, has prayed the earlier and later litanies, has sung the *glorias* and *misereres* of exultant or penitent millions, has lifted the sweet hymns of East and West, has organized missions and sent forth their messengers, has called councils and subdued nations to the cross, has conserved the order and reformed the abuses of imperfect administrations, and has presided over the learning, the philosophy, and the poetry in the literature of the Christian centuries. Throughout all these diversities of sacred operation, this old and vital truth, reaffirmed, hardly questioned, if omitted soon resumed again, kept clear and confident, has wrought, has builded, has preserved. And then, if we enter into the private experiences, the griefs, and strifes, and sorrows of the unnumbered multitudes that have been born in pain, and died in the midst of tears, it is this truth which has kept its vigils by the weary processions of sufferers, and consoled them. All this is the undeniable report of facts. That there have been some, in different places, limited communities, or scattered individuals, avowing belief in the religion, and honorable in character, who have rejected the doctrine, is evident. Yet it keeps its place, — never more firmly established, or widely welcomed, with its related and attendant truths, than to-day. Grateful for a support so comforting, and a sympathy so large, its advocates can afford to leave all impatience and intolerance to less privileged men.*

The object of the present discourse is not to offer a systematic, much less an exhaustive statement, of the grounds, Scriptural or extra-Scriptural, for a belief in the Divine Trinity. Such of these as may appear are incidental to the different and practical purpose of showing how that belief ministers to the spiritual life, salvation, and comfort of the believer. Only to prepare the way, possibly, for a more favorable entertainment of this latter attempt, we introduce it with the briefest sketch of the form of the doctrine

* Hardly anything respecting the history of the Trinity is more remarkable than the substantial agreement amidst the large variety of forms and shades under which the doctrine has been theologically presented. In the face of the libraries of close controversy, and the number of schools, — all of them signs of the intense vitality and power hidden in the inmost spiritual economy of the article, — the strong thinkers upon it are, after all, essentially and persistently at one: the early and mediæval Fathers, the Continental and English reformers, the Anglican scholars, the Puritan and American divines, — Athanasius and Tholuck, Fénelon and Knox, Augustine and Anselm, Calvin and Taylor, Luther and Bossuet, Bull and Baxter, Horsley and Howe, Pearson, Newman, Pascal, Cudworth, Wolf, Butler, Tauler and Hopkins, Waterland and Edwards, Sherlock and Dwight, Stuart, Neander. Nice, Trent, Augsburg, Westminster, Princeton, Andover, New Haven, with their symbols, notwithstanding their differences, are Trinitarian.

as it is accepted in our own thought, always striving to remember, and entreating the reader to remember, the inadequacy of both thought and language to comprehend or to define what is too high for everything in us but faith. With another we can say, in no ostentation of modesty, that we "do not undertake to fathom the interior being of God, and tell how it is composed. That is a matter too high for us all." And, with the penetrating and healthy mind of Robertson, in no strained sense, we can say, of the things of religion, "the doctrine of the Trinity is the sum of all that knowledge which has yet been gained by man."

In the transcendent, removed, and awful depth of his Absolute Infinitude, which no understanding can pierce, the Everlasting and Almighty God lives in an existence of which our only possible knowledge is gained by lights thrown back from revelation. Out of that ineffable and veiled Godhead, — the groundwork, if we may say so, of all Divine manifestation, or theophany, there emerge to us in revelation the three whom we rightly call persons, — Father, Son, and Holy Ghost, with their several individual offices, mutual relations, operations towards men, and perfect unity together. Holding fast the prime and positive fact of this unity, we have given us, as an equal matter of faith, the Threeness. We know of no priority to that Threeness; of no epoch when it was not; of no Deity independent of that threefold distinction. A question at that point takes us over into realms utterly inscrutable to thought. We conceive of God always, not as Absolute Being, but as in relations, in process, in act. And in such relations, process, act, we behold him only as Three: — the Son eternally begotten of the Father, not subordinate in nature or essence, nor created, nor beginning, but consubstantial with the Father: — the Holy Ghost ever proceeding from the Father and the Son, not in time, nor made out of nothing, but one in power and glory and eternity with them both.* Christ comes forth out of the Godhead as the Son, the Saviour, and, being born of Mary, is Jesus, the Messiah. We could not know him in those very characters which he must sustain in order to be our Redeemer except as he really takes upon himself our nature, a voluntary human subjection: as it is precisely written, "the image of the invisible God" in humanity. This is the mystery of the Incarnation. This was the precise mercy to be wrought for the solution of the problem of the world's sin. He was to leave "the glory which he had with the Father before the world was," and "be made in fashion as a man," be "tempted like as we are, yet without sin," be "a High-Priest that can be touched with the feeling of our infirmities," "God manifest in the flesh," "God with us." To this agree all the Scriptures.†

It was to be expected that, in repeated instances, this incarnate Son, engaged on his redeeming and intercessory work would be shown as dependent on the Father, who now represents to us the unseen personality of the Godhead, — as submissive, suffering, deferential, obedient even unto death, perfect in humiliation. Volunta-

* "These (Nicene) documents do not mean that God, at some date called "Eternity," begat his Son and sent forth his Holy Spirit, but that, in some high sense undefinable, he is datelessly and eternally becoming Three."

† The author's reasons for believing in the proper Divinity of Christ have been partly stated in "Sermons for the People," — XVIII., XX., XXII., XXVI.

rily, to this end, and for the time, things which only the Father knoweth are veiled from the Son, and he says (in language which we have only to suppose put into the mouth of any other being to find it in fact a proof of his divinity), "My Father is greater than I." He prays; how else could he be the Intercessor? He obeys, is sent, lessens himself to dependency for the sake of mediation. How else could the Divine will and perfection be displayed under human conditions? Hence the whole of that instrumental inequality between Son and Father, which is wrought into the Biblical language, remains in all our devotional habit, and which ought to remain there to give us a realization of the wondrous fact of the redemption, that we may apprehend our Saviour both as God and as man. Nor is there any great practical difficulty, as experience abundantly shows, in disconnecting from this endearing conception the notion that this is a permanent or subjective subordination. The apprehension is by faith, or by the spiritual power. And yet the understanding itself receives help and illumination from this Scriptural and consistent view of the whole august theme. A Trinity of co-equal persons, with diverse offices, is, if we may so express it, the sublime working-scheme of Revelation and Redemption.

Minds just passing away from the opposite view, and first adopting the faith that Christ is verily their Lord and God, are liable to a kind of surprise when they are called back from this new contemplation of his actual divinity by those texts which represent him as doing nothing "of himself." But a deeper reflection will discover that this very language is one way of referring up the springs of his personal action into the Godhead;

and that the human representations are just as essential to the completeness of the twofold view of the Saviour in his incarnation, — the mediator sharing the two natures of the parties mediated, — as the language which tells us so distinctly of his divinity. Consider, too, — if the Incarnation was to be a fact at all, — how the Saviour could possibly lead the rude and unprepared men about him, who saw him every day "in fashion as a man," to conceive of him in his higher character, except by exactly the gradual and accommodating process of language which he employed.

Nothing is much easier, of course, when the spiritual faculty is not in harmony with the truth announced, than for the critical reason to go to work and thrust upon it any number of difficulties. All readers of theological controversy know well enough beforehand what they will be. And if the deeper want has been awakened in them, they know presently just as well how unsatisfying these objections are, as well as their steady proclivity to a bold and extreme negation of what they regard the peculiar glories of the religion of the Gospel. Still, we must expect to hear them announced, again and again, with all the conscious complacency of a supposed originality. We shall have arithmetic, mechanics, common sense, psychology, diligently invoked to prove our absurdity. Meantime, faith will be probably just as little disturbed in the future as she has been in the ages past, and those excellent mathematical and metaphysical sciences will keep their places of utility, with no serious damage from the false appeal made to them. To all such oppositions, the believer has to make a single and sufficient answer: "I know in whom I have believed;" and if he may do so without presumption, he will repeat those great words of the Apostle, written from 1 Cor. i. 23 to the sixteenth verse of the second chapter, beginning, "But we preach Christ crucified."

For those who do not see the literal divinity or deity of Christ it appears difficult to entertain the idea that the Saviour's perfect humanity is just as dear to the Trinitarian, and just as theologically important as his perfect divinity: indeed that each is indispensable to the whole mediatorial office. For him who has "all power in heaven and earth" to say "Of that day and hour knoweth not the Son" is condescension indeed! It brings God near, as in his unabated attributes he could not be brought. But the objector, if he recognizes the Scriptural authority at all, will still have other passages, just as explicit and undeniable, to dispose of, before he has adjusted the scheme of his Christology. The Eternal Son is seen remaining rooted forever in the Godhead, having the basis of his being unchanged, deific, uncreated. Then he speaks to say, "I and my Father are one;" "He that hath seen me hath seen the Father." With these decisive affirmations accord a large class in the New Testament, both direct and indirect. Paul speaks of Christ as set "far above all principality and power, and might and dominion, and every name that is named, not only in this world, but also in that which is to come." Can this be a creature? "That at the name of Jesus every knee should bow, and every tongue confess that he is Lord." Is not this a being to whom prayer is to be offered? "The God of our fathers raised up Jesus; him hath God exalted," preached Peter and the rest, "to be a Prince and a Saviour for to give repentance to Israel and forgiveness of sins." Is it not right to *ask* him who gives "repentance and forgiveness of sins" to do it? "He is the propitiation for our sins," writes John, "and not for ours only, but also for the sins of the whole world." A man, a mortal and finite nature, the "propitiation for the sins of the whole world!" At last, when all the purposes of the propitiation are accomplished, — in that dim, far-off, well-nigh inconceivable future toward which a prophetic eye once ventures to reach, — this incarnate "Head over all things to the Church" will render up the kingdom to the Father, and resume his place in the co-equal Three, the indivisible One. Mark the expressions (1 Cor. xv. 24, 28). It is the Son who hath put "all things under his feet," "all rule, authority, and power," who is "subject unto God (ὑποταγήσεται, "arranged under"). Just after, it is God that "hath put all things under him." In this sense, therefore, God and the Son are the same, for the same mastery is asserted of each. But the Son, in his character of Sonship, is retaken, so to speak, into the everlasting, almighty, ineffable, undivided One, where the distinctions of office which had aided us so greatly in apprehending the glorious Trinity are lost to our sight. It is not anything peculiar to one of the Three Persons, but God in whom they all are One, who then "is all in all." *

* The following paragraphs, indicating a particular and original line of proof, are taken from Bushnell's "Nature and the Supernatural."

"There is yet another point related to this, in which the attitude of Jesus is even more distinct from any that was ever taken by man, and is yet triumphantly sustained. I speak of the astonishing pretensions asserted concerning his person. Similar pretensions have sometimes been assumed by maniacs, or insane persons, but never, so far as I know, by persons in the proper exercise of their reason. Certain it is that no mere man

Both in the interior necessities of the evangelical system as a consistent whole, and in the ordinary habit of theological thought, a proper acceptance of the doctrine of the Incarnation and of the true Divinity of the Second Person is attended with a prompt assent to the Divin-

---

could take the same attitude of supremacy toward the race, and inherent affinity or oneness with God, without fatally shocking the confidence of the world by his effrontery. Imagine a human nature saying to the world, 'I came forth from the Father,' — 'ye are beneath, I am from above;' facing all the intelligence and even the philosophy of the world, and saying in bold assurance, 'Behold a greater than Solomon is here,' — 'I am the light of the world,' — 'the way, the truth, the life;' publishing to all people and religions, 'No man cometh to the Father but by me;' promising openly in his death, 'I will draw all men unto me;' addressing the Infinite Majesty, and testifying, 'I have glorified thee on the earth;' calling to the human race, 'Come unto me,' 'follow me;' laying his hand upon all the dearest and most intimate affections of life, and demanding a precedent love, — 'He that loveth father or mother more than me, is not worthy of me.' Was there ever a man that dared put himself on the world in such pretensions? — as if all light was in him, as if to follow him and be worthy of him was to be the conclusive or chief excellence of mankind! But no one is offended with Jesus on this account, and, what is a sure test of his success, it is remarkable that, of all the readers of the Gospel, it probably never occurs to one in a hundred thousand to blame his conceit or the egregious vanity of his pretensions.

"Nor is there anything disputable in these pretensions, least of all, any trace of myth or fabulous tradition. They enter into the very web of his ministry, so that if they are extracted and nothing left transcending mere humanity, nothing at all is left. Indeed, there is a tacit assumption, continually maintained, that far exceeds the range of these formal pretensions. He says, 'I and the Father that sent me!' What figure would a man present in such language, — I and the Father? He goes even beyond this, and, apparently without any thought of excess or presumption, classing himself with the Infinite Majesty in a common plural, he says, '*We* will come unto him and make *our* abode with him.' Imagine any, the greatest and holiest of mankind, any prophet or apostle, saying *We* of himself and the Great Jehovah! What a conception did he give us concerning himself when he assumed the necessity of such information as this, 'My Father is greater than I;' and above all, when he calls himself, as he often does in a tone of condescension, 'the Son of Man.' See

ity of the Third.* A just Christology carries with it a just Pneumatology. The baptismal formula, in the text, would alone put the personality of the Holy Spirit on a ground of reasonable certainty, through the most natural understanding of the words. If He is personal, no considerable number of men have ever been found to question that he is God, nor to hesitate at the Tri-unity. How forced would be the suppression, — and putting what a repulsive ambiguity on this final and momentous commission of the Lord's followers for the conversion of the world, — if he first mentioned two names which, as all alike agree, are names of distinct persons,

---

him also on the top of Olivet, looking down on the guilty city and weeping words of compassion like these, — imagine some men weeping over London or New York, in the like, — 'How often would I have gathered thy children together as a hen doth gather her chickens under her wings, and ye would not!' See him also in the Supper, instituting a rite of remembrance for himself, a scorned, outcast man, and saying, 'This is my body, — this do in remembrance of me.'

"Come now, all ye that tell us in your wisdom of the mere natural humanity of Jesus, and help us to find how it is, that he is only a natural development of the human; select your wisest and best character; take the range, if you will, of all the great philosophers and saints, and choose out one that is most competent; or if, perchance, some one of you may imagine that he is himself about upon a level with Jesus (as we hear that some of you do), let him come forward in this trial and say, — 'Follow me,' — 'be worthy of me,' — 'I am the light of the world,' — 'ye are from beneath, I am from above,' — 'behold a greater than Solomon is here;' take on all these transcendent assumptions, and see how soon your glory will be sifted out of you by the detective gaze, and darkened by the contempt of mankind! Why not; is not the challenge fair? Do you not tell us that you can say as divine things as he? Is it not in you too, of course, to do what is human? Are you not in the front rank of human developments? Do you not rejoice in the power to rectify many mistakes and errors in the words of Jesus? Give us then this one experiment, and see if it does not prove to you a truth that is of some consequence; viz. that you are a man, and that Jesus Christ is — more?"

* See Hare's "Mission of the Comforter."

and then slipped in, without notice or explanation, a name which purports to be just as much the name of a person as the other two, but which is only a common noun signifying an immaterial influence! How desperate the shifts of a determined theory! The fifteenth and sixteenth chapters of John are equally explicit. No personality was ever more clearly pronounced, by the appropriate attributes and pronouns, than is that of the Comforter there. In those tender and solemn conversations, charged with the only hope and counsel to the disciples about to be bereaved, and indeed to the world of mankind, is it possible our Saviour was dealing in dark paradoxes or uninterpreted figures of rhetoric? Many other passages in the Gospels and Epistles can be wrested from their obvious meaning only by a similar violence. It is so with the Apostolical benedictions, which were evidently intended to be, what they have so generally proved, the familiar repositories and often-repeated symbols of the great central facts of Christian theology. Apart from some preconceived purpose, who would ever suppose there was a sudden lapse or deviation from the personal to the impersonal style, on getting half or two thirds through that worshipful and pre-eminent blessing: "The grace of our Lord Jesus Christ, and the love of God, and the *fellowship* of the Holy Ghost, be with us all evermore"?

That the influence emanating from that Person should be sometimes represented as subject to impersonal or passive conditions, — as "poured out," "given," "transmitted," "shed abroad," and the like, is not strange; nor that these influences should be so personified that they and the Person they proceed from should be sometimes designated under the same term. We say of the spirit of a man that it is diffused, imparted, communicated, in the same manner. But who supposes that this denies the personality of the man? On the other hand, there is no usage nor analogy to justify us in reversing this popular practice of language, and concluding that because principles may be personified, persons, clearly described and shown to us as such, may be stripped of their personality, and refined away into impressions. The other class of passages remains undisturbed, where this personality is affirmed, — passages to be disposed of, on the anti-Trinitarian hypothesis, only by constructions to which Reason herself should be very reluctant to offer her protection.

Thus, in the internal and permanent basis of their eternal being, the Three are one and the same, as much so as three different intermingling oceans, underflowing and encircling the continents, are one sea. In God revealed these three personalities issue forth to take up their merciful and glorious offices as Father, Son, Spirit. It has been justly observed that the strictly evangelical origin of the term "Father," or its application simultaneously with the appearance of Christ, and in immediate connection with the new economy of the Incarnation, is itself a suggestion of the Tri-une belief, as implying that not all of God is expressed till the "Son" also, the necessary correlative of "Father," is known. And thinking patiently a little further, we shall see that human language could not so well represent these infinite realities as by using the same term, "Father," sometimes for the absolute Godhead, and sometimes for that relative paternal Person in the

Godhead brought to view only when the Son and the Spirit appear; as also by using the term "Son" sometimes for the condescending and accommodated nature of Christ in the flesh, "tempted like as we are," and sometimes for the Christ who is "the same yesterday, to-day, and forever," "in whom dwelleth all the fulness (*pleroma*) of the Godhead." The qualities of the unutterable, deific substance are present in each. Christ Jesus, as we imperfectly say, brings God near to us.* So that the suspicion that any homage, reverence, gratitude, worship, paid to the Son is so much taken away from the Father will instantly betray its origin, as arising in another conception of the whole subject. To the Trinitarian, as to Christ himself, it is impossible. "That all men should honor the Son even as they honor the Father. He that honoreth not the Son, honoreth not the Father which hath sent him." †

---

* "The Son of God became incarnate in order that man might have a way to the God of man through the Man-God." — St. Augustine's "City of God."

† Olshausen's exposition of our text may, perhaps, furnish some assistance to a willing apprehension of it; and we quote from it at some length. "But it is worthy of notice that the Saviour does not here give the name of God directly, but the names of the Father, Son, and Holy Ghost, as the exalted object to which the votary of baptism becomes pledged. This is the only passage in the Gospels in which the Lord himself names the Three Divine persons together. In many passages the Saviour, it is true, describes both the Son and the Holy Ghost individually as Divine personalities. Here, however, they appear together, and are styled in common the object to which believers bind themselves by baptism. The elements of the doctrine of the Trinity are thus given in Christ's identical words. But the dogma is presented in an entirely undeveloped form, and the unfolding of the mystery is committed to the scientific activity of the Church. The established doctrine of the Church on this subject is essentially that of the Bible also, but the symbolically derived term *Person* involves a degree of inconvenience, and may easily lead to error. Human language, how-

Consistent, simple, and sublime as this ancient and prevailing doctrine is thus made to appear to us, it is none the less a mystery offered to faith, on faith's own evidence. It is obvious that most of those difficulties which puzzle the mind in attempting to grasp it spring from some form of our notions of personality. Hence it is pertinent to remember that, strictly speaking, personality is a human conception, applicable to God at all only by an extreme liberty, and not at all competent to include the measures of Infinitude; and that this is so generally held by all Trinitarian scholars that any attempt to press them into embarrassment by the consid-

---

ever, furnishes no expression by which the connection between a unity of essence with an independence of consciousness in Father, Son, and Spirit can be more appropriately indicated. We cannot therefore charge the teachers of the Church with error because they have made choice of this expression. We can only lament the imperfection of human language, which renders it inadequate to designate the most exalted and absolute relations which are clearly comprehensible to the purified reason only by precise ideas and words corresponding to them. The chief error to which the word 'Person' leads, and which has constantly been opposed by all the more profound teachers of the Church, and especially by Augustine, in his acute and profound work on the subject of the Trinity, is this. We are led by it to conceive of Father, Son, and Spirit as locally or mechanically distinct from one another, whilst we *should* view them as livingly interpenetrating one another. To this view we may advantageously oppose whatever there is of truth in Sabellianism (which rightly recognizes this unity in the existence of the Deity), yet without adopting at the same time its erroneous denial of the individual independency of consciousness in Father, Son, and Spirit. The only means we possess for illustrating the unity of the essence, and the severalty of consciousness in the Godhead, consists in the corresponding analogy which we find in the spiritual nature of man, the image of God. As in man there is not only spiritual being, but also the knowledge of that being, so also in the Divine nature, if we apprehend it as a living God, not as a dead notion, we must suppose both being and the knowledge of its peculiar being. This knowledge which God possesses of himself is designated as the Son: in him dwells the Father himself, and through him effects everything that he does effect.

eration now before us is nugatory to the last degree. It is now as commonly admitted by the highest philosophy as it is cheerfully confessed by religious humility, that a proper, intellectual conception of the personality of an Infinite Being is impossible. Yet it graciously pleases our Heavenly Father to show himself to his children, as we are soon to see more fully, in a personal character. Nothing in all our religion is so precious and so powerful as this manifestation. We are taught, and we all believe, that God absolute is a being who has no form, motion, place, measure, color, and never literally thinks, reasons, remembers, plans, considers, or believes. Yet

---

But, as all the powers of the Father concentrate themselves, as it were, in his self-consciousness, so do they also continually revert from the Son to their primary source, the Father, and this return is designated as the Holy Ghost. This view explains the phraseology of Scripture, where it is said that 'the Father draws to the Son,' but, 'the Son leads, in the Holy Ghost, back again to the Father.' 'All knowledge of God proceeds *from* the Father, as *absolute power*, *through* the Son, as *perfect love*, to the Holy Ghost, as *complete* holiness. But, regarded conversely, the Holy Ghost leads back directly to the Father, so that the end again issues in the beginning.' And thus in Father, Son, and Holy Ghost is represented the eternal being of God in its essential, internal movement and interaction. To apprehend, however, the idea of the *individual* as something limited and bounded within itself, and totally separated from all other spiritual life, would be the very error which has been already pointed out; and the Scriptures, in their entire mode of expression, show that *in this sense* it apprehends neither the Son nor the Holy Ghost as a person. The Son, indeed, appears individualized in the person of Jesus, but he labors by regeneration to transform all humanity into his own nature, on which account the whole Church is simply called Christ (1 Cor. xii. 12); and the Holy Ghost also appears shed abroad in the hearts of all believers, like the Father, who is omnipresent throughout the whole universe. As, therefore, the consciousness of God in itself can be conceived of only as all-comprehending, so also must the notion of *Person*, under the true idea of the doctrine of the Trinity, be understood in an all-comprehensive sense. By this means a great deal of the difficulty which, from the earliest times, has surrounded the doctrine of the Trinity, will be obviated."

what thought have we which is absolutely able to clear itself of these limitations, and still hold fast the notion of a properly personal existence? None the less are we so made under Christ as by a secret force of conviction to believe and affirm that God is both Infinite and a Person. None the less do our Christian Scriptures continually draw up and lead on our souls to a loftier and clearer communion with our God by setting him before us, heart to heart, through human relations and images, as having in him, and towards us, that which answers to thoughts, emotions, and experiences in ourselves. The inference is not remote nor obscure. We have no more reason to disbelieve God's declared Tri-unity, on the score of any inadequacy in our rational conceptions of it, than we have to disbelieve his infinite personality. We know both only in revelation, where the one is disclosed in immediate connection with the other. What we have to do is to be sure we do not either offend religious reverence, nor assert a literal tri-theism, by fastening on a metaphysical idea of persons.* "As we can say that God is a Person without any real denial of his infinity, so we can say that he is three Persons without any breach of his unity." A great deal of our common allegation of "mystery" as an objection to believing is the most shallow self-illusion. In this parlance, mystery

* So says Dr. Taylor, "Who does not know that Trinitarians claim, in the statement of their doctrine, to use the terms *being* and *person*, not in their ordinary, but in a peculiar meaning, demanded by the nature of the subject?" A considerable part of his course of lectures on the Trinity is devoted to an elucidation of this peculiarity. It is to be hoped that it is by a defect of information, and not of candor, that, in the face of similar statements from Bishop Butler, Whately, Neander, and other leading writers on the Trinitarian side, their opponents persevere in overlooking the fact that any such distinction is made.

means something like a compound of the unfamiliar and the unwelcome. But we live amidst mysteries, keep house with them, walk over them, lie down and rise up with them, are folded in by them, are born out of them, breathe them, and die into them. When we have told ourselves *how* the tree that shades us gets out of the seed blown from our finger's end, or when we have explained how one person influences another without sight or touch, we may perhaps be emboldened to make our comprehension the criterion of the verities of God.*

---

* To refer to Mr. Mansel's very full and striking illustrations and demonstrations of the general principle that the human consciousness is unequal to the speculative conception of a Being at once absolute, infinite, and personal, while yet faith in such a Being is the soul's privilege and duty, does not involve an assent to all the conclusions he reaches in the same remarkable course of reasoning, much less to all those which impetuous and unfair critics have attributed to him. That Sir William Hamilton's view of the Philosophy of the Unconditioned, and his pupil's, of the Limits of Religious Thought, contain original ideas which are calculated, with whatever modifications, to encourage the coming generation in Scriptural convictions of the Divine Nature, is what nothing but either the Rationalism or the Dogmatism which they both so powerfully assail can venture to deny.

"The objection, 'How can the One be many, or the many one?' is so far from telling with peculiar force against the catholic doctrine of the Holy Trinity, that it has precisely the same power or want of power, and may be urged with precisely the same effect or want of effect against any conception, theological or philosophical, in which we may attempt to represent the Divine Nature and attributes as infinite, or indeed to exhibit the infinite at all." "How can there be a variety of attributes, each infinite in its kind, and yet all together constituting but one Infinite? or how, on the other hand, can the Infinite be conceived as existing without diversity at all?" "The doctrine of the Son of God, begotten of the Father, and yet co-eternal with the Father, is in no wise more or less comprehensible by human reason than the relation between the Divine essence and its attributes." "If there is sufficient evidence, on other grounds, to show that the Scripture, in which this doctrine is contained,

If, however, there are any who will insist on the supports of intellectual consent, let them be so far met by the facts of history as to be obliged to own where the real strength of men's thought has deposited the power of its testimony. Against all pretences of rational advantage or literary patronage, let it be freely said that this doctrine has been cordially accepted, and in countless illustrious instances zealously advocated, by the vast majority of the logicians, philosophers, statesmen, men of the largest dialectic and thinking energy, of the keenest penetration and most comprehensive faculty of generalization, that have lived in Christendom: and let the fact stand for what it is worth, and persuade whom it will. Respectable cases of exception can, it is true, be readily referred to. Constitutional biases, or those of education, the passion for difference or innovation, inevitable reactions from extreme positions; — all these have occasioned an anti-Trinitarian party, including examples of sincere, able, honorable dissent from the

---

is a revelation from God, the doctrine itself must be unconditionally received, not as reasonable nor as unreasonable, but as Scriptural. If there is not such evidence, the doctrine itself will lack its proper support; but the reason which rejects it is utterly incompetent to substitute any other representation in its place." "Let religion begin where it will, it must begin with that which is above reason." "We may seek as we will for a religion within the limits of the bare reason, and we shall not find it, simply because no such thing exists," &c., &c. — MANSEL's Bampton Lectures, VI.

"But if he denies that three can be predicated of one, and one of three, let him allow that there is something in God which his intellect cannot penetrate, and let him not compare the nature of God, which is above all things free from all condition of place and time and composition of parts, with things which are confined to place and time, or composed of parts; but let him believe that there is something, in that nature, which cannot be in those things, and let him acquiesce in Christian authority, and not dispute against it." — ANSELM.

accepted belief of the Church. But when we look from these we emerge into an almost boundless field of the eminent names of moral and intellectual science, history, theology, and general Christian letters, all undoubting in that article of faith of which one of their number, Coleridge, says, "The article of Trinity is religion, is reason, and its universal formula;" and another, Neander, "It is the fundamental article of the Christian faith, — the essential contents of Christianity summed up in brief." The ascendant school of philosophical thought to-day is unequivocally Trinitarian. Even the most imperial intellects of unchristianized antiquity recognized a truth corresponding to this as a necessity of the great laws of being, — Plato speaking as distinctly in the belief of a Trinity as Aristotle in that of the Unity, — the "One Lord who ordaineth all things." Not much stress can be laid on any mere scientific manipulation of a truth so dependent on spiritual revelations as this. And yet it may be something, — especially as against a contrary assertion, — to see that where the heart *is* made ready for it, the ablest heads have been just as willing to credit it as the simplest.*

* Possibly there may be some reader of these pages who will be the more favorably inclined to admit the spirit of this paragraph for finding it uttered from a soul so clear-sighted, so purged of all cant or hearsay notions, of all make-believe and deference to mere tradition, so appreciative and large in sympathy, and so widely loved and trusted, as Rev. F. W. Robertson. In several of his sermons he avows his faith that in God there are "three distinct personalities, consciousnesses, yet all these three are one;" that "Trinitarianism is true." He also pleads: "There are those who are inclined to sneer at the Trinitarian; those to whom the doctrine appears merely a contradiction, a puzzle, an entangled, labyrinthine enigma in which there is no meaning whatever. But let all such remember that, though the doctrine may appear to them absurd, because they have not the proper conception of it, some of the profoundest thinkers and some of the

It would seem, then, to require some audacity to toss about such charges as "absurdity," "self-contradiction," "impossibility," "scholastic figment," and others even more opprobrious, as fitted to a faith on the most unspeakably momentous and affecting of the themes of thought, deliberately adopted and earnestly expounded by nine tenths of those master-minds whose logic and learning have been applied to the subject at all. What shall be said of the mental proportions of men who persist in the dull fallacy of imputing to believers in the Trinity of "God, who is a Spirit," the notion of an arithmetic relation, with the complacent inference that this vital and everlasting confession of Christendom is to be silenced or dispossessed by a frivolous allusion to mathematical incompatibilities? Can it never be considered that, when all our current ideas are sifted and analyzed, every attribute and act of the Self-existent One is exactly as inexplicable to us as his Threeness? *

---

holiest spirits among mankind have believed in this doctrine, have clung to it as a matter of life or death. Let them be assured of this, that, whether the doctrine be true or false, it is not necessarily a doctrine self-contradictory. Let them be assured of this in all modesty, that such men never could have held it unless there was latent in it a deep truth, perchance the truth of God."

* When the philosophical line of investigation is carried out still further, it will doubtless be made to appear, as ancient and modern thinkers have more than once intimated, that it is three, not less, not more, which, in the nature of numbers and of forms, admits the greatest relative combination of simplicity and variety, and especially meets the abstract conditions of the ontological problem. Some minds are also able to hold the doctrine in such a way as to find a comforting relief in it from a certain cheerless impression of solitude in Deity, gaining the idea, as they think, of a sharing of counsels, a reciprocity of affections, and a divine joy of participated, reflected, and so intensified beatitude, as a part of the conception of Trinity in Unity. But these are speculations beyond the Bible.

Of quite a different character is the objection sometimes alleged against the doctrine, that it belongs to a class of opinions which are of no practical consequence, and which may be received or rejected with equal unconcern, provided men are careful to maintain a correct conduct. Granted that this cheap estimate borrows some plausibility from dogmatic exaggerations and intolerant pretensions too often associated with the advocacy of the most important ideas, — partly because they are important. Yet when we are pointed by doctrinal indifferentism to right living as a proof of the insignificance of right believing, we have to ask some questions in return. How are we to achieve that not altogether easy or every-day matter, *right* living? What are the powers, and whence come they? Is it living rightly to live ignoring or denying realities which our God has graciously unveiled, by costly revelations, touching his own nature and our salvation? Is it living rightly to fail of gratitude to Divine benefactors, as Divine, withholding praise from the Son and the Spirit, into whom we are bidden to be baptized? Do almsgivings, kindnesses, moral integrities, noble as they are when springing from the sacred stock of true faith, release us from "coming to Christ," "receiving the Holy Ghost," trusting in the Cross, and walking humbly with our God? Or, since the boldest egotism in any man will hardly pretend that his own life is now "right," has ever been "right," or ever will be "right," or otherwise than terribly wrong, is it not a very reasonable thing, and the very first thing, for a soul in this position of conscious weakness, guilt, and shame, to be searching earnestly after the Divine relief? Following in the path of these inquiries, let us notice some of the practical fruits of the doctrine before us, especially in furnishing a positive foundation for piety, the way of deliverance from evil, and an animating inspiration to Christian service.

I. The Tri-unity of God appears to be the necessary means of manifesting and supporting in the mind of our Race a faith in the true personality of God, — a faith indispensable to the foundation and to the vital operation of Christianity. The impossibility of a speculative cognition of the infinite personality has already been adverted to, and apart from that, neither the resources of philosophy nor the demonstrations of history encourage us to believe that anything like a Christian monotheism could keep its place in the world from generation to generation, through all the divergencies of speculation, and the degradations of materialism, at least beyond the limits of direct manifestations like those granted to the Hebrews, save by the revelation of God as One in Three and Three in One. The actual departures from this faith have been in two directions. On one side, the religious sentiment, subjected to a process of intellectual generalization, has resulted in Pantheism. God ceases to be a person. Everything is God, and God is everything. We are ourselves a part of him, and in such a sense that he would not be complete without us: we are not subjects of his personal will, created, directed, swayed, led, punished, saved by the act of that personal will toward us, lying very humble before the supreme majesty of his infinite holiness, or walking in the light of his conscious love, and ascribing all that is good and great on earth, "not unto us," but to his personal power. We are rather partners in his omnipotence. We are in him, not by faith or spiritual possession, but as setting up rights. So with the universe.

Responsibility ceases. Prayer is absurd. Worship is a lost idea, even if the form survives by force of old tradition or of better instincts that refuse to be killed by a domineering and perverted understanding. The heart of faith is chilled. Conscience is systematically divested of the sense of personal retribution. Sorrow has no comforter. Nature is admired, and this admiration of her beauty and order is called religion. All the ten thousand blessed influences which attend the feeling of religious dependence gradually sink away, and a poor, restless, unsatisfied, self-asserting conceit takes their place.

On the other side, the religious sentiment, subjected to a process of sensual limitation, results in some form of idolatry. Something less than God is taken for God, and worshipped as God. It may not be a visible object. Paganism is not confined to fetichism and image-worship. Some man, some hero, some fabulous story of a man, or some conception of humanity in a single individual indefinitely enlarged, is set in God's throne and adored.

These two errors have divided the unchristianized world between them. They do still. Either the personality of God is sacrificed to the infinity, or the infinity is sacrificed to the personality. In the former case, men may imagine they recognize an Infinite Being; but it is only an abstraction, or a principle, or a bundle of laws, or a loose mass of sequences and phenomena, from which the attribute of infinity itself as well as of personal consciousness is soon found to have ebbed away. In the latter case, the innate longing for a veritable Divine Person, with personal traits answering to ours, may be met; but it will soon begin to appear that, though a Person remains, the Eternal and Uncreated and Almighty God of Glory is gone. The advancement of learning, the scientific mastery of outward nature, and other characteristics of modern times, have shifted the danger very largely from the latter to the former of these tendencies, as every thinking mind must see, and as so many tongues are saying. But probably both the errors spring from desires and demands of man's nature which in themselves are right. This human *soul* will ever seek in some way to identify God with the humanity in which it shares. This human *mind*, exploring the method and magnificence of the external universe, will ever seek to identify God with the different works of his hand. Or, to state the matter in different relations, despairing to conceive of personality without limitation, some men rush over to Pantheism. Others, despairing of retaining a Deity near enough for love and sympathy who is literally infinite, stop short with a deity who is not God.

These implanted wants are wonderfully satisfied in the Divine Trinity. In the Absolute and one only Godhead, all man's highest, purest, largest, most far-reaching conceptions, stretching away into the regions of Infinitude, Eternity, Almightiness, have their full and complete exercise. In the incarnate Christ, taking up our humanity, the longing for a personal, sympathizing, companionable Deity, is blessedly answered, — and yet God is there; there is no loss of the essential and veritable Deity. In the Holy Spirit, the natural desire of the devout mind to connect God with all the operations of the present world, the processes of creation, the welfare, renewal, revolutions, sanctification, of the Human Family, finds its lawful verification. If they only would, the reverent Pantheist, humanitarian, naturalist might here, in the beauty and symmetry and fulness of the Gospel doctrine, obtain the true and grand interpretation of their several yearnings, see their partial and fragmentary views of the Divine filled out, and their mistakes corrected. For the dangers of the separate systems are here forestalled. If in the ardent attachment to the historical Christ, the "Word made flesh," the disciple is tempted to deny the Unseen and Ineffable, to forget that no man hath in a complete sense "seen God at any time," this doctrine holds ever up before him the God and Father of our Lord and Saviour, from whom the Son comes eternally forth. If, again, we incline to let our speculations wander in the cold and rare atmosphere of a purely deific energy, joining the deistic multitude so easily misled by the audacities and flatteries of a false philosophy, we are forthwith brought back to the warm and cheerful household of Faith by beholding the face of the Gracious Shepherd and Bishop of our Souls, and being assured that whoso hath seen Him hath seen the Father. Or if thus fixing our inward gaze either on the Infinite above, or on the Jesus of Nazareth and of history, we come to locate our Lord only in the heights, or in the limited enclosures and events of a visible Messiahship, then we are taken again into the juster thought of the New Testament; the Holy Ghost is witnessed in His everlasting and blessed goings forth into the world of men to regenerate and comfort it, the Paraclete proceedeth ever from the Father and the Son, thus taking up and including the powers of the Incarnation, — not an impalpable essence or airy influence, but the third and living person of the ever-blessed and glorious Trinity.

The adorable mystery becomes a practical and precious fact to the toiling and praying soul. The baffled intellect rests from the aimless beating of its wings, and while it discovers fields of boundless contemplation for the expansion of all its powers, abides in the peace of that holy benediction, — "The grace of our Lord Jesus Christ, and the love of God, and the fellowship of the Holy Ghost be with us all evermore."

Nor have we any record of even the more negative of these effects, namely, the escape from the pantheistic and the mythologic paganism, nor any reason to suppose that would take place, on any extended scale, in the religious experience of mankind independently of this doctrine. Christendom furnishes the only instance of this security, and Christendom has been Trinitarian. If the Christian conception of God's personality has survived in minds or localities or periods where the Trinity has been denied, it must be remembered that in such instances the conservative energies of the surrounding and general belief always exert a considerable power. The logical consequences of a doctrinal denial do not appear at once; they are often largely counteracted, even where the denial is not revoked. But it certainly is a fair and serious question whether the denial of this particular doctrine has not carried, at least in a striking proximity and association with it, a special movement toward the extremes of deistic, pantheistic, and rationalistic conclusions. Bereaved of their real Lord, men grope after some vague, sublimated entity, like Brahma, "sleeping on eternity and the stars," or "literary freethinkers begin to speak familiarly of 'the gods,' repairing their loss of a Trinity by embracing a classic Pantheon."

II. The Trinity of God is the necessary groundwork of the whole Scripture doctrine of the atonement for sin, or the reconciliation between God and man. Under the former head, man has been regarded in his normal conditions, needing a development through Divine grace and worship, irrespective of the fact of his lapse and bondage under evil. But transgression has introduced, from the beginning, a new element and a new relation. Sin is not an act only, but a state, a state of the individual and a state of the race. Hence the great need of the race was that God should come into it anew in a quickening, healing, life-giving, personal mediation. Lost humanity was to be restored, how plainly! only by an Incarnation of God himself in the Son, making a perfect union of it with his own spirit by the "Word made flesh."

One of the chief practical dangers of our life, as well as one of the chief sources of laxity, confusion, and weakness to theology, is that we are so apt to contemplate the disorder, mischief, and enormity of sin only from our human point, with only natural and immediate notions of its character and effects, without estimating its deadly antagonism to the holiness of the Almighty, the good of all that live, the integrity and peace of the universe. There never can be a religion of vitality and commanding majesty, where enfeebled conceptions prevail of those two primal and terribly hostile forces, — the sovereign holiness of God and the wicked will of man. The depth of that wickedness, the all-pervading taint of ungrateful iniquity, the unreasonableness and profanity of disobedience in the child of a Parent so gracious and so good, — these are not to be described, nor can any adequate and lively impression of them be made except as the soul is startled and awakened from insensibility by the strong touch of that renewing Spirit, which convinceth of sin, of righteousness, and of judgment. Yet it would seem as if a tolerable degree of intelligence and thoughtfulness applied to the simple and plain conditions of the problem might so discover the sanctity of God's immaculate will, the venerableness of his law, the absolute indispensableness that his government should stand firm and unimpeachable, in the sight of all his subjects, in order to the welfare, stability, and joy of his whole family in earth and heaven, as to remove all reluctance at receiving the sublime demonstrations of the method of redemption revealed in the Cross. When their look is first directed to the lofty heights and purity of that law, and then to the utter ugliness of the transgression, men avert their eyes; they call it a hard and gloomy system. Till some profounder feeling is moved, till some spiritual sympathy is kindled with the whole mercy and blessedness of the plan, they find no beauty nor loveliness in it that they should desire it; they pronounce it harsh, forbidding, strange; they turn away to what they consider a milder and pleasanter scheme. But hast thou not learned yet, O sorrowing man, born of woman, of few days and full of trouble! that the hard and sad way is very often the short, sure way to comfort and light? that it must be hard and sad only because thy own heart is hard, and thy sinfulness is sad? Has it not begun to dawn on thy soul that the very severity and terror of the law are the stern necessity which yields afterwards the unutterable peace of renunciation, the gladness of submission unequalled by all the gladness of self-will, the bliss of reconciliation, the rest of faith? Cheerful views are views that bring the true and everlasting cheer, not those that cheat us with the image of a fond or indulgent deity, too soft-hearted to punish, too weak to execute justice, — views that cry "Peace!" when there is no peace, only to leave us at last mocked and betrayed. Nothing that is milder than God's word and will is happy for us in the end. Nothing is gained by winking out of sight the facts. God's way is the brightest way, for he is perfect love. The uniform and accordant testimony of the millions from the morning hour of the Church, who have believed in this redemption and known it in their experience, is that it brings the soul to joys beyond all that can be spoken in language, beyond all the joys they had ever found in the assurances of an easier salvation, and a more indiscriminate compassion. Is that testimony nothing? Would to God it might be borne in upon all our minds by his own Spirit, how much wiser, how much more cheerful, is the strong piety that is won through intense and painful experiences of the real contradiction of God's will against self-will, creating the need of a Divine sacrifice, than the superficial contentment which mistakes the benignity of Providence for a repeal of his statutes, and misinterprets all his promises of forgiveness into a denial of his repeated declarations that he hateth iniquity, that his wrath abideth on the impenitent, and that the sinner shall not stand in his sight. Forgiveness! If our God were the yielding and ever-repealing Lawgiver that some teachers sedulously represent him, he would have nothing to forgive!

The atoning sacrifice of Christ may be regarded either in relation to the needs of the individual soul, or in relation to the whole paternal and royal administration of the government of God. In each of these relations it will be found that the Divine Tri-unity, including the actual and complete divinity of the Redeemer as the second person of that Tri-unity, is the secret of the power.

In any really deep Christian experience, the great feeling of need, the energy of repentance, the agony of conviction, connects itself with a conscious estrangement from the Heavenly Father, through a violation of his holy and merciful law; not merely a single act of sin; not merely a series of such acts; but a state of the nature and a habit of the life ungratefully and wickedly separated from God. Of course, so long as there is a feeble or lax sense of God's holiness, of the sanctity of his requirements, of the exceeding height and breadth and length of his commandments, and of the wide-spread mischief and unutterable wrong even of a single infraction of it sending its jar of discord through the spiritual world and directly offending such a Being as God is, so long this piercing and bitter conviction will not be realized. Some lighter and easier solution than the Cross, therefore, will satisfy the mind, or seem to satisfy it, till a deeper movement agitates the heart and breaks up its inmost fountains. Whenever that hour comes, there comes with it a cry for full redemption, such a redemption as only the suffering of Him who is both man and God can give. The different theories of Christ's nature and sacrifice appear and pass before the stricken and self-condemned soul. Is Christ a consistent man only, a brave martyr, a glorious instance of a well-finished career, meeting an inevitable death with exemplary firmness? But what is that to a sorrow and remorse like this? However animating to other moods, after the alienated conscience is reconciled and knows that its condemnation is blotted out, such an example can now be only an aggravating and unattainable vision, mocking the disabled and disordered will. Besides, however blameless and disinterested the death of Jesus may be, if we speak of human firmness or courage, these have been apparently equalled, as has often been noticed, by other sufferers. The scenes of Gethsemane and Calvary have been surpassed in the mere quality of silent, human endurance, more than once. On the humanitarian hypothesis, the tears and prayers and groans and shrinkings of the "Lamb of God who taketh away the sin of the world" sink to an inferior place in the victories of fortitude. It is only as we find there the nameless and inexpressible anguish of a Divine and Infinite Being, bearing the iniquities of us all, and purposely taking up all the tenderest sensibilities of our ordinary frame, in the benevolent mystery of the Incarnation, that the signals of the Passion are lifted into any genuine honor. Without this, they are less than they assume to be, and fail even of respect. Nor is the grand want supplied by supposing the Saviour to be exalted into some superhuman dignity of endowment, yet remaining only a creature and a subject. Subject he certainly was in his mediatorial and earthly office. But the union of the two natures was real, organic, not apparent only, not dramatic, nor mechanical; so that when the Saviour suffered, God suffered. God did not perish: how strange and sad that the thoughtless perversions or wilful misrepresentations of hostile theologians should have ever made such a statement necessary. But when the mortal part of the Saviour died, God suffered in him. The shedding of the blood of such a body was more than a human sacrifice. The sundering of that eternal life-principle from that sacred flesh was a divine death. This is what faith means, when, rising into its unquestioning joy, and breaking forth into lyrical thanksgiving, it sings its holy hymns of praise to a "dying God." He died as man, who also liveth ever as God. And in that dying, by the intimate and transcendent sympathies of the divine and the human in him, — incomprehensible indeed, but just as truly comprehensible as any creative act of the Infinite, — there was involved God's anguish for his sinning children, and his free sacrifice for the broken law. The sacrifice was not confined to the ninth hour. It was in the garden; it was on the heavy journey thence to Calvary. It began to be manifest even at the supper and the judgment-hall. It was consummated at the cross; for "without the shedding of blood" there could be "no remission of sin."

And now this is precisely what any inferior faith fails to gain. Raise your conception of Christ's rank in the scale of created being high as you may; carry it to the mark of Ebion or Arius; assign the point of Christ's beginning at whatever period in time you will: still both practically and logically the needed atonement fails. The eternal Lawgiver is not bearing the disinterested pain and wondrous penalty for all his creatures "in that all have sinned." God is not himself in the suffering. This was the requirement of the case. This was the longing of the guilty heart. This is what the Gospel, from end to end, in plain and full and glorious language, declares. Read it again, and see how in the interpretation of this principle all becomes consistent and simple; all occasion for forced explanation and abatement ceases; all the strong and earnest speech is luminous with meaning, and abounding in comfort. It is not meant that the understanding, in the presence of a work so vast and a goodness so august, should be able to describe every part of the wonder, and put in place every element of the redemptive power. But enlightened by the Holy Spirit, which delights to teach and satisfy so docile a mind, it does seize enough to cling to, and cheerfully hands over the remaining marvel to a Christian trust. And trust gladly accepts the charge. The soul is free. Conscience is at the same moment released and roused to an unprecedented and sanctified activity. Duty never looked so dear. Obedience was never so eager. Practical righteousness was never so noble, because never animated by so grand a motive. "The cross" has now no accommodated, strained, perplexing signification, but its entire evangelical force rings clearly and directly on the inmost sense of faith. And underneath is a peace, which, as they that have found it humbly testify, differs from all the consolations ever felt before, and surpasses them all, as the love of God in Christ passes the love of man.

To undertake here an exposition of the inseparable connection of the truth of the Trinity with the doctrine of the atonement which has prevailed in the Church, in respect to the integrity of the Divine government and the general welfare of the race, would lie somewhat aside from the immediate design of this discourse. Indeed, it is one great danger of treating this governmental aspect of the subject, that it is apt to pass into hard, unspiritual, economic representations. The almost necessary employment of terms borrowed from civil polity, and the departure of the discussion one remove from the personal interests and affections of a human experience, create impressions of a cool and legal handling of the theme offensive to the deeper religious instincts. Yet there is a very short and simple process of thought, by which nearly every person is capable of arriving at the conclusion that, after all claims to the contrary, the exact and fearful problem of the world's redemption is not solved, and cannot be, save as Christ is seen to be "very God of very God." There was a thorough alienation of the subject race from the Sovereign. So deeply rooted was it, so universal, so interpenetrating all institutions, relations, faculties, activities of man, that no insurrection or rebellion against human government, in all history, serves for a reasonable or proximate illustration of the disobedience. How was this lapsed and lost race to be restored? Words, declarations, promises, would not do it. Human virtues, converted generations, godly lives, bright examples, however multiplied, could not heal this unrighteous Past, nor atone for it. Not in the race any more than in any one individual among us, could any amount of future goodness weigh one iota towards discharging all this foregoing waste and guilt. Let man obey thenceforth perfectly, if he could, and he would do no more than each moment's own duty; and even less than that he is sure to do. The load accumulates instead of being lightened. Now, for the Ruler to say, "No matter about all these days of rejection and disobedience; no matter about all these wanton and repeated affronts against a blessed Will in which stands not only the veracity of God and the honor of your King, but the welfare and stability of the world;" this will certainly have a very singular effect on the reverence and faith and virtue of mankind. No: it is God, the wise and gracious Lord of the worlds, who has been disobeyed and offended. Both for the moral renewing and the retrospective satisfaction the atonement must clearly come forth then from God. All the obediences of ten thousand legions of saints would not touch one unreconciled heart's position, either to regenerate or acquit. In the person of the Messiah the Divine Life was to stream again into the withered and crippled body of humanity. In his Sacrifice, who alone was competent to make a sacrifice which should at once satisfy and transcend the law, taking all its penalty and leaving it unharmed in majesty, the restoration was to be made complete, and the pardon free forever and forever. Now man lives again, and lives a new and glorious life. He sees and feels what is done for him. Indifference melts away. Ingratitude is changed to consecration. The dull and sluggish heart of humanity is quickened to repentance and newness of life. The streams of human thought and feeling and aspiration begin to set sublimely heavenward again. Faith looks, and lives. As the serpent was lifted up in the wilderness, so the Son of Man is lifted up; and whosoever gazes, believing, is healed, is saved. It is as if the Father said, "All else has been done; I have created, guarded, guided, supported, blessed, forborne; Providence and revelation, in nature and in the inspired oracles of Moses and the prophets, have exhausted their possibilities. Lo! one mercy more; the last and mightiest. I can suffer for my children, I can come in the flesh, I can be one of them. In that incarnation I can ache and weep and sorrow for them and with them: all their stripes can be laid upon me. All their infirmities can cling to me. I can die as they die, — the last of the evils they dread, — the penalty of the broken law. This shall both move and release them. This shall be the regeneration and the redemption of all mankind who will believe it." O infinite compassion! Herein is love! This is the "mystery hid from the foundation of the world." The Holy Spirit ever comes, from the Father and the Son, to make the whole work effectual for the Church and the heart. We behold, we begin at least to behold, why God is forever ONE, — is forever THREE.

III. We have now seen the need and the power of this truth in the positive operation of the personal Fatherhood toward man, and in the remedial action required by man's fall under sin. A third element of its practical efficiency is found in the manifold and vital connections it establishes between itself and the historic development and practical piety of the Church. The fact of its prevalence in Christendom, — a prevalence so general that it may be taken as a characteristic and a law, has already been noticed. Each of the great Christian movements, from the apostolic age to our own, whether for the missionary extension of the Gospel, or for the reformation and revival of its spiritual power in communities where it was nominally received, has held up the Triune confession as the inscription on its standard. But that confession has been more than a conventional battle-cry or password for the hallowed aggressions of the Church militant. It has expressed realities very precious to the heart, and its chief potency has been in the moral energy of those realities. It is in vain to say that other views of the New Testament, other interpretations of the Bible, other conceptions of the Divine nature, are equally effectual. The impressive and obvious fact stands forth, that they have *not* been. Whether we are able to account for this or not, a rule so uniform in its operation becomes itself an argument. It is true, no prevalence of the anti-Trinitarian belief in Christendom has existed on so wide a scale as to furnish a very large opportunity to test its self-sacrificing, organizing, and converting capabilities, and this in itself is significant testimony. Amidst all its other changes of form and dogma, of administration and policy, of culture and simplicity, however violent or radical the revolution, the Church has remained in this respect essentially unaltered. Oriental and Western, mediæval or modern, it has been equally clear, confident, and full in the recognition, nay, in the ever-repeated and jubilant affirmation, of this great practical mystery of faith. Protestantism has been essentially just as Trinitarian as Romanism; the spontaneous modes of worship, as the Liturgical. From age to age, from land to land, the living Body of the Lord has delighted to take up the substance of that only primal creed, given by the Saviour himself in the text, on which her other creeds have been justly founded, and to repeat, to reiterate, to lift in reverential praise, to sing in holy triumph, voice answering to voice, and multitude to multitude in the lofty chorus,—"Glory be to the Father, and to the Son, and to the Holy Ghost,—as it was in the beginning, is now, and ever shall be, world without end." *

* Testimony to the reality of *effects* here only briefly touched, as unexpected as it is eloquent, has lately been given by one of the gifted writers of our day whose whole public career has been associated with denominational connections opposed to the Trinitarian faith,—Rev. James Martineau, of England. What *cause* he would assign for those effects we are at

But we are not left without insight into reasons for this result. The inwrought implication of the doctrine in all the great steps of man's spiritual education and recovery from sin to God, as we have already observed it, would alone be reason enough. The farther down into the heart of the matter our study is carried, the more directly will the strength and the satisfaction of the Christian life be found indebted to the forces proceeding from this source. Then there is great religious

---

a loss to imagine. Speaking of those who deny the Trinity, he says: "I am constrained to say, that neither my intellectual preference nor my moral admiration goes heartily with their heroes, sects, or productions of any age. Ebionites, Arians, Socinians, all seem to me to contrast unfavorably with their opponents, and to exhibit a type of thought and character far less worthy, on the whole, of the true genius of Christianity. I am conscious that my deepest obligations, as a learner from others, are in almost every department to writers not of my own creed. In Philosophy I have had to unlearn most that I had imbibed from my early text-books, and the authors in chief favor with them. In Biblical interpretation, I derive from Calvin and Whitby the help that fails me in Crell and Belsham. In devotional literature and religious thought, I find nothing of ours that does not pale before Augustine, Tauler, and Pascal. And in the poetry of the Church it is the Latin or the German hymns, or the lines of Charles Wesley, or of Keble, that fasten on my memory and heart, and make all else seem poor and cold. I cannot help this. I can only say I am sure it is no perversity; and I believe the preference is founded in reason and nature, and is already widely spread amongst us. A man's 'Church' must be the home of whatever he most deeply loves, trusts, admires, and reveres, — of whatever most divinely expresses the essential meaning of the Christian faith and life; and to be torn away from the great company I have named, and transferred to the ranks which command a far fainter allegiance, is an unnatural, and for me an inadmissible fate. That I find myself in intellectual accordance with the Socini, or Blandrata, or Servetus in one cardinal doctrine, — and that a doctrine not distinctively Christian, but belonging also to Judaism, to Islam, and to simple Deism, — is as nothing compared with the intense response wrung from me by some of Luther's readings of St. Paul, and by his favorite book, the 'Theologia Germanica.'"

value in keeping ever prominent before the mind of the believer a formula like this, which perpetually reasserts the superiority of the things of faith to the realm of intellectual comprehension. It offers a ceaseless testimony to the inspired character of Revelation. It is a kind of moral monument showing that the regions of knowledge and of faith, and also of natural and revealed religion, while perfectly harmonious, are yet distinct. It administers a strong and wholesome rebuke to the "wisdom of the world" which, even with devout minds, is so terrible a temptation to self-conceit and a pride of the brain. It is a merciful safeguard to veneration and humility, — not beyond the reach of abuse, and not always restraining the arrogance of human nature even in those that formally admit it, — but, on the whole, of large and saving influence. Besides, a certain solemnity of tone invests the symbols which convey the doctrine, certainly to such as receive it, of unwonted and elevating grandeur, lifting the soul very near to God. Definiteness is given to the religious experience. Under the distributing and ordering effect of this central, threefold fact, all the parts of an intelligent, evangelical belief fall into place. The ideas of divine justice and love, requirement and forgiveness, legislation, ransom, and sanctification, play freely within the tri-personal activity, each strong and full, each in balance with the others. Theology has a more scientific development, worship a more unhesitating confidence, each sacrament a more opulent grace. Preaching appeals to a surer authority; it is charged with a more authoritative and Biblical unction; it contemplates a more specific end; the undertone of a more conservative and apostolic fervor is heard in it.

Whether the theme is man's want or God's greatness, the Father's perfections, the Son's condescension, the Spirit's influence, there is found prepared a great adaptation of thought and word, a lively apparatus of instruments, phraseology, imagery, symbolism, all growing out of this threefold conception, arranged by the Spirit for reaching and moving each portion of man's manifold constitution, — reason, imagination, sympathy, trust, hope. The doctrine of the personality of the Holy Ghost becomes the indispensable inspiration of all those special and social revivals of religious zeal, which quicken the slumbering vitality and replenish the wasted fires of a formal or worldly ecclesiastical community. Does sensual laxity dissolve, or material prosperity paralyze, the spiritual faculties? Here is a teaching of the Almighty, and his unyielding, retributive law, which sends its terrible warnings upon the careless conscience, and arouses to repentance with Pentecostal power. Does the penitent heart long and seek for the way to the Father's house? Here is a voice, saying, "Whosoever shall call on the name of the Lord shall be saved." Do earnest inquirers after eternal life begin to look with sympathy on one another, and see the windows of heaven opened, and welcome the Messenger of the covenant who comes as a refiner and purifier? The assurances, the promises, are heard, "Jesus hath shed forth this which ye now see and hear;" "The times of refreshing shall come from the presence of the Lord."

On the other hand, when this view is denied, — if one may offer such a criticism with no affront to Christ's own charity, the bond of Christian perfectness, — it appears that, besides the direct loss of positive evangelical resources, there is also a general decline of Christian efficiency. There is a diminished attachment to the person of the Saviour, a cooler loyalty to him, a feebler sense of indebtedness to him with a corresponding abatement of all those inspiring and grateful emotions toward him which the thought of God "found in fashion as a man and humbling himself to become obedient unto death, even the death of the cross," is calculated to sustain. Moral obedience takes on a prudential, calculating aspect. The exultant thankfulness at release by the cross from a deserved misery is gone. Even the belief in Christ's personal presence with his people often becomes an abstract notion, and the joy of it fades away. In not a few instances, a living faith in any divine personality gives place to a frigid intellectual nature-worship, and God either subsides into a philosophical abstraction, or is tied up in the changeless and fatal continuity of his own physical laws. The supernatural grows unreal; its glories vanish from the scenery of the soul, and all the tangible communications it opens between heaven and earth are shut. Deism is followed by naturalism, naturalism by materialism, a materialism not a whit the less Pagan because adorned with taste, learning, and a liberal application of those terms of Christian phraseology, and those external habits of decorum, which are the inestimable boon and heritage transmitted from the disowned creed of the Gospels. The doctrine of the Holy Ghost dwindles into an attenuated, æsthetic impression of a regular, natural Providence. The special act of that Person, regeneration, is dwarfed into a self-improvement by the human will. The liberty of genuine prayer is shortened, — if prayer survives in articulate forms at all, — into a dull and barren process of self-stimulation which yields effects like dropping new or multiplied buckets into empty wells; — for a fixed order of events cannot hear supplication, praise, or thanksgiving. The life dies out of both private and public devotion. Man's part of the business usurps the interest that belongs to God's part; — the professed worshipper is more anxious to be enlightened or entertained or electrified by figures of rhetoric or bursts of declamation or ethical lecturing, than to be pardoned for his sins, or to have his soul borne up in self-forgetful homage. Through a sentimental fear of charging God with severity, a cruel blow is struck at his equity, — and his majestic attribute of mercy is construed to mean a fond indulgence of all sorts of people in all sorts of things. The very possibility of mercy or forgiveness is taken away, for where there is no penalty there is no clemency; indifferentism has nothing to forgive. A general infirmity creeps into religious action. A taste grows up for that sort of instruction which leaves all consciences equally at ease, substituting descriptions of a desirable goodness for the Apostle's abrupt and searching rebuke, "Repent, and be converted, that your sins may be blotted out," or the Saviour's own, "Except ye repent, ye shall all likewise perish." Other themes than those which lie close to the heart of the Gospel are the popular subjects of the pulpit, till Paul's magnifying of his office is exchanged for an effectual obscuration of it in a wonderful variety of offices. Of course the distinctive ecclesiastical honors are lowered. Missions are languid or unknown. Enthusiasm is chilled. Not replenished by the reactionary strength of an aggressive and progressive zeal, the parishes are deadened at home. Discussions or diversions occupy the empty room of the prayer-meeting. The Sunday school fails to supply its pupils with an answer to those that ask them what they believe. "The world" reaps an easy harvest. And of course, where these tendencies predominate, the question whether anything which can properly be called a Church of Christ will continue is only a question of time.*

Were it to be affirmed that these tendencies always work themselves out immediately, or in all individuals who reject the Triune declaration, the insult to common sense would be as gross as the breach of catholic amity. Devout men and women who turn a revering and affectionate heart to Christ, and yet persist in that dogmatic rejection, are found in our day as they have been in other days. To us they seem exceptional cases, standing somewhat apart from the vigorous currents of Christian life in the Church, indebted after all to hereditary influences which they do not acknowledge, not very successful in handing down their piety from one generation to another, and denied some opportunities and privileges which, in a clearer doctrinal agreement with the ancient standards, would enlarge their usefulness along with their satisfactions. They also seem to

* That the *term* "Trinity" is not Scriptural furnishes no argument against the Scriptural authority for the doctrine, so long as the truth is asserted and reasserted in the Scriptures. So the terms "Divinity," "Deity," "Humanity," "Incarnation," "Missions," even "Christianity," and many more, are not less used as true because not found in the Bible. The veneration for the letter of Scripture which thus insists on a mere name, if consistent, would involve other conclusions for which the supposed objector would hardly be prepared.

us, — if the remark may be allowed, — to suffer soon or late under a degree of theological inconsistency, exalting Christ in their reverent affections to a place which they refuse him in a deliberate and express confession. But it must be a narrow construction of the substance of faith which does not cheerfully and gratefully recognize in them a sincere and beautiful imitation of much in the Master's example. We are aware that there are those who fail to connect the evils we have just enumerated with the cause to which we have ascribed them. But when we consider how marvellously God binds causes and effects together, and how at last he blends all revealed truth with righteous practice and accepted institutions, it does not seem very strange that an error respecting so supreme a reality as the nature of God, Christ, and the Spirit, should entail damaging consequences not readily traced in all the links of their succession, by the eye, on all the interests of personal and social religion. Undoubtedly, too, there are faults enough in those branches of the Church where the truth we are advocating is fully held. But the common imperfections of human nature are not to blind us to the existence of real contrasts, nor justify us in ignoring conclusions equally enforced by the interior nature and the exterior history of the Christian system.

Having thus set forth, too cursorily and too feebly, the principal points designed to be included in the present discussion, it only remains to mention two or three more incidental religious advantages of this element in "the faith once delivered to the saints."

1. It is found to be an aid to clearness of thought in respect to the nature and place of Christ, and thus indi-

rectly an encouragement to reverent sentiments in religious discourse and worship. Clinging tenderly to his humanity, with Fénelon "adoring even the childhood of the Word made flesh," and finding at every step of his earthly way some fresh touch of sympathy, we are also assisted to a less perplexing view of him on the Throne of his Glory. It is not uncommon for those who regard the Trinity of God as inconsistent with his Unity, to allege that the devout mind is confused and perplexed by the Threeness. And where the understanding presses itself in so cogently as to subordinate the proper office of pure adoration, constantly taking up and turning over, as in the fingers of its intellectual curiosity, the relations or rank of the persons, this is not unlikely to occur. What is claimed, on the contrary, is that this very thing is a departure from the just attitude of the mind in prayer; that the selfhood of the mind is meant to lie looking very humbly upward; to be still and know that its Lord is God. And further, it is claimed that the objection cited is apt to be urged only by those who have not first entered into the conception with sympathy, but judge it from without; whereas such minds as first receive the doctrine, and then worship in it, discover not only that this objection disappears, but that the liberty and satisfaction of their devotions are much advanced by their belief. It suits, in fact, the actual states of most worshippers to turn in different moods to each of the Three in the One, and, according to its joy or need, to praise and entreat each with the whole heart, — the Father as Creator and Providence, the Son as Redeemer and Embodied Friend, the Spirit as the Dispenser of a diffused and sanctifying influence which permeates and comforts the sensitive soul. More or less clearly there arise thus, before the thought, and impress the feeling, in these hours of high communion, the grand and moving facts of the evangelical history. The holy imagery that peoples the audience-chamber of the Eternal and the mansions of heaven stirs itself in the presence of the suppliant. Ere it is aware, the heart is encompassed with the verities and events of the redemption. Then, there is the very precious mystery of Christ's Intercession, the power of which it is exceedingly difficult to support in a mind which consistently rejects the Trinitarian view. It would be, perhaps, the easiest, though not the most agreeable or grateful method of exhibiting what we would here bring forward, to refer at length to the difficulties encountered by persons of that class in adjusting any definable, satisfactory account of their actual estimate of the Saviour. We often hear it asserted that the anti-Trinitarian view is the simplest, as just now observed. But it is a "simplicity that brings disappointment," the "clearness of a wintry day." Take any form of it, from the highest to the lowest in the honor paid to Christ. Is it easy for the earnest and thoughtful mind to rest in it, — we will not say intellectually, but religiously? If it is the theory, now somewhat prevalent, which attributes moral as well as natural limitations and even moral imperfections to Jesus, then of course the language of his Gospel, including what he expressly says of himself, is ruthlessly abandoned. If the common humanitarian hypothesis is assumed, the honest devotee will be sorely puzzled in taking upon his lips such language as we have quoted, the Saviour's own declarations, the Apostolical ascriptions, the epistolary benedictions, the litanies of the heavenly host as given in the Revelation, the ancient chants, lauds, anthems, or the familiarized and almost universal homage of believers. Ascend to some view more nearly conformed in its terms of statement to the Evangelical standards, whether Arian, Sabellian, or any modification of these, and does not the same sense of inadequacy linger? Does any such conception fill out, fairly and naturally, the language of the New Testament, — as that in Christ dwells all the fulness of the Godhead bodily? We put it as a matter of personal experiment. Does not praise halt or hesitate at this wide diversity between the theological opinion and the evangelical homage? At one moment the mind coolly concludes that Christ is a created being, made in time. But it is seen very soon that this really reduces him at once from all proper divinity, and, by crossing the immense gulf between infinite and finite, the Creator and the creature, it places him essentially on the human plane, however high up upon it. Turning unsatisfied from this conclusion, driven from it by the terms of Scripture, and of the Saviour himself, who must at least be supposed to have known who and what he was, the doubters seek to find some position for their Christ midway between the human and divine, but really belonging to neither. And here they may seem to pause. You ask, then, "What think ye of Christ?" and they answer, they believe he is "not God, but the Son of God." But press the inquiry what they mean by "the Son of God," and there is no answer. Does the Son follow the nature of the Father? Is he the Son otherwise than as created? Is he superangelic? But how well can the boasted "definiteness and simplicity" tell us what a superangelic being is, who is not God? Is he omnipresent? If not, how speak of his presence with you and the Church? If he is, is omnipresence an attribute of any but God? Do you confine his personal stay on earth to his visible ministry? But then you take up the Epistle to the Ephesians, or that to the Philippians, or his own conversations with his followers just before he suffered, or his parting words, "I am with you always," and you have to drop that idea instantly. You pray for his intercessions as your Advocate; but how can he intercede and advocate if he does not know your thoughts and all your personal history? You think to escape your confusion by adhering strictly to the language of Scripture; but as soon as its glorious sentences begin to fall from your lips, the startling inquiry forces itself back, *Whatever I may make these words mean now, would they ever have been chosen and used in the first place on any other belief than that Christ is properly and truly divine, Eternal, Almighty, as the Church of his Heaven-guided people has believed and taught?* So tossed between one untenable supposition and another, the strength and the peace of faith are sadly missed, unless, indeed, through a happier admission of God's grace, the truth which was lying all the time plain and persuasive before the eyes *is seen*, that Christ has the nature of God and the nature of man perfectly united and spiritually wrought together in his glorious Person; having "all power in heaven and earth" as God, even as it is written, — and having that power "given" to him, as man; and thus "God is in Christ reconciling the world unto himself." *

2. The truth here presented goes far to exhibit the mutual interdependence of the parts of Revelation, and to confirm the historical and moral unity of the Bible.

---

* See Note at the end of the volume.

That volume appears in a character of greater dignity and consistency in the light of it. All its successive disclosures and utterances fall into one symmetrical plan. The Incarnation begins to appear, in its preparations and foretokenings, at the very beginning of the Biblical period, as the one central fact and supreme glory of the whole. The Redemption is the theme of the sublime chorus of inspired voices from Genesis to the Apocalypse. As on the Mount of Transfiguration, so in the high seats of Prophecy, Psalm, Sacred History, and typical anticipation, the elders speak of the decease which should be accomplished at Jerusalem. Those difficulties of exegetical explanation, which lay so elaborate and puzzling a task on the anti-Trinitarian, lift and disappear, like mists before the morning. "The Light of the World" scatters them. Christ is the Lord of the Old Testament as well as of the New; and because he is the universal Lord, ruling over the souls of the heathen as well as the souls of Christendom, it is he who saves every heart that is saved, to the utmost corners of the earth, even of those who, not having heard his name nor knowing his law, yet do the things contained in the law, and feel the secret workings of his Spirit. Those traces of the Divine Trinity in the former Scriptures, which are not arguments, are yet natural and beautiful illustrations or confirmations. The plural name of the Creator, his speaking of himself as "we" and "us," the repeated appearance in vision of the Jehovah-Angel as anticipating the visible Messiah,—these things, to the believer, have a meaning as symbols if not as proofs. They appear at a divine call. The royal and sacerdotal figure of Melchisedec arises before us in the Patriarchal age, and moves through the twilight of history, as being, according to the great argument of the Epistle to the Hebrews, the living type of the new king of Righteousness and Peace, and of the "Priest forever," after the heavenly order of priesthood, which is "without descent," "having neither beginning of days nor end of life," "not after the law of a carnal commandment, but after the power of an endless life." Abraham *did* see the Saviour's day and was glad. Moses, as Lawgiver, did predict the Redeemer, and the law given him was the purposed preparation for the "truth and grace by Jesus Christ." Shiloh does come, with his never-departing sceptre of peace, as Israel promised. All the immense and costly system of sacrifices does verily serve its predestined end as the "shadow of better things to come," things which did come in him who "once offered up himself," the Refiner and Purifier of all the sons of Levi, at once High-Priest and Victim, "made higher than the heavens," "continuing ever," "having an unchangeable priesthood," "ever living to make intercession." David, chieftain of kings, takes his singular exaltation, not only from the personal worth of his penitence and the inspiration of his song, but as the regal ancestor of the human part in the Prince of all the kings of the earth. The prophecies, from age to age, and along the pages of the Bible, resound the ever-strengthening and ever-clearer cry, "He cometh! The Wonderful Counsellor, Mighty God, the Everlasting Father, the Prince of Peace! Hosanna to the Son of David! Blessed is he that cometh in the name of the Lord! Hosanna in the highest!"

Now the disciple, taking his stand on this immutable and far-reaching ground of interpretation, finds it a vantage-ground of incomparable superiority. The entire domain of Scriptural revelation spreads itself out under a more luminous sun and a more hallowed air. Let literal criticism ply its needful and honorable labor as it will; let this and that other and less broad explanation be adduced; let cavillers dissent and deny because that is not demonstrated which the Spirit offers only to the reception of faith; nevertheless, once seen, the all-pervading and underlying Christian oneness of the sacred writings is inestimably impressive. They become a new creation to us; not a disjointed, dissevered, unequal, heterogeneous compilation; but, in the express design of God, a manifold and many-voiced affirmation of a single message. They are read, in all their parts, even those remoter in subject from ourselves, with fresh enthusiasm. The poor presumption that proposes to set aside any member of the one sacred whole comes to appear a flippant, superficial tampering of unholy hands with what God has joined together. No wonder the Saviour says of the older Scriptures, "These are they which testify of me!" The *volume* of the BOOK *is* written of HIM; of the "Lamb slain from the foundation of the world." The Forerunner, last in the line of Hebrew prophets, exclaims, "Behold the Lamb of God which taketh away the sin of the world!" And as the record closes, amidst the ineffable openings of the Apocalypse, the worshipping multitude about the throne, many angels and elders, and every creature from heaven and earth and sea, ten thousand times ten thousand, and thousands of thousands say, with a loud voice, "Worthy is the Lamb that was slain to receive power, and riches, and wisdom, and strength, and honor, and glory, and blessing!"

And finally, we also, yet on the earth, taught and reassured by these heavenly and holy voices, take up our praise and prayer, saying, "Glory be to God in the highest, the Creator and Lord of heaven and earth, the Preserver of all things, the Father of mercies, who so loved mankind as to send his only begotten Son into the world to redeem us from sin and misery, and to obtain for us everlasting life! Vouchsafe, O our God, to represent thyself and all the excellences of thy nature, and all the testimonies of thy love, so powerfully to our souls, that we may seriously reverence thee, unfeignedly love thee, and worthily praise thee; rejoice in thee incessantly, trust in thee heartily, adhere to thee zealously, and serve thee devoutly all the days of our lives!

"Glory be to the Eternal Son of God, who for our sakes was made man, and dwelt among us, and died for us: who purged away our sins by the sacrifice of himself, and hath given his body and blood to be our spiritual food and sustenance! Glorious things are spoken of thee, O Jesus, the image of the invisible God, the Light of the World, the Lamb of God that takest away sin, our Great High-Priest who art set down on the right hand of the Majesty on high, and appearest in the presence of God for us, and art our advocate with the Father: who also shalt come again with glory to judge both the quick and the dead; and whose kingdom shall have no end: O blessed Jesus, we acknowledge thee to be the Lord, the Holy One of God. We adore and worship thee, and look for all blessings through thy hand alone, who hast all power in heaven and earth. Out of thy fulness, O most gracious Lord, let us receive grace for grace! Give us humility and meekness; purity, holiness, and universal charity; reverence and constancy in devotion; attentiveness and recollection of mind in hearing thy word; patience in waiting upon thee; weanedness from the world; resignation to thy holy will and contentedness in all conditions; sincerity and uprightness of heart towards thee our God, and towards all men.

"Glory be to the Holy Spirit, of the Father and of the Son, who regenerates and sanctifies us and unites us unto Christ; who enlighteneth our understandings and disposeth our wills; who helpeth our infirmities, strengtheneth us against temptations, and maketh us to fulfil our duty; who directeth us in doubt, and comforteth and supporteth us in troubles! Blessed Spirit, pardon, we beseech thee, our grievings of thee and our rebellions against thee! Be not provoked to leave our souls destitute of thy heavenly influence. Graciously assist us, and make us meekly and readily obedient to all thy holy inspirations. Cherish and increase any good motions thou hast ever wrought in us towards a more complete participation of the Divine nature. And so sanctify us throughout, that our whole spirit, soul and body may be preserved blameless unto the coming of the Lord Jesus Christ!

"Glory be to the Father, and to the Son, and to the Holy Ghost; as it was in the beginning, is now, and ever shall be, world without end! Amen.

[For the sake of giving as faithful a representation as possible of the attitude of the subject as it has offered itself to the author's mind, and as a due acknowledgment of many valuable impressions upon it, the following extracts are made here from a Sermon on "The Christian Trinity a Practical Truth," by Rev. Horace Bushnell, D. D., — himself, in his own language, though not applied to himself, "a lover of the doctrine as related to the life of religion and the working of Christian experience, — preaching, praying, worshipping, climbing up unto God through an experience shaped in the moulds of Trinity "]

"There is yet another class of witnesses, even a great cloud of them. We mean those living myriads of God on earth and above, who, apart from all scholarship and philosophy, have been raised to a participation of God so transcendent in the faith of this adorable mystery. Why or how it is a truth they have not been able, it may be, and as little cared, to find; for it had proved itself to their experience in such a raising of their consciousness, and a communication to them of the Divine nature so indisputably witnessed, as to make them inaccessible to all the colder assaults of scepticism. Sometimes they have stated a Trinity to which there have been abundant reasons for exception, and yet they have found such practical virtue in that, as to be raised quite above the encumbrances added; and seem even to have had it for a part of their joy, to see how the fires of their faith could burn up all the chaff of their head. The wise ones of the Church and the speculative schools sometimes give them pity; or, what is not far different, set them forth as the weaklings of the faith, who make a virtue of their ecstasies over what has been imposed upon their superstition; but the revelations of eternity will show who were weakest and most on a level with pity, — they who could so readily fall into the abysses of the Divine mystery, or the wise pretenders who stood questioning over syllables and refining in distinctions, till they had shut away all mystery, and taken up for God a dull residuum just equal to the petty measures of their understanding.

"Could we bring up this great cloud of witnesses, and hear them speak to the question we have here on hand, or could we but gather up the words in which they have recorded their experience in the faith, even these would contribute a weight of evidence to the truth we are asserting, and shed a glory over it such as to quite forbid the need of any other argument. Thus, for example, we should hear, at Heidelberg, two centuries and a half ago, the distinguished Professor of Divinity, Francis Junius, testifying that he was in fact converted from atheism by the Christian Trinity, or by the sense of God rolled in upon his soul by means of that stupendous mystery of the Gospel. Having fallen into great looseness of living, and become an atheist in his opinions, his Christian father kindly puts a New Testament in his hands, requesting him to read it; and the result is, that, opening on a passage most of all likely as it would commonly be supposed to offend and fortify his scepticism, he is visited, in its mysterious and sublime words, by such a sense of God as overwhelms and instantly stifles the doubts which no mere argument of books and treatises had been able to remove. He shall give the account in his own words: 'Here therefore I open that New Testament, the gift of heaven; at first sight and without design, I light upon that most august chapter of the Evangelist and Apostle St. John, "In the beginning was the word, and the word was with God, and the word was God," &c. I read part of the chapter, and am so affected as I read, that, on a sudden, I perceive the divinity of the subject, and the majesty and authority of the writing, far exceeding all human eloquence. I shuddered, was confounded, and was so affected that I scarce knew myself. Thou didst remember me, O Lord my God, for thy great mercy, and didst receive a lost sheep into thy flock.' (Bayle's Dictionary)

"The testimonies of Christian experience rejoicing in this truth are of course more frequent. Thus the mild and sober Howe, explaining in what manner the Trinity is to be connected with Christian experience, says, coincidently with what we have advanced concerning the relational nature of the fact: 'When, therefore, we are to consider God as related to us as our God, we must take in and bring together each of these notions and conceptions concerning him; we must take in the conceptions of each of the persons, — "God the Father, God the Son, and God the Holy Ghost, is my God." How admirable a thing is this! How great and high thoughts ought we to have concerning the privileged state of our case! Indeed there is nothing that we have to consider of this God, or to look after the knowledge of, to answer the curiosity of a vain mind, but everything and anything that may answer the necessity of a perishing soul. Whatever is requisite to our real felicity and blessedness, we may look to all that is in God, as determined by a special relation unto us.' (Works, p. 1100.)

"Jeremy Taylor, holding the truth of the Christian Trinity to be a truth entirely practical, apprehensible therefore in its real evidence only by experience, says: 'He who goes about to speak of the mystery of the Trinity, and does it by words and names of man's invention, talking of essences and existences, hypostases and personalities, priorities in coequalities, and unity in pluralities, may amuse himself and build a tabernacle in his head, and talk of something he knows not what; but the good man who *feels* the power of the Father, to whom the Son is become wisdom, sanctification, and righteousness, and in whose heart the Spirit is shed abroad, — this man, though he understands nothing of what is unintelligible, yet he alone truly understands the Christian doctrine of the Trinity.

"Again, the Marquis de Renty, a distinguished French disciple of the seventeenth century, opens the secret of his own living experience in these words: 'I bear in me ordinarily an experimental verification and a plenitude of the most holy Trinity, which elevates me to a simple view of God; and with that I do all that his providence enjoins me, not regarding anything for the greatness or littleness of it, but only the order of God, and the glory it may render him.' (Life of De Renty.)

"The testimony of Edwards, a man whose intellectual sobriety and philosophic majesty of character are not to be disrespected, corresponds: 'And God has appeared glorious unto me on account of the Trinity. It has made me have exalting thoughts of God that he subsists in three persons, Father, Son, and Holy Ghost. The sweetest joys and delights I have experienced have not been those that have arisen from the hope of my own good estate, but in a direct view of the glorious things of the Gospel.' (Life, pp. 132, 133.)

"The celebrated Lady Maxwell, a follower of Wesley, is more abundant in these revelations. She says: 'Yesterday he made his goodness to pass before me in a remarkable manner, while attending public worship. I was favored with a clear view of the Trinity, which I never had before, and enjoyed fellowship with a triune God. I was in the spirit on the Lord's day, and felt my mind fixed in deep contemplation upon that glorious incomprehensible object, the ever-blessed Trinity. Hitherto I have been led to view the Holy Ghost chiefly as an agent, now I behold him distinctly as the third person of the Trinity. I have, in my own soul, an *experimental proof* of the truth of this doctrine, but find human language perfectly insufficient for speaking or writing intelligibly on the subject. Eternity alone can unfold the sacred mystery; but in the mean time what we may and do comprehend of it is replete with comfort to the Christian.' (Life, p. 258.)

"It is impossible not to admire the Gospel formula that can so flood the human soul in its narrowed and blinded state with the sense of God, and raise it to a pitch of blessing so transcendent. The amazing power of the Trinity, acting thus on the human imagination, and the contribution thus made to Christian experience, cannot be overestimated.

"After we have discovered, in this manner, how closely related the Christian Trinity is to Christian experience, and all the highest realizations of God, it will not be difficult to account for the remarkable tenacity of the doctrine. No doctrine is more paradoxical in its terms. None can be more mercilessly tortured by the application of a little logic, such as the weakest and smallest wits are master of. None has been more often or with a more peremptory confidence repudiated by sections of the Church and teachers of high distinction. The argument itself, too, has always been triumphant regarding the mere logical result; for the fact is logically absurd, and there is no child who cannot so handle the words as to show that no three persons can be one. And yet, for some reason, the doctrine would not die! It cannot die! Once thought, it cannot be expelled from the world. And this for the reason that its life is in men's hearts, not in their heads. Impressing God in his true personality and magnitude,—impressing and communicating God in that grand twofold economy, by which he is brought nigh to our fallen state and accommodated to our wants as sinners, showing us God inherently related both to our finite capacity and our evil necessity, what can ever expel it from the world's thought? As soon shall we part with the daylight or the air, as lapse into the cold and feeble monotheism in which some teachers of our time are ready to boast as the Gospel of reason and the unity of a personal fatherhood. No: this corner-stone is not to be so easily removed. It was planted before the foundation of the world, and it will remain. It is eternally woven into the practical economy of God's kingdom, and must therefore stand firm. Look up, O man! Look up, thou sinner! in thy fall, and behold thy God, eternally Father, Son, and Holy Ghost, bringing all his vastness down to thy littleness, all the power of his will to release thee from the power of thy will, acting, manifolding, circling round thee, inherently fitted, though infinite, to thy finite want, and so to be the spring of thy benediction for ever!

"We are fully conscious of the tameness and poverty of the illustrations by which we have endeavored to set forth this greatest of all subjects. What can a mortal say that is worthy of this transcendent mystery of God? Even if he should some time seem to be raised in it quite above mortality, how can he utter that which is so plainly unutterable? Well is it if he does not seem rather to have blurred than cleared the glorious majesty of the subject, by the consciously dull and feeble trivialities he has offered. Indeed we could not dare to offer a discussion so far below the real merit of the theme, were it not for the conviction that there is a lower and feebler inadequacy, in our common holding of the theme, from which it is scarcely possible to detract. To hold this grand subtonic mystery, in the ring of whose deep reverberation we receive our heaviest impressions of God, as if it were only a thing just receivable, not profitable; a dead truth, not a living; a theologic article, wholly one side of the practical life; a truth so scholastic and subtle as to have, in fact, no relation to Christian experience; nothing, we are sure, can be less adequate than this, or bring a loss to religion that is more deplorable, unless it be a flat denial of the mystery itself. We can wish the reader nothing more beatific in this life than to have found and fully brought into feeling the practical significance of this eternal act or fact of God, which we call the Christian Trinity. Nowhere else do the bonds of limitation burst away as here. Nowhere else does the soul launch upon immensity as here; nowhere fill her burning censer with the eternal fires of God, as when she sings, —

One inexplicably three,
One in simplest unity.

"Who that has been able, in some frame of holy longing after God, to clear the petty shackles of logic, and the paltry quibbles of a world-wise speculation, committing his soul up freely to the inspiring impulse of this divine mystery as it is celebrated in some grand doxology of Christian worship, and has so been lifted into conscious fellowship with the great celestial minds, in their higher ranges of beatitude, and their shining tiers of glory, has not known it as being, at once, the deepest, highest, widest, most enkindling, and most practical of all practical truths?

"Regarding it, then, as such, it is only a part of the argument by which we undertake to commend it to faith and a practical use, that we indicate, in a few brief suggestions, the manner in which its advantages may be most fully received, and with fewest drawbacks of hinderance and perplexity.

"First of all, then, we must hold fast the strict unity of God. Let there be no doubt, or even admitted question, of that. Take it by assumption that God is as truly one being as if he were a finite person like ourselves, and let nothing ever be suffered to qualify the assumption; for the moment we begin to let in any such thought as that the Father, Son, and Holy Ghost are three beings, we shall be thrown out of all rest, confused, distressed, questioning what and whom to worship, consulting our prejudices and preferences, and suffering all the distractions of idolaters.

"Holding firm the unity in this manner, use the plurality with the utmost unconcern, as a form of thought or instrumental verity, by which you are to be assisted in receiving the most unrestricted, fullest, most real and sufficient impression of the One. We must have no jealousy of the three, as if they were going to drift us away from the unity, or from reason; being perfectly assured of this, that in using the triune formula, in the limberest, least constrained way possible, and allowing the plurality to blend, in the freest manner possible, with all our acts of worship, preaching, praying, singing, and adoring, we are only doing with three persons, just what we do with one, — making no infringement of the unity with the three, more than of the infinity with the one. Let God be three persons forever, just as he is one person forever, and as this latter is a truth accepted without difficulty, and held as the necessary truth of religion, so let it be our joy that he is a being who needs for other purposes equally dear to be and be thought as three.

"Meantime we must avoid all practices of logic on the persons. We must take them as we take the one, which, if we will put our logic on the term, will immediately turn out to be only a finite being, — a man. They are to be set before the mind at the outset as a holy paradox, that only gives the truth in greater power of expression that it defies all attempts at logic or definition. Seizing thus upon the living symbols, we are to chant our response with the church, and say, — 'God of God, Light of Light, very God of very God;' and, if we cannot reason out the paradox, to like it the better that it stops the clatter of our speculative mill-work, and speaks to us as God's great mystery should, leaving us to adore in silence. Not that we are here to disown our reason; God is no absurdity as three persons more than as one. Fully satisfied of this, we are only to love the grand abyss of God's majesty thus set before us, and rejoice to fall into it, there to bathe and submerge our finite love, rejoicing the more that God is greater than we knew, taller than our reach can measure, wider than our finite thought can comprehend.

"Neither will it do for us to suffer any impatience, or be hurried into any act of presumption, because the Trinity of God costs us some struggles of thought, and because we cannot find immediately how to hold it without some feeling of disturbance or distraction. That is one of the merits of the Trinity, that it does not fool us in the confidence that we can perfectly know and comprehend God by our first thought. Simply because God is too great for our extempore and merely childish comprehension, he ought to be given us in forms that cost us labor, and put us on a stretch of endeavor. So it is with all great themes. The mind labors and wrestles after them, and comes into their secret slowly. Let no shallow presumption turn us away, then, from this glorious mystery, till we have given it time enough, and opened to it windows enough by our praises and prayers, to let in the revelation of its glory. Let it also be an argument of modesty with us, and a welcome commendation to our reverence, that so many friends of God and righteous men of the past ages, such as bore a greater fight than we, and grew to greater ripeness in their saintly walk, bowed themselves adoringly before this holy mystery, and sung it with hallelujahs in the worship of their temples, in their desert fastings, and their fires of testimony. And as their *Gloria Patri*, the sublimest of their doxologies, is, in form, a hymn for the ages, framed to be continuously chanted by the long procession of times, till times are lapsed in eternity, what can we better do than let the wave lift us that lifted them, and bid it still roll on?"

SERMON XXI.

THE PROMISE AND ASSURANCE OF SANCTIFICATION.

MY SHEEP HEAR MY VOICE, AND I KNOW THEM, AND THEY FOLLOW ME: AND I GIVE UNTO THEM ETERNAL LIFE; AND THEY SHALL NEVER PERISH, NEITHER SHALL ANY MAN PLUCK THEM OUT OF MY HAND. — John x. 27, 28.

BOTH in the common business of Christian living, and in the discouragements of Christian failure, there is an inestimable power in the assurance so explicitly given in these words of the Saviour. And this is the assurance: All who have become his by the communication into their souls of his secret and divine life through faith shall be securely and inviolably kept in that communion. They are not on the same ground with the rest of the world. They live in no uncertainty. They have believed to some purpose. They have not made their good confession for a disappointment. The promises of God have not imposed upon them a delusion. The laws of their spiritual nature are not going to play them false. There are privileges, there are safeties, pertaining to them, not to be had in any other way than this new way. The salvation they are told of means something. The almighty friendship of the Saviour, pledged to them when they consented to be his friends, amounts to something. They are not outside, but inside a commonwealth, or fold, which has defences, foundations, immunities. Over it is a Guardian who is not a covenant-breaker, a Shepherd that is a King. No man is able to pluck them out of his hand. Say nothing of that deep experience which is the only competent interpreter in the case, since it brings with it a new organ of discernment; who of us, even by the common knowledge of common things, does not see that a new and invigorating character must be given to the whole action of the religious life, when this conviction about it is established as a living habit in the soul?

Take first the moods of religious dissatisfaction. These are various in their occasions, various in form, color, and degree, according to individual temperament and situation. They range over the whole scale of man's marvellous sensibility to doubt, to fear, to palpable accusings of conscience and nameless depressions. They gather up their painful elements from without and from within. They shape themselves, with a multiformity of suffering that is wonderful and fearful, to all our individual ideas of what the Christian life is, and of what God requires. If you conceive of this chiefly as an obligation, you see with dismay that the command outreaches your obedience. If you regard it as a privilege, you are mortified that you abuse it. If you take the legal view, you feel the sentence of death in your self-judgment; if the ethical, your moral standard mocks and shames you. If the disinterested compassion of Christ's sacrifice moves you, you are humiliated at the poverty of your return and even the dulness of your gratitude. If you are inclined to look mainly into the Bible for your direction, then the distance between that Book and the record of your own doings is the distance between Heaven and earth, between holy and unholy. Or if you listen reverently for the voices of intuition, springing in the oracles of your own immortal spirit, still the ideal dwarfs the performance, and the honest conscience cries, " Unclean, unclean ! " — " Miserable man that I am," " who shall deliver me ? "

If these were only moods of discontent, and nothing more, they might be taken as a wholesome portion in a necessary discipline ; an interior crucifixion into that meekness which is of the very essence of Christian submission ; or else as a stimulus to a stronger work and warfare. For it is inevitable that a faith whose characteristic spirit is eternal aspiration should be more or less a sorrowing faith. If any of us shrink from committal to it, or toss off its Divine invitations, because we are such cowards as to dread these attendant shadows of its glory, still we do not mistake its grand conditions; we only forfeit what the timid and servile soul could not hold at any rate till it is transformed and new-born by the Spirit of courage and of liberty, the Spirit of power, and of love, and of a sound mind.

Nevertheless, friends, Christians, in whom this spirit has begun, you know there is a bound where all this dissatisfaction and unrest ought to end. Beyond that limit it becomes a hinderance to Christian growth, a fetter upon Christian liberty, a chill upon Christian zeal. Instead of inspiriting, it debilitates. By an easy and dangerous transition it passes into a morbid self-occupation, which shuts off charity for men and service to Christ. It becomes a practical denial of the supporting strength and the pledged grace of God. There can be little freedom, or heartiness, or efficiency, in the worship or the living, under this overshadowing anxiety. Better far always than indifference or unconcern, it is not the natural, healthy state of a disciple. If it is an inevitable stage on the way to that state, yet it should always be treated as just that and no more, — temporary, instrumental, immature: tending ever to peace; looking for the joy of believing; waiting for the promise of the Comforter; pressing on, with confident expectation, from the transient "spirit of bondage to fear," which asks, "Who shall deliver me?" into the abiding "spirit of life in Christ Jesus," where "there is no condemnation," and into the blessed "spirit of adoption whereby we cry, Abba, Father:" "if God be for us, who can be against us?" "Neither death, nor life, nor things present, nor things to come, nor height nor depth, nor any other creature, shall be able to separate us from the love of God which is in Christ Jesus our Lord." If it be possible, every Christian heart will feel it to be a part of its Christian endeavor and prayer to lay off the weight which burdens the race, exchanging it for this undoubting, full assurance of faith.

And to a greater extent than even many earnest, sincere people believe, it certainly is possible. The Lord of our salvation has made it possible. It is possible, not in our might, or wisdom, or self-lifting, but by his own Spirit, given to those who seek in simplicity. It is possible, by our seeing him as he is, receiving him as he is offered, following him, not for our own sake, but for his sake. It is possible that we should "be of good cheer," because he has overcome the world's tribulation. It is possible we should "fear not," because "it is the Father's good pleasure to give us the kingdom." It is possible we should "fear none of those things which we shall suffer," because our Saviour has suffered for us. It is possible for us to do our work cordially, without misgiving of failure, without dread of a separation from the great Source of our safety and strength, — because "no man shall be able to pluck" his people "out of his hand."

There is an anecdote of the saintly and learned Archbishop Usher, not unfamiliar to religious readers, which is meant to illustrate his spiritual modesty. It relates how a friend frequently urged him to write his thoughts on Sanctification, which at length he engaged to do; but, a considerable time elapsing, the performance of his promise was importunately claimed. The Bishop replied to this purpose: "I have not written, and yet I cannot charge myself with a breach of promise, for I began to write; but when I came to treat of the new creature which God formeth by his own Spirit in every regenerate soul, I found so little of it wrought in myself that I could speak of it only as parrots, or by rote, but without the knowledge of what I might have expressed; and, therefore, I durst not presume to proceed any further upon it." Upon this his friend stood amazed to hear such a confession from so grave, holy, and eminent a person. The Bishop then added: "I must tell you, we do not well understand what sanctification and the new creature are. It is no less than for a man to be brought to an entire resignation of his own will to the will of God; and to live in the offering up of his soul continually in the flames of love, as a whole burnt-offering to Christ; and O, how many who profess Christianity are unacquainted, experimentally, with this work upon their souls!"

As an example of personal self-distrust, this is touching and beautiful. But to infer from it that there are themes of spiritual thought unfolded in the Gospel really and finally beyond the reach of sincere and consecrated souls would be a perversion of it. By large confidences in the Saviour's promises Christians do not extol themselves, but honor him. The New Testament writers never misapprehend man's spiritual nature. They never overstate God's encouragements. Sanctification is an actual and frequent theme of Evangelical meditation and exposition. Sooner or later, therefore, a declaration of "the whole counsel of God" requires that it be gratefully and solemnly and reverently opened. If we stammer and blunder, the same "Faithful Promiser" will pity, correct, forgive. There is a shortcoming of faith which nothing else will enlarge. There is a religious anxiety that nothing else will console. I spoke of the variety of forms that religious anxiety assumes. Yet down at its deepest source it is probably very much one and the same thing, having one and the same cause. It springs from a feeling of one fact, — the distance between what we ought to be and what we are. In one way of putting it or another, that is the solemn difficulty: the great, deep gulf that still opens between what the Holy Father in heaven must require of us, and the lives we live: a gulf so great and deep, and so imperceptibly narrowed, if at all, that it threatens to keep us apart forever. Apart! Patiently examine, analyze, and confess it, and see if this is not the secret of the fear. Quicken any soul into a more delicate sensibility, and this is the real question that distresses it. To be left apart from its Lord! It is deeper than any selfish alarm. It is grander than the suffering of any material penalty. It is the sorrow of love, of loyalty, of devoted and honorable friendship. It belongs to the noblest view, and the most generous philosophy, of Christian truth.

Hence it is that the passage where the text occurs meets profoundly just the inmost nature of the trouble, in all its diversity of action. Christ is conversing with his disciples about their future. He knows, and they begin to feel, that in that future is involved one secret which contains all other interests, hopes, terrors. What is to become of their connection with him? Is it to cease? Is it to last forever? Tell them that, and you solve the one darkest doubt that haunts them.

Their Master tells them. Already he had revealed to them, as their slowly opening minds were prepared for it, one and another of his great designs and offices in their behalf. He had told them, in imagery beautifully and touchingly diversified, many sublime marvels of his Messiahship; that he was "the Door," by which alone every man must enter in; "the Light," by which every man who sees must be lighted; the "Living Water," quenching every thirst; and, at last, rising to a more personal and intimate representation, that he was the "Good Shepherd" of all souls, in heaven and earth, keeping the frail, recovering the lost. Still something remained untold. Doubtless the very object of these startling statements was to arouse their thoughts to further inquiries, and so prepare them, by a natural education, and not a blind compulsion, for the greater truth to come; — just as he still often waits to bestow on us his richest blessings, till ripened affections are stirred to seek them. The Jews come at last, and say, "How long dost thou make us to doubt? If thou be the

Christ, tell us plainly." He answers their unbelief plainly; and then, turning to the few hearts which he knew were struggling with the weight of a more serious premonition: "My sheep hear my voice, and I know them, and they follow me. And I give unto them eternal life, and they shall never perish; neither shall any man pluck them out of my hand." Let who will among them take comfort from the assurance!

Even so far back as the Patriarchal period our Lord began to reveal himself as a Promise-maker and a Promise-keeper, — a God of covenants. And not only were these promises literal and Scriptural. Sublime signs attested him. The stars of the Eastern sky were marshalled into his witnesses over the Mount, when the angel pointed Abraham to them in the redemptive promise of his posterity: "In thy seed shall all the nations of the earth be blessed," — "as the stars of heaven for multitude." Bethel, the solemn pasture-ground whence the ladder of light sprang up to heaven while Jacob slept, was bright with the same eternal promise, and when he awoke into the splendor he cried, "How dreadful is this place," — "house of God and gate of heaven." Peniel, where the Patriarch wrestled in the long, dark night, and cried at length, "Let me go, for the day breaketh," and gained his new name, "Israel," as a pledge of "power with God," became a monument of promise. The whole Mosaic apparatus, from the "circumcision in the flesh" to the Temple on Moriah, and from the Garden of Eden to the Garden of Gethsemane, was a system of historic symbols and instruments to persuade men they had to do with a Jehovah that remembered his pledges. All the sacred lands were dotted over with the tokens of these divine covenants, like the signature to a bond. That Oriental territory became a kind of outspread scroll, its hills and rivers printed with promissory memorials speaking from one generation to another. It vivified the people's faith and strengthened their hands to fight for the personal God who had agreed to stand by them. And when the Messiah was born, the old promises were at once fulfilled and grew more articulate, while "new," "more glorious," "better" promises were added. "God was manifest in the flesh, justified in the spirit, seen of angels, preached unto the Gentiles, believed on in the world, received up into glory." United now with humanity, his assurances had a human sound as well as a divine authority, and every word was "glad tidings." It was a Testament, a covenant. Its great pledge was that of a redemption to the ends of the earth and the end of time. A Personal "Comforter," "a Paraclete," was to come, to "abide," apply it, and give it an everlasting practical energy. He was promised to come from Christ, and dwell in the Church, and carry forward its reconciling work forever.

If we begin to read the New Testament for the first time with this truth for a key, we shall find that the light of a new meaning begins to shine along the pages. Take, for example, those conversations Christ held with his disciples just before his separation from them, written in John. Do we not all acknowledge that, in our human sympathies, the first sad thought which intrudes, after the establishing of a new and valuable friendship, or the assured possession of a coveted affection, is the question about its duration? What will endanger it? Can anything break it? To meet that fear, Jesus took much of those last hours of communion to reassure his friends, in every form of promise, that he would not leave them exposed or forsaken or comfortless, but come back to them, abide with them, watch over them, deliver them. "That where I am, there ye may be also." Nay, it shall be an internal union. "At that day ye shall know that ye are in me, and I in you." There shall be not only union, but love, — Almighty love. "He that loveth me shall be loved of my Father, and I will love him, and will manifest myself to him." "I and my Father are one." Hence all alarm must disappear. "Let not your heart be troubled, neither let it be afraid." Nor shall it be merely a negative thing, — this absence of terror, — but a positive and settled peace: "My peace I give unto you." And this shall pass into active, productive righteousness. "Every branch in me that beareth fruit, he purgeth it that it may bring forth more fruit." Besides, all new wants shall be supplied: "Abiding in me, ye shall ask what ye will, and it shall be done unto you." "The Spirit of truth will guide you into all truth." "Father, I will that they also whom thou hast given me be with me where I am:" "No man shall pluck them out of my hand." What promises are these!

Turning, then, to the corresponding confidence created by them in the mind of the Apostles, we have resplendent instances of the assurance of faith responding. Hear Paul to his fellow-witness: "I suffer; nevertheless, I am not ashamed: for I know whom I have believed;" — the tranquil and triumphant answer to all persecution, sophistry, hatred, ridicule, to all unbelief, in all ages: "I know whom I have believed, and am persuaded that he is able to keep that which I have committed unto him, against that day," — the day that brings "life and immortality to light."

Or listen to those majestic affirmations of assurance, in the Eighth to the Romans, — a kind of echo to the promise of our text, — assurance answering to assurance, rising and gathering power as it rolls on, each clause coming with the certainty of a decree, — solemn at once and jubilant: "For whom he did foreknow he also did predestinate, to be conformed to the image of his Son. Moreover, whom he did predestinate, them he also called; and whom he called, them he also justified: and whom he justified, them he also glorified. If God be for us, who can be against us?"

Now all these passages, and too many more to be even mentioned, present our most holy religion to us in a light not only very different from what our feeble faith, sinking below its high calling, is too apt to linger in, but one that is of unspeakable interest in the actual and necessary difficulties of the Christian life. We are not left to ourselves, with a mere guide-book in our hands, and the mere reminiscence of a vanished voice behind us. The grand peculiarity, the divinest characteristic, of the Christian Gospel is, that it does not stop with telling us *how* to act, but enters in, by the living person of the Lord, and becomes an indwelling force, *by which* we act. It is not only a precept before our eyes, but a power in our hearts. The spiritual world is not only an expectation, but all its channels of inspiring influence have been set open by the Mediator, and, through him, henceforth, the believer lives in direct relations and immediate intercourse with God. The disciple is encircled and touched with the celestial presence. Another will than his own has begun to work *within* his own, — both to will and to do. In proportion to his faith in that, he can do all things, —

"through Christ strengthening him." Nothing shall by any means hurt him. So much stronger is this Holy Spirit felt to be in him, than anything self-derived, that he says with Paul, "It is no more I that live, but Christ that liveth in me." The superficial delusion of the senses passes away; this invisible reality is more plain to his consciousness than anything the senses take knowledge of. He has nothing to fear; for nothing can pluck him from that Hand of Power in which he rests.

Furthermore, the true disciple's faith is not a means nor a merit by which either salvation or peace is bought. The Gospel says, "Believe and live." And the moment any soul hears that, it believes, if it believes at all, simply because it must. It is true, the assurance, the peace, does not come till the faith comes. But neither does it come if the faith is brought as a deserving equivalent for it. In other words, we are not to believe for our own sake, but for Christ's sake: because he supremely deserves it, by his infinite love and sacrifice. The mind of Christendom has yet to undergo a great change at just this point, as well as the preaching. We are not sanctified in order to be justified, but sanctified because we are justified. This is the Divine order. Faith; more faith; assurance; sanctification; peace. This makes the Christian service and progress a free, joyful tribute of gratitude. "He that hath this *hope* in him purifieth himself." The believer is not still struggling, down under the bondage of compulsion, trying sorrowfully to get faith enough, any more than works enough, to be saved by. He is up on the heights of spiritual liberty, no longer under law, but in grace. He has lost sight of self and its solicitudes. He knows in whom he has believed, and is assured that he is "saved already" in that he does believe, — "passed from death unto life." And thus, being emancipated from the hinderance of self-interest, he obeys from love, brings his body more and more under, for the pure Master's sake, goes from grace to grace, and has "peace with God through our Lord Jesus Christ." In the same way it may be said that we have not to go in search of a Saviour, but only to be found of him who so tenderly has come out into the cold mountains of our pride and unbelief, in search *of us*, according to that affecting "hymn of faith and hope" of Bonar, —

> "The Shepherd sought his sheep,
> The Father sought his child,
> They followed me o'er vale and hill,
> O'er deserts waste and wild.
> They found me nigh to death,
> Famished, and faint, and lone;
> They bound me with the bands of love;
> They saved the wandering one!
> They spoke in tender love,
> They raised my drooping head,
> They gently closed my bleeding wounds,
> My fainting soul they fed.
> They washed my filth away,
> They made me clean and fair;
> They brought me to my home in peace, —
> The long-sought wanderer!"

It is not to be forgotten that with some of the sincerest disciples in the world, misgivings not only exist, but even take up a defence more complex, more subtle, and harder to yield than those we have examined. Such persons know indeed that religion is not a set of legal or ethical requirements. They tell you they do not expect to save their souls by keeping all the commandments, nor by anything they can do. That system of self-righteousness, or judgment by merits, they have seen through and left behind. Still, they believe that acceptance has its conditions, and these conditions they fear they have not fulfilled. God's forgiveness, Christ's reconciliation, are not given, they say, but to a soul that really seeks. Progress too they know to be a law and test of conversion. And daily they sorrow with conscientious grief, lest their faith should be a delusion, their hopes unfounded, and all "the blessedness they knew when first they saw the Lord," as "a dream when one awaketh."

Granting, then, the value of whatever earnest self-examination these questionings may prompt, granting that there are conditions and tests, and, most of all, that condition which consists in a self-renouncing consecration once for all to God; yet there is another line of thought, equally Scriptural, equally humble, equally adapted to impart energy to effort and fervor to prayer. It starts in the conviction that our Father coming to us, and coming for us, in his Son, does not want our loss, but our gain; not our destruction, but our life eternal; not our performances, so poor at the largest to his Infinitude, but our affections, confidence, gratitude, and such earnest service as these filial feelings will inspire. Christianity, let us remember, is from first to last a divine movement in our behalf. It is an offer, promise, compassion, help, redemption. Love for us was the motive, sacrifice for us the means, and an opportunity to pour out into receptive and willing hearts the same infinite and everlasting affection is the end. Suppose, now, any soul comes to feel this, and believe it. Can it then believe it the object of him who has died for us once, to thrust us back, and cast us away? to set up measurements of exercise for our new-born and thankful faith? to enter with captious criticisms into the failures and shames of our faltering but quite earnest discipleship? to say back to us with frigid severity, — "Yes, you believe or try to; you love me, or you think you do; you long to resemble me and live my life, or honestly suppose you do; yet you are not quite up to the mark I require, and so I am watching to catch sight of every flaw, and score every shortcoming, and shall shut the entrance against you, if by any possibility of justice I can?" Is this the sound of the Gospel? Is this the language of a Saviour who has once shed his life-blood to recover us? Is this to be a "Door" and a "Light" and a "Good Shepherd," to his own feeble flock? No! His words are: "I know them, and they follow me; I give unto them eternal life; they shall never perish; neither shall any man pluck them out of my hand!"

Consider, finally, whether all this undue distrust, besides being far less nutritive to a useful and active piety among men, is not in danger of holding in it some ingratitude and irreverence to Him whom it professes and really intends to honor. Which honors him most; to believe that he will keep those that have sincerely come penitent and longing to him, or that he will scorn them? that he will fulfil his promises, or break them? When shall we learn this, — till we do learn it we have missed the one deepest and most special and distinctive thing in the Gospel of our redemption, viz. — that Christianity does not expect of us to be perfect people first, in order that we may be entitled to salvation, nor Christians first, in order that we may earn

Christ for a Saviour; but quite the opposite thing,—that we should believe we have a Saviour in order to be consciously saved; and that we should know the needful way to be already opened, that we may walk in it by the attraction of our Leader's spirit? Every miracle the Saviour wrought on earth, every sentence he spoke, every pain he bore, is a new ground of assured comfort for every soul that has once come heartily to him confessing, "I believe; help thou mine unbelief;" or asking, "What shall I do that I might work the works of God?" Hear his explicit answer: "This is the work of God, that ye should believe on him whom he hath sent." "Whosoever believeth in me, though he were dead, yet shall he live." "Him that cometh to me, I will in no wise cast out." "No man shall pluck them out of my hand." "Why art thou cast down, O my soul? and why art thou disquieted within me? Hope thou in God, for I shall yet praise him who is the health of my countenance and my God!"

Whichever way you look, with the purpose of looking, you see persons with whom you are confident the one strong and ruling desire of life is to be Christlike, and to know him in whom they believe, yet troubled, uncertain, anxious,—and very often painfully anxious, about their acceptance with him. Some time ago,—a year or years,—they resolutely, thoughtfully took up their choice,—half a cross and half a recompense, but all a joy,—and yet they sometimes return to the beggarly elements of the question whether their Master will keep that which they then committed to him! Does not this betray some erroneous conception of the very nature of his faith, putting something of our own in place of him,—some will-work for childlike humility, some self-hood instead of the gracious Spirit whence every good thing comes?

To each of these the Redeemer tenderly approaches, saying, "Fear not; I have called thee; thou art mine; this work of thy great redemption is done; it has not to be done again; I have overcome the world; be of good cheer. Thy work is first to believe, and then out of thy faith, impelled by holy thankfulness and love, undoubtingly, to do daily all the will of God thou knowest, which shall then be known to thee more and more. That which makes thy work effectual is the Spirit I have given thee, and the pardon with which I have pardoned thee. Fear nothing, O weary and troubled heart! any more. Doubt nothing any more. Forget the things that are behind. The ascension day has come. Thou hast an advocate with the Father. Thinkest thou not I have as much desire and interest to keep thee as thou hast to be kept? Already thou mayest say, 'Abba, Father!' Peace waiteth for thee. Thy Lord is in earnest with thee. 'Behold what he has told thee about the finished work of thy redemption. Return, and be at rest. Enter again thy forgotten home, and take thy prepared place, for all things are now ready, and rejoice with them that rejoice over thee.' Fear nothing. I have called thee by thy name. I know my sheep, and am known of mine. I give unto them eternal life. No man shall pluck them out of my hand!"

SERMON XXII.

THE SOCIAL CONSCIENCE.

CONSCIENCE, I SAY, NOT THINE OWN, BUT OF THE OTHER. — 1 Cor. x. 29.

THE form of the expression is accommodated and idiomatic. Strictly it would be, "Conscience, not *only* thine own, but of the other as well." For it is only through my "own conscience" that I can morally respect the conscience of that "other." If I regard his, it must be by obeying my own; and my thoughtfulness for his must be proportioned to the sensibility of my own.

By all who believe that there is any such thing as a moral authority for human life, that duty is a word with a meaning, and that responsibility is a fact, it will be granted that each of these three propositions is applicable to our intercourse and connections with each other; that is, that the moral significance of life is nowhere more vitally manifest than in what we do or fail to do for the characters of our neighbors; that a large part of what is included in the term duty is what we owe to other men's welfare, or their goodness, which is the same thing; and that society presents a scene of personal responsibility, peculiar to itself, where the materials of judgment are always accumulating.

But, as in other cases, so here: the consent to a general statement of a principle is one thing, while a courageous loyalty to its personal requirements is another. There may be a wide gap between the storehouse where we keep a supply of respectable abstract notions loosely laid away for quotation, — something between the earnestness of conviction and the inconvenient disrepute of scepticism, on the one hand, and the living embodiment of these notions in a self-denying practice, on the other. It is easy enough to agree that we ought not to weaken and damage and degrade other men's consciences; but to give up the gratification, the amusement, the pleasant and *otherwise* harmless habit, which will certainly damage and mislead them, is not always very easy. Besides, there are some questions of right, how far, in particular cases, this ought to be done, or is demanded to be done. These questions may really complicate the matter to honest minds; or they may only furnish a subterfuge for cowardly and evasive natures to escape a disagreeable sacrifice, without at the same time losing all self-respect by abandoning the general principle. The New Testament takes pains to provide directions for a settlement of both these classes of difficulties. Whether it will be of any use to appeal to that source of instruction will depend on another point, viz. whether we have determined to make the spirit and word of the New Testament, when we have found them out, the law of our lives, let them cut in upon whatever comfort or indulgence; let them rebuke, and chasten, and humiliate, and tax our fortitude as they may.

We begin with the broadest obligation belonging to the matter. This is, that every man shall make his relations to other men's characters, and the effects of his actions on other men's actions, a direct part of his regular religious culture. It shall be more than a sentiment, — a concern; and more than a speculation, — a practice. To this both the nature of the case and the word of the Gospel agree. On the ground of the nature of the case, it can be denied only by one of three classes of objectors. It may be consistently denied by asceticism, by indifferentism, or by the mere impulsive theory of morals. A monk, or rather an utter anchorite, might refuse to pay a religious regard to social relations, on the ground that in solitude, as a higher state of man, the relations do not exist. A thorough-going indifferentist, or practical fatalist, or antinomian, might refuse, on the ground that the result of things is beyond the influence of ethical distinctions as recognized by the human will. Or a believer in the absolute legitimacy of sheer impulse, whether sensual or supersensual, might object, on the score of the philosophy which, in professing to follow Nature with peculiar fidelity, confuses her legislation of just liberty, and turns the beauty of her economy and the order of her subordinations into a mob of ungoverned desires. These three are intelligible defences of that recklessness of other men's principles which denies that we are answerable for our influence on every life of those around us.

Quite as clear as the reason of the case is the word of the Gospel. The Christian faith is eminently a social principle. Its ideas are social ideas. Its development is a social development. It contemplates each heart as having interdependencies and communications with its fellows. The forms it takes on are domestic and associative. It proposes fellowship. It founds a church. It advocates the common weal. It is always asking, from the beginning, of every cruel Cain, "Where is thy brother?" It calls every exclusive, oppressive, abusive, corrupting community, or person, to account for the lost, the neglected, the betrayed, the weaker members of the household. It says, with the solemn voice of God, "Thy brother's blood cries from the ground," — the blood of his soul no less than of his body. One half of its twofold commandment is, "Thou shalt love thy neighbor as thyself." If it declares, in one breath, that "every man shall bear his own burden," in the next it says, "Bear ye one another's burdens." It predicts an infinite misery for them that tempt, betray, misguide, deprave one another, — for them that form companies, clubs, societies, to make each other frivolous, profligate, dissolute. It treats with terrible severity any one that presumes to reply, when called to reckon for such outrages, "Am I my brother's keeper?" virtually rejoining, "Yes, you are; all men are each other's keepers, educators, helpers or hinderers, saviours or seducers." It requires all to give not only food, clothes, and money, but the ministry of encouraging words, patient endurance, honest living, aspiring thoughts. So, negatively, it forbids theft and killing; and if we study the whole religion through and through, we shall see that this means the robbery of any particle of virtue, honor, temperance, truth, — the killing of the spiritual and immortal part, quite as much as the theft of a garment, or the murder of the body it covers. In fact, all the pages of our Book of Faith are marked with these earnest counsels and expostulations about caring for other souls. It is always adjuring us to work for, to think for, to suffer for — and to that end to love — other people. Such is the compass of its charity. Whether it commands or forbids, its intent is the same. If you examine both prohibitions and injunctions, you will find they run into each other, and are only the two sides of one bright truth, — the positive and the negative being only measurements in opposite directions of the universal law of affection and service. The lives of the Apostles were throughout consecrated, abstemious, self-sacrificing labors for the souls of their fellow-men. And we have only to look into any period of the earthly ministry of Christ to see how constantly and scrupulously he acted for the internal state of those he met. He did, and refrained from doing, he spoke and kept back, he came into danger and went away from it, all for the sake of the souls of others. Nay, his whole earthly career, his humiliation into a body, and his human suffering, are instances of what a true and faithful Spirit will do for human need. Suppose he had said, "Why should I take the form of a servant, make myself of no reputation, become obedient unto death, bear the ignominy of the Cross? Men must live according to the laws and condition of their own being. My communion is above. My joys and tastes are heavenly; why condescend to these miserable, unintellectual, uncultivated creatures? They have their own pleasures, associations, their own *set* in society. Why should I deprive myself of some of my best and highest enjoyments for them?" Do we never hear language a little like that about us here? *His* doctrine was that nothing on earth or in heaven can possibly be higher than serving, lifting up, saving the spiritual life of God's children; and that, compared with that, all social fastidiousness and all intellectual self-seeking are vulgarity and shame.

Or is it said that in this respect the Son of God is no example for us? This is practical infidelity, — to make excuse that we are not called to live in the same spirit in which our Saviour lived. That is the very thing we have to try to do; and if we try devoutly God will help us to it more and more. But even if the Master's self-sacrifice were set aside as too exalted, the same condemnation of our letting other people's virtue take care of itself would come down from every nobler and holier life of his great followers and confessors of every age. And were this testimony to fail, I should still be sure of a nearer witness to the essential reality of the doctrine, — even a voice speaking in the loftier moods of your own breasts. This silent decree within will reaffirm the living oracles of the Evangelists. Together they will pronounce him to be the only truly conscientious man who is ever applying the discriminations of his sense of right to new regions, new connections, new questions of conduct; and will pronounce that it must be a very limited conscience indeed which only inquires, of a course of action, how it will affect the individual performing it. "Conscience, I say, not thine own, but of the other."

Now, the helps men render to one another's virtue are, for the most part, rendered without any express attempt at what is called "setting an example." That is, all excellence is more impressive when it is seen living and acting by a certain independent force from within itself, looking for its motive above the world, than when it is prepared and put on exhibition for a pattern. At the best, a man can give only what he has, and work only with what is in him. To begin a correct life with the notion of being a model is, to say the least of it, beginning a good way from the heart of the matter, and is likely to end with a mere surface morality.

In agriculture and mechanics, producers do sometimes raise stock, or finish fabrics, merely for a show; and if they do it to stimulate other brains and muscles in the line of their profession, it is plainly more honorable than to do it for the premium or the admiration. So it is higher to conquer passion for the sake of encouraging other strivers for that mastery, than for self-interest, or a politic vanity. But goodness is a more delicate thing, and has quite another nature than machinery or animal symmetry. The danger is, that if we undertake to manufacture it for a pattern, we shall spoil it in the making. It will not be genuine. The very idea of making it a spectacle will have taken the authenticity out of it. Pattern-behavior, putting the foreign effect before the spiritual essence, is Pharisaic,—just as any declaimed righteousness, where speech gets before conviction, is cant. When words are felt, or sincere, they instantly and infallibly become efficacious,—as health always is. Of Sterling's saying, "First realize your cant, then put it off," the last half is not wanted; for cant turned into reality is put off already; when vitality or sincerity went into it, the thing was changed, and it ceased to be cant. Besides, goodness is not a conveyable or merchantable substance. It has to strike its root deep in an individual consciousness, a personal faith. And for all these reasons, men are very far from being morally acted on, to the best purport, by what is aimed directly at them.

But this does not at all deny the quick sensibilities of the social constitution, nor our obligation both to do some things, and not to do some other things, out of a simple regard to their social effects. "Thine own conscience" is not thoroughly active, unless it bears a sacred respect to the conscience of the "other." In fact, the case seems to be clearer about refraining from what will injure others, than about doing what they may imitate. Christian modesty may shrink from the thought of being exemplary; but Christian principle will eagerly renounce what is hurtful. Is it not likely that we are set into society for this very end, that by sacrifices for others' *moral* purity as well as their physical comfort, — by relinquishing some pleasures for our brethren's inward as well as outward abundance, we may be disciplined into a more Christlike disinterestedness? I can see no great sense in the maxim of Cecil, that "society shows us what we are, and solitude what we should be." If we only catch up its overt manifestations, its current criticisms, or look into the mirror of its manners, society *will* only show us what we are, and in fact very imperfectly show us that. But if we look at it on the side of its moral powers, and moral wants and exposures, it will eloquently teach us what we ought to be, and furnish the very school for making us that. He has not half awaked to the majesty and the mystery of his being, who can tolerate in himself the atrocious levity of living as if the integrity of his companion's conscience were never a cause for the abridgment of his own pleasures.

The complicated case, undoubtedly, is where some habit, or some indulgence of taste, or some gratification of appetite, is felt to be perfectly safe to yourself, but would probably be unsafe to others by reason of their less guarded position or weaker principles, while they are the more likely to go astray for your practice. There is the real issue and strain. Have we no guide, in the Christian teaching, to a right decision, even there?

The defence set up for a continuance of the gratification is this: 'Rules of meat and drink, amusement and display, are not definite nor absolute. Each must adjust his habit to his constitution and circumstances, and stop there. Everything is likely to be abused that is used. I cannot look after all abuses, nor people, nor positions. I am to strike out a way of living that seems lawful enough for myself, and expect everybody else to do the same. I am not the appointed guardian of my neighbors, and need not forego what I consider the good things of life lest some weaker heart should be ensnared or enslaved by them.'

This answer will carry different degrees of plausibility to different persons. Christianity certainly comments upon it.

In the first place, it may be said, without argument, that to many ears this language has, in its very tone and its first impression, a sound of hardness and selfishness. A certain intuitive moral judgment pronounces that it is not the final nor the highest view of duty; that, whatever the truth may be, this is not the whole of it; that, whatever the difficulty may be, this does not go to the bottom of it. It is not a disposition of the case that satisfies the best demands of a self-denying religion. It is not the sort of response we expect from the nobler order of men, who live for the good of their race, and not for themselves, — live before their times and beyond their fellows, — prophets and apostles. But this is only an appeal to sentiments, which may not be universal.

Another remark, not conclusive but pertinent, is that this defence is not one very likely to be presented by any of us, where the party endangered by our gratification should be very near to our affections, — a child, or a brother by blood. There the gratification would probably be waived. But Christianity recognizes no such limitation of responsibility as this: it declares all mankind one family; and, by the lips of its Divine Founder, affirms that, for the purposes of doing God's will, every human being is a mother or a brother or a sister.

But furthermore, when it is said that all things used, however lawful, must be abused, let it be remembered that this tendency to abuse by no means excuses him who *so* uses, beyond the line of actual necessity or imperative duty, that the abuse comes in. If "offences must needs come," none the less "woe to him by whom the offence cometh." The question now is, not whether men are extremely liable to do wrong on occasion, but whether I shall add to that liability by offering a fresh occasion, and under the plea that other men do so, or will do so, if I do not. In full view of that likelihood Christ said, "It were better for a man that a millstone were hanged about his neck, and that he were drowned in the depths of the sea, than that he should cause one of these weak ones to offend."

And further still, if you say that, so long as your act is not in itself wrong, Providence, in the general ongoing of affairs, must see to it that no harm comes of it: may it not reasonably be put back to you that Providence is quite as likely to see to it that no harm comes to you when you deny yourself, as that no harm comes to those weak natures when your self-indulgence has tempted them? Besides, when we speak of an act as "right in itself," let us consider what is included in "itself," and take in all its necessary elements and relations. For no act can be said to be right in itself which is so done that the spirit of the doer or the situation of its occurrence binds it up inseparably with wrong.

And further yet, if it is urged that nothing ought to be given up which makes for the genial and happy processes of social life, — then let it be fully established that the practice, the luxury, the pleasure in question, does belong to the best order of life, and is essential to it, and that its advantages are not outweighed by the evils that spring directly out of it. Above all, let a solemn examination of the motives and sources of action make it clear, whether the thing is really done from a conscientious and comprehensive regard to the public good, or whether that is only an afterthought of apology, — a sophistication to palliate what is *actually* done only because it is agreeable and entertaining.

There may possibly be instances — let it be granted — where the mind honestly hesitates whether the good to be done by a compliance with a luxurious custom will not overbalance the possible mischiefs of leading others to transgress. But if the foregoing principles are kept steadily before us, — if, in every such emergency, we go directly to the Master, who never mistakes, to correct and clear up our moral judgments by communion with his unselfish and blameless soul, we shall find that class of perplexities reduced to a very narrow line. And if then we are ready, with self-command enough, in every case that is only doubtful, to resign our ease or entertainment, and stand on the side that is sure to be safe, rather than run the risk of putting any human soul on that which is wrong, if we make and keep it a matter, not of inclination, but of conscience, we shall hardly go far astray, — "Conscience, I say, not only thine own, but of the other," — for light will fall from the unerring Sun on a spirit so seeking and so sincere.

Let us now set over against the defence we have supposed the following words of the Apostle Paul, — submitting it to each hearer, which seems to ring clearest from the heights of Christian clearsightedness and truth, and which sounds most as if the heavenly testimony was in it, — "None of us liveth to himself, and no man dieth to himself. Let us therefore judge this, — that no man put a stumbling-block, or an occasion to fall, in his brother's way. If thy brother be grieved with thy meat, now walkest thou not charitably. Destroy not him with thy meat, for whom Christ died. It is good neither to eat flesh, nor to drink wine, nor anything whereby thy brother stumbleth, or is offended, or is made weak. When ye sin so against the brethren, and wound their weak conscience, ye sin against Christ. If meat make my brother to offend, I will eat no flesh while the world standeth. For the kingdom of God is not meat and drink, but righteousness, and peace, and joy."

The more frequent obstacle to this thoughtful and generous behavior, at least among decent men, is the absence of any glaring evidence that our luxuries do tempt our neighbors. What is the delight of a palate, or of an amusement, that any of us would not hurl from him with all the intensity of disgust, if he *saw* before his eyes one fellow-creature, however weak or ignorant, who, from an unhappy childhood, or any misfortune of condition, was plunged over the edge of safety into all the shame and wretchedness and filth of profligacy by a questionable liberty of his own? But surely, in such a matter, a doubt is grave enough to dictate a Christian's conduct. A very earnest moral nature will not be willing to imperil a fellow-creature's purity on the slender difference between a conjecture and a certainty. The likelihood of a poison taking effect will be pondered, not without a prayer for help. And, as if to assist us in such discoveries, human beings are often thrown together, in such local connections, such closeness of contact, and such peculiarity of relationship, as to bring out and exhibit plainly these mutual interactings of moral conduct and impression. Of that kind is every collection of givers and receivers, of teachers and pupils, every seminary of learning, or family, or class associated for a common pursuit. There spring up new obligations, new occasions for restraint, new calls for cheerful and voluntary sacrifices, peculiar to the structure of the society. He that does not feel them, or is not equal to them, may well reconsider the fitness of his presence. There, too, as he will find who ever takes pains to inquire, these influences come to light. The older is quoted by the younger; the more advanced by the new-comer; the instructor by the pupil. There the laxity of an esteemed acquaintance is made to take sides with some appetite that burns in the body. There the neglects of the more experienced are thrown up as shields for the irregularities of the novitiate. There the irreligion of the mature fosters and encourages the recklessness of youth. And little as they may suspect it, who eat, drink, and are merry, without a religious scruple on their pleasures, all the while, in many a building not far away, the beginnings of vice are taking a terrible warrant and license from their freedom. "No man liveth to himself, and no man dieth to himself. Let us judge this, — that no man put a stumbling-block, or an occasion to fall, in his brother's way."

Brethren, there is no self-denial deserving the name that is not willing to give up any privilege of the palate or the passions rather than endanger the least or lowest of God's children. And then if it is demanded, "Why should I be deprived of the lawful use of some agreeable thing, merely because some less guarded, less experienced, or less coolly constituted neighbor will abuse it?" we will leave the ground of justice altogether, and come upon that of magnanimity and of privilege. We will ask, not what we have *a right to do*, but what is to be gladly chosen because it is *right to be done*. In the estimates of God and eternity, the generosity that shields a human heart from shame will stand above a genial style of hospitality. Not till comfort shall become the creed of Christendom, can free living be the testimony of faith.

After all, we must raise our minds before a higher judgment than our own. We need not terrify ourselves with an imaginary tribunal; it is enough to anticipate the reality. There is to come a time when no one of us will be satisfied to have been here eating and drinking and making merry, sporting with the virtues of our companions, quenching the better life of those for love of whom Christ was willing to die, or entertaining ourselves at the cost of their integrity. Again, the voice of the Lord God will be heard at the end of the day, asking of you and me, "Where is thy brother?" How little will it avail us then, having that brother, and all the past, standing revealed before us, to stammer with the impotent mockery of self-defence, "Am I my brother's keeper?" His blood will cry from the ground, and Heaven will hear. Whosoever shall cause one of these to offend, it *were* better that a millstone dragged him into the sea.

Too little, too little, will there appear in that day of any positive achievements of ours for God and his truth, proportioned to our opportunity. But at least let it not be found that, when some frail fellow-creature was inclining to baseness and to ruin, any frivolity or unconcern of ours made his downward way easier and swifter; or, if any other soul was struggling up into light and victory, that our faithlessness discouraged him, our inconsistencies confused him, our self-love drew him back.

SERMON XXIII.

CHRISTIAN CITIZENSHIP AND HONEST LEGISLATION.*

FOR HE LOVETH OUR NATION, AND HATH BUILT US A SYNAGOGUE. — Luke vii. 5.

THE two thoughts are joined, not accidentally, not artificially, but by a natural law. In the habit of the Hebrew mind, which was speaking, — in the character of the public-spirited officer for whom that praise and that plea were spoken, — those ideas lived harmoniously together, a bond of organic unity between them, and each more vital for the other. By the march you have just made from the State-House to this sanctuary, you have given another deliberate confession, and offered one more public symbol, that both ideas were true, and that their mutual relation is a truth also. The love of country and reverence for God; their conjunction here was no rhetorical device, nor local Judaistic sentiment, but a permanent, philosophical, unchangeable reality. It was not a fact then for the first time, or the last. No matter though the centurion was a citizen only by adoption. The association was just as vivid, for that,

* Delivered before His Excellency Henry J. Gardner, His Honor Henry W. Benchley, the Honorable Council, and the Legislature of Massachusetts, at the annual Election, Wednesday, January 6, 1858.

between the people's good and the worship of the Most High. It is not the rule, but it happens, — it happened then, — that the foreigner, by the very freshness with which the genius of an advanced economy salutes him, and by its contrast with oppressive institutions that he has outgrown, enters farther into its real meaning than the sluggish and sordid native. Probably the centurion was more profoundly imbued with the central life of the Hebrew system than many of the straitest of the Pharisees. It seems he was discontented with Paganism, and found his aspirations encouraged and his affections attracted, by the sublime monotheism of Moses; it seems he loved a slave, and was so catholic as to bestow his liberality on a nation of which he was not born; it seems he was so modest and reverent as to shrink from letting the Lord of life come under his roof. These are not slight nor provincial virtues, in any age or land, certainly not too common in our own. Nor ought it to surprise us to find, in a nature so lofty and comprehensive, a practical faith that patriotism and religion, — the State-House and the synagogue, — belong together.

We can go farther yet. Down at their lowest roots and life-springs, these principles not only interlock, but become essentially one and the same. Patriotism, that is, when it *is* a principle, and not a mere blind instinct of the blood, is an outgrowth and a part of the faith and honor of the Almighty. Analyze it, and you will see it so. For patriotism is only disinterested devotion to the justice, the power, the protection, the right, embodied, after a certain fashion and degree, in the State and its subjects. It is not attachment to the parchment of a constitution, to the letter of an instrument, to the visible insignia of authority, to a strip of painted cloth at a masthead, to a mass of legal precedents and traditions, nor always to the person of the sovereign. It is not a personal interest in the people of the nation, for the most of one's fellow-citizens are unknown, and the few that are met may awaken no special regard. Instituted ideas, — as justice, power, protection, — organized into a national government, and lifted up for the defence of the country, are what inspire an intelligent loyalty, and the same ideas have their perfect embodiment in the person of God. On the other hand, religion, veneration for the Creator, involves a consistent regard for the welfare of great bodies of his family. By the laws of the human nature he has fashioned, this will mount to enthusiasm, as our relations to any one body grow intimate, or look back to an antiquity, or own a history of common sufferings. Less elevated elements may intermix. But whichever you take first, — the feeling for the State, or for the God of States, — the other clings to it, and comes logically with it.

So the State, through you, its temporary representatives and civil ministers, bends here to-day before the Ruler of rulers. Legislation comes to the Church, not primarily to hear a sermon from a man, but to adore the Supreme Lawgiver, and to supplicate light. Our fathers, best builders of empire, on the whole, that the world has ever seen since the great Emancipator of Israel compacted a commonwealth of fugitives, of which Jehovah was the head, — our fathers, taking *that* for their model, when they ordained this ceremony of Election worship, believed in it. With them the ceremony was a faith. If it ever sinks into a mere routine, — the ghastly effigy of a departed sincerity, — it will be because some generation has not honesty and courage to drop the form with the life, but is willing to keep credit with superstition by continuing, for considerations of policy, a sanctimonious pageant out of which the soul has ebbed away. For, saying nothing either of religion or of patriotism, it is only when man is emptied of his manliness, that he consents to go through a solemn performance that is emptied of its heart. And, let it be added just here, when there are cant and make-believe at Church, it will not be strange if presently there are fraud and falsehood at the State-House; for it can scarcely be expected with reason that men who undertake a deception on the Omniscient, and act a part before themselves, will be restrained from overreaching one another, and cheating the people.

I have no occasion, therefore, to wander far for my subject. It lies before me in your coming here, and we are shut up to it. I have to speak first of the personal character of a Christian citizen, and then of the honest legislator; and since it is the blessing of our system that citizen and legislator are united in one, — our rulers, as the prophet put it, being of ourselves, and our governors proceeding from the midst of us, — the one of these topics will pass, by a natural transition and progress, into the other.

I. Nor need I detain you with much amplification on the propensity in all partially Christianized states of society to separate what are here joined, — to divorce public affairs, that is, from the control of the Gospel, and so to unchristianize government. Such a tendency may be briefly disposed of in this way. If it will stand out in the light and defend itself, — and not merely creep under the poor shelter of an unthinking timidity, or an irrational selfishness, — it must pursue one of three lines of argument; for there is no fourth for it. It must maintain either, 1. That religion is *inferior* to politics, as an interest of humanity, — which would be virtual atheism, — a denial of God, as God, supreme; or, 2. It must maintain that religion and politics are naturally hostile to one another, the admission of religious obligation damaging political success, — which is practical infidelity, i. e. a denial of the absolute character which religion takes in the teaching of Christianity; or else, 3. It must maintain that, while both are legitimate ideas, and capable of being represented by legitimate institutions, their provinces are distinct, and their objects best achieved by keeping them apart; which, so far as it is not atheistic and infidel both, is simply absurd; because it amounts to saying that a man, or a community of men, can have such a thing as a Christian character separate from those vital social relations, and those duties of life in which the character is formed. So much of attempts to wrench asunder what the Divine constitution of things has married into one, and what, as I said, *were* one in the centurion of the text, as in every Christian citizen.

But what is more deserving of your careful notice, because a truth apt to be disguised by subtler kinds of sophistry, is, that every such attempt, whether open or occult, ends practically in the first of the three errors just supposed, — i. e. in *subordinating* the claims of religion to the claims of politics, — which then instantly become, by that act, false and vicious politics. When a people begin to sever their obligations as Christians from their obligations as citizens, it is never long before the first class of obligations become secondary, and they are ready to break the laws of God, in managing the machinery that dispenses the offices and patronage of the State. God and Mammon never become co-ordinate powers, nor even enter into treaty; and as soon as any department of life, like political action, bereaves itself of religious guidance, it becomes at once unmitigated mammon. If they divide, religion sinks into a mere client. Because, there are always commercial advantages which Government is able to multiply, and material interests which it can secure, — trade, ustom-houses, corporations, post-offices, public works, legal protection to property, — and these will be had *at any rate*, by men who are willing to turn religion into a corner, or lock it up in a meeting-house.

In such a sense as this, the subjection of the Church to the State is a mischief of much larger extent than the theory technically known by that name. In the time of the civil wars in England, the doctrine took a specific shape, and, reaching out from its Germanic origin, formed a British sect that made it known to history. But there is a *virtual* Erastianism, where there is no church establishment, and no crown to wrangle for its patronage. Let the Church represent the Christianized life, power, and principles of a people; and let the State represent those regulations that provide for the external welfare of society, — which was Mr. Webster's definition, — and there has been no age when the State has not aggressed upon the Church. For there has been no age when men's outward comfort has not seduced their conscience; no country where grasping passions have not made war upon righteousness; no people in the whole period since the office-seeking sons of Zebedee applied for places at the right hand and left of the expected Prince, down to the city of Washington as it has looked since the first of December, in which multitudes have not been more willing to attest their affection for their nation by accepting its emoluments, than, like the centurion, by building its synagogues.

And yet what warrant is afforded, either by experience, or by the word of Heaven, or by the nature of things, for supposing that national safety is compatible with any less strictness of moral life than individual safety is? or that those retributive rules of God, which require the loss of power as a penalty for the abuse of privilege, which drag every secret abomination to judgment, linking sin to damnation, will be somehow evaded by *masses* of men, while they hold for men one by one? as if God's hand were too unskilful to feel through the intricacies of a crowd, or his eye so infirm as to be bewildered by the pompous iniquity of office! Whenever America shall be thoroughly committed to a line of policy that rejects those officers which are peace and those exactors which are righteousness; whenever it shall resign the election of its law-makers and rulers into the hands of cunning cabals, to the chicane of talkative persons whose only principle of suffrage is a determination to put certain labelled candidates in, right or wrong, and to keep certain proscribed candidates out, wrong or right, — so giving over its Capitol and Cabinet to brawling tongues and embezzling fingers; whenever it shall consent to seat on the high Bench of Justice political debaters instead of Judges of the Law, and to take from that Bench sophistries and special pleas of partisan self-interest instead of impartial interpretations of the Constitution, — whenever it lifts to power those who care more for the world's applause and money than for God's worship, so violating the *condition* given in the text, then, infallibly shall the warning also of the context be fulfilled. Enemies shall come from the East and West, and God shall take away the kingdom from you, and give it to a nation bringing forth the fruits thereof.

God knows who can be trusted. Bad governments seem to succeed for a while; but their fame only lifts them up into a more conspicuous post, that the mockery of their coronation and fall may be more widely instructive. For the permanence of power there needs a select sacramental band, and enough to control the community, of brave-hearted, God-fearing, consecrated men, — needs these more than the amplest revenue, the most splendidly appointed navy, the mightiest fortifications, or the loftiest roofed arsenals. If "saints" meant, as it ought to mean, men of manly righteousness, and not men of cunning or cruel piety, we might all join the Fifth Monarchists, and pray for "the reign of God's people." The best system of national defence is the organization of character. No State-House presents a venerable front, after it becomes a nest of unclean birds, — demagogues who have bartered their principles to get there, or carried them there for a market. If Congress is to be the country's council, — or indeed if it is to leave any country long to be counselled for, — you must stock it with hearts whose faith is vital, and not traditional, in the justice of Almighty God. No judiciary can decree law or equity from a durable bench, if the men that sit there, however learned or large of brain, have forgotten that they are themselves forever on trial at the great assize of eternity. It is little that the members of a cabinet talk in twenty tongues, or issue diplomatic papers that rouse domestic pride and foreign jealousy, if they never speak the one simple language of childlike hearts to the Father of Truth, with whom lies are abominations. And what is spiritual law for the president and his secretaries, for judges and legislators, is law for the humblest of the subjects. It will be seen yet, truly as the maxims of passing dynasties and parties must be adjourned for the ideas of the New Testament, that every faithful disciple, standing in his lot for the command to love God and man, is a better patriot than the statesman who seeks every kind of honor but that which comes from on high. For the *statesman* ought also, and first, to be *Christ's man;* patriotism without Christianity is not a strong sentiment; he who has resolved to stand on the side of God is the best friend of his country that any country can have; and there is no earthly country good enough to be loved safely, except the love of it be hallowed by faith in a better country, even an heavenly.

In this spiritual sense, not by an ecclesiastical or prelatical control, the State is really but a dependent on the society of Christ. Instead of the church being a subaltern to the government, government is ancillary to the church. The church is the religion of Jesus organized, of all sects where faith in Jesus is, going forth to redeem and bless humanity with the heavenly doctrines of freedom, equality, holiness, and love. Has the civil State any higher function than that? Has any empire so exalted a sovereign? So far the theocratic idea is just, that every nation should have God for its acknowledged Ruler, and make every custom and institution in it loyal to that heavenly supremacy. We can imagine no loftier conception of human society than that. Every avenue of the national life should be a channel for the free course of the Divine Spirit, every legislature a school of practical theology, every court-house a solemn vindicator of the oppressed, and every city, village, and home, a nursery of strong and beautiful souls.

II. Christian citizenship, then, is the true foundation of national greatness. But who are Christian citizens? Something more definite and determined than mere men of compliance with the conventional decencies of civilization, — not mere "barbarians in broadcloth."

Something more is necessary to being the citizen of a Christian State than barely living in it. Because I tread under my feet, as I go about my private business, a certain soil which has been marked off by surveyors, and called by the geographic name of Massachusetts, and because I avail myself of its various local provisions for the more advantageous pursuit of certain selfish ends, do I therefore deserve to be recognized as one of the State's proper citizens? In matter, mere physical presence constitutes a claim to be called by a local name. Holyoke, whatever the character of the prospect from it, is a Massachusetts mountain; and Cochituate, whether its waters be pure or foul, is a Massachusetts lake, — as a quantity of building materials fashioned into a dwelling within the limits of this city makes a Boston house. So, for the mere purposes of a census, or for the assessment of a capitation-tax, or for convenience of description, it may be said of a person that he is a Massachusetts man, irrespective of his convictions or his character, his loyalty or his treachery. But you will see that the moment you take up such a designation for thoughtful reflection, or a sober analysis, you must make it cover something besides the bare fact of inhabiting. You can apply the term citizenship, then, only to such as possess a certain Massachusetts spirit, and are morally assimilated to the genius of the State's institutions.

We shall begin at a safe point if we say that the first qualification consists in *an intelligent understanding of the principles which the government organizes, and of the ideas which it represents.* Every political institution is the visible exponent of an invisible thought. Every charter, compact, bill of rights, written law-book, or established custom of civil administration, is an attempt to realize in practice some idea in the governing mind. If that governing mind is an autocrat, or even monarch, you will have embodied the idea of irresponsible dominion, or pure despotism, like the old eastern tyrannies, or like modern Russia, where only the smallest check is imposed by the prerogative of the nobles. If it is a landed aristocracy, of caste, conquest, or hereditary rank, you will have Feudalism, as in the middle ages. If it is a combination of royal prerogative and popular will, you have a limited monarchy, with parliament and crown, as in Great Britain. If it is a majority of the people, you have a limited democracy, as with ourselves. Sometimes this central and radical idea of the government is formally set forth in a declaration, as with a constitutional power like the United States. Sometimes it is expressed only in the aggregate of usages, precedents, and maxims of an empire, or of some petty court or chieftain's castle. But whether its utterance be direct or indirect, in words or practices, it does somehow get uttered, and by its consequences it is felt. The business of an historical student is not merely to learn the outward succession of events, the sayings and doings of the several kingdoms, but it is to comprehend those hidden principles lying below the surface like seeds under the ground, out of which empires and their epochs have germinated, and sprung up, opening their beneficent or baleful foliage, bearing their nutritious or poisonous fruit.

So also of the present. It is one thing to go through the mechanical functions of voting for law-makers year by year, or obeying laws after they are made, and quite another to enter into an intelligent apprehension of the great thoughts which lived in the minds of the men by whom the whole structure of the government was founded, and which still live in the heart of the government itself. It is this last which every man ought to have attained before he is worthy to be regarded as, in any lofty acceptation, a citizen.

Libanius, quoted by Montesquieu, says, that at Athens a stranger who intermeddled with the assemblies of the people was punished with death. If this was summary and cruel, it proved the sanctity attached to political action, — the faith that a distinctive civil education was indispensable to it, — that the popular sources of power should be kept pure, and thus it attested the reality of the democratic profession. An illegal vote was usurpation, and ignorance was a milder form of rebellion.

I am not referring here to the advantages of a general education. I accord, of course, heartily with all that can be argued in behalf of that. There can be no right citizenship at this day without intellectual activity. But over and beyond this I insist on the importance of a special branch of science, — of a better understanding of the fundamental principles which underlie and animate our political system. Proudly as we boast of our promiscuous cultivation, I believe that we are in great danger of national damage from indifference just at that point. We take too much for granted. We are driven to the ballot-box once a year in gangs, by little knots of self-constituted leaders in caucuses, who mean, by indirect process, to dictate the votes and take the offices. Or else we follow some party champion, who, let him know never so much, is certainly not endowed with a vicarious knowledge that shall atone for our ignorance, and who may possibly, on the very theatre where he has gained his experience and his eloquence, have encountered temptations, too strong to be resisted, to imbibe the duplicity and the trickery of a demagogue.

I would have every child, therefore, carefully and conscientiously taught those distinctive ideas which constitute the substance of our constitution, and which determine the policy of our politics. He should know wherein his own government differs from other governments. He should be able, on his own information, and not depending on any interested meddler, to tell when there is a departure from the true course, where an abuse begins, and where a peril threatens. And to this end, there ought forthwith to be introduced into our common schools a simple, comprehensive manual, adapted to juvenile minds and to the whole country, whereby the needed tuition should be planted at that early period. It is absurd that our pupils should go on, through the whole term of their preparation for life, committing the rules of a grammar, the facts of geography, and the calculations of arithmetic, to the total neglect of the principles of the legislation under which they are to live, of the facts of the country to which they belong, and of the constitution of their liberties. It may be the low instinct of a money-making age to desire only a knowledge how to reckon profit and loss. But will it not be at least as sensible, and far more patriotic, to covet an acquaintance with those grand laws of social order and protection under which all our traffic is prosecuted, by which all our prosperity is shielded, and which alone can make any successful or honorable enterprise possible ?

Among us, a neglect of this sort of culture is without excuse. It is made so, equally by the freedom of opportunity, guaranteed by all the arrangements of our educational apparatus, and by the simplicity of the government itself, which is to be studied. An Austrian peasant, a Russian serf, Italian lazzaroni, have a plausible apology for being in the dark respecting the laws they live under, for the laws themselves are kept in the dark; and then the subject is held *so far* under them, that he cannot lift himself up to look at them. In some of these cases, no school-house door stands open to him; a stifled press defrauds him, or a mercenary one hoodwinks him; an "*Index Expurgatorius*" screens from him what he most wants to know, and tyranny silences the instruction which he has the best right to hear. To say that it is otherwise with us, is only to repeat the commonplace of two hundred and twenty-seven election sermons. Yet professional and trading politicians, for purposes of their own, have the effrontery to tell us that nobody is fit to legislate, nor to form parties, nor to discourse on public matters, but those who, like themselves, hold a professional key to the secret. Doubtless, if legislation consists in making the many the tools of promoting a few, if drilling parties is tantamount to framing a conspiracy of plunder, and if discoursing on public matters is the art of compounding falsehood, detraction, and insolence, then they may be left to enjoy a monopoly of political science. Such characters flourish among us, — just as the rankest weeds grow in the fattest soil, — for the very reason that our admirable system of government is so well able to go alone, that the consequences of individual apathy are slow to appear. But those consequences will not be postponed forever; the everlasting laws of national retribution are not to be defeated: ignorance and carelessness are seeds that will yield their harvest of calamity and shame.

The next qualification for good citizenship I mention is *a sympathy with the spirit of the government.* There needs a feeling in the heart for one's country, as well as a comprehension of its presiding principles and its informing ideas by the intellect; because a nation, which is only a kind of collective and conscious person, has, in some sort, a heart of its own, as well as a brain, — and so a characteristic temper, or quality, to be loved or hated, to be sympathized with, or repelled by. It is on this moral sympathy between citizen and government, that loyalty and patriotism depend, hardly less than on intelligence. You know how loyalty is roused to enthusiasm, how patriotism flames up into an ardent passion, at the sight of a national edifice, fortification, ship, or the sound of national airs or watchwords. There is no intellectual process in these cases, — no deliberate recurrence to ideas, — but a sudden rush of feeling, a throb out of the heart. Hence the mere sentiment of loyalty, half-blind but enthusiastic, has often been found most impetuous and most heroic in those periods of the world and those states of society when there was little thinking, but an abundance of feeling. Still, any government is weak which has not this vital sympathy between the spirit of its institutions and the spirit of the citizens.

Now it often happens in a State, as it does in a family, that individuals are found in it who are out of all harmony with its prevailing sentiments. There is mere physical presence, — but a moral discord, an absence, or alienage, of the heart. The body is native, but the soul foreign, — and needing some other naturalization than a formal oath of allegiance or subscription before a magistrate. Wherever there is one or more of such uncongenial inmates in a family there is a chill on the intercourse of the household, an iceberg in its sunny climate. And wherever there is such an element of estrangement and distrust in a State; there must be so much hindrance to its prosperity, so much material for disorganization in trying times. It reminds us of what De Maistre, by one of his lively paradoxes, calls France, at one period of her history, — "A republic without republicans."

In this country we are exposed to two classes where this want of sympathy has a tendency to appear. One is a class of essential anti-republicans, partly monarchists and partly aristocrats, sometimes cast in upon us by accident, and sometimes growing up among us by anomaly. People are found in our democratic society who belong, by natural affinity, under a transatlantic emperor, among ultramontane ecclesiastics, or back in the feudal centuries. They are full of the pride of caste, full of hereditary ambition, coveting exclusive privileges, fond of badges of rank, absolutists in their real notions, and ridiculously contemptuous of their fellows who suffer external disadvantages. Such persons, however democratic their professions, have no more place here than a cardinal's hat has in a Methodist meeting, simply because they are out of all affinity with the inmost life of the land. If they have their way, unrestrained by custom or policy, they yoke the weak and the poor into a vassalage, they pamper their estates and add splendor to their equipage out of the earnings of the laborer, they would toss up their caps for a bold and conceited adventurer with a crown of gems on a brainless head, or they would institute a selfish oligarchy, taking good care to be themselves inside its counsels. A great many restraints may keep this class from ever openly acknowledging themselves; but they are none the less out of all hearty fellowship with the true spirit of the country, and are bad citizens.

There is another class, who, instead of being anti-republicans, are ultra-republicans; or rather they are disorganizers and destructionists, and so are as truly anti-republicans as their opposites; for their wild and irresponsible notions are incompatible with any order or law, and so are among the worst enemies a legitimate democracy has to dread. The main desire of this class is a total solving of all restraints on the passions and the individual will. Their first postulate is that everybody is as good as anybody. The liberty they lust after is liberty to swallow their fill at the first stall,—the liberty of untamed animals.

There grows up among us an excessive and morbid individualism, begetting an arrogant irreverence. It obstructs domestic discipline, going down into the brains of young children, and inflaming in them a prurient eagerness to spurn at parental authority. It runs into destructionist speculations on theories of social order. It caricatures the generous conceptions our national existence grew from. It writes an egotistical, fevered, passionate, foolish literature. It rallies mobs. It perverts democracy into demonism. It longs for no Christian republic, but a wild riot of the lusts in its heated blood. Sometimes it sits in its study and philosophizes unbelief; sometimes it haunts a German beer-shop, — sometimes a reckless pulpit; sometimes it simmers in social bogs and fogs; sometimes it sparkles brilliantly on the top of the rocks. Everywhere it is a traitor and a rebel to the country, and because it spoils the Christian citizen, robs the nation of its rights. Construe independence to mean an unlimited license to do as you please, and instead of the just arbitraments of law, with precedents and experience, calm adjustment and sober equity, you retreat, at best, upon the summary instincts of the injured party, and the matches of brutal violence. Paul, of Russia, when a French ambassador incidentally spoke to him of some man of consequence in St. Petersburg, instantly and impatiently replied, "There is no *man of consequence* in this empire, save the man with whom I happen at any moment to be speaking, and so long only as I am speaking to him is he of consequence." Where every man in the nation feels himself of the size of an emperor, that language will be in the bearing if not the mouth of all the crowd. And what is impertinence in manners soon becomes insubordination in temper. It is the misfortune of all liberal movements to attract about them malcontents and radicals. Such false alliances try the strength of a government. If it takes up this crude ingredient, wisely regulates it, converts it and assimilates it, it is strong. But if the disordered matter proves too much for the digestive energy of the constitution, and remains discordant, then it poisons the whole health of the body.

A third qualification for a right citizenship, besides an understanding of the principles of the government and a sympathy with its spirit is *a practical respect for the operation of its forms.* One might suppose, indeed, that where the first two exist the third must necessarily follow. I think we do find instances, however, where the government is both understood and loved, while its regular and necessary functions are treated with a neglect amounting very nearly to contempt. Because the forms are free, and the acts are voluntary, it does not follow that they are trivial, but the contrary. Among us respect for the government is shown in performing all the primary duties that attend the right of suffrage. Our early fathers certainly enjoy a reputation for dignity quite as high as we can emulate; yet they did not deem it beneath them, whatever their station, to take the most active participation in all the initiatory steps of an election. Those of our citizens who stand aloof from the little local meetings and movements which are the fountains of all democratic power, are actuated by a very false view of their responsibilities, or else by a very foolish pride; and they are handing over the reins of rule or misrule, as fast as they can, into the fingers of jobbers and charlatans. Neither business, nor pleasure, nor unconcern, nor disgust at vulgar proceedings, nor any other cause ought to deter you from this duty. If it does, the country holds you chargeable for its disgrace, and you are not good citizens.

III. So we pass up from the citizen to the legislator, which two, by the felicity of our system, meet in the same person, — the citizen-legislator.

Nothing belongs more precisely to this occasion, than a fresh conviction of the necessity of a high personal character, in the public makers of law, to the honor and safety of the Commonwealth. Let us not be deceived. There are laws of moral influence and moral life, above those that are voted and recorded, so inwrought into man and his institutions by the Eternal God, that nothing can tear them out without dislocating the joints of the structure, and nobody can break them without being an "architect of ruin." One of these is, that wrong principle, in every workman whose work is moral, creeps over, and subtly spreads itself, to contaminate and damage the thing he works in. Now, the legislator's work is largely moral. It has constantly to do with the everlasting distinction between right and wrong. It professes to guard and foster equity and truth. It is the avowed organ of justice. It is the terror of evil doers, and the praise of them that do well. It touches the most sacred interests of society. Its special and legitimate sphere is rectitude, peace, order, between man and man. It deals with the very first demonstrations of overt integrity and systematic morality, so far as external measures can. Nor are the laws merely an enactment and execution of the moral convictions of a people, as is so often implied: they are an indirect but effectual educator of these convictions also, constantly forming the public conscience, and raising or lowering the tone of moral life. They are not only an expression, but an influence, — not only a sign *of* morals, but a power *upon* them.

Now, a business so august and so sacred as that cannot be intrusted to any but good men, — righteous men, — sound at heart, right with God, true to humanity, — men that can neither be bought off, nor reasoned off, nor frightened off, nor flattered off, from the simple and immutable right.

The State and the law, persons and property, education and industry, marriage and life, are not safe in the hands of any other order of men. You say, good laws may be made by unprincipled men. So may pious sermons be preached by a Godless clergy. But that does not affect the truth, that down at the secret channels of things, and finally, in the long run, up on the open fields of history, what man *is* works itself into what man *does* — spirit determines life — principles shape institutions. Public virtue does not graft nor grow on personal iniquity. Men do not gather figs of thistles, nor of a bramble-bush grapes, nor of tricky and profane legislators a noble and Christian State.

True, the *form* of the government is by no means a matter of indifference. Here it is not likely to be underrated. Yet personal character will sometimes override even the sharpest distinctions in that, and it is certainly a grander element. A Mexican republic can hardly be pronounced better than an English monarchy. Unless we live in some consistency with the pure ideas out of which the Revolution sprang, we shall have gained no more by a change of rulers than Rome gained by the expulsion of the Tarquins. Despotism may be "democratized," but it is still despotism. A people may destroy their tyrants without destroying tyranny; so the Romans did; but they cannot corrupt their law-makers without debilitating their laws.

See, by a little careful notice, how the mischief results, and why a Massachusetts legislator should be practically, as well as nominally, an honest, Christian man. First of all, you, whom the people have chosen to represent them in the government are set, in some measure, to be exponents of public virtue. An authority is committed to you. Each of you in his own town, village, or city, is marked by his election as a man that may be trusted. Responsibility widens with respect. The young look to you for example. The unsteady quote your practice. If you are self-indulgent, mean, coarse, double-tongued, you will harm your neighborhood on a larger scale, you will diffuse corruption with a more fatal facility, and to a heavier judgment, for your office.

Again, a legislator's personal sins disgrace the institutions he tampers with in the eyes of the community, and so they are unpatriotic as well as impious. Reverence for the appointments of law is certainly not too common. It declines alarmingly. The generations are not growing up with an excess of loyalty. For this waning veneration toward the dignity of government, the "powers that be," the place, the assemblies, the processes of governmental control, it is for you to consider how far the bearing of official persons is accountable. You say, institutions may be revered whether their managers are noble or vulgar. But it happens that men are influenced by the living representatives and spokesmen of things, quite as much as by the things themselves. Mental association is a fact; and a government is judged by the governors.

Thirdly, moral weakness blunts the intellectual perceptions. Every time a man is false to the highest leading of his soul, he dwarfs his mind. Law-makers need every faculty their Creator gave them, and in something better than the natural condition, — sharpened, stimulated, made solid and strong. Measures come before you that require the mind's nicest touch and boldest stroke, — the keenest discrimination and the firmest grasp, — the quick insight and the patient reason. These are intellectual abilities that go only with habits of truth, temperance, chastity, honesty. The man that drags himself up to his seat after a night of convivial carousing, his brain still foggy and his eyes vacant with the profligacy that has drenched his soul, is no fit servant to stand for the interests of man or the powers ordained of God, — among wise statesmen or pure patriots, — in the encounters of dignified debate, or the difficulties of entangled times. Clearsightedness of the head waits in the end on clearsightedness of conscience. The sentence of retribution against that evil work may not be executed speedily, but it comes at last. The voluptuary will not abrogate the immutable penalty. God is the God of our whole life. Pure waters of pure fountains. Never wisdom out of folly; never right by compromise or collusion with wrong. The cunning and selfish bargainer of the shop and the market, the farmer that cheats in weight or measure, the fraudulent mechanic, the lawyer that makes exceptions in Heaven's command of truth for professional lies, the exorbitant money-lender, the gambling broker, — all these will carry their disordered natures and their mutilated honor with them to the legislature, and there they will barter away rectitude and themselves for fees or votes. Then a carnival of the appetites will supplant the dignities and sterner joys of our beginnings; then we shall be ashamed to recur to our ancestral annals, just as the Roman authorities, of a corrupted age, were afraid to show the populace the old code of Numa, after it had been dragged from its obscurity, lest the palpable inconsistency should rouse indignation into rebellion; then pleasure will become the scandalous substitute for patriotism, — just as enervated Athens, when truth and honor were lost, "dreaded Philip, not as the enemy of her liberty, but of her luxury," — or as the emasculated subjects of Augustus, angry at his severities, quelled their factions, and were tamely pacified, when he let Pylades, the comedian, come back to make sport for them in the theatre. It will avail nothing that we have built up a splendid prosperity, and that our numbers have increased eightfold since we were a people and a power. Numbers and property and territory are as effectual to break an overgrown and corrupt policy to pieces as to confirm a sound one; and we shall sink under a law of God framed before Numa meditated, or Philip fought, or Columbus sailed. My friends, you will see the ancient glories of our Commonwealth restored, just as far as you restore the scrupulous conscience and the righteous character — and with them the high-bred manners and commanding thought — of those men who approached the magistrate's trust with awe, as a temple holy to the Lord.

Would to Heaven we could only realize this simple and everlasting law of moral life; that the stream cannot rise above the fountain! There is an unsightly spectacle, not unknown in our own legislative annals. In some fitful mood of conscience, of philanthropy, a people, or its representatives, legislate some measure altogether beyond the average and common level of their moral life. What then? How long can such a statute stand? What will be its efficacy while it remains? Statute-book and people both are only disgraced presently by a retreat into their inferior morality. Anybody that professes, in creed, or in civil decree, above its faith, is guilty of cant, if not of hypocrisy, and its life silently eats out the heart of its written law. We do nothing effectually but what we do from the full head-waters of honest conviction. Bring up the personal sources of goodness, and your acts will put on a consistent grandeur.

The complaint appears to gain emphasis and currency, that both in the National and the State bodies, the course of independent and impartial legislation is seriously obstructed by the use of ambiguous machinery, and by appeals to sordid motives. I do not profess to know the absolute or the relative reason for this complaint. This, however, is certain, and challenges consideration; within a few years past, in our State legislature, the subject-matter of legislation has undergone a remarkable change. There is a vastly increased proportion of private bills — measures that look to the immediate interests of individuals or corporations. At the last regular session, considerably more than half the Acts and Resolves were of this nature. Partly this is inevitable; with the passage of time, the growth of commonwealths, general laws get settled. The same advance calls into being an increased number of special enterprises, seeking the protection, or patronage, of the State. Obviously there comes in, with this tendency, an accumulating temptation to external interference with the opinions, judgments, consciences of senators and representatives. This needs no proof. The lobby speaks for itself, and whatever may be said of its tactics, its geography needs no description. Now, let it be granted that gross bribery, that open and direct bids of money or of custom in business, are rare. Granted that in this honorable body of men before me, there is not one that would not spurn such an approach away from him as an atrocious insult to his manhood, and with shame and pity for the depravity capable of proposing it. Much, I say, yet remains behind all that. It remains, I suspect, proverbially and notoriously true, that a bill is by no means secure which is left simply and solely to its merits. It remains proverbially and notoriously true, that not a few measures are no sooner proposed, than a systematic arrangement and plan of attack are made to carry it, without or within, by other appeals than those to the clear judgment, the unbiased will, the impartial and honest sense of the members. Committees may be packed, weeks beforehand; prejudice may be enlisted; base passions — envy, jealousy, avarice — kindled. Make what allowance or qualification you please. If such things happen only once in a session, it is cause for anxiety and alarm. Or, make the case one of pure hypothesis; your notice of the matter will still be profitable.

Remember, then, first, that every possible question, proposition, grant, charter, or measure whatsoever, that can come before you, has in it the elements of right or wrong, justice or injustice, and is to be judged by you accordingly, and not by any inferior judgment. Remember that it is as true to-day as in the days of the Hebrew legislator, that "a gift," that is a bribe, "blindeth the wise," and that the capability of being bribed has ever gone with treachery, signalized a decaying state, and has been held the sure precursor of anarchy and overthrow. Remember that bribery is none the less bribery for coming, not in the shape of gold or bank-notes, but in that of an electioneering lift, or a professional assistance, or a supper party. Surely it must be a strange and intolerable morality that distinguishes whether the price of dishonor is paid into an itching palm, or on to a proud pair of shoulders, — paid to a man's pocket, or his politics, or his palate. Financial, political, professional, convivial, they are all of one debauched and accursed brood.

I know it may be said, many measures are brought forward that seem to have no specific quality of good or evil; it is immaterial whether you vote for or against them; you do not see far enough into them, or trace them out to such consequences, as to make it an imperative duty to favor or to oppose them, and so you may follow your own interest in doing the one or the other. This seems to be taking refuge from moral responsibility in intellectual stupidity. But it will not serve, in fact, in logic, or in ethics. The truth is, no measure proposed is thus indifferent. Every one you *ought* to countenance, or you *ought* to oppose. Understood, the bill, however small, will reveal that positive character. And to begin to tamper with your power of discrimination, your legislative fidelity, your private manliness, by balancing off your own interest or your pet project with some fellow-member's, — helping your railroad in the western county by supporting his, justified or not, in an eastern one ; carrying a bank charter at home by helping out an infirm bridge-corporation for your neighbor ; or making an insurance company in the city, or next autumn's canvass, pay the way of a company where you are a stockholder, or your nephew is a director, or your political friend wants to be president, — all this is to pronounce yourself below the level of the moral dignity of your place. These are only the tempter's plausibilities, — Satan transformed into the angel of mutual accommodation. More than that, it is just as profligate, and just as dishonest, to be hired to run from your seat, when a vote is to be taken, as to be hired to stay there and vote on the wrong side, only in that case you add the meanness of a coward, with the ignominy of a truant and a trimmer, to the guilt of a knave. Gentlemen, whatever else we lose, let us cling to our brave, unspotted, ancestral honor. No one measure can possibly be put before you, by governor's message or people's petition, in all this session, so vital, so momentous, so supreme, as that principle. Imagine James Otis and Samuel Adams foisting projects through the forms of law by mutual compensation! Imagine John Adams and Benjamin Lincoln dodging a vote! You must pardon the half profane hypothesis. And that you may spare the State a reproachful contrast, take care that the time never come to us, when it can be said, in our capitol, as by an old statesman of another stamp and grade, that he could never obtain the grant of sixpence for a poor and deserving claimant, but that he could always carry a felony without benefit of clergy.

Doubtless it is a deplorable condition of a people if they do not recognize their divinely appointed leaders, — do not know their best men when they see them, and, having the republican privilege, do fail to put them at the head of affairs. But it is a sadder sight yet, when those who have been raised to power under the impression that they were the best, noblest, purest, falsify that confidence, betray that trust, and turn the glory and the hope into shame. That happens when men imagine they can neglect the law of a heavenly estate, because they are chosen to enact laws for an earthly. That happens, if they dream that they can lay off their principles when they take up an office, or because they begin to be legislators cease to be men. That happens, when they forget that from the moment they enter the Halls they become the unpurchasable servants of the least and lowest of the people of the State, and can take no other furtherance to their private fortunes but their lawful salary. That happens, when they come to the Capitol of the State to practise in secret, out of sight of their families, the vices that always corrupt commonwealths, and then go back to their constituents unclean and guilty. That happens when they postpone the integrity of the soul to political Shibboleths, making it a test where a man was born rather than what he is, or else subordinating the mighty virtues of humanity to the cabals and caucuses of a party. Above all, do not be enticed into any measure, direct or indirect, which can possibly be construed into connivance at the overshadowing American crime, — the enslaving or re-enslaving of man.

I go back just a century in the history of Massachusetts. It is striking to see how the sins of one age are the sins of another, because the same old human heart remains. There is no extinct species in the *Flora* of iniquity. A hundred years ago the 25th of last May, before the election day was changed, and when the first duty of the Colonial Legislature was to elect the councilmen, the minister of the New Brick Church, in Boston,* preached the anniversary sermon. Calling on the magistrates before him to "arise and teach the people," to "fear God and keep his commandments," that it might be well with them and their children forever, he continued his faithful exhortation thus: "Animated by this divine principle, we trust you will proceed this day to the choice of His Majesty's Council, and give your votes for men who have an awful regard for the laws of God. You will choose men of wisdom to discern the times, — more zealous to advance the public welfare than their private advantage, — men who will hazard their credit and estates rather than unite in any schemes of oppression and injustice, — men who will venture to displease the highest authority upon earth, rather than give a vote for a person unqualified for the office to which he is nominated, — men that will not sell their country for a bribe, but will generously neglect their private affairs when the public requires their attention, — men that will recommend religion, not only by wholesome laws, but by their instructive example."

This immaculate, invincible uprightness in public station is no dream of visionaries. We cannot dismiss it as a glory of the Past, impracticable and fabulous at present. That is infidelity to Providence, to history, to

---

* Ebenezer Pemberton.

the ever-living heart of Christ. Besides, instances stand forth, illustrious and imperial, in every Christian nation, — the honor of statesmanship, the defence of governments, the strength of their age against all partisan or selfish conspiracies. Look, for a single example of that power, into the last generation and the legislative halls of England. Trained in the best refinement and learning of his time, coming forth from the midst of London fashions and palaces, where the frowns of the world are most formidable and its flatteries most seductive, familiar from his childhood with the luxuries of fortune and the policies of a false expediency, yet with his vision quickened by Christian faith, and his whole nature lightened and invigorated by the lessons of Olivet and Calvary, Wilberforce enters Parliament. Many a hard test tries his steadfastness. Erect, and yet courteous, he never swerves. He sees straight through every moral sophistry, and no chicanery can cheat him into one doubtful compliance. Hardest of all, Melville is impeached. Friendship, favor, interest, social alliance, popularity, all importune this Christian statesman to take up the cause of the accused. There was the eloquent countenance, and the trumpet tongue, of Pitt, pleading the same way. But there was one voice on the other side, stiller, grander, the voice of a righteous sincerity, and from that "he was accustomed to take no appeal." He knew Melville was wrong, the accusation just. Not an instant's hesitation. He stood up to speak for Right, stripped bare of all enchantments, and he knew that, speaking for that, he spoke for man, for his country, for God; because he who obeys a law higher than that of states, obeys a law in which alone any state is safe. Proud and powerful men looked on with disappointment, not to say with wrath. Every sentence was like hacking away old and precious bonds of fellowship. Melville was condemned, and how? Let the words of another's history answer: "It was felt that in a question of simple integrity, where casuistry had to be eluded and plausibility swept aside, this religious tongue was the last authority in England. In the British Senate, in the nineteenth century, when a point of morality was to be settled, it was not to the man of duelling honor, it was not to the philosophic moralist, that men looked for a decision; it was to the Christian senator whose code was the Bible," kneeling every morning before the All-seeing Eye, "going up to his seat from his closet," through all the perplexities of his place saying ever secretly to his God, "Lead me only by thy Light."

I am sure, gentlemen, you respond this day to any earnest call for public fidelity, and welcome any exalted standard of public duty. You are at the outset of great perils as well as great labors. Whether you make a conscientious study of all measures and schemes and subjects put before you or not, be certain there are those who are already making a politic and interested study of you, — your prejudices, tastes, habits, associations, your weaker and stronger side. You are in danger of losing your single-mindedness, your independence, your manhood. You are charged to-day with the responsibility, first of keeping a Christian conscience, and then of Christian legislation for Massachusetts. Immense trusts both, — the last vain without the first. So you need this hour of prayer, and are thankful for it. If any of you, on the other hand, are carrying up to the Capitol now such poverty of principle, or such salable convictions, that you will be seduced into making merchandise of your soul to the first or richest buyer in the passage-way, then, in the name of the State, — in the name of all public credit and faith, — in the name of common decency, — in the name of the truth of God, I adjure you to resign and go home to-night. It will be the best service you ever rendered to the Commonwealth, and more to the advantage of the statute-book than all the votes and speeches of a session.

Gentlemen, these are solemn hours for our country, for this Commonwealth, for the whole Republic. They are solemn hours for you, who hold for a little while the awful trust of the character of one member in the great confederation. It is no vision of alarmists that sees tendencies busily at work which will sweep us first to political prodigality, and then to oblivion of freedom and justice both, and then to revolution, unless some new-born conviction of the eternal rectitude comes to check the madness of the hour, and restore religion to her control. Be the immortal honor of building the order which the early patriots founded, yours. Yours also are the fathers, and yours the adoption, the glory, the covenants, the giving of the law, the service of God, and the promises; and to you Christ has come. The just nation, the just state, like the just soul, shall live by its faith. No height of privilege, no swelling census, no width of territory, no perfection of political construction, no wealth or splendor of cities or of citizens can save the faithless people from perishing.

Lovers of the nation, then, still build its synagogues! Ye that would be patriots, be believers. Have men of veracity for your officers, men of intrepid uprightness for your law-makers, men that fear only God and keep his commandments for your citizens. For he that reverences our holy religion in the sanctuary, and replenishes it in the closet, and acts it in his life, is a more effectual priest in the temple of our liberties, than the cunning statesman that diplomatizes in a cabinet, or the orator that talks administrations and parties into power or out of it with a crafty tongue. For it is as true now, in our ancient, beloved, Christian Commonwealth, as in the days of the eloquent prophet-king, that "over the faithful of the land the eyes of Mercy keep watch."

Let us conclude, then, with the most comprehensive affirmation of our subject. Above and beneath all civil constitutions, — the foundation of their stability, the dome of their protection, their corner-stone, their wall of defence, their genial and sheltering sky, is the religion and Gospel of our Lord Jesus Christ. Virtue is loyalty. Goodness is patriotism. The best citizenship is the best Christianship. The best legislator is the truest and wisest man. Character is the strength of the State. They are the friends, the ornaments, the defenders of the country and its constitution, who will not swerve from its three original, immortal ideas, — Faith, Freedom, Fraternity. These, rightly interpreted, comprehend the wealth of our heritage, the boundless promise of our Future. We spoil that heritage, we forfeit that Future, only as we disobey God, injure man, and worship ourselves.

To the retiring Chief Magistrate I offer the respectful salutations of the place and the hour, congratulating him on the honors of his office, on the successes of its administration, on the release from its cares, on every independent and unselfish act in its discharge, on every inward or outward testimony of fidelity.

For the honorable Senate, Council, and House of Representatives, I invoke here the spirit and blessing of the God of our fathers, the God of our beloved Commonwealth, the God of Honor, Justice, Truth, and Peace. May all their members be honest legislators, Christian citizens, lovers of the nation, servants of Christ and his Church!

SERMON XXIV.

LIFE THE TEST OF LEARNING.*

WHO IS A WISE MAN AND ENDUED WITH KNOWLEDGE AMONG YOU? LET HIM SHOW OUT OF A GOOD CONVERSATION HIS WORKS WITH MEEKNESS OF WISDOM. — James iii. 13.

IF we remember that the term here rendered "conversation" bears a larger signification than we commonly attach to that English word, — meaning the whole action of life, the development of character, the way a man works, turns, or behaves himself in the world, — *ἀναστροφή*, — and if we remember that on that term falls the main emphasis of the sentence, we shall get from the whole passage a general declaration of remarkable point, and quite appropriate to the special bearing of this service.

The scope of the writer's thought, paraphrasing the statement a little, will be something like this: — You speak of knowledge. You value intellectual attainments. You honor wise or learned men. But why do you value those attainments? Who are your wise men? Let Christian truth tell you. The use of

---

* Delivered before the Graduating Class of Harvard College, June 15, 1856.

knowledge is to guide and elevate the life. Wise men, or well-educated men, are those that make what they know illuminate and enrich what they do. The proper end and aim of study is a strong, simple, consistent character. The best attainments always produce a certain humility, or reverence, — a sense of dependence on the great Source of Light, God, — what is called " the meekness of wisdom." This feeling is an inspiration to religious actions. The more learning a true man gets, the more widely, the more accurately, the more profoundly, he will see and think ; and so, by consequence, the more he will *see* what earnest labors there are to be done ; the more he will *think* of the claims of God and man upon him to turn all his resources and energies into the channel of a beneficent activity. His attainments will be worth having, just in proportion as they are assimilated with the vital forces of his manhood ; and, by entering into the currents of spiritual purpose and affection, they will inspire and nourish his soul. If you would find out who among you is endued with knowledge, and who is not, you can apply this proof. Inquire who puts his knowledge into a " good conversation," — a noble or beautiful manner of living, — καλὴ ἀναστροφή. In a word, Character is the final cause of study. Life is the test of learning.

I cannot help asking you to notice, in passing, how exactly this idea fits in with the peculiar characteristic of James, the Apostle that wrote this letter to the churches. There is always a moral interest in a coincidence between a man and his speech. It makes the man more valid, and the speech more credible, besides confirming and comforting our faith in human sincerity generally. The New Testament is full of these marks of genuineness. And they are nowhere seen in a more striking and unconscious appearance than in James. Pre-eminently, he was the Apostle of practical service. The first question about everything with him was, What will it render of living, human goodness? Or, in our common phrase, How will it work? Let it be opinion, or faith, or preaching, or charity. What are its fruits? What does it come to? So, here, of knowledge. Conduct is the criterion of knowledge. Unless it yields a goodly harvest here, much study is only a weariness to the flesh, and a vanity of the mind.

A moment has come when you, my friends, whom it is my privilege to address especially to-day, can hardly help putting to yourselves the question, whether your education, thus far, is worth what you have given for it. The providence of God, who interests himself so paternally and solemnly in every new step we take, and who puts a voice of his own into every event, though it seems the most regular, or natural, or incidental, is urging that question home upon you. The interruption of a routine that has lasted several years casts us back upon individual choice and absolute principle. It is divinely intended to. And so the closing up of one long and important term of intellectual training, so costly of time and means, and faculty and strength, presses in the Christian inquiry, whether what has been gained is equal to such pains expended.

An unprofitable and possibly a dismal question, if the answer were not still in your own power! But it is. The great test of life is yet to be applied. And the time is coming. Whether what you have gathered here is to lie a crude and unproductive mass, in sluggish brains; or whether it is to be perverted to the baleful purposes of a selfish and headstrong will, — all the elaborate apparatus of education turned into an engine of more effectual mischief; or whether it shall be given to the noblest objects of human hope, and thus consecrated to Christ; — this is the threefold choice that awaits your determination, not to be evaded by any ingenuity, not to be forfeited by any neglect. It is certainly a fit time, then, to meditate the true and righteous uses of a Christian scholarship. Three easy and tempting mistakes seem to me to lie directly before you, — I might say before us all, — exposing all our past industry to failure.

I. The first danger is indifference. False objects in life are positive destroyers: but the absence of any clear object is a waster almost equally consumptive, and with one order of minds even more seductive. It would seem as if the natural effect of a comprehensive system of discipline must be to rouse the will and direct its aim. Why translate the tongues of so many tribes of men, if not to collect from them some completer interpretation of the riddle of our destiny? Why explore the mysterious geography of the mind itself, and interrogate the wondrous faculty by which all knowledge comes, if not to gain new data towards the solution of the oldest and deepest problem, — Why was I born? Why do I breathe? Whither do I tend? How is it possible to trace the moving processions of the ages, through paths seeming so trivial while they were trod, but so solemn in the echoes of their desertion, and not be sent back to watch with a wiser eye which way our own steps lead? The whole contemplation of history is an incitement to live purposely and earnestly. It is the very dignity of science, that it reads off to us not only the thoughts but the plan of God, — a plan whose unity and method demand some reflection and some copy, even in natures so fantastic and wayward as ours. Every lesson from creation proposes a task to be done. Every disclosure of the Creator presents an end to be achieved.

Yet I need hardly remind you how often we miss this practical and personal issue of the most intelligent study, — ever learning, but never coming to the knowledge of that simple truth! The lives of scholars, so peculiarly solicited and stimulated to the straitest determination, are given over, as often perhaps as others, sometimes it appears oftener than any others, — and certainly with a more palpable and melancholy abortiveness, — to aimless, nerveless, desultory chance. How the treasures rust in our hands! The smooth stones out of the brook drop unused from our grasp. The sling hangs loose at our side. Giant Error walks defiant and unchallenged at the head of his Philistine troops. The years run on, and no resolute helm guides the rocking keel toward a land of distinct and sacred promise. We are idly busy with living, careless of life. Two causes encourage this apathy.

One is, that the structure and habits of our industrial commonwealth expose the recent graduate from college to a period of uncertainty in his employment. It cannot be denied, I think, that at present there is some want of happy adjustment between the academic career and the public stations it precedes. The places of the higher and more intellectual labor are not organized in proportion to the mechanical and trafficking vocations. The developments of modern civilization have much widened the range of selection, and almost bewilder the judgment. Two or three clean-cut professions, technically learned, do not, as formerly, distribute and absorb the whole educated force. The same professions, meantime, for better or for worse, cease to be technically, if not in any other sense, *learned*, and are occupied by candidates who have rushed up to their gates by a shorter road. The fact, however it comes about, seems to stand, that an increasing number of college-bred men wait, with an awkward pause, after their graduation, undecided yet of what their "commencement" shall be the beginning. Unless some positive predilection or early bias has happened to settle their choice for them, an interval of doubt disturbs and enfeebles the steady drift and tenacity of their resolves. It is a crisis of trial and peril. Some men are hurried by it into a choice that is foolish and profanes the after-existence. Others are diluted by it into a spongy softness, and fall off into habits of literary generality, or sentimental imbecility. What is wanted is a Christian efficiency of purpose, — a Christian decision not to let haste spoil the material, — a Christian decision not to be content with vacillation. Delay too long, and there creeps upon the soul a fatally satisfied unconcern. The descent is easier, because the goads and exactions of a systematic discipline have just been taken off; the indolent free-will often finds the charming liberty to do what it pleases a wretched liberty to do nothing. Be guarded against this dull catastrophe. Let not the bright beginning slouch into a stupid sequel. What thy hand or thy brain findeth to do, do it with thy might. For he only is the wise man, and endued with knowledge among you, who keeps his life lively, and shows fruits of his study in a goodly conversation.

Another cause of indifference to any lofty and religious uses of education is a subservience to the routine of professional tasks. When the profession has been chosen and entered, it may still put on a yoke. Recurring drudgeries deaden enthusiasm. The first ardor fades off. Monotony sings its drowsy tune. Commonplace efforts will do for commonplace business; why stretch the powers beyond their wonted mood? Mediocrity is safe and practicable; why spur the aspirations by a swifter measure? Because, answers Christianity, they are the glory of your being. Because unbounded powers are insulted by arbitrary limits. Because the conquest of the possible into the actual is the keenest fascination of true courage. Because God never made us, and his institutions never nurtured us, to be sluggish grinders in the mill of repetition, but fellow-wrestlers with the heroes and apostles, — striving for the great mastery, pressing toward the mark. And there is but one victory, but one mark. However sloth may sleep, or cowardice despair, or infidelity deny, there is nothing less than a practical and progressive ripening of the whole man for the glory of God that can fill out the passion of the really "wise man endued with knowledge among you." The first sentence of Milton's tract on the Reforming of Education is an exposition of my text: "I am long since persuaded that, to do or say aught worth memory or imitation, no purpose should sooner move us than simply the love of God and of mankind. . . . . . The end of learning is to repair the ruins of our first parents by learning to know God aright, and out of that knowledge to be like him, — as we may the nearest be by possessing our souls of true virtue, which, being united to the heavenly grace of faith, makes up the highest perfection." And how well he insists on this definite and living purpose of the scholar, when he speaks of "that methodical course wherein our gentle and noble youth must proceed, by the steady pace of learning onward, till they have confirmed and solidly united the whole body of their perfected knowledge, like the last embattling of a Roman legion!"

II. But beyond indifference whether learning has any grand object, — and sometimes, indeed, this side of it, — lies the hindrance of a poor self-seeking. Undoubtedly it is one of the most appalling proofs of the vigor of the selfish passions, that they survive as they do through all the liberalizing influence of a catholic culture, and resist the generous impressions of science, and even triumph over the charities of good-fellowship, in the base hunger for luxury or comfort. The Apostle does not say it is in a lucrative conversation, or a famous conversation, or a comfortable conversation, that the works of the real wisdom are shown forth, but in a "*good* conversation." Nor is it in the pride, the distinction, the notoriety, or the emoluments of wisdom, — the office, the salary, the applause, the furniture, — but in "the meekness of wisdom. It is Wisdom for her own pure and precious sake, — or rather for His sake who possessed her of old, in the beginning, when he laid the foundations of the earth, — that he loves and pursues. If scholarship holds itself affronted by being degraded into the low wrangle of appetites, religion has a sterner rebuke, and calls it sacrilege. The question, when you are laying your plans for the future, is not, Which will yield me the best living? but, Which will yield me the best life? It cannot be that you have been out in the fields of learning seeking jewels, to bring them in and lay them down as purchase-money for equipage or compliments. The legitmate children of Mammon, schooled, not as you have been, in the ample and serene atmosphere of unselfish thought, but in the closer chambers of mercenary calculation, — trained, not, as you have been, in the royal company of great persons from antiquity downward, but in the scramble and devices of gain, — will beat you in that rivalry; and they ought to. How your educated strength shall be devoted, should be settled by another reference than the stock-list or the tax-bill. All honest callings are honorable. If you carry your acquirements into commerce, you may enter into a worthy and magnanimous competition. There is scope there for your largest faculty, and there is need there of the broadest philosophy. But you cannot decently go to turn your talents *into* merchandise, to forget the communion with high examples, to square your notions of civil affairs by the self-interest of the market, to sell the nobility of art and letters for some rich bargain, to barter conscience for tariff or dividends, — to let your independent duty as citizens and as patriots be appointed for you by the narrow gossip of the exchange or the contracts of brokers' boards. Bear into whatever mercantile engagements or profitable alliances you encounter a spirit that is genial with the sympathies of all the peoples you have conversed with, — self-denying with old sacrifices, fragrant with the mountain air of meditation, sacred with the veneration of holy traditions. Breathe the spirit of your studies into the haunts of trade. Touch the rough customs of shops with the grace of a genuine refinement. And do all that modesty will allow to raise the strifes of property into a statelier degree, by asserting everywhere the supremacy of thinking man over his possessions, and of simple justice over all the policies and expediencies of the hour. Maintain everywhere the absolute dignity of Truth who has chosen you once as her disciples and heralds, — and never forget, however affluence bids for your souls, that you were here set apart and dedicated as priests in the unsordid Temple of Learning.

Consider, too, that there is a greediness of praise just as radically selfish, if not quite so carnal, as the lust for money. And precisely because it wears a more intellectual look it is a sin that offers a more acceptable bait to cultivated men. But there is nothing in it of "the meekness of wisdom." The selfishness of vanity is at its root, and the selfishness of ostentation is in its branches, — and green jealousies are canker-worms on all its leaves. He is not half-educated, not the wise man, nor endued with knowledge among you, who suborns the common largesses of the past into a stepping-stone to personal renown, and prizes the light that is sent to warm the whole race into a brotherhood, only for the distinctions it reveals between himself and his kind. Not that is the genuine scholar's temper, nor the goodly conversation.

III. Thirdly, it is no business of the liberal and Christian scholar to become the hired servant of party prejudice or sectarian interests. Science is given and got for no such contemptible uses. Students are congregated in a still and separate spot, on neutral ground, remote as may be from all political and ecclesiastical chicanery, on purpose that they may grow and expand, aloof from the warping forces of controversy. But, in a social state like ours, it would take more than a Chinese wall, or the rules of monastic seclusion, to shut out even from academic groves the intruding conflicts of the forum and the convention. Before you have passed out of the hearing of the College bell, the recruiting officers of state and church will besiege you for your pledge. Consider carefully, I pray you, before you give it to any of them, how much you give with it, — whether your manhood, whether your individuality, whether your liberty of speech, whether the sanctity of a fearless conviction. Here again scholarship and Christianity both unite to put you on your guard. There are little coteries enough, in art, in letters, in social opinion, in public policy, in theologic speculation, that will be delighted to enroll a new name on their lists. Their captains will electioneer for you while you are free, — flatter you when you consent, — patronize and cajole you when you are caught, — use and pay you while you succumb, — abuse and torment you when you rebel. Can you afford that servitude? Can learning afford it in your persons? And who, in all these truckling and hard-drilled times, shall be honest and free, if not they whose minds have been balanced and poised by contemplating the reasons of things?

It is not against the more *open* and *offensive* aggressions of such combined interests that these warnings are directed, so much as against devices that are more specious and plausible. We have committed ourselves, in our social experiment, to the government of public opinion, even more than of public law. Unless the original fountains of it are kept healthy and pure, we are in the most complicated and disastrous of anarchies. Already, thoughtful men cannot look far about them without seeing what beginnings of ruinous and despotic power, of misjudgment, of defamation, of vituperation, are craftily growing up in these bigotries of our democracy. Truth is scarcely seen for what it is, but only for the image and superscription it bears, nor prized for its beauty, but for its currency. The few that venture on a practical assertion of the boasted liberality, have to be catechized, and menaced, and ostracized, so far as the puny persecutions of wordy violence can ostracize. Oppose to these degrading dictations all the massive resistance of your knowledge, the muscle of your manhood, and the sincerity of your faith.

Faith, I say. For it is not the independence of self-will, not the vain ambition of peculiarity, not the insolent contempt of the past, or of other men, or of righteous authority, that I exhort you to. It is the honest loyalty to the one only Authority, instead of mortal counterfeits. It is the appeal from custom to Christ, — from party and sect to the Holy Spirit, — from mortal majorities to God. There is no right religious reverence which does not fear the one only Master more than unpopularity or reproach. What we want is that humility, growing ever deeper with all growing heights of attainment, — that penitential confession of sins, that meekness of wisdom, which bends with unutterable awe before the secret voice of the Most High, before the open command of the Bible, and which, being turned "into a native and heroic valor," makes men "hate the cowardice of doing wrong."

Let us ponder, then, the great claims that are laid on our educated men. The country has claims, — never more than now. We need more of that sort of education which stirs and fosters, from beginning to end, a loyal zeal for the central and dominant ideas that lie at the foundation of the Republic. The scholar is not well trained that has not been formed day by day into a Christian patriot. Our universities ought all to be nurseries, not of national exclusiveness, or national vanity, but of a just national honor, virtue, and devotion. They should rear and send forth prophets for the American Israel, — prophets brave and blameless, and speaking ever with a "Thus saith the Lord," — prophets that no sophistry can bewilder, no tyrant silence, no bludgeon terrify, no flattery blind. Out of libraries, and out of laboratories, and out of the forearming contests of debate, let them send forth, for each impending struggle of Right with Wrong, thinkers and speakers "fraught with a universal insight, ingenuous and matchless men." For, as said that stanch old English republican of two centuries ago, in language suiting us to-day, There is a study of politics worthy of Christian scholars, "that they may not, in a dangerous fit of the commonwealth, be such poor, shaken, uncertain reeds, of such a tottering conscience, as many of our great counsellors have lately shown themselves, but steadfast pillars of the state."

Universal humanity has claims. That "good conversation" of the Christian scholar condescends to converse with the lowest offshoot of the human stock. That "meekness of wisdom" stoops gladly to help the weakest wayfarer; to hear the story of wrong or weakness from the faintest or most unlettered lips; to sympathize with the wants of the vagrant, or the sorrows of the slave; to bring all the sublime resources of culture, the magic of invention, and the facilities of genius, to ease the burdens of penury, to open the path to the helpless, to pay respect and wages to unpaid toil, to inspire brute force with intelligence, to marshal idle men and women and children into ranks of self-sustaining labor. This is a worthy end for the best scholarship of the age, —

> "How best to help the slender store,
> How mend the dwellings of the poor, —
> How gain in life, as life advances,
> Valor and charity more and more."

Above all, Christ has claims. And his claims are supreme. They transcend, they underlie, they encompass, all beside. The Lord of souls is Lord of the sciences as well. Common gratitude challenges obedience and love for Him, in whose name every hope of civilization moves to its fulfilment, and every affection of mankind realizes itself in peace. It must be a personal obedience, — a personal love. No general and cold confession, no vague and rhetorical loyalty, no heartless and high-sounding praises, can satisfy that Gospel of regeneration on which salvation depends. Penitence, trust, consecration, prayer, righteousness, — these will; for God is Love, and his forgiveness waits. Every thought and imagination must be brought into captivity to the holy obedience of the Son of God. All knowledge that is not rooted and centred there vanishes away. "Who is a wise man and endued with knowledge among you?" He is the believing student, the studious disciple.

Gentlemen of the Graduating Class, our doctrine culminates here.

Every considerable change in the *form* of our life is

meant to suggest to us something original as to its spirit. The dissolving of one set of relations moves the question by what law new sets shall be organized. When farewells and distance threaten manly friendships, what is more unavoidable than to think what arm shall keep the friend that is parted from, and whether there is not one Friendship in whose Eternal and Almighty clasp every human affection finds its safety? The separation of classmates opens spaces about each one's personality which let in light from above on all your plans and habits. A change of residence puts us to asking why we live at all; how long we shall need any earthly dwelling; whether we deserve any. How shall your tuition justify these years, and your future be adequate to the past?

That question, like every other that an earnest experience asks, God's Book of Life answers.

Life *is* the test of Learning. Character *is* the criterion of knowledge. Not what a man has, but what he is, is the question, after all. The quality of soul is more than the quantity of information. Personal, spiritual substance is the final resultant. Have that, and your intellectual furnishings and attainments will turn, with no violent contortion, but with a natural tendency and harmony, — a working together, conversation, *ἀναστροφή*, — to the loftiest uses. Add faith to knowledge, and your education will be worth what it has cost. Your lives will honor and justify your preparation. Say, every morning, with the simple confidence of the holy child in the Temple, "Lord, here am I!" and he will send you to noble and effectual victories. Your wisdom will tell to issues that are divine, and that wisdom the Eternal Providence will watch, because it is matured in the spiritual school of Him who knows all that is in man.

"Lift up your eyes to the fields; they are white already to harvest." With the blessing of that Providence, go to the field of your slow, patient work. That slowness of the result may be the bitterest element in the discipline.

> "To-morrow, and to-morrow, and to-morrow,
> Creeps in this petty pace from day to day,
> To the last syllable of recorded time."

Be content to wait for Him with whom ages are days.

> "If but this tedious battle could be fought,
> With Sparta's heroes, at one rocky pass,
> One day be spent in dying, men had sought
> The spot, and been cut down like mower's grass.
> If in the heart of nature we might strive,
> Challenge to single combat the great power,
> Welcome the conflict! But no; half alive,
> We skirmish with our foe long hour by hour."

Nevertheless,—nevertheless,—in due season ye shall reap, if ye faint not. Go out with faith, with supplication. Ye shall come again in the Jubilee and Sabbath of the Resurrection rejoicing. And then, be content if it shall be with you as with the solemn pictured figures of the returning warriors, in the historical galleries of the Italian city, where the reverent and pious victors are seen, not in chariots, nor with sceptres, nor on thrones, nor with crowns on their heads, but kneeling, the crowns lifted in their hands, looking upward, and giving thanks to God.

SERMON XXV.

THE HOUSE OF PRAYER.*

MY HOUSE SHALL BE CALLED THE HOUSE OF PRAYER. — Matthew xxi. 13.

By the permission of the Infinite One, through whose wisdom the first purpose was shaped, of whose love the bounty was given, and in whose strength the builders have labored, this sacred work, begun a little more than two years ago, stands complete. It betokens a truth old as the human soul. It registers a want of our nature ever-new and ever-present, — communion with our Creator. It attests a life at once above and before us, of loftier joy and everlasting goodness. It helps perpetuate the promise of man's redemption from his only real evil and of his forgiveness for his only terrible wrong. It is, in design, a copy, all unworthy, but such as our mortal penury could bring, of that mysterious Pattern of perfect social adoration "in the Mount," of which the praise is pure, whence they go no more out, "eternal in the heavens." May the Ancient of Days, the Father of all that now live, and the God of all

---

* A sermon preached at the dedication of the "Appleton Chapel," of Harvard University, in Cambridge, October 17, 1858.

hope, God and Father of Jesus Christ our Lord, who was dead, and is alive again, and who liveth evermore, accept it into his keeping, save it from profanation, guard it from misuse, and hallow it as his own House of Prayer!

It would seem to form a fit introduction to the course of thought best suited to this service, and at the same time duly honor the noble spirit of Christian beneficence which, from one generation to another, provides and renews these instruments of faith and inlets of a heavenly inspiration, if we notice first the events that led to the rearing of the edifice, and the special generosity that has been thought worthy to give it the name by which it is to be known.

Since the time of the amicable withdrawal of the College community from its connection with the First Parish, in 1814, the public worship of the Lord's Day and other religious services have been held in University Hall. That building, as is well known, was reared and has been occupied for the united purposes of recitation-rooms and a Chapel. For a time, also, there were uses of some of its apartments still less in keeping with the designs of a sanctuary than the ordinary secular exercises of the week. Two of the rooms were devoted to a commons ordinary, and the basement was given over to a store-room, a kitchen, and lodgings for servants. To invest such a spot with the select and hallowed impressions of a sanctuary would be quite too difficult for minds the most disciplined and a devotional habit the most mature. To attempt it amidst the less fixed convictions and the forming influences of a seminary for the young seems still more hopeless.

The inconvenience and interruptions were felt and

deplored long before a way could be found for their remedy. A specific official notice of these unfavorable arrangements appears to have been first taken in a report to the Overseers from the Treasurer of the Corporation, Samuel A. Eliot, just twelve years ago last week, October 12, 1846. They are there mentioned as "the most important of existing deficiencies" connected with the Institution. "The present Chapel," says this judicious paper, "is at once too small, and ill adapted, from its appearance and its connection with adjoining apartments, to its peculiar purpose. It may seem to those accustomed to the severe simplicity of our Puritan church architecture that the effect of the mere appearance of a room used for religious worship could not and ought not to be great, and it may be freely admitted, that, if it were used for once or for a few times only, it would not be important; but nothing which must be often repeated is insignificant, and it is therefore of no doubtful utility that the worship of God, which is to be often renewed, should be so conducted as to attract and not to repel." On the last day of the same year, President Everett, in the first of his annual reports, distinctly recommends "the erection of a Chapel exclusively consecrated to religious exercises," as "one of the most pressing wants of the Institution." An earnest recurrence was made to the subject in each of the two remaining reports of the same presiding officer. At the close of the last of these documents, his large observation and thoughtful regard for every higher object of education, of learning and the State, led this devoted son and friend of the University to remark as follows: "Wholesome habits, salutary traditions, winning examples, revered memories and generous sentiments, are more important toward effecting the great purposes for which the societies of men are formed, than the letter of the law. But of influence more vital and controlling than all are the softened temper and gentle spirit which nothing but a religious principle can create. The devotional exercises of the Chapel are the foundation of the discipline of the place, and apart from their higher office, are all-important in this respect. Nothing which can make the Chapel-services interesting and duly affecting should, in the judgment of the President, be spared. They should be regarded, throughout the Institution, as the first of duties. The aspect and arrangements of the Chapel should invite to meditation, and the organ and a solemn chant of select portions of the Psalms, or 'the imperishable hymns of the Church,' should be united with the reading of the Scriptures and the offering of prayer." He further expresses his belief that a service of this description, with auxiliary measures for the spiritual culture of the students, "would, by the blessing of Providence, do more to increase the usefulness" of the seminary "than an indefinite multiplication of means and appliances purely secular."

It was found, however, and reluctantly confessed, by the author of these views and by all the departments of the government, that such a structure as was needed was entirely beyond the funds at the command of the Corporation, and that, if the object was to be effected at all, recourse must be had to the Christian liberality of "the children and friends of the University."

From the enlightened dispositions of a few men belonging chiefly to the last of the two classes here designated, — the friends, wise and liberal, of the University, though not its children, the patronage so deeply needed was, not long after, to be gratuitously proposed.

Samuel Appleton, a merchant of Boston, was of a family of which it has been noticed that from a very early period in the colonial settlements it has been remarkable for the "uniformity in the character of the individuals embraced in it;" and of that character it may be said, with equal justice, that among its prominent traits have been integrity, firmness, enterprise, and patriotism. Two of its members have been eminent in their relation to the interests both of learning and religion in New England. The first settler of that name emigrated in obedience to the stanch convictions of a Puritan believer. He afterwards refused to share in the persecution of the Antinomians and Mrs. Hutchinson, and lost office for that liberality. It is an agreeable association in the thoughts of this occasion, that one of his descendants, as this audience will remember, was for the long period of about sixty-seven years of the last century the pastor of this College, as the minister of the First Parish in Cambridge, was the brother-in-law of one of its most efficient and celebrated Presidents, Edward Holyoke, and was the second divine on whom it conferred a degree for theological and ministerial eminence, — the faithful Christian teacher, a record of whose simple-hearted wisdom, apostolic devotion, and patriarchal dignity, is to be sought in the after-lives of the two thousand graduates that listened to his preaching and observed his life; and whose motto, "Orthodoxy and Charity," was recorded not only on the canvas of the portrait which still preserves his likeness in our gallery in Harvard Hall, but on all his profession and discourse and labor, as a servant of the College and the Church.

Another of the kindred was, at a later period, a candidate for a theological professorship in this University, received one of its honorary degrees, and was twelve years President of Bowdoin College, in Maine.

A common ancestor of theirs, Samuel Appleton, was in public service at an earlier time, was appointed commander of the Massachusetts forces in Philip's war, because he was a person "very sensible of ye cause and people of God," was counted factious by the Royal Governors Randolph and Andros, on account of his republican principles, and appealed to the people from a rock at Lynn, still called "Appleton's pulpit." His despatches, dated at Hadley, abound in proofs of skill, bravery, and piety.

Our benefactor belonged to that worthy class of New England men who are born in frugal homes, gain their balanced power of character by a modest conquest of many hardships, and pass out into large usefulness through a course of discipline and achievement as favorable to the attributes of a genuine manhood as almost any in the world. Forbidden a personal share in the culture of the higher seats of learning, they become the patrons of letters, the founders of institutions and chairs of instruction, and command the esteem and confidence of scholars. Bred to habits of acquisition and calculation, they rise superior to the meagre prospects of a mere mercenary ambition, not only dignifying commerce by their public spirit, but forwarding science itself by their practical sagacity and energy. For that part of education which consists in the study of books Mr. Appleton was limited through his early years to the district school and such private hours as made the margin of a busy and laborious employment. But by assimilating and using what he learned, by an intelligent intercourse with men, by travels abroad, by a self-knowledge and sterling sense ever prohibiting in him the assumption which is the fatal mark of ignorance, and by that conscientious discipline of his faculties which is the nobler part of wisdom, he entered in unchallenged among our foremost order of men. The fullest and highest heads found a manliness in him that made him their peer. In the stainless justice and frankness that ruled his dealings, "he knew but one way of speaking, and that was to say, straight on, the truth." In a suit at law, a jury once found in his favor, even against some apparent odds of evidence, on nothing but the plain declaration of his word, — with this almost unexampled explanation of their verdict, that "they were quite sure Mr. Appleton would not dispute the payment of the note, except on the certainty that he did not owe it." Eager gainseekers, bewildered by financial success, or enslaved by a lucrative opportunity, saw in him the fine example of a self-control which subdued the passion for wealth just when it is most apt to grow despotic, voluntarily withdrew him from all the tempting prizes of fortune before he was sixty years old, and devoted the rest of his life to doing good. There was, indeed, as all who knew him will confess, and as it is more than proper here to remember, a singular sweetness and simplicity in the old age of this venerable, benevolent, unpretending citizen and Christian, — master of his possessions and of himself. There were sufferings and infirmities of the body, but he could better bear all these than the pain of turning back the humblest deserving applicant from his door, or closing his bountiful hand on a dollar that was needed by Christ's poor. Such cheerfulness did this charity breathe through his household, that it would seem as if all the new gladness and the hearty benedictions of the wretchedness he brightened came back and pitched their permanent tents about him. Simple as a child, the generous steward of God's bounty sat there amidst his affluence, listening, pitying, giving, till sordid riches were transfigured before him, till the pursuits that we commonly call worldly looked divine, the curse that clings to Dives's lot was loosened, and even money wore the stamp of Jesus of Nazareth. Let me say that the only time I ever saw him I went to ask help for the education of a minister of the Gospel; and that when I went away, with his willing gift, he said these rare words, rare even from generous people, "When you know of some other very good object, I wish you would come to me again." Mercy, in each of its benignant forms, and religion, and literature, and great industrial enterprises full of benefit to the people, felt the force of his disinterested purpose. As little narrowed by the vanity which makes a merit of straitened beginnings as by the other vanity which is ashamed of them, he only said, when he heard the circumstances of his youth and age contrasted, that but for a physical constitution naturally feeble he should have been as well content with the early labor as the later leisure. He remembered the humble workmen in the Eastern woods who used to lend him their arms in lifting logs beyond his strength, and even their children saw kindnesses falling into their dwellings from the same unknown and unforgetful giver. For several of his last years he consecrated the entire income of his estates to charity. And when nature was putting a term upon his personal munificence, by his will, after numerous and ample specific legacies, he bequeathed two hundred thousand dollars in trust to his executors, — in the language of the instrument, "to be by them applied and distributed for scientific, literary, religious, and charitable purposes." He died on the twelfth of July, 1853, in the eighty-eighth year of his age.

Both by the consistent practice of the original donor, then, sustained through a long career of benefactions in this kind, and by the special directions of his last testament, we are justified in honoring Samuel Appleton of Boston as the source of this welcome accession to the resources and right conduct of the Institution. Happily, however, for the University, the discharge of these trusts fell to executors who partook of the liberal designs and temper of the testator. In November, 1854, these trustees, Nathan Appleton, William Appleton, and Nathaniel Ingersoll Bowditch, communicated to the Corporation their decision to appropriate the value of fifty thousand dollars of this fund for the purpose of erecting "a building of granite, freestone, or marble, as a Chapel for religious services." The gift was accepted, in the words of President Walker, as "timely aid to supply a pressing want of the University." At the same time it was voted by the President and Fellows "that the Chapel to be thus erected shall be named the Appleton Chapel, in memory of" this "munificent benefactor of learning and humanity." The plans were soon after proposed and submitted; the ground was broken in July, 1856, and the corner-stone of the structure was laid, with suitable ceremonies, on the second day of May, 1857.

We are gathered to thank the providence of God, to acknowledge the faithfulness of good men, and to set the building apart as a "House of Prayer."

The College has not waited these two hundred and twenty years for the appointment of God's worship within its walls. Knowing well that grand article of its faith, that "God is a spirit," and that "they that worship him must worship him in spirit and in truth," its guardians have provided for the daily homage of each generation, within such plain substitutes for the separate sanctuary as poverty, or other needs, and the times allowed. Through a line of reverend teachers, its presiding and other officers, and the ministers of the churches, it has striven not to falter from the elevated standard of its two early charters: the first of 1642, proposing as the object of the seminary, "piety, morality, and learning;" the second, of eight years later, "knowledge and godliness." From the dawning hour of its distinction it has never been wholly unmindful of its loyalty to the Messiah. The leaves of the vine planted by the hand of the Son of Man have been patiently dropped into this fountain of learning. At last a day of better outward appointments has come: God grant it may prove a day of nobler spiritual zeal! We see laid on these grounds, sequestered already to science and letters, this stately token of another reality, — faith in things not seen; and this we are to consecrate to the King Eternal, Immortal, Invisible, the only wise God!

The chief meaning of our assembly and the first cause of this day's festival is that this building represents Religion. And since Christ has come, and died, and risen, we apprehend religion only in him. Historically we know the Father only in the "Word made flesh." Experimentally, we know the power of the Spirit only by the life Divine communicated to ours. The upward-looking welcome of that Spirit, with its fruitful transmission into a practical and consistent action, is the organizing law of the Church; a social body with conscious members, under its living Head. Here is the one essential principle of a devout, humane, indestructible church-life. A sanctuary is one of the chambers of its retirement, one of its places of replenishing and strengthening, one of its oratories of prayer: not its only home: *that* is the whole field of the world where men work, and love, and suffer, and sin, and die. The house of the spiritual Church has no roof but heaven: no walls but the ever-widening bounds of space and time; nay, it abides in infinitude; "the true tabernacle which the Lord pitched, and not man."

Now, this religion is of three elements, with a need, a nurture, and an expression for each.

First, it is an idea; and as an idea, held by the understanding, its need is to be cleared; its nurture is instruction; its expression is doctrine. Perfect this, and you rid the Church of intellectual error.

Secondly, religion is a faith, and as a faith, held in the soul, its need is to be purified. Its nurture is spiritual communion; its expression is worship. Perfect this, and you rid the Church of superstition on the one hand, and unbelief on the other.

Thirdly, Religion is a life; and as a life, bred in the practical force of the will, its need is freedom; its nurture is action; its expression is righteousness. Perfect this, and you rid the Church of its selfish indolence and mammonism.

For each of these elements a place is found in the well-ordered symmetry and solemn beauty of a genuine Fold of Christ. To lend each of them energy, simplicity, constancy, is the direct end of the public meeting of the sanctuary.

Interests like these, according to the common dictates of our nature, and the best interpretations we can put on God's providence with man, tend to clothe themselves in institutions. The State, the Family, Education, Commerce, and the less definite and less systematized form of human intercourse that we call Society, furnish sufficient analogies. History, heathen hardly less than Christian, is the record, — for, mixed with all the surface-dust of the globe moulder the fragments of altars, priests, temples, shrines. Results are the argument. Round the world, and through the centuries, men embody their strong thoughts and dearest hopes in shapes presentable to the senses. If reasons are asked, the plainest seems to be that men, at present, are neither ghosts, nor brutes, but are of both body and spirit. With such convenience as their culture has contrived, with such grace or majesty as their taste can admire and their skill create, with such durability as the transient materials or fugitive fashions can command, they found and build and adorn the dwellings of their deep desires. Legislation, armies, marriage, learning, exchange, and the social custom that ever varies but never dies, all seek shelter, method, signs, forms. So along with statesmanship and generalship, — with the husband, the soldier, the scholar, the merchant, and the neighbor, religion also, in the persistent organization of its designs, taking on the externals of a Form, sends for the architect: and to Him who is a spirit, filling the universe, invisible, temples are built "with hands."

Passing, then, from the interior view, by the steps of an analysis so obvious, we come to inquire the precise objects of the outward structure of God's house. They may be gathered from what has already appeared.

I. First is Worship: worship, old as humanity; yet a worship springing for us only at the call of that Gospel of reconciliation which blends Fatherhood, Mediation, and Brotherhood together, — its threefold and absolute Revelation. "Whom therefore ye ignorantly worship, Him declare I unto you:" how right that this should have been spoken from the Athenian Areopagus, — the hill-top of that luminous centre of the old Pagan civilization: where stoics and epicureans and soldiers, — philosophy and pleasure and power, — Alexandria and Corinth and Rome, and the three continents, could hear! The kneeling devotees must bend in a lowlier prostration, and then rise to a wiser work. The wondering sages, — men of intellects so mighty and imperial that no after-age discredits the originality and comprehensiveness of their genius, — must confess a diviner wisdom than the Academy's. The most seeing poets, like that Aratus whom Paul's scholarship could quote, must awake from dreaming to the solid convictions that no daylight scatters. The patient sufferers must turn their aching eyes to a more miraculous oracle, to feel their pain touched and released by the great Healer of Nazareth. And the prayer and the praise were thenceforth to ascend with the promise ever falling, "Seek, and ye shall find:" "Whatsoever ye shall ask in my name, I will give it you."

Worship is the docility of the soul. Whence does it

come? It is of reverence, the most august and profound of man's capacities, because it reaches instantly from his humblest self-distrust to the loftiest sufficiency, laying the trembling arm of his infirmity on the Almighty throne. An attribute of all the stateliest and broadest men from the beginning! How justly it has been said, "Whatever is wise, or strong, or loving enough in this world to outlive the changes of human admiration, will be found to have the tincture of intense faith. They who have most affected the fates of mankind have not attained their great dimensions without bearing a divine secret in their souls; they have been men of trust and prayer; and, familiar with an Infinite presence, have reached the stature which throws so grand a shadow over history." It is of aspiration; — the filial, fallen spirit longing and struggling for its source and its rest again; this aspiration differing from ambition as soaring straight up, with open mind, from creeping obliquely with a face averted in shame; or as self-promotion is different from sacrifice. It is of confession, crying out of a prodigal's penitent home-sickness, and a publican's sincerity, "I have sinned against Heaven, and in thy sight;" "God be merciful to me, a sinner."

Without worship our knowledge grows arrogant, and therein grows weak, crawling back by vanity to ignorance, hiding its own lamp, and cheating itself with knowingness, or sciolism, for wisdom, — a blunder that more than one chapter of the sullied pages of literary biography recites. Without worship enterprise is forever investing for final failure. Just as undevout science, in the largest view of creation, is unscientific, because it stops between causes and the Cause, (is geocentric, or at most heliocentric, but not theocentric) so invention and labor deny their true principles and ends by Atheism, because they retreat unbelieving from the one "open secret," and forfeit the supreme blessing. Their rebellious architecture is of the order of Babel and Babylon, in every country they colonize, in every city they crowd. For in rearing the mansion of their civilization and multiplying its machinery, they lose the one world-wide language of brotherly love. They get confounded with the dialects of caste and hate. They weave purple and fine linen for oppression and lust. They pile their walls so high that they shut off the beams of heaven. Without worship manhood is dwarfed, for it ignores the only supreme intelligence, the only irresistible power, the only infinite love, — the Highest, the Greatest, the Best One ; and he who ought to open out on every side of him, by every breathing pore of his constitution, and every thirsty passion of his immortality, towards the boundless realm that encompasses, invites, and waits to transfigure him, shrinks self-limited. His very acquisitions and accomplishments, which ought to lift his position and ennoble his attitude, by the veil they interpose between his inmost life and Heaven only cramp his proportions and blind his eyes. The curse of pride and the fall, on the fruit of the tree of knowledge, returns.

Corresponding to human worship, its object, its answer, is the influence of the Spirit. This is the Comforter Christ promised and gave, to abide forever, to testify of him, to help our infirmities; to convince of righteousness, of sin, and of judgment; to revive the hearts of the humble and contrite; to renew, to quicken, to sanctify; — to make intercessions for us with unutterable earnestness. Faith in that heavenly gift, which would seem to be the simplest act of Christian consciousness, is now the foremost want of the Race, — within the Church, I think, and without. All the graces of a richer and more genial piety wait on its growth. It would be at once the restoration of primitive zeal in the brotherhood, of simplicity in administration, of holy fire in the preaching, of pure and noble manners in society. It would melt the Pantheist's frosty speculation. It would vitalize the formalist's routine. It would irradiate the dulness of materialism. It would shame sectarian suspicions and silence the bigot's malediction. It would reinstall the apostolic catholicity amidst the "diversities of gifts" begotten of these periods of discovery and inquiry. "Ask, and ye shall receive" it. To the Holy Spirit, then, we dedicate this place.

II. Secondly, Ordinances: — Those slight but steadfast bonds which join the successive spiritual generations together, and by the mysterious adjustment of their simplicity to our twofold constitution, as of an outward and inner life, becoming, — what Augustine called them before falsehood put them in *between* the heart and God, — "life-giving sacraments" *to* the heart *from* God. Surely experience is lost, and Christian progress is hopeless, if we cannot retain what was of reason and of grace together amidst the mistakes of our fathers, — nay, if we cannot find the limit where reactions exhaust their office, and so recover, after a reformatory suspension, any of those affecting ceremonies, which Truth had to tear off when she played the iconoclast for God and stripped away the fetters of idolatry.

The special function of our two sacraments, as setting

forth to the believer, at impressive intervals, what is most personal in our Lord's ministry and redemption, harmonizes certainly with the deeper intuitions of nature. Seizing on the universal emblem of purification, it pours the water of baptism, — finding the great example of Christ's humility, in condescending to it that he might "fulfil all righteousness" and be in all things an example to his disciples, to lie at the very beginning of his public ministry, — while the charge was issued, just when he was about to ascend up out of their sight, "Go ye and teach all nations, baptizing them in the name of the Father, and of the Son, and of the Holy Ghost:" the one universal formula of the creed of Christendom affirmed in its initiatory rite. Then, retiring, with awe and wonder, to the shaded upper chamber, just before the agony, — Gethsemane to-night and Calvary to-morrow, — it receives from the same "holy and innocent and immortal hands" the common food and the common drink of his countrymen and his time, the sign of the body broken, of the blood poured out, — the living, redeeming, infinite sacrifice for man. And there hearing him say, "This do in remembrance of me," with gladness and trust and love quite unspeakable, penetrating, thrilling, exalting all the heart, faith cries eagerly in answer, "This, Lord, this now and ever, and with all thy saints on earth, will I do in remembrance of thee!"

For the impressive celebration of both these uniting and animating ordinances of the Church wise and generous thought has been taken, as you will witness, in the arrangements of this building. — To Christ Jesus, then, whose personal life regenerates, whose death redeems, and whose intercessions redeliver his people from all the bondage and misery and waste of sin, making them that were dead alive, and causing that "whosoever loveth and believeth in Him shall never die," we dedicate it.

III. Thirdly, Human Duties, both in men and towards men. All worship and ordinances, Divine influence and the Messiah's mission, terminate, for man, in the production of holiness, in the growth of character, and thus in the glory of God. Disturb that uncompromising law, break utterly apart the solemn solitudes of devotion from the market and the household, sever the mount of vision from the multitude where justice and mercy are tempted, and then the sanctuary becomes only the cowardly retreat of an imbecile religious sentimentalism, or else the shameless parade-ground of hypocrisy. Derange the just proportion; let form encroach on substance; let the letter that killeth overlay the spirit that giveth life; let an indolent expectation of supernatural compulsion mistake itself for the energetic trust which rests vigilantly in the Lord, laboring for him, and then the deadliest conceivable sacrilege has desecrated your temple, and undone the deed of to-day. Be it not forgotten, that this Chapel is raised for the proclamation of liberty, purity, charity, of right for all men, truth in all action, temperance in all pleasure, — the keeping under of the body, the eternal ascendency of conscience. In the early ages of our faith, the victim of wrong, fleeing from his oppressor, took refuge in the sanctuary of Christ, and was safe. Let his cause still find security, hiding in that pavilion. I read again that warrant of the preacher, published in the Synagogue of Nazareth, "The spirit of the Lord is upon me, because he hath anointed me to preach the Gospel to the poor. He hath sent me to heal the broken-hearted, to preach deliverance to the captives, and recovering of sight to the blind, to set at liberty them that are bruised, to preach the acceptable year of the Lord."

Wherever this communion has been forgotten, there was a failure, not of Christianity, but of its unfaithful trustees. Wherever it was evaded, by self-love, by cowardice, by an excess of ceremony or an exaggeration of dogmatic conformity, there was a betrayal of the Son of Man. And there may be no end of that dreary contradiction, till the very rubric and eucharist become monuments of a lie, or till the barbarous priesthood of infatuation and cruelty, like the Mexicans, build even their temples with bloody hands, and build them of the skulls of men. But wherever the Commission was heeded, the genuine fruits of the celestial seed sprang up in the good soil of the world, an hundred fold,—love, joy, peace, long-suffering, gentleness, goodness, faith, meekness, temperance. There the twofold completeness of the kingdom,—the love of God and of the neighbor,—was witnessed, not in name only, but in deed; there faith was not in word, but in power; there all the blessings of the beatitudes clustered and turned the wilderness into Eden; there the eternal life began. "Where two or three are gathered together in my name," saith the Master, "there am I in the midst of them." And therefore we dedicate this Chapel to humanity, in all its weakness and suffering, in its want and aspiration, in its tears and its triumphs, in the grandeur of its capacity and its immortal destiny.

But, my friends, the purpose of this edifice is not merely to provide a shelter for our persons, while our spirits unaided meditate, commemorate, and adore. The structure itself is a part of the homage. Or rather it is a part, most expressive and helpful, of the sacred symbolism by which the homage is made real. We have mistaken the whole relations of the form of our devotions to their spirit, if we regard this house as only a physical accessory, a dead wall between our senses and the noises of the street or the inclemencies of the sky. Fitness and decoration, and emblems and images, in form or color, already do, or hereafter will, more and more, disown that poor subordination of art, in its most consecrated creations, to the dull demands of the animal economy. A dread of the exaggerations and perversions of the Past, not less penitential, nor less merciful in intention, perhaps, after all, than the Present, shall not always disarray and disfigure the Church.

Nor is this Chapel merely a show of veneration before the criticism of men, meant to put our professions of piety on exhibition. We have not laid these stones and spread this arch, I hope, to notify passengers that we, for our part, have concluded to believe in God, and can afford to spend something handsome to prove it. No! the building itself is a part of our conversation with Heaven: it is an invocation of trust: a sentence of praise: a voice uttered to the Maker of heaven and earth, no less than the hymn we sing, or the verbal petition we speak. It is an article in the confession of our faith. It stands in the solemn, hereditary line with the stone of Bethel, in the Eastern pasture, that Jacob called "House of God," — with the Shekinah over the cherubim, the temple on Mount Moriah, the synagogue of Nazareth, where the Saviour stood up to read, "The

Spirit of the Lord is upon me," — with the upper chamber where the bread from Heaven and the blood of the true Vine furnished the sacramental supper, — and with the room at Jerusalem where the tongues of fire preached at the dedication of Christendom, and the Pentecostal spirit inaugurated the visible Church for the nations.

And if any object that this makes a superfluous form, then what do all our signs of adoration signify? our postures, our ordinances, our very words of supplication? What has a vocal sound to do with any heart's secret communion with Him, who heareth in secret, and needs no voice? What but this, — that He who alone knows, and who alone has a right to require, has adapted mortal means to immortal ends, and has made the fulness of the blessing to depend on the appointed way?

For this reason, and to such an end, the very place itself is sacred; and we find a precept for the veneration in which every reverent mind will hold it and every hand that is ever lifted or clasped in prayer will treat it. By humble postures and subdued tones, by the suppression of levity and haste, by steps that remember to follow His who purged of its profanations even the temple enshrining a Ritual that was to vanish before his New Covenant, — by the Christian thoughtfulness which never enters but to confess, "Lo, God is here," and yet is none the less but more sure that he is everywhere, — by the stillness that hears a voice ever saying in the separated air, "The Lord is in his holy temple, let all the earth keep silence before him," we shall gladly, gratefully, hallow the courts of the House of our Lord. Like all things set apart to reserved and holy uses, it will evermore repeat to us the silent admonitions of Him from whom we came, of Him who came to us, — of the eternity and the Judgment that are yet to be. The more these holy associations gather about it, the more natural, the more irresistible will they grow. The faith of generations will invest and crown it.

Assembled here, therefore, with these occasions of praise, within the walls that a Christian munificence has reared in honor of Religion and Learning, assisted by the officers and members of the several departments of the University, in presence of those who represent to us the founder and the efficient agents of his design, of the majesty of the Commonwealth, the Government of the Institution and its past Presidents, — in humility and trust and gratitude, confessing, "Lord, we believe," entreating, "Help our unbelief," recalling the high examples of ancestral piety, — blessing the God of our history, — in the same names into which the true believer is ever bidden to be baptized, of the Father, and of the Son, and of the Holy Spirit, we now dedicate this Chapel to the Maker of all, to the Saviour of the world, to the Comforter. We dedicate it to its hallowed uses, — a fervent and reverent worship, sincere and holy ordinances, an earnest and enlightened study of all wisdom and righteousness. We dedicate it to the immortal heart, conscience, soul of man. We dedicate it to Faith, and Hope, and Charity. We dedicate it, as the successive inscriptions of the College Seal have taught us, — to Truth, to the Master's glory, to Christ and the Church.

NOTE TO SERMON XX.

The course of the author's experience, — if such a reference may be allowed, — prompts a few words further on two or three difficulties connected with the subject in minds hesitating to receive the form of the doctrine, while yet inclined by their reverence to offer to the Saviour exalted honors. The phrase "Son of God," by an inadequate conception of the Sonship, and a neglect of other Scriptural terms, is sometimes made to obscure instead of disclosing our Lord's real Divinity. A vague view is taken which is not high enough for the Trinitarian, as the Trinitarian must say, is too high for any other, and is either too high or too low for self-consistency. A less lofty place cannot be assigned to Christ, with the Bible lying open and with Christendom in sight; nor, on the other hand, can so much of dignity and majesty be consistently ascribed to him without a full recognition of his absolute and proper Divinity; that is, without confessing that the basis or ground of his being is so identical with that of the Father, so truly Deity, that his personality is "very God of very God," from eternity, self-existent, and supreme. The whole issue is close and brief. Jesus is either the Incarnation, not of an abstraction, a quality, or a principle, but of God, or else he is a created being, who *began* to be in time, so that there was a time when our Lord and Redeemer was not. There is a devout class of men who speak earnestly of Christ as divine, and who yet acknowledge that they date the beginning of his being from the hour of his birth as the Son of Mary. But is it possible that such offices and prerogatives as the New Testament assigns to him could belong to a creature, coming into existence in the midst of the little history of this planet, after multitudes of its inhabitants had lived and vanished? Could the very life of Him to whom belong judgment, omnipotence, intercession, the gift of eternal life, and the pardon of sin, date from any late or any early day in mortal calendars?

Closely analyzed, the idea of Incarnation which is advanced by some writers, who yet deny that Christ is God, seems to signify nothing really distinct in kind from what takes place in any living child of human birth. We may partially cover the question up with sounding words, or try to exalt the subject by dignified generalities; but unless there was a Divine Personality incarnated, there were only those abstract notions or ideas which, in some sense or other, may be said to be incarnated in every human character. More than this is certainly affirmed in the mighty sentences of the Gospel. More than this would seem to be demanded by hearts that the Gospel has quickened and enlarged. In the attempt to maintain that middle position there appears to be a constant struggle between the moral posture of the student and the intellectual; between his sentiments toward the Saviour, which are essentially adoring, and the abating definitions of his formal statements. The right conclusion of that struggle is a great joy.

In the view under remark, it is common to represent the original substance or groundwork of Christ's being as human, and the divinity as supervening upon that; whereas the strong declarations of the Record put the truth exactly the other way, making the original substance, or the root, of his being to be divine, and his humanity to be assumed. So he "took on" the form of man. He "humbled himself" to be human. He "came forth," "came down," "was made flesh," "left the glory he had with the Father before the world was." This representation is so continual, the statements are so multiplied, so varied, and so natural, that the argument would be irresistible even if it were not supported by the more distinct and emphatic passages, such as "Before Abraham was I am," passages disposed of by the objector only through exegetical expedients which illustrate at once the emergencies of a hard-pressed theory and the ingenuity of its defenders. These passages establish a personal preexistence; and establishing this, they establish a proper Divinity; for Arianism is so untenable that it is well-nigh extinct. By the Church doctrine we are furnished with a conception of the Incarnation far more clear, and more religiously inspiring, as well as more Scriptural, than by any other. Our Lord's humanity was a development;

his Divinity is perpetual, "from everlasting to everlasting." As man, and as men speak, he "grew in wisdom and favor;" but as God he is "Jesus Christ, *the same yesterday, to-day, and forever*," and is therefore worthy to be worshipped.

In these observations, we are not making "rationality" a test for the reception of this doctrine, any more than of other religious and revealed truths. We only exhibit it as an advantage of the doctrine, that when faith has welcomed it, the intellect has its reward also in discovering its internal harmonies and the beauty of its relations. The faith of the Church and the ages, while confessedly outreaching the finite intelligence, satisfies our highest reverence, and feeds and gladdens the inmost soul of piety, while the other has no such offset to its obscurity, but would leave us in the double grief of an unsettled mind and unsatisfied affections. The backwardness shown sometimes in reconciling this adoration of our Lord with the terms of dependence and limitation which are applied to him in connection with his mediatorial mission and earthly ministry, arises largely from an education in opposite habits. Yet, when we consider the real problem and conditions of that mediation, how can we fail to behold the simple necessity and complete naturalness of all these representations? What other explanation do we need of the Messiah's earlier reserve in unfolding the fulness of the Godhead which dwelt bodily in him, — a reserve laid more and more aside, however, as the time of his crucifixion and glorification drew near? That he did take this method of a progressive disclosure of his truth, adapting it in a degree to the condition of his hearers, appears from many instances; as from his saying, "In the beginning I said not" thus and thus "unto you;" "Ye cannot bear them now;" "When he, the Spirit of Truth, is come, he will guide you into all truth." Suppose that while appearing in that human form, among the rude men of his day, he had been continually affirming, in the most unqualified, sudden, peremptory manner, his divine supremacy. How could it fail to confuse and bewilder them, if not to exasperate them, all unprepared for it as their ignorance was, and while his visible shape appeared before them? Even the comparatively few expressions which he did employ, made more distinct and frequent as his "hour" approached, threatened to put an end, and did finally help to put an end, to his ministry in the body. The truth could not shine forth at once, in its peerless glory, upon eyes so dull. He contented himself, in his wise and tender condescension, with pronouncing these comprehensive and weighty declarations of his complete oneness with the Father, and left the further doctrine of his mysterious nature to unfold itself in the ripening wisdom of his Church, under the Holy Spirit which he promised. This it would accomplish more simply and powerfully than was possible while he was associating as man with his untaught countrymen. Yet we observe also that he did not refuse to be worshipped when worship was offered him. He suffered Thomas to call him Lord and God. He declared himself the Judge of all souls. He is "Emmanuel." He "hath power to forgive sins." He is "the propitiation for the sins of the whole world." "All power" is his "in heaven and earth." The Being of whom the Bible says this is to be worshipped in his glorified state and majesty. "All things that the Father hath are mine," he says. This raises him to the height of adorableness. Even "the Comforter," he declares, "*shall glorify me.*" How can we believe that he meant to refuse his disciples the dear delight of praising him and entreating him "in the midst of the throne," yet near and tender as when he wept for those he loved on earth, and bade them come unto him, and told them that "without him they could do nothing," and was never sought by any sincere petition in vain? He said, too, speaking of the sad impending hour of separation, when he foresaw that the hearts and minds of his followers would be torn with anguish and doubt, half paralyzed by fear, and alternating between fond remembrances of his bodily appearance and new thoughts of the spiritual relation to subsist thenceforth between them, — "*In that hour* ye shall (or will) ask me nothing." But, he adds, very considerately, to console them, Nevertheless, your halting faith shall not forfeit the blessing. "Whatsoever ye shall ask the Father *in my name*, he will give it you;" and again, "If ye shall ask anything in my name, *I will do it.*" The whole passage evidently relates to the distinction between his outward and his eternal presence, between the visible and invisible intercourse of his followers with him. In a remoter and calmer period his worship would take its place spontaneously in their hymns, ejaculations, and litanies. Meantime, he points them to the Father in whom they are already believing with a more settled and definite faith. Whoever prays truly to that Father prays to God, and fulfils the spirit of prayer; for God is one. There is no division and no jealousy there. Some Christians never pray to any other than the Father; yet if they pray heartily, and "in the name" of Christ, that is, with *true faith* in Christ, and do not merely repeat his literal name at the end of their petitions, they surely must be heard and accepted. Still, there comes to many other disciples a time, and not seldom, when their devotional aspirations seek a more direct and personal communion with their Saviour, to whom they owe their everlasting life, their peace and hope and strength. They long to utter the language of this communion, in gratitude and supplication; and theirs, if they do utter it, is the richer worship. It is not so much enjoined as an obligation as it is offered graciously as a privilege. It is not to be forced, nor rejected. The believers who share this veritable and unquestioning fellowship, the fellowship between the suppliant and the Lord, who set forth the holy fruit thereof in their daily living, and "show it accordingly,"—these have the blessing peculiar to those who, in this respect as in others also, keep the Master's own word, and "*honor the Son even as they honor the Father.*" "Not unto us," not unto them, "but unto thy name, O Lord, give glory!"

THE END.

www.ingramcontent.com/pod-product-compliance
Lightning Source LLC
LaVergne TN
LVHW021301110826
845150LV00003B/453

* 9 7 8 1 4 2 5 5 5 9 8 7 8 *